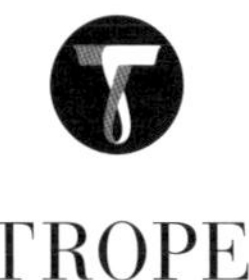

TROPE PUBLISHING Co.

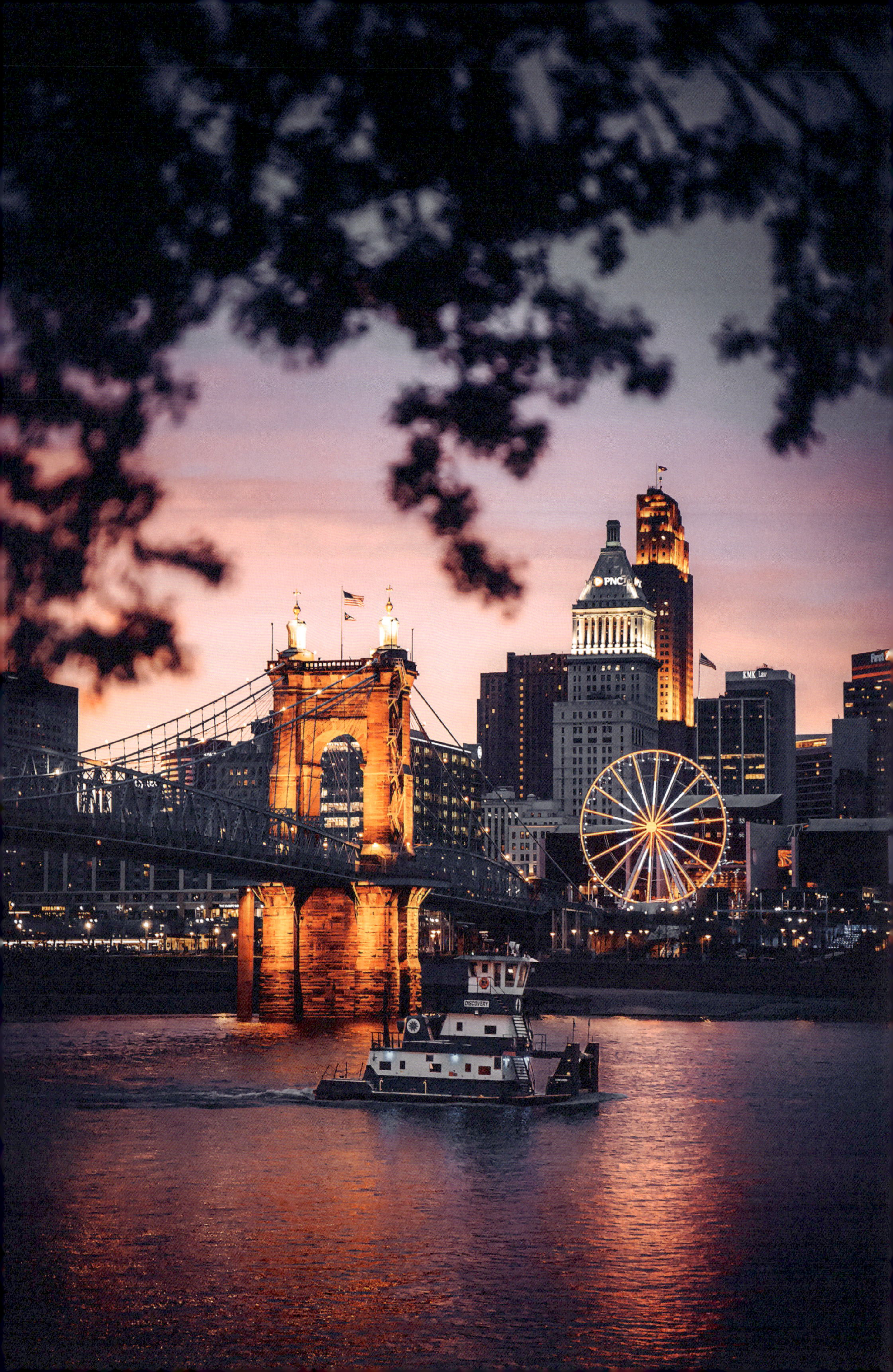
PNC
KMK Law
DISCOVERY

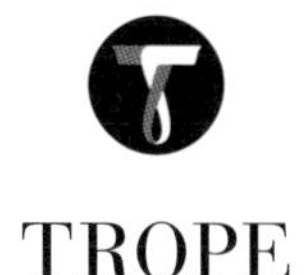

TROPE

CINCINNATI DREAMING

MIKE POGGIOLI

TROPE PUBLISHING Co.

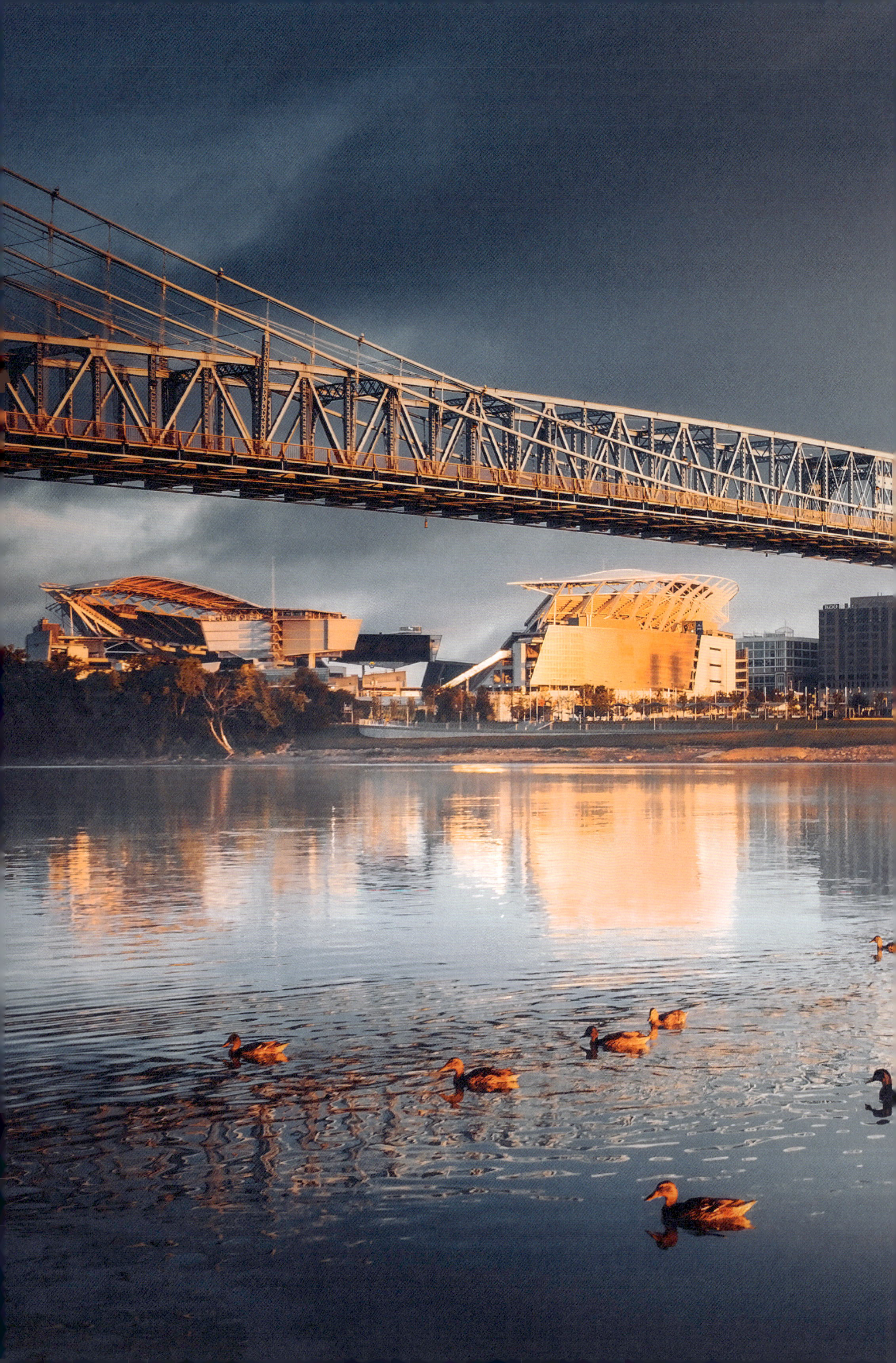

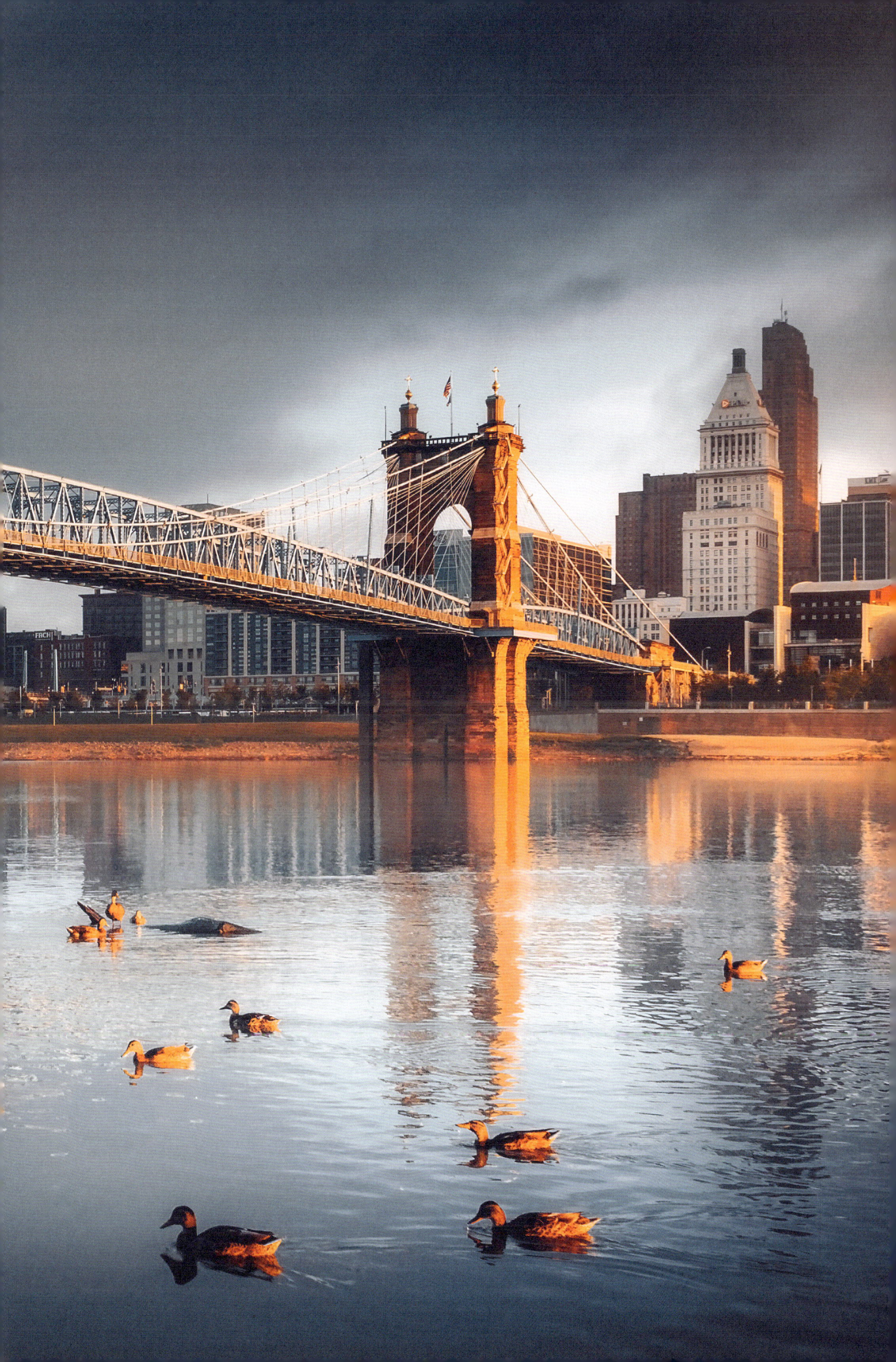

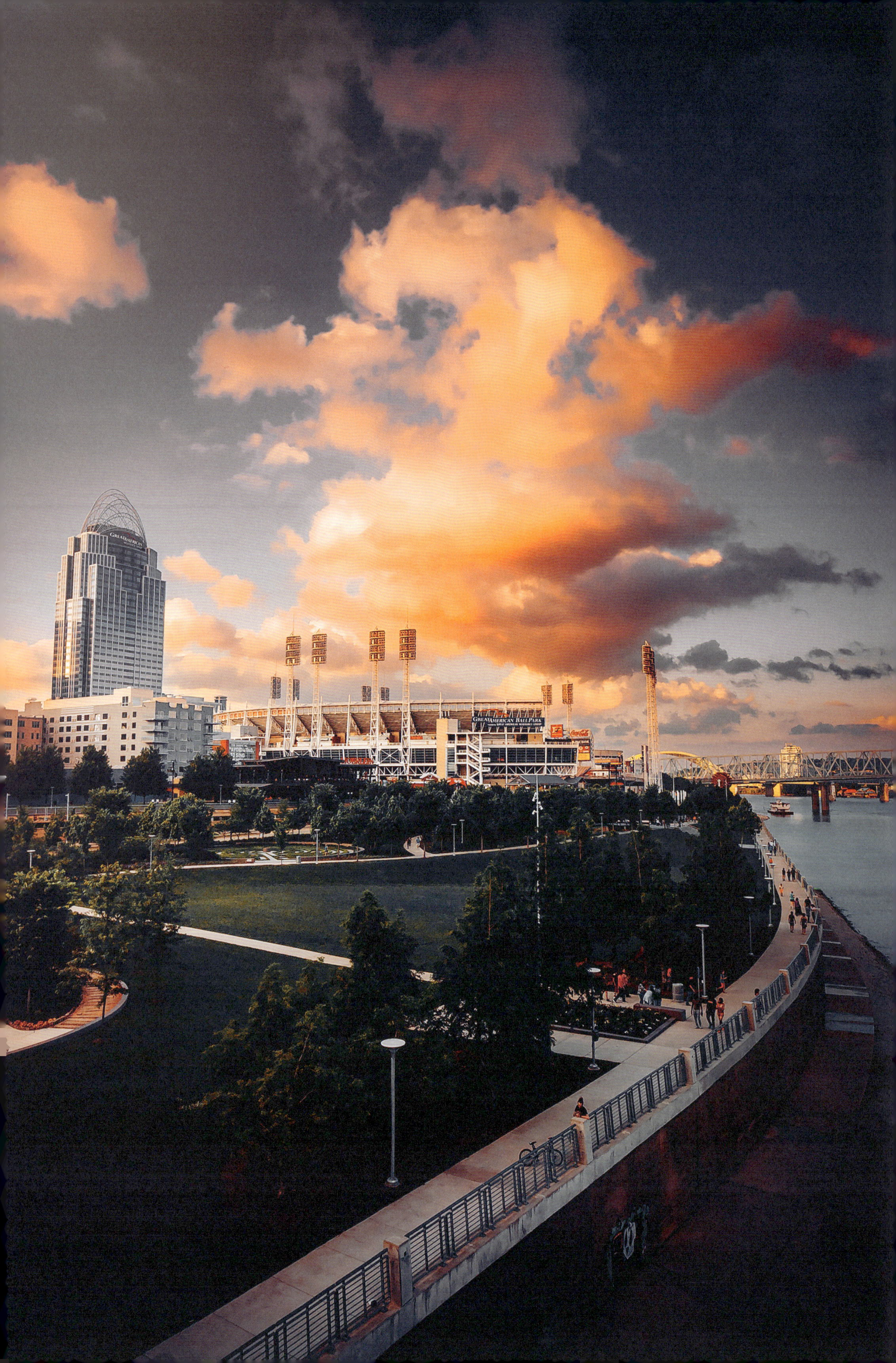
GREAT AMERICAN BALL PARK
GREAT AMERICAN INSURANCE GROUP
Coca-Cola

FOREWORD KRISTEN ERWIN SCHLOTMAN

I am fortunate to be a native of Cincinnati, a city that elegantly balances the charm of its rich history with the vibrancy of modern life. My family and I have grown up appreciating this Midwestern gem, a tapestry woven with diverse cultures, stunning architecture, and a warm sense of community. It's a place where I've made countless memories, explored hidden corners, and found joy in the familiar sights and sounds that define this remarkable city.

One of the first things I fell in love with about Cincinnati was its distinct neighborhoods, each with its own unique personality and flair. From the historic streets of Over-the-Rhine, with its stunning 19th-century architecture, to the artistic energy of Northside, there's a richness that invites exploration. Strolling through the streets of Over-the-Rhine feels like stepping back in time, with its beautifully restored buildings housing an array of trendy boutiques, vibrant bars, and eclectic eateries. The murals that adorn the walls speak to the city's creative spirit, each telling a story of its own.

The food scene in Cincinnati is another jewel in its crown. Yes, we all know about that Cincinnati-style chili that everyone highlights as a "must try" while visiting. But over the last few years we have welcomed and developed master chefs who have been recognized by the prestigious James Beard Awards, appear regularly on national TV, and have brought a sense of culinary class to our city. It's a treasure that delights both natives and guests alike and continues to showcase our amazing diversity.

My love for Cincinnati extends to its lush parks and outdoor spaces. The Cincinnati Parks system is a true treasure, with each park offering its own sanctuary from the hustle and bustle of urban life. Eden Park, with its stunning views of the river and the city skyline, is my favorite spot for a peaceful afternoon. Whether it's a leisurely stroll, a picnic with friends, or simply enjoying the beauty of nature, this park is a reminder of the serenity that can be found amidst the city's vibrancy.

Then there's the cultural heartbeat of Cincinnati, embodied in its world-class museums and theaters. The Cincinnati Art Museum and the Contemporary Arts Center showcase both classical and modern works, offering inspiration and insight into the creative spirit that thrives here. The Cincinnati Symphony Orchestra brings the gift of music to life in a way that transcends time, providing an unforgettable experience for those fortunate enough to attend a performance. And, of course, our homegrown film community continues to attract major motion pictures and world-renowned directors to our area. Cincinnati continues to be a top destination for filmmakers—a testament to the talent we have both in front of and behind the camera.

Lastly, the sense of community in Cincinnati is what truly makes it special. The annual events, from the Taste of Cincinnati to the Cincinnati Music Festival, bring people together to celebrate the city's rich cultural tapestry. It's during these gatherings that I've seen the city shine, filled with laughter, joy, and an unmistakable sense of belonging.

What's my favorite of these? It's something simple like going for coffee with my daughters and chatting about their day. These quiet times are special, and I treasure those mornings when we can talk about their day, their activities, their hopes and dreams. As we drive around the city, soaking up the morning sunshine, sipping our lattes and laughing about nothing, I know these are the images I'll take with me my entire life.

As you journey through the pages of this book, I invite you to explore my favorite places around town and uncover the hidden gems that make Cincinnati a city like no other. From its vibrant neighborhoods to its culinary delights and cultural offerings, I hope you discover the same love for this city that has inspired my life. Welcome to Cincinnati—where the historical meets the modern, and every corner tells a story.

KRISTEN ERWIN SCHLOTMAN

President-CEO, Film Cincinnati

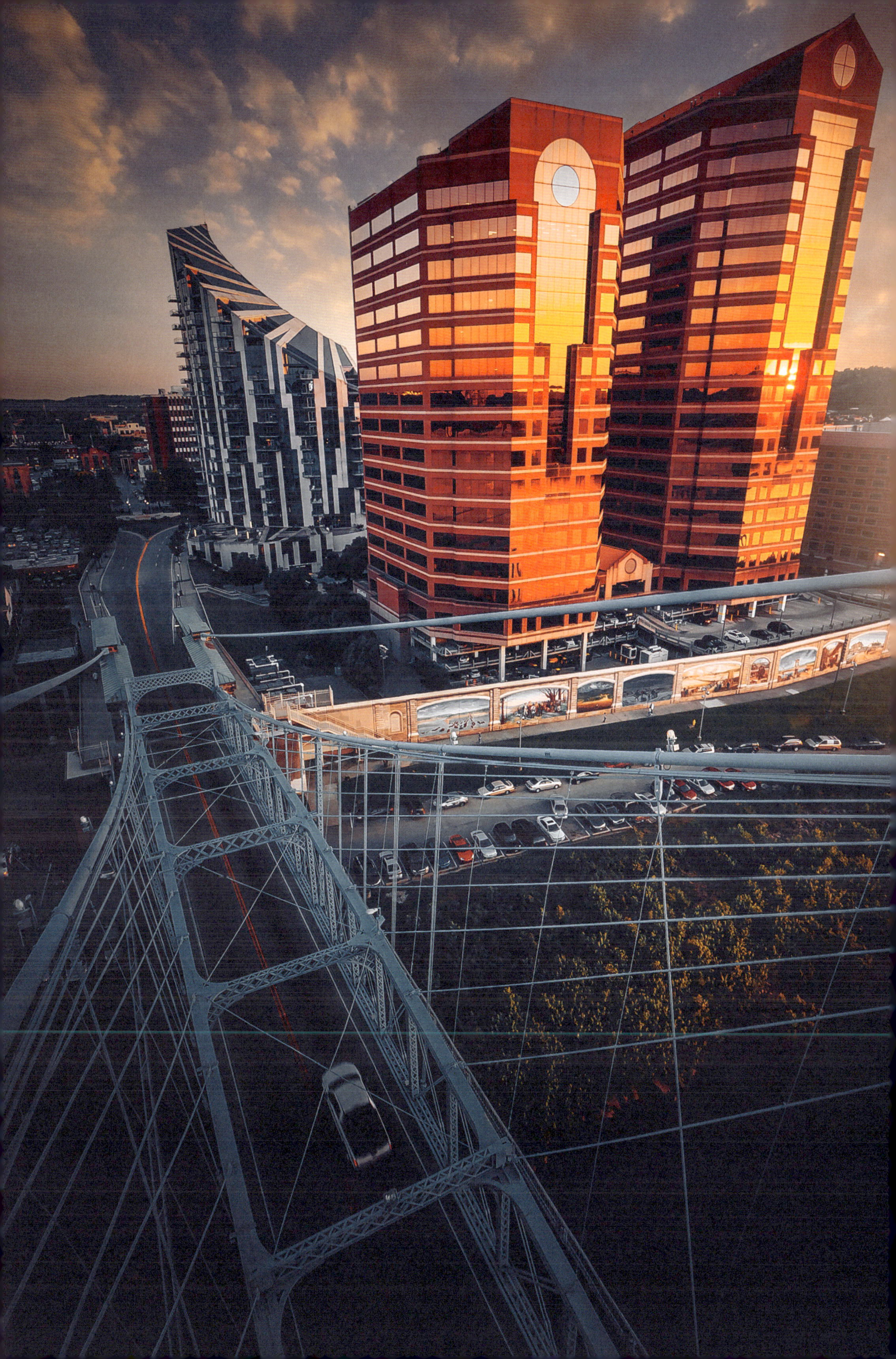

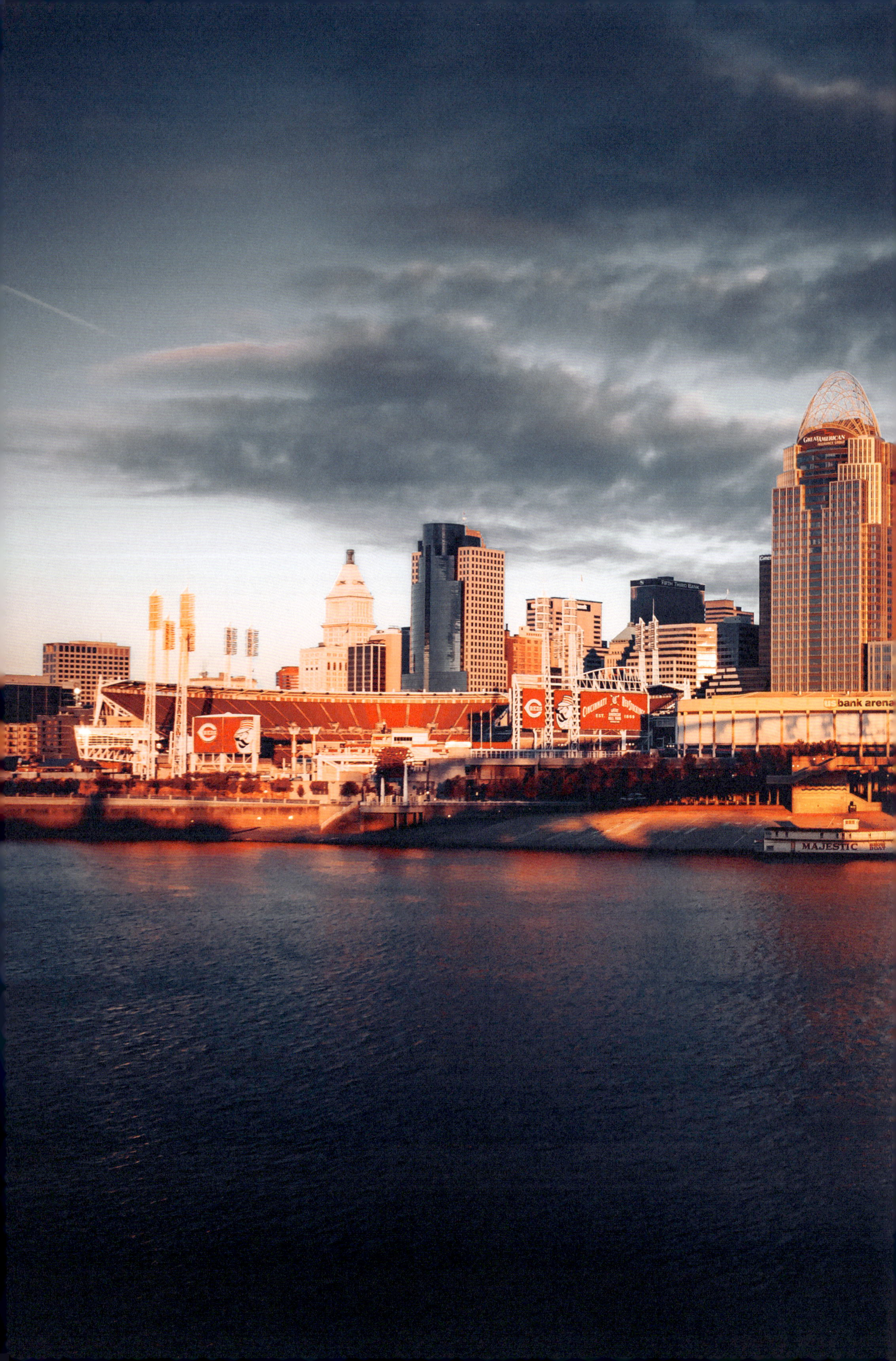

usbank arena
CINCINNATI RED STOCKINGS
EST. 1869
MAJESTIC
SHOW BOAT

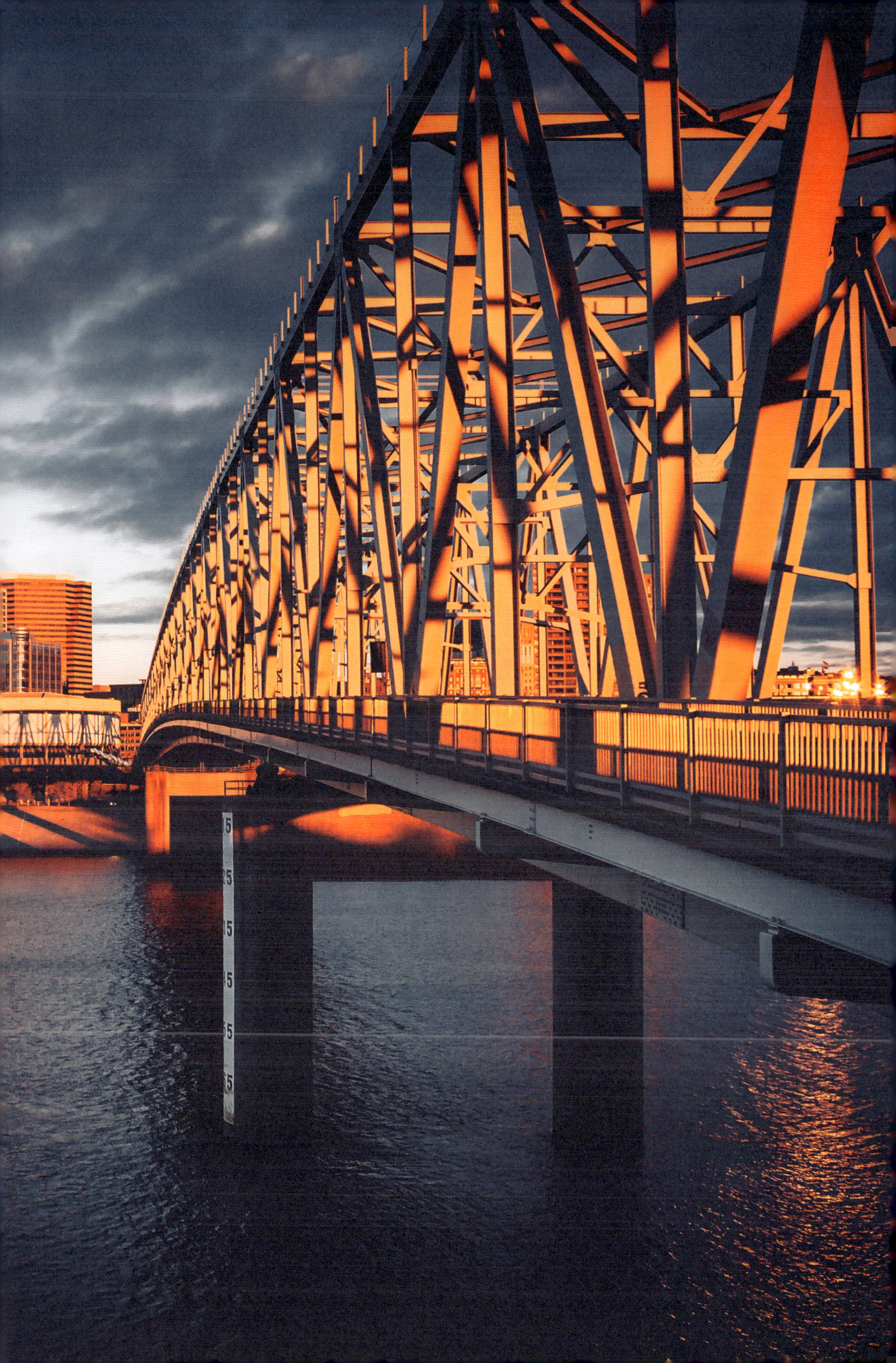

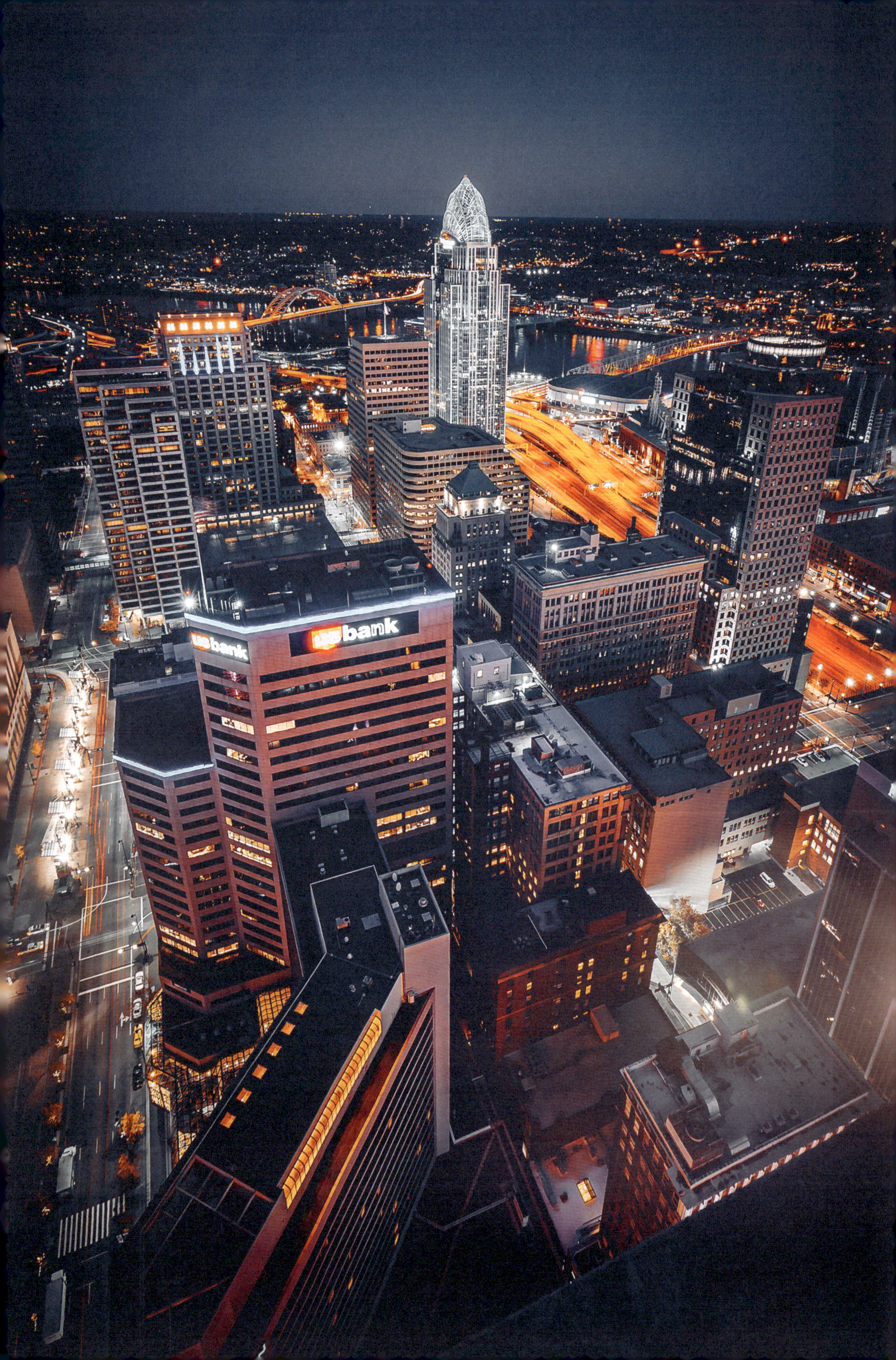
bank
bank

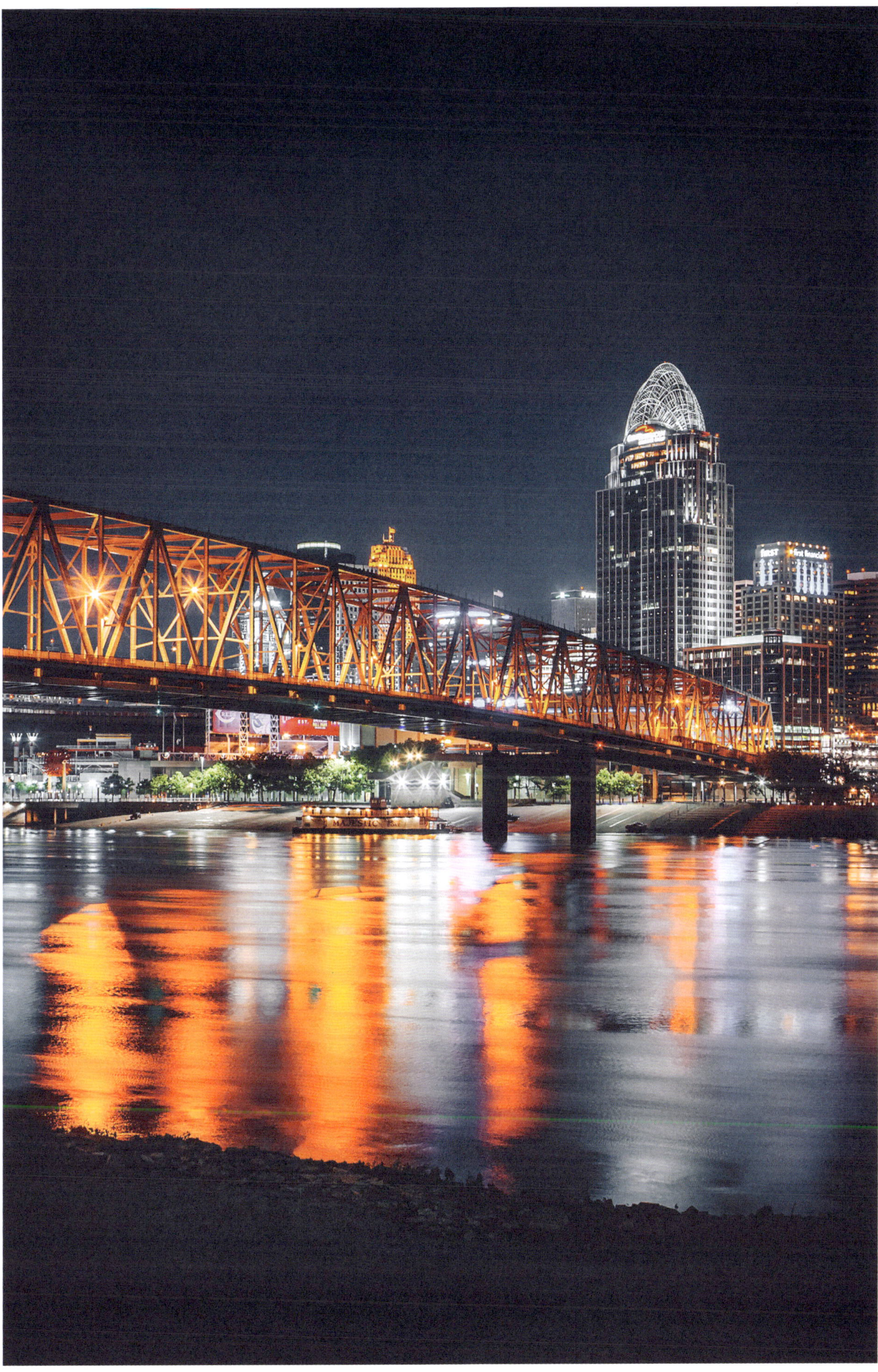

Cincinnati, I thought, was the most beautiful of the inland cities of the Union. From the tower of its unsurpassed hotel the city spreads far and wide its pageant of crimson, purple and gold, laced by silver streams that are great rivers.

WINSTON CHURCHILL

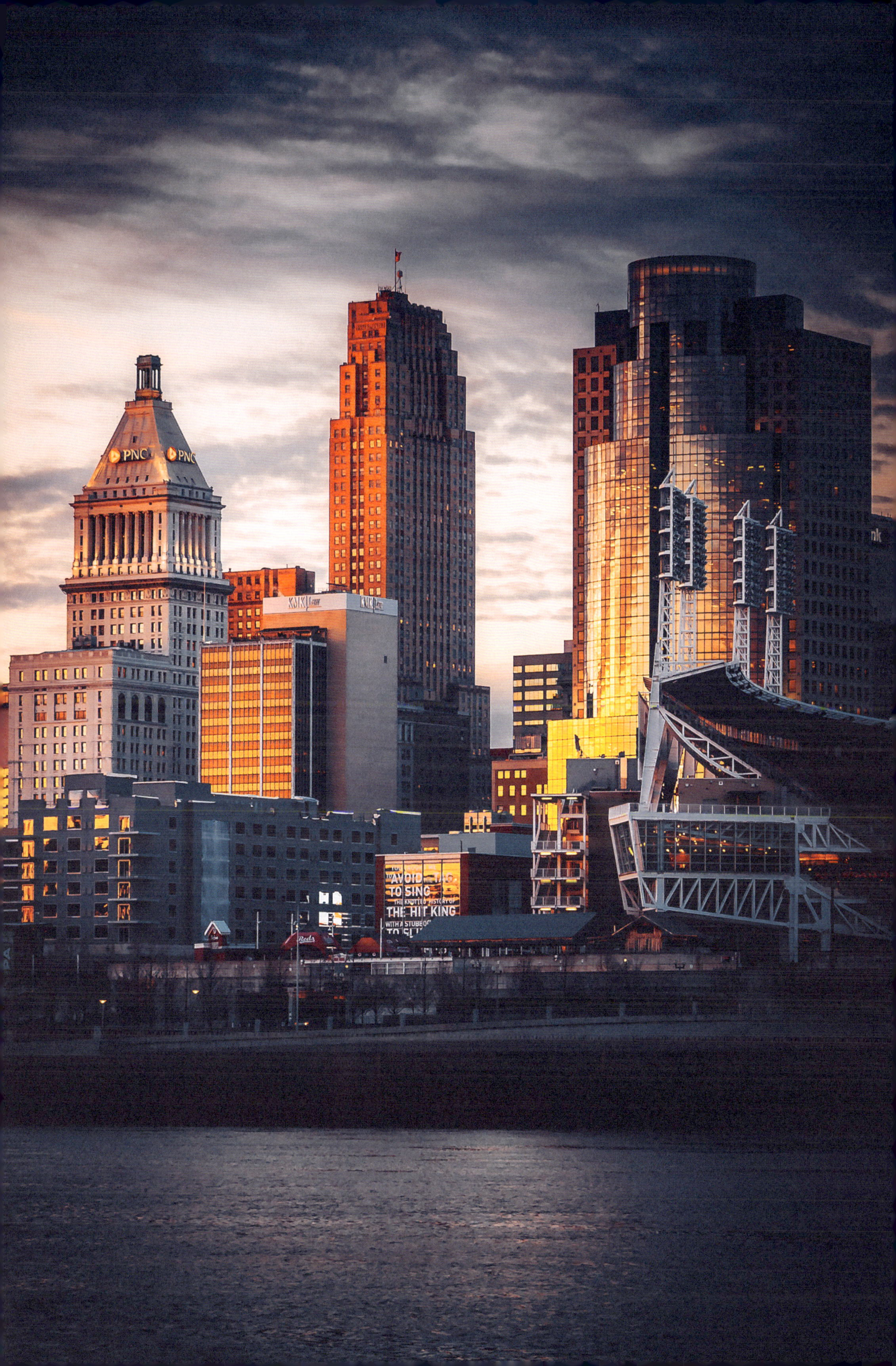
PNC
PNC
AVOID
TO SING
THE KNOTTED HISTORY OF
THE HIT KING
Reds

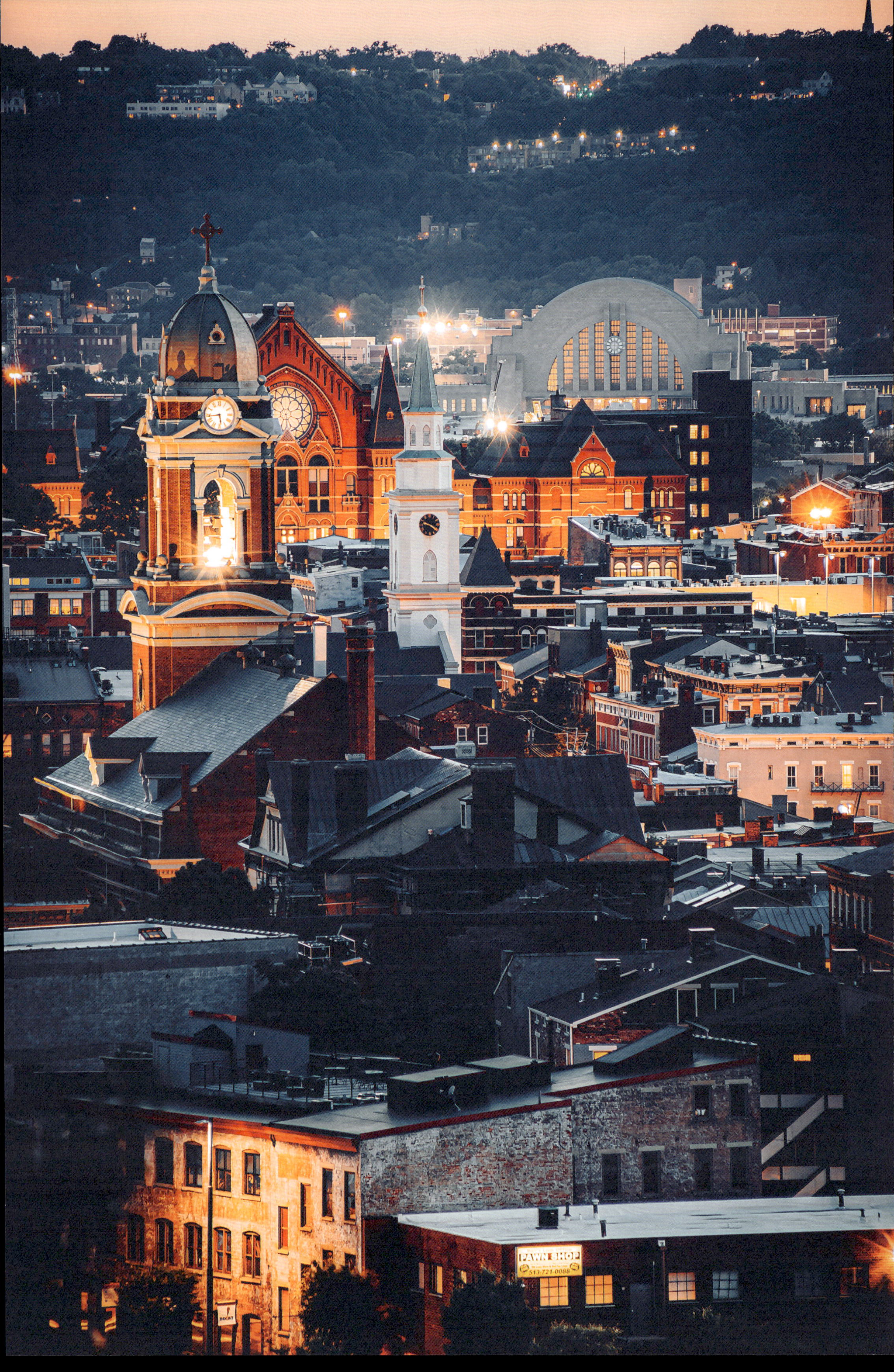
PAWN SHOP
513-721-0088

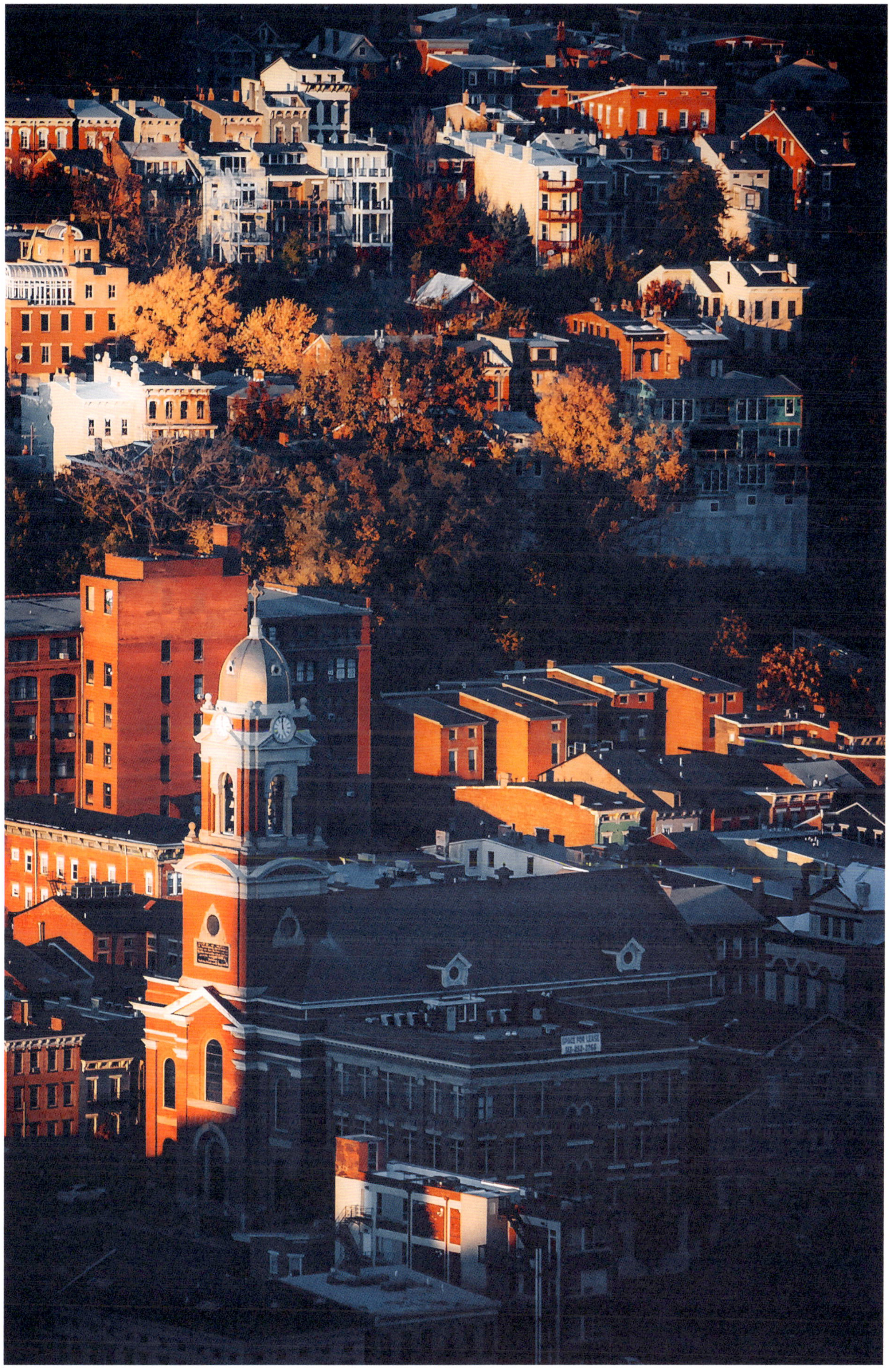

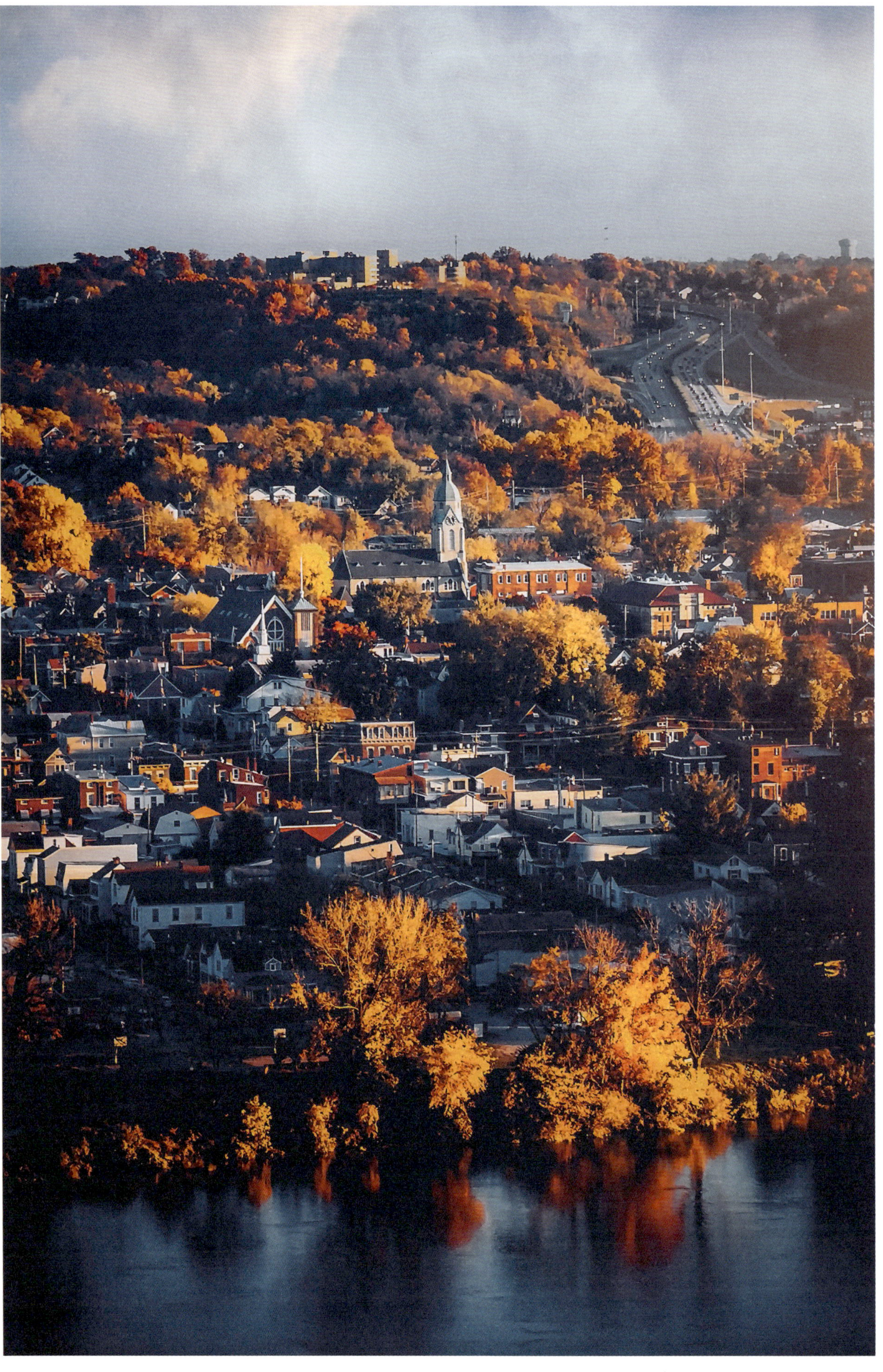

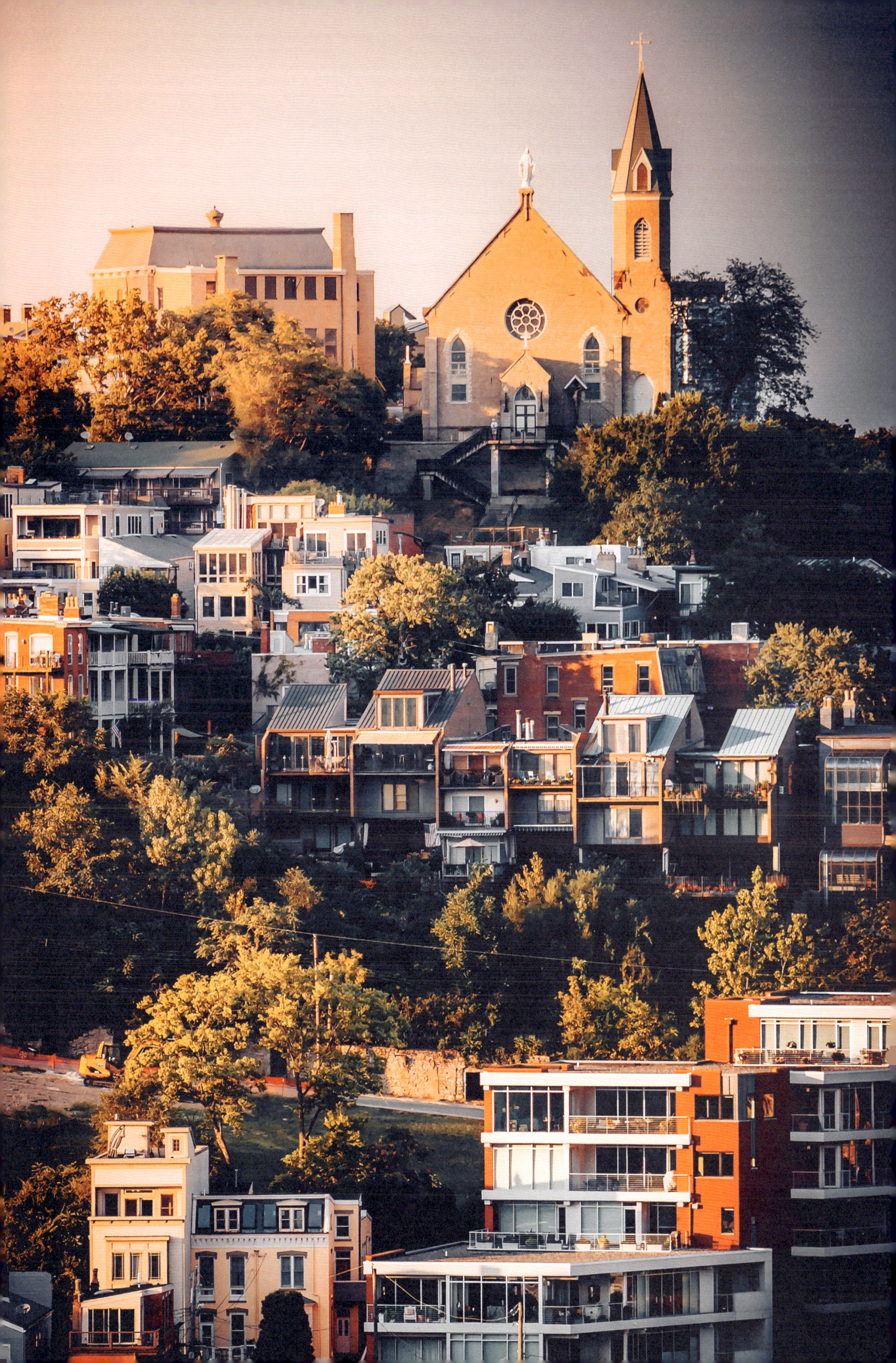

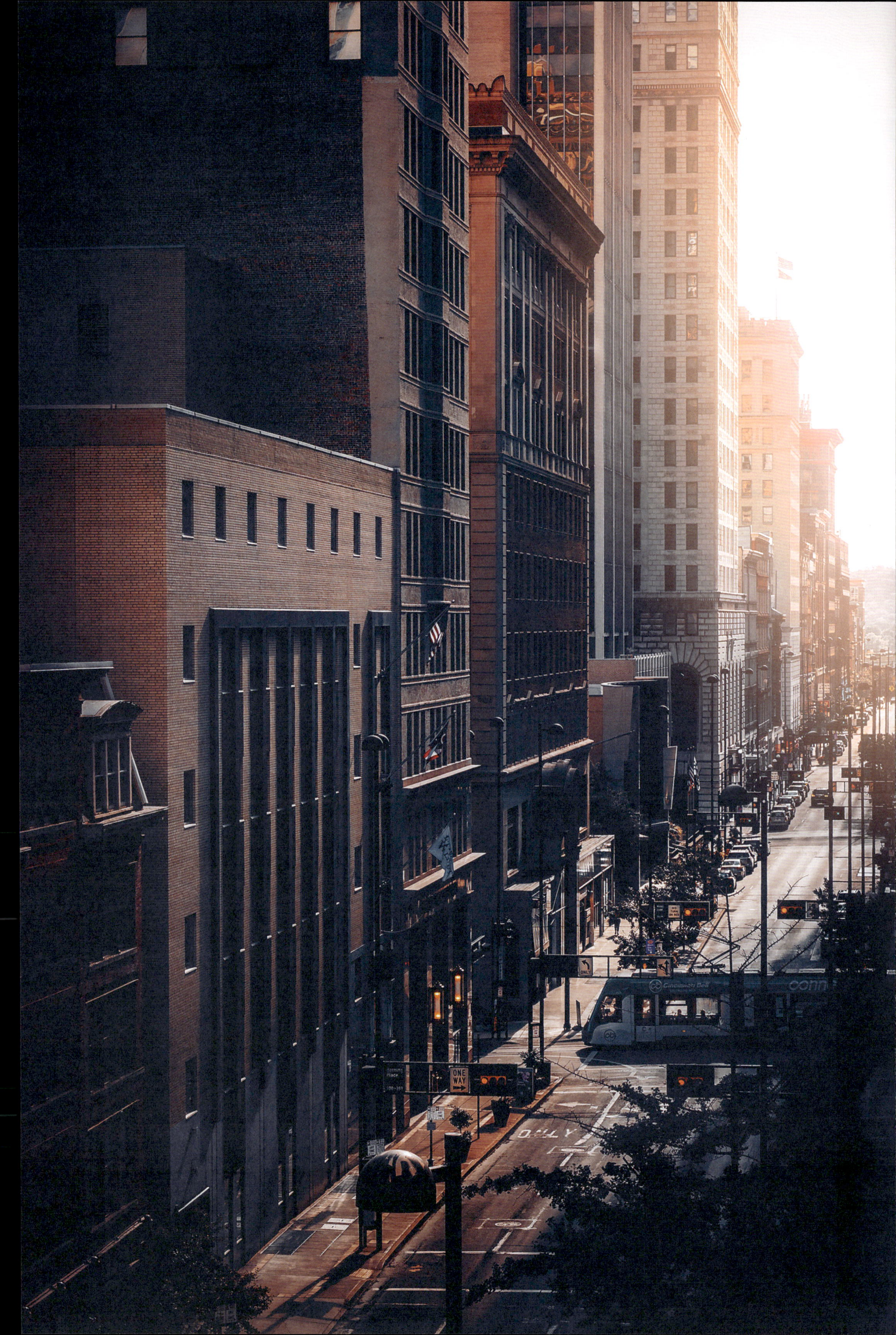
ONE WAY
Cincinnati Bell

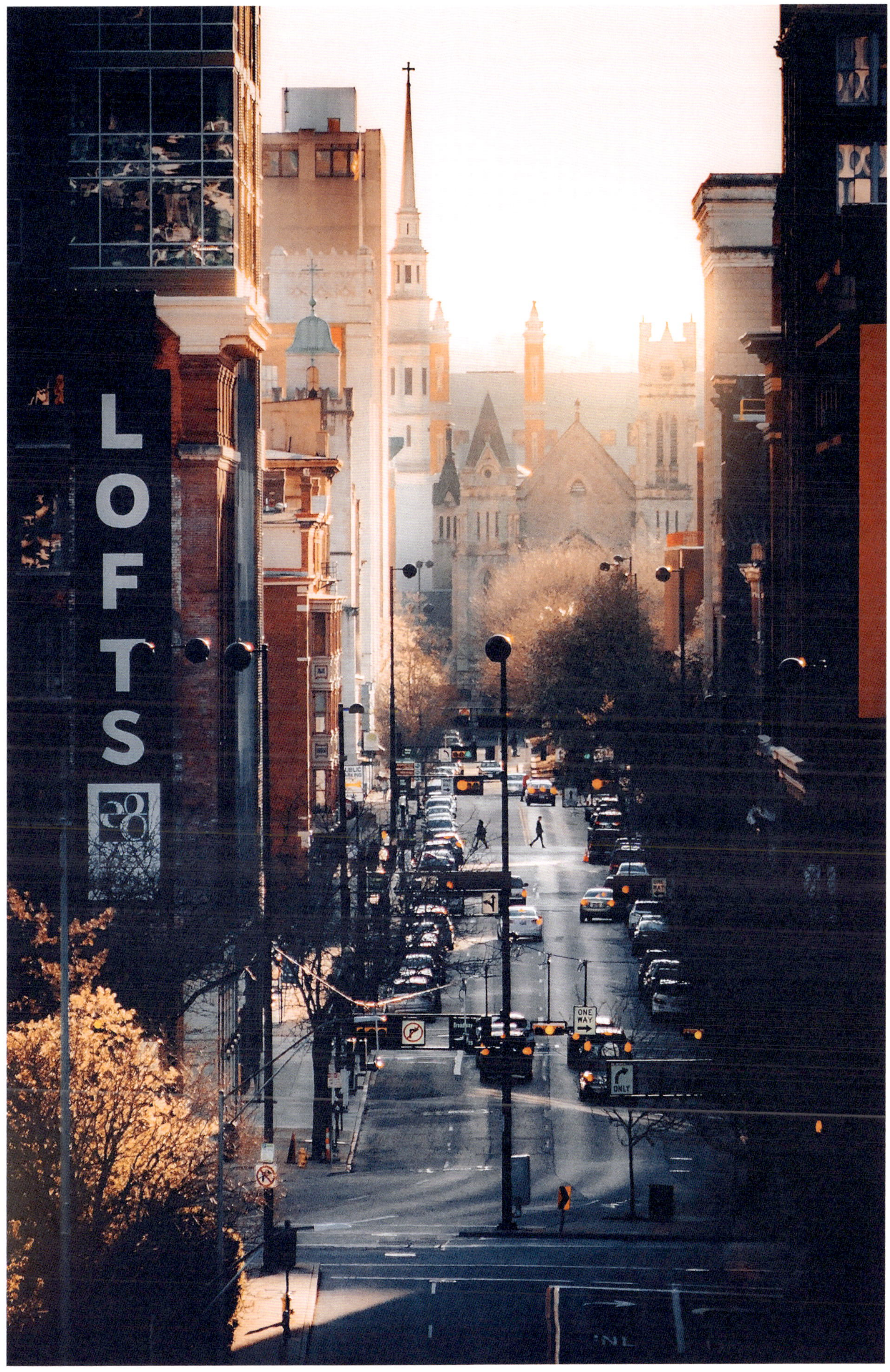
LOFTS
ONE WAY
ONLY

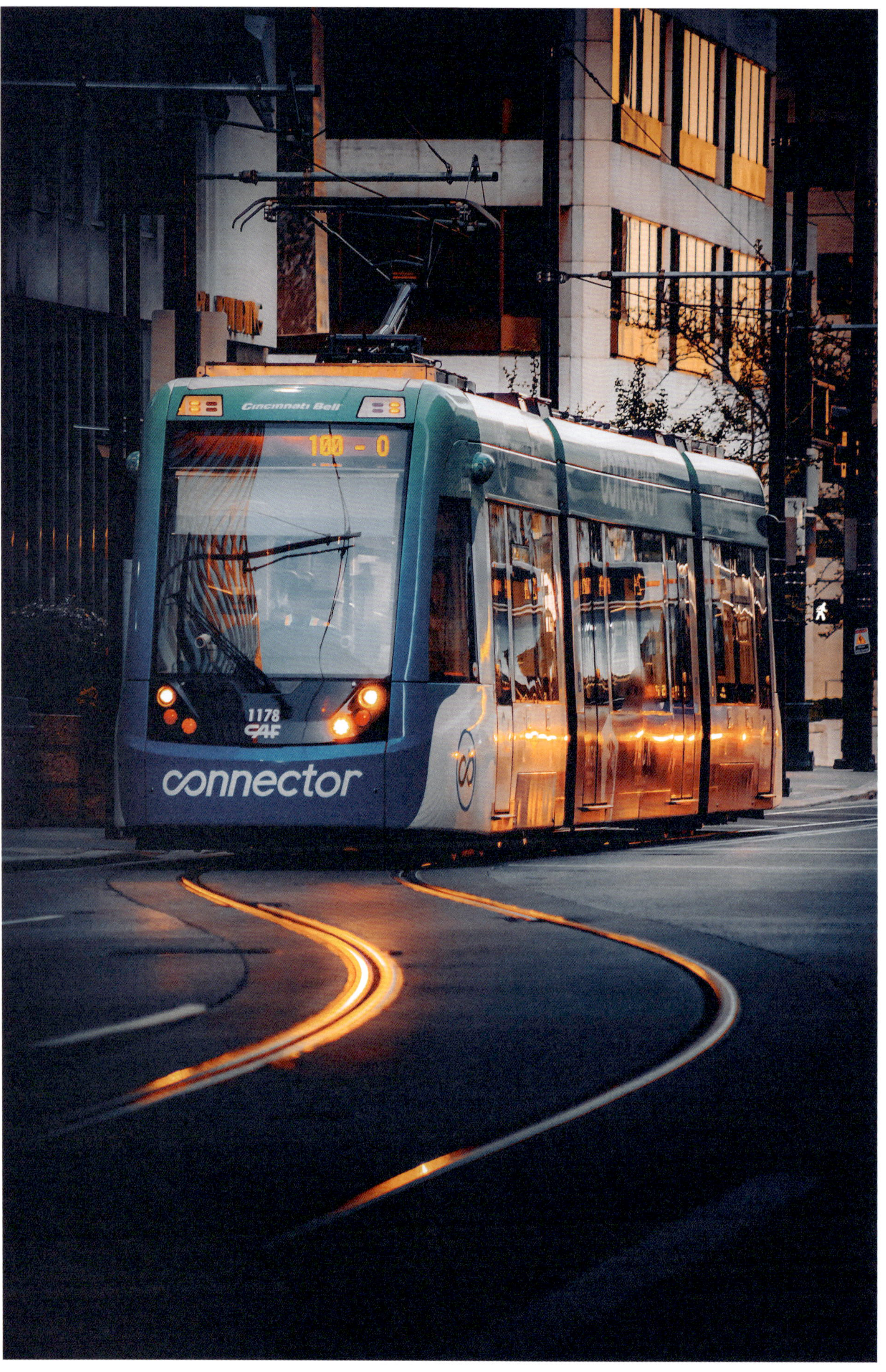
Cincinnati Bell
100 - 0
1178
CAF
connector

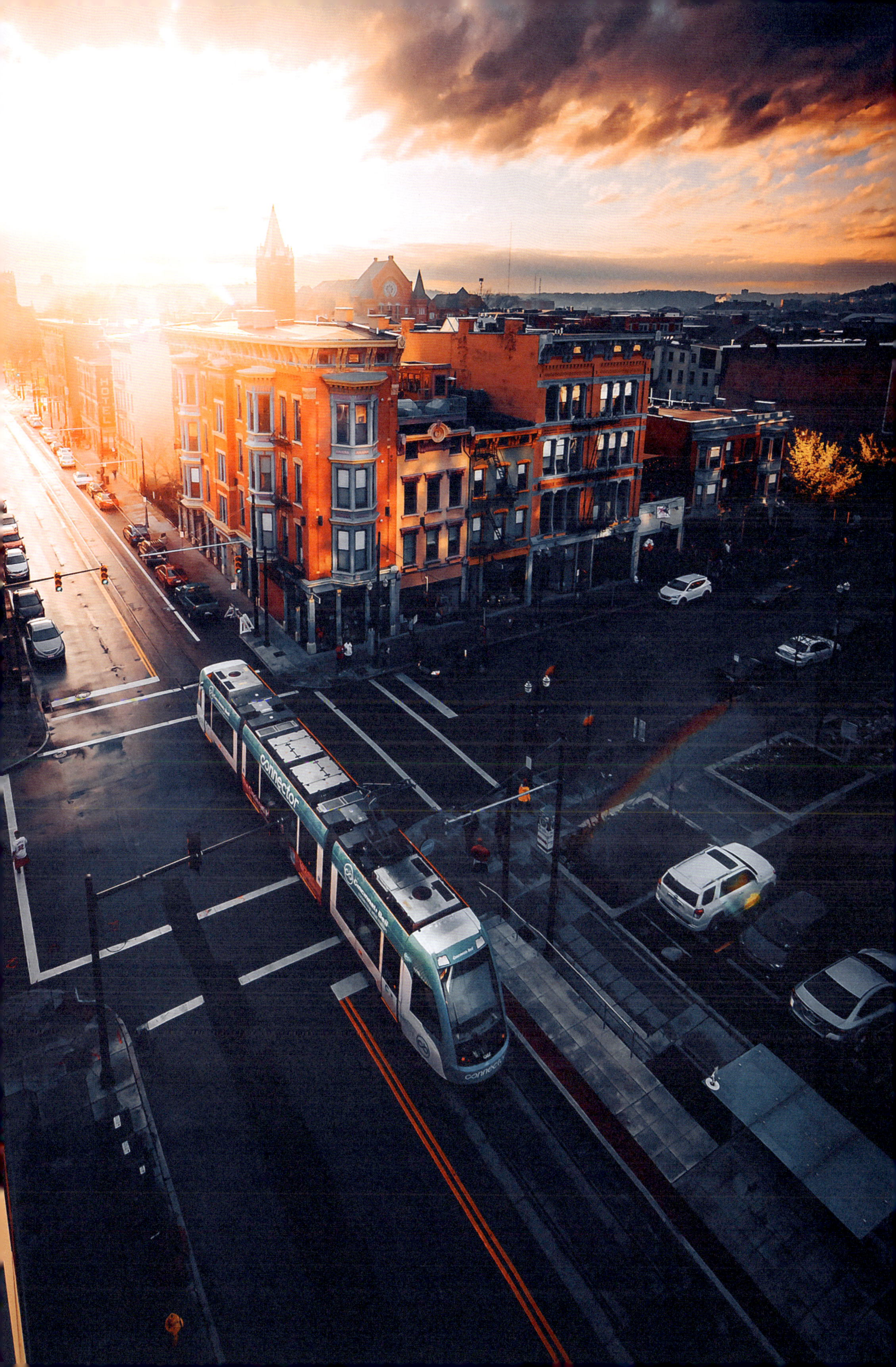
connector

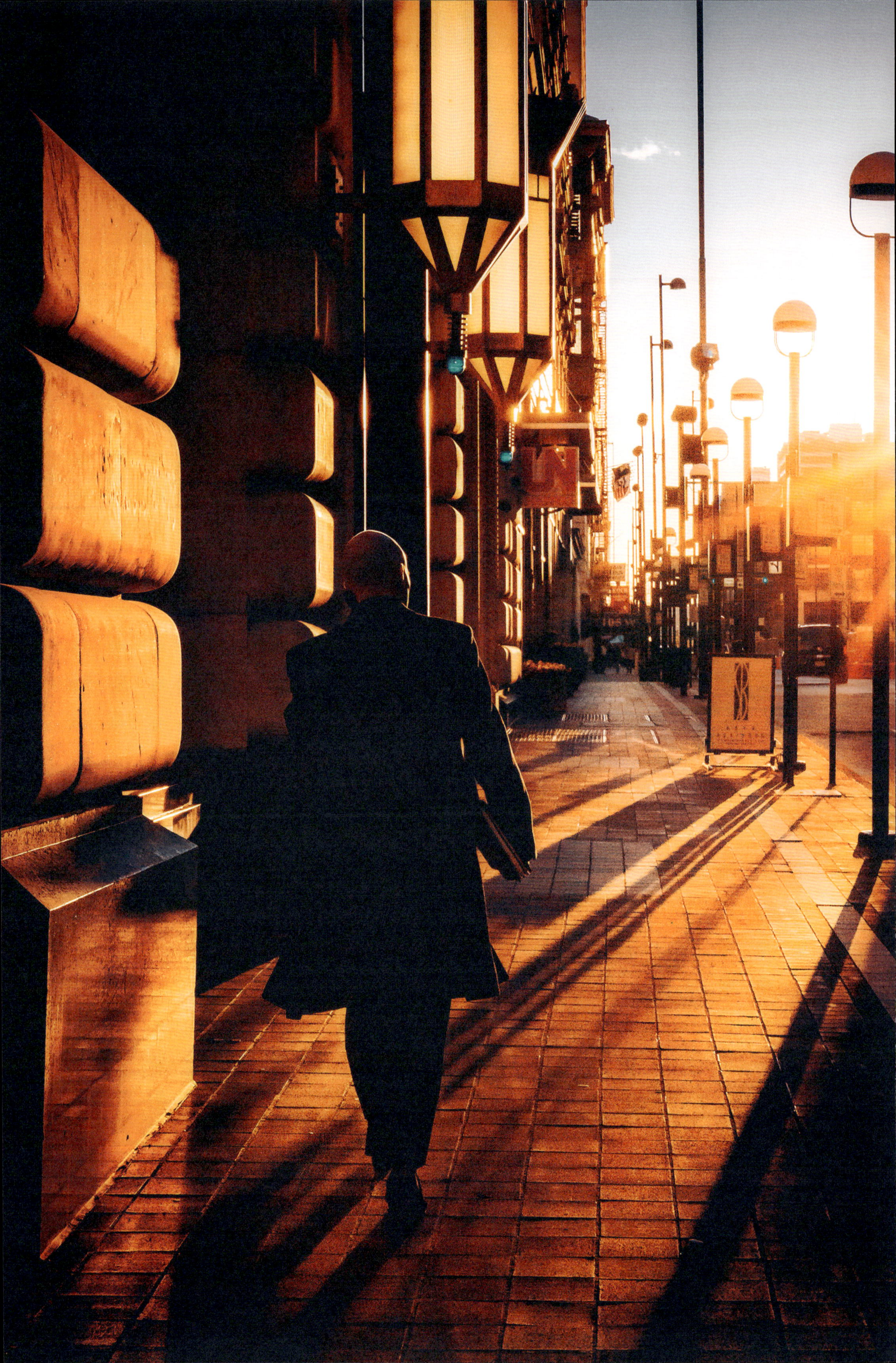

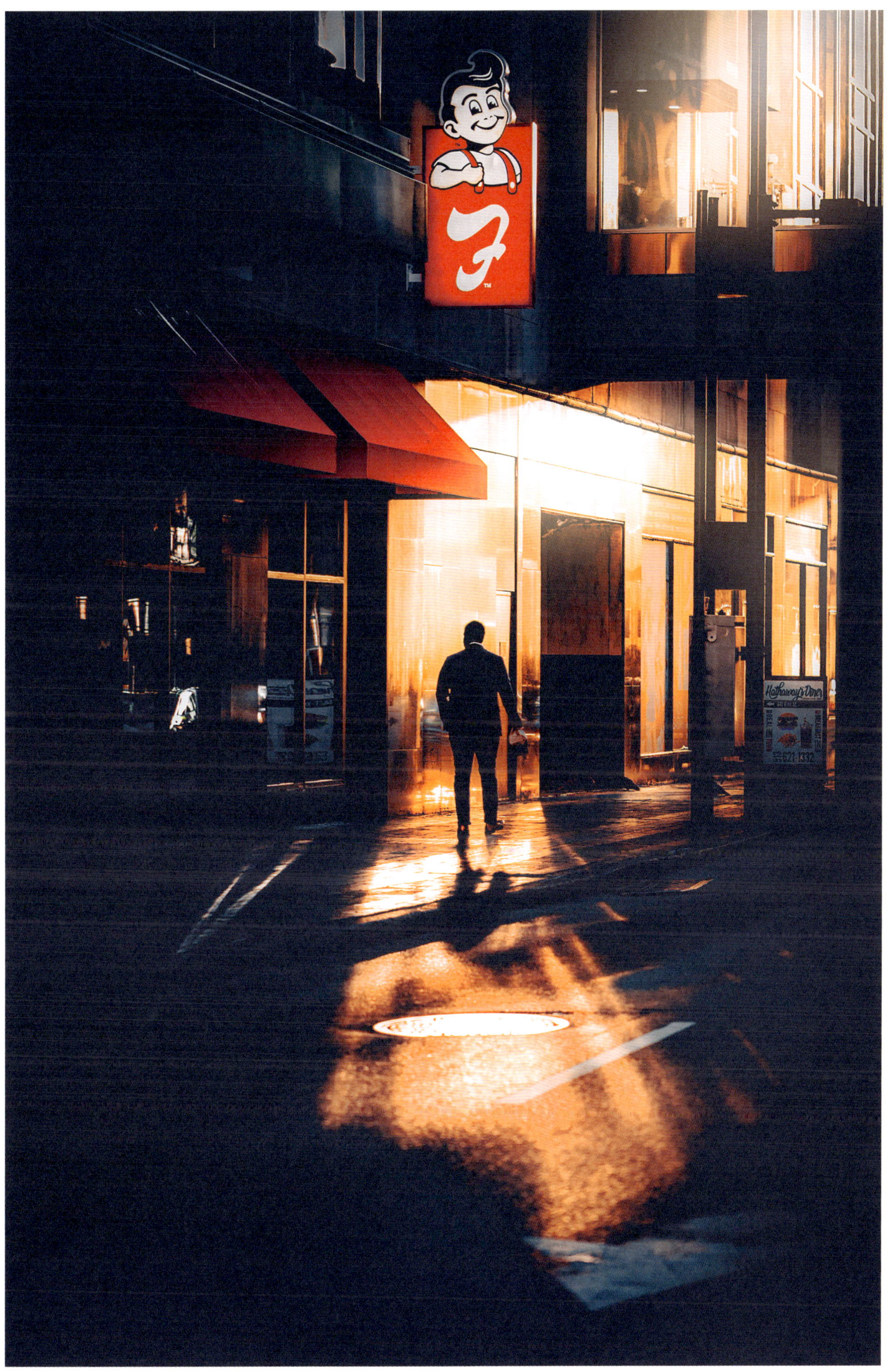
Hathaway's Diner

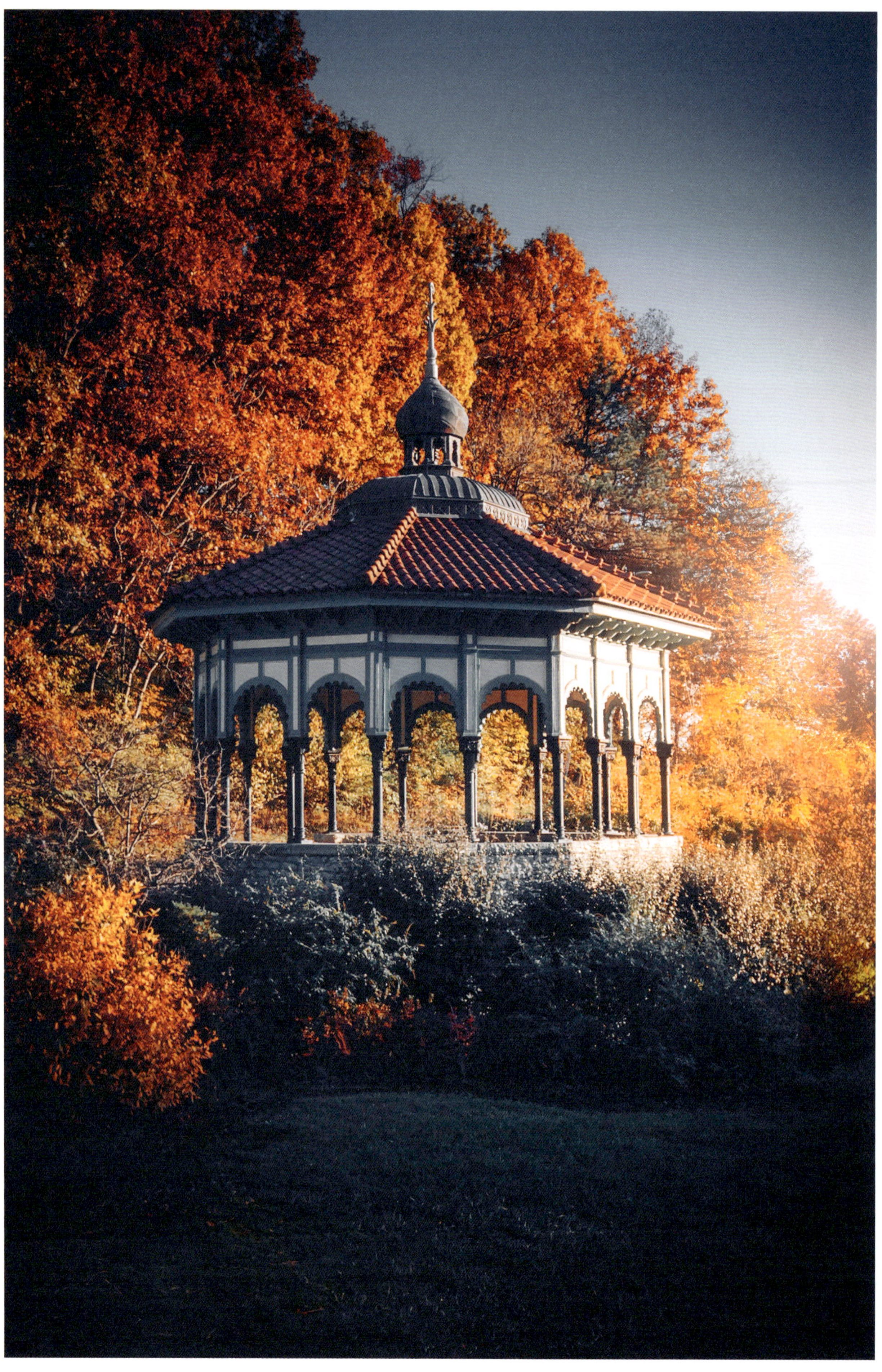

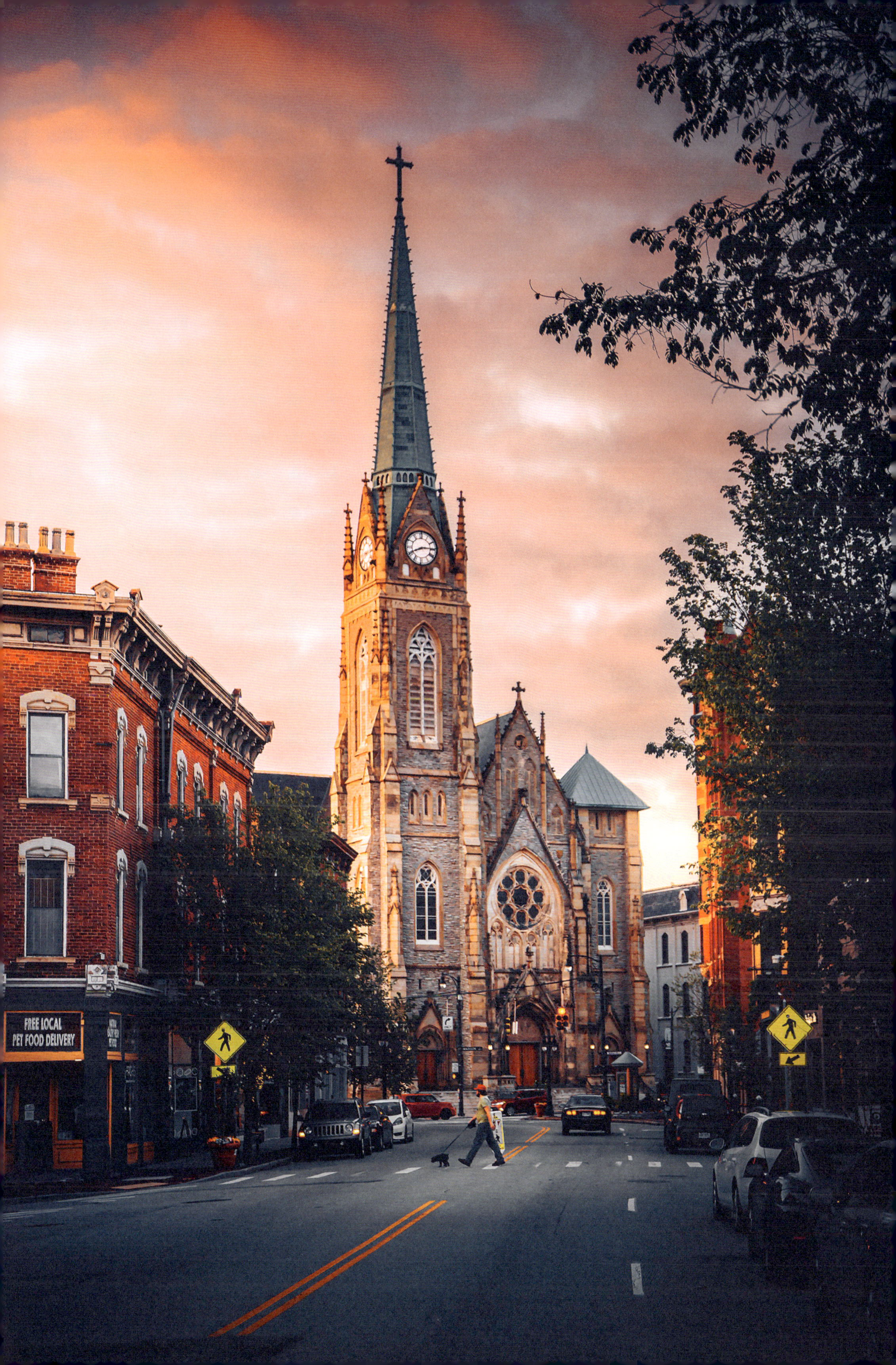
FREE LOCAL
PET FOOD DELIVERY

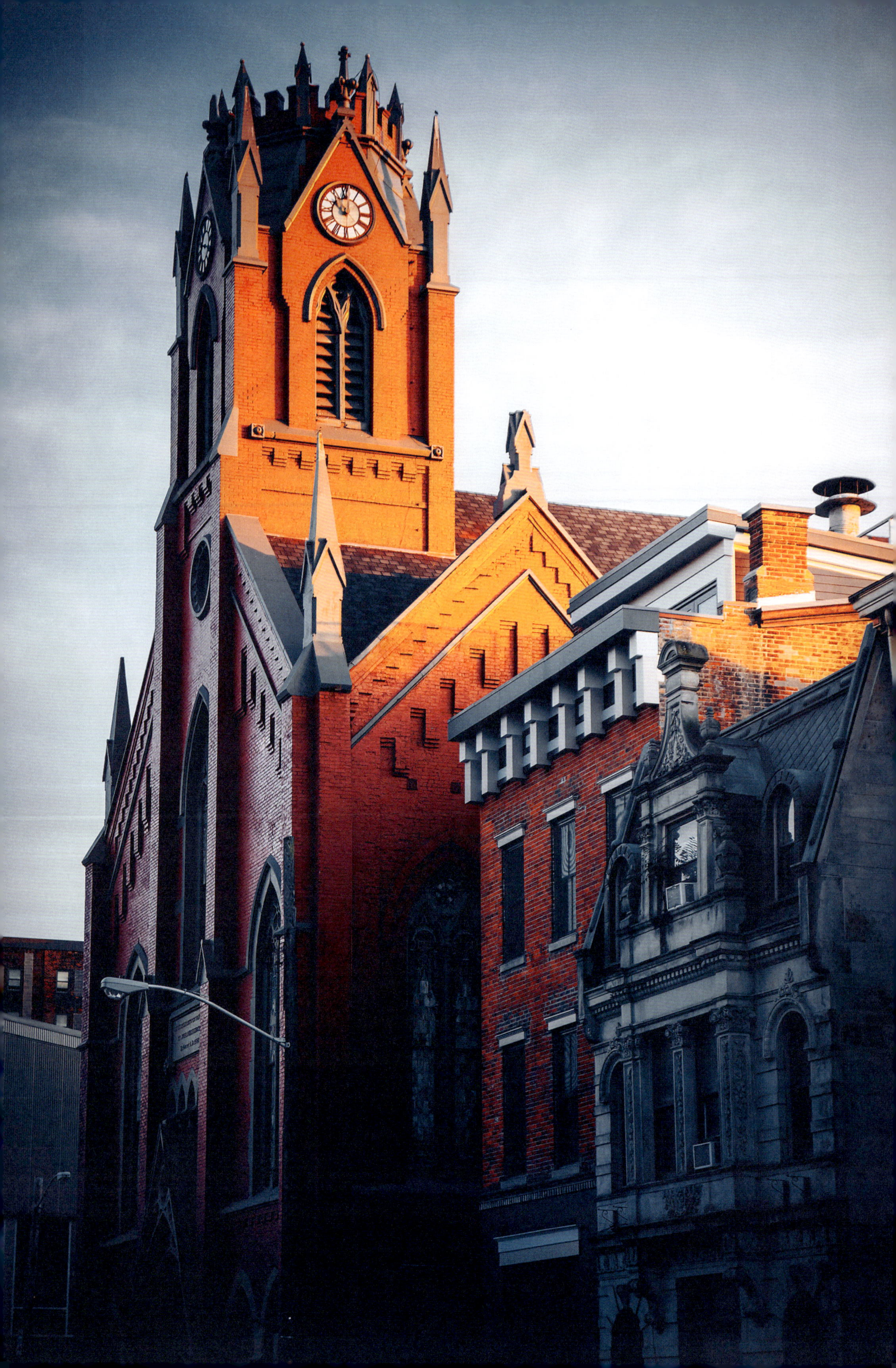

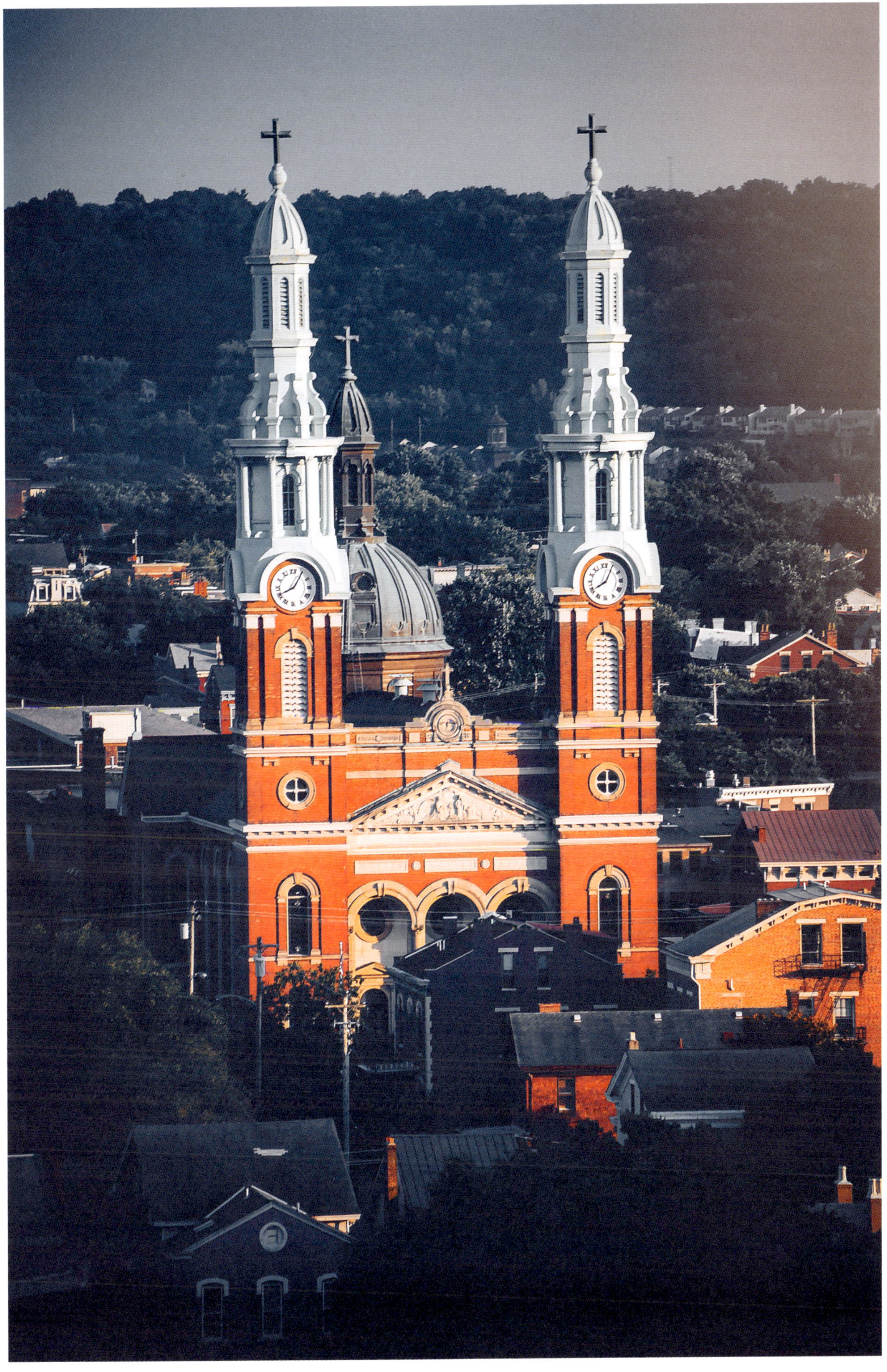

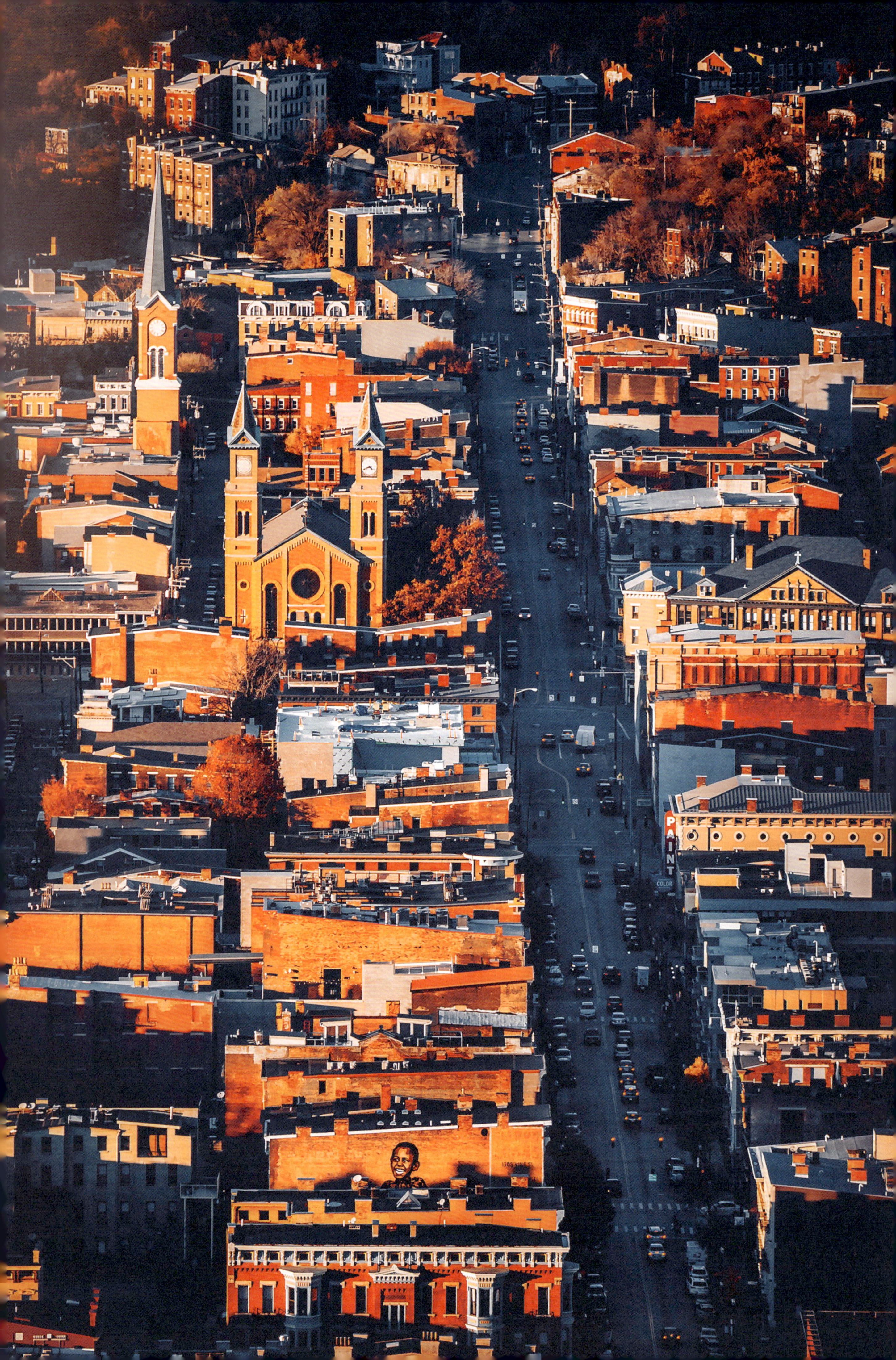
PAINT
COLOR

Cincinnati is a beautiful city; cheerful, thriving, and animated. I have not often seen a place that commends itself so favourably and pleasantly to a stranger at the first glance as this does.

CHARLES DICKENS

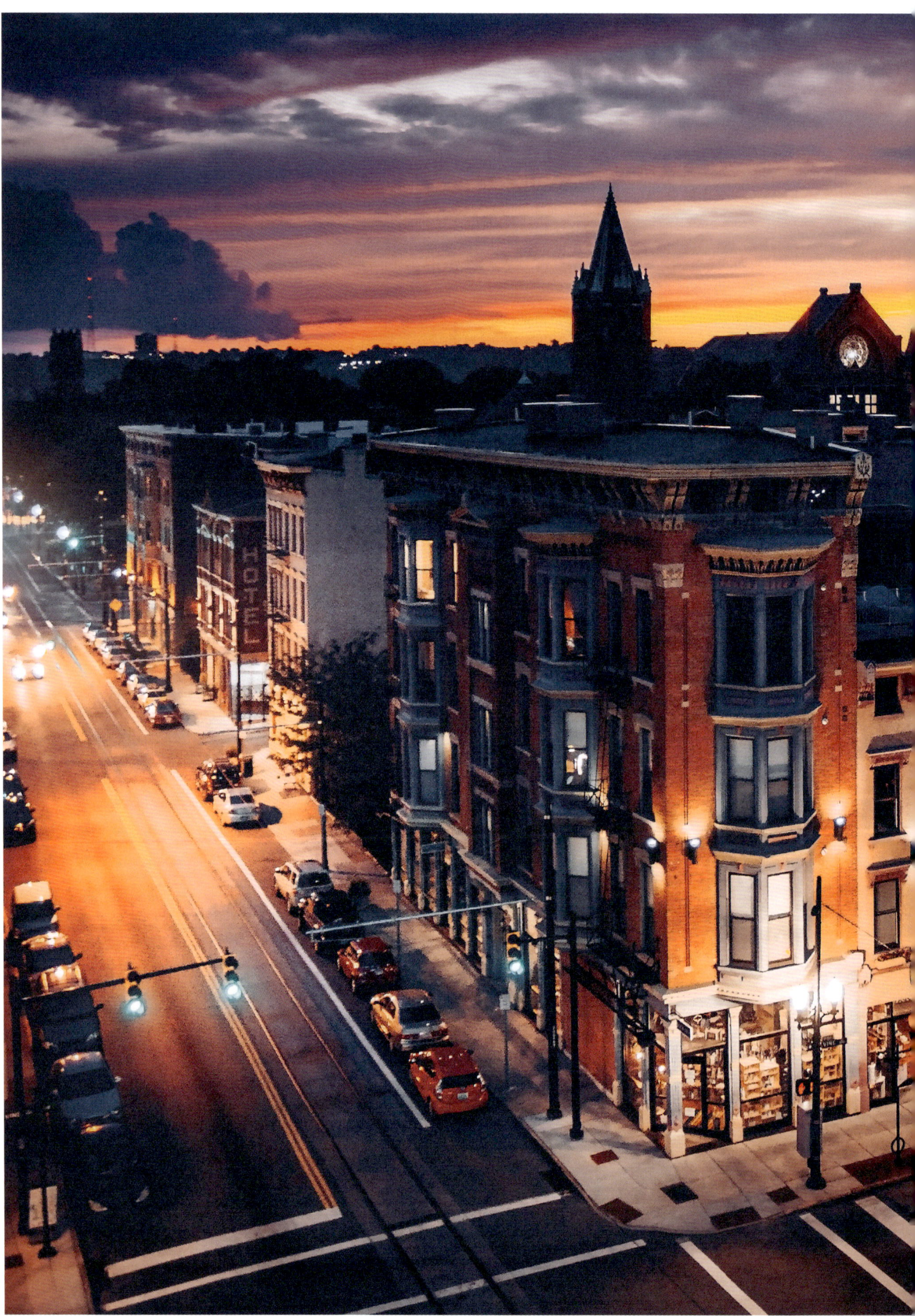
HOTEL

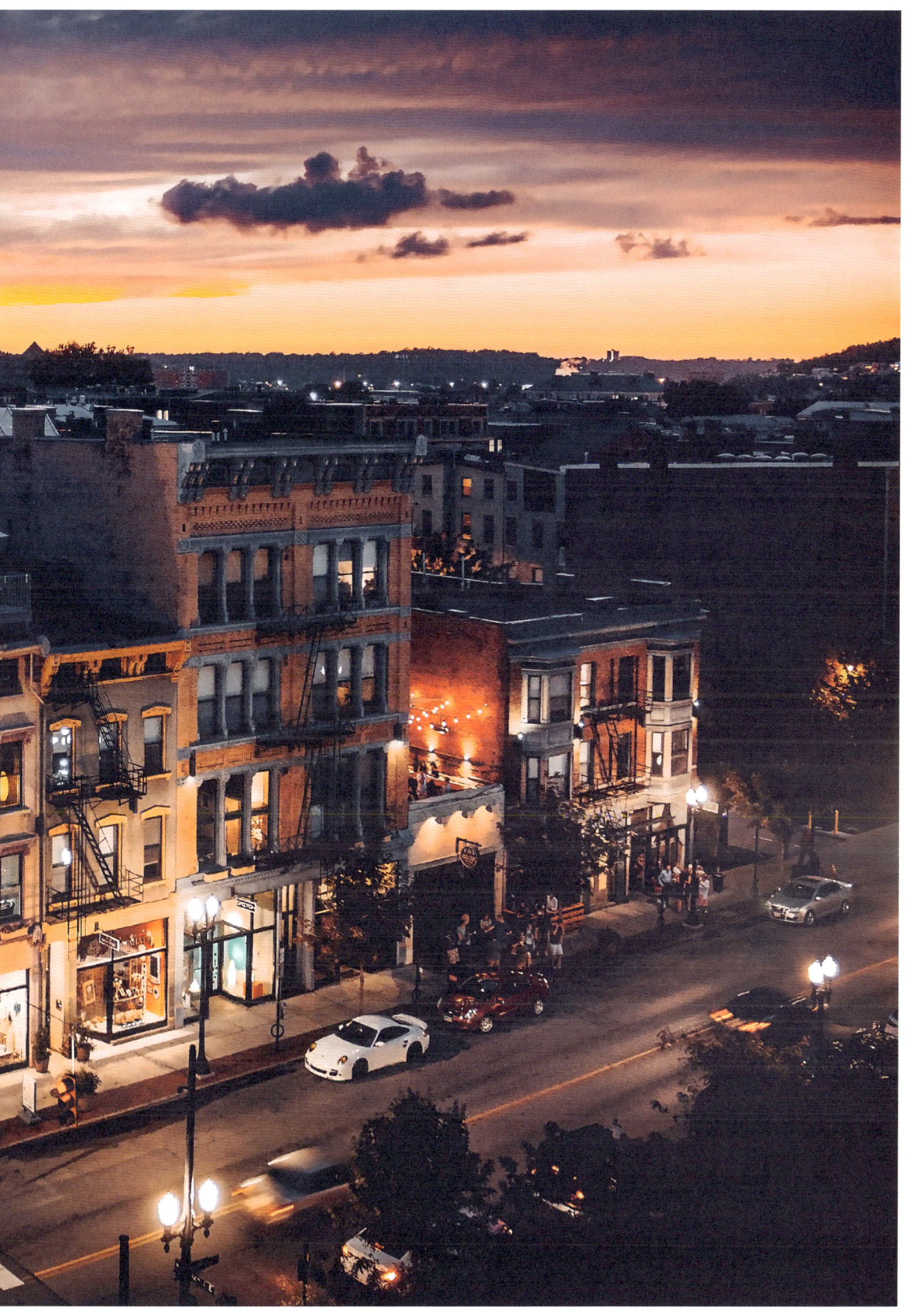

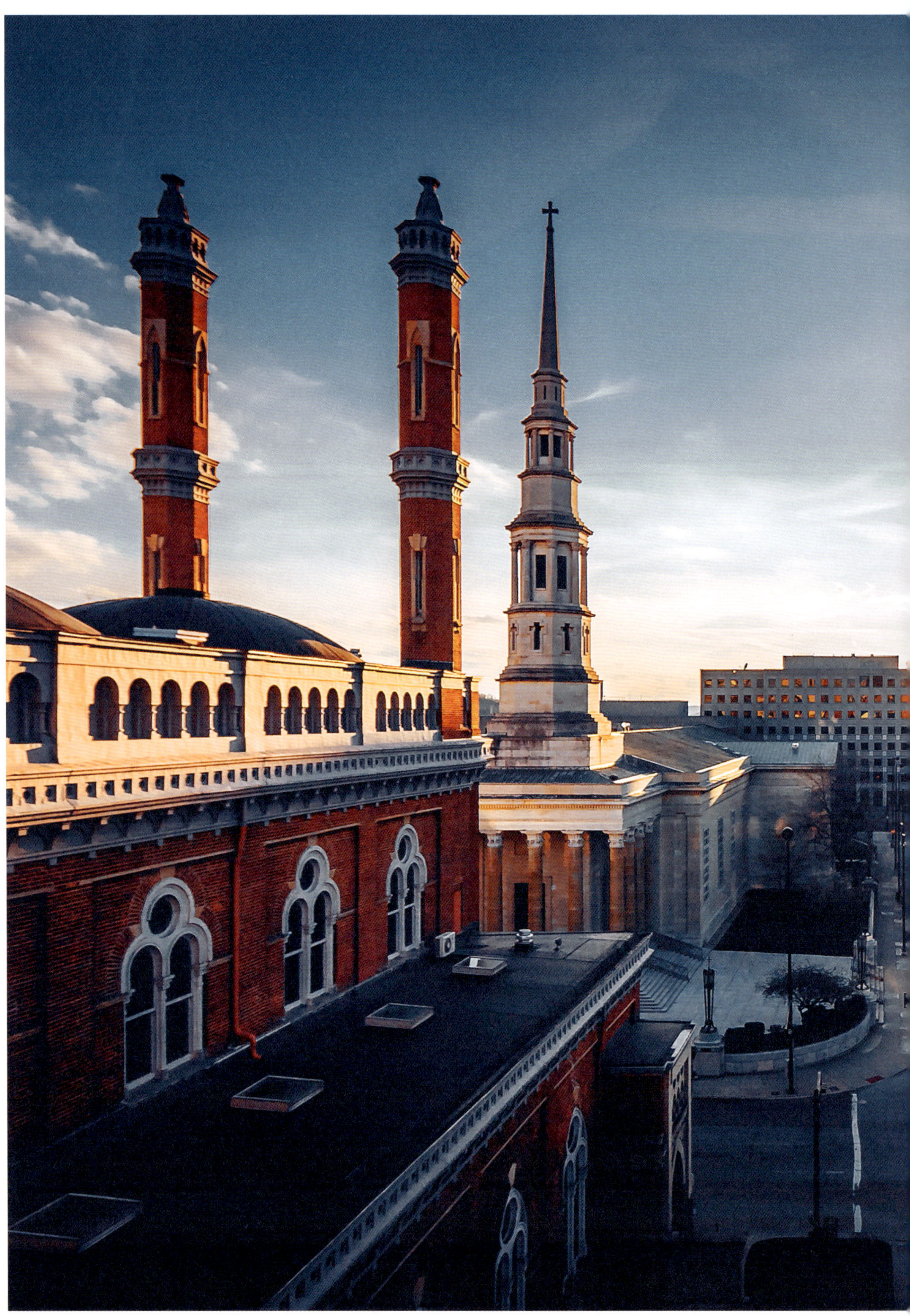

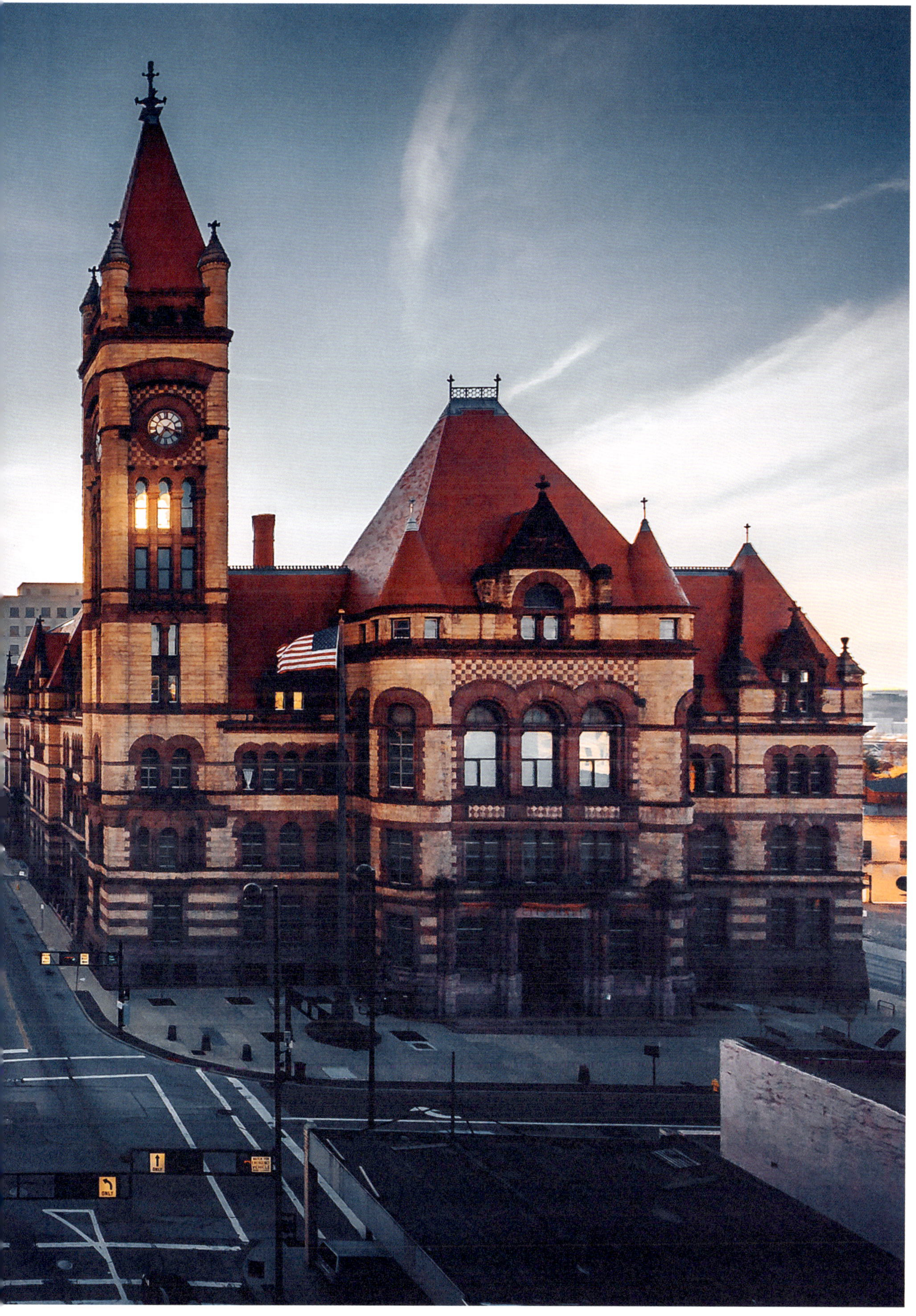

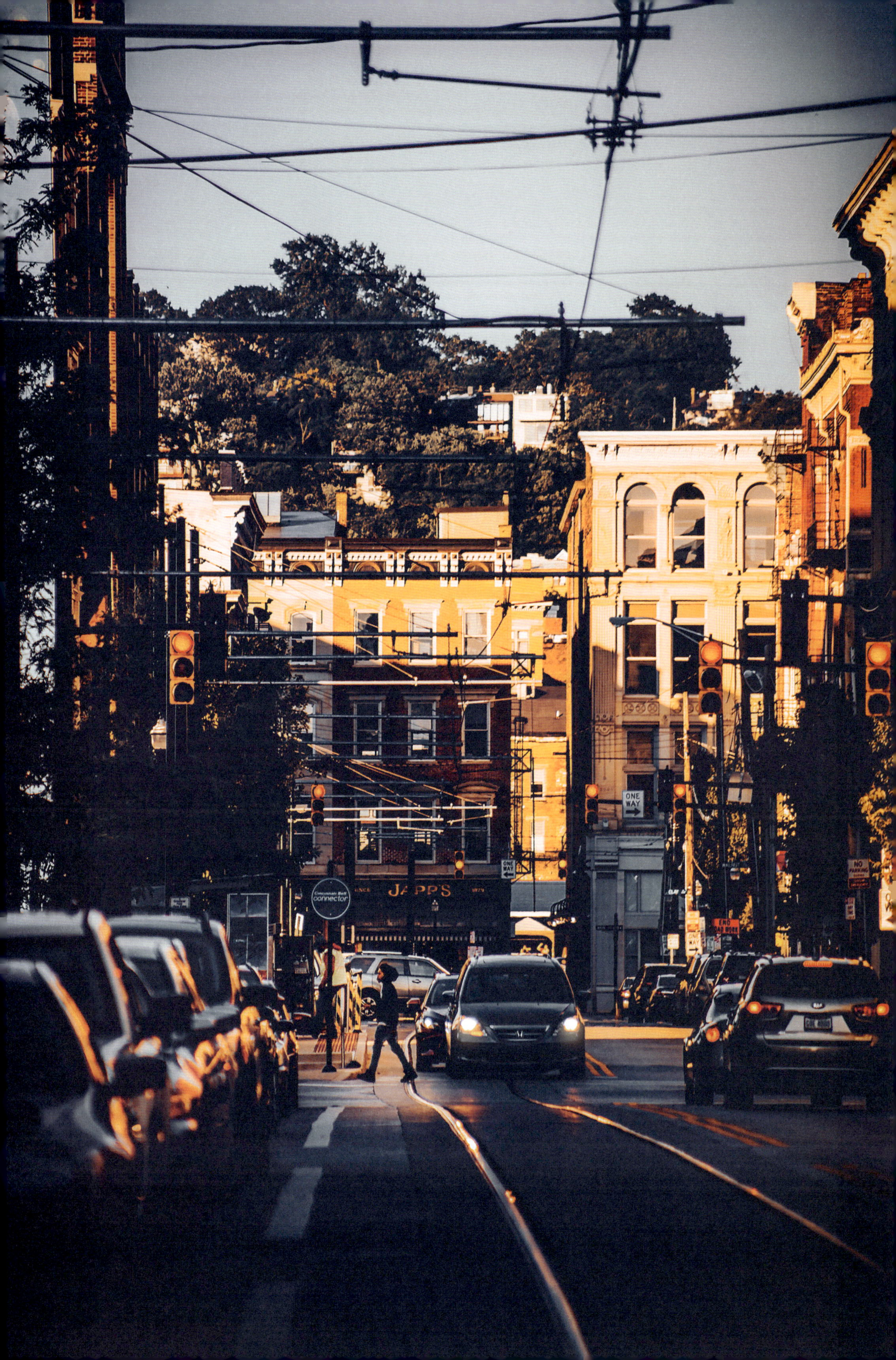

Cincinnati Bell
connector
JAPP'S
1879
ONE WAY
ONE WAY

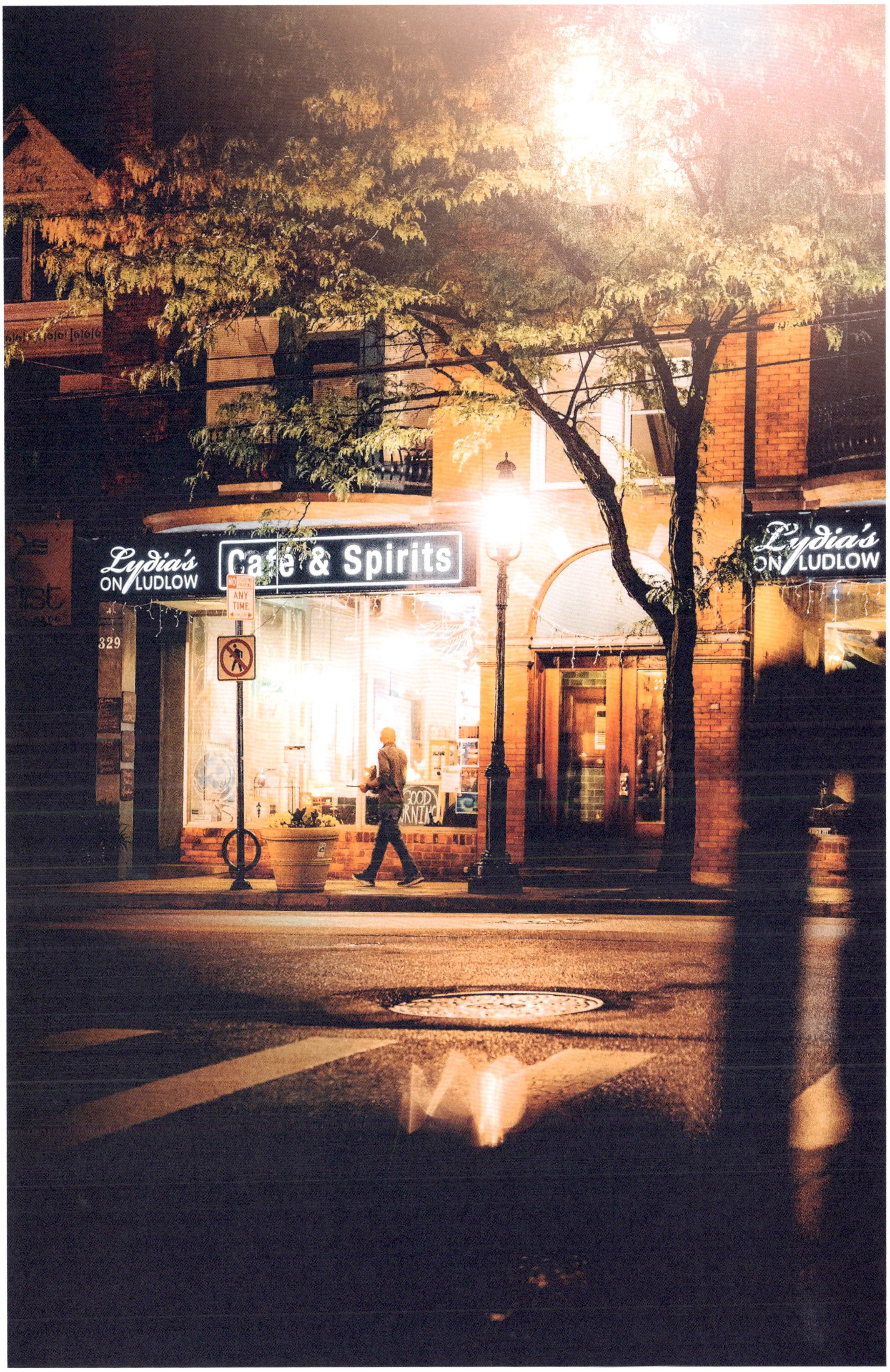
Lydia's
ON LUDLOW
Café & Spirits
329
NO
ANY TIME
Lydia's
ON LUDLOW

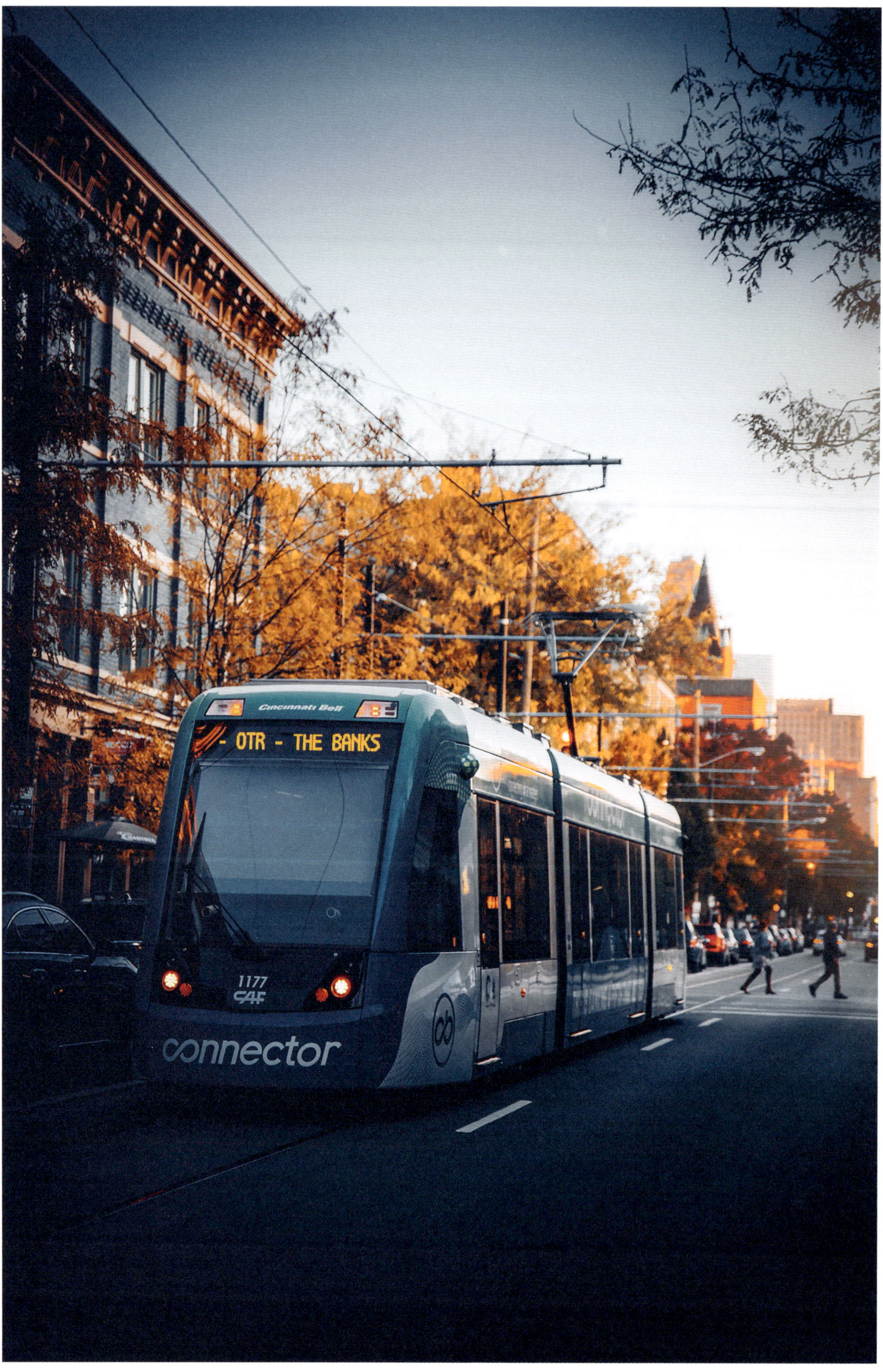
Cincinnati Bell
- OTR - THE BANKS
1177
CAF
connector

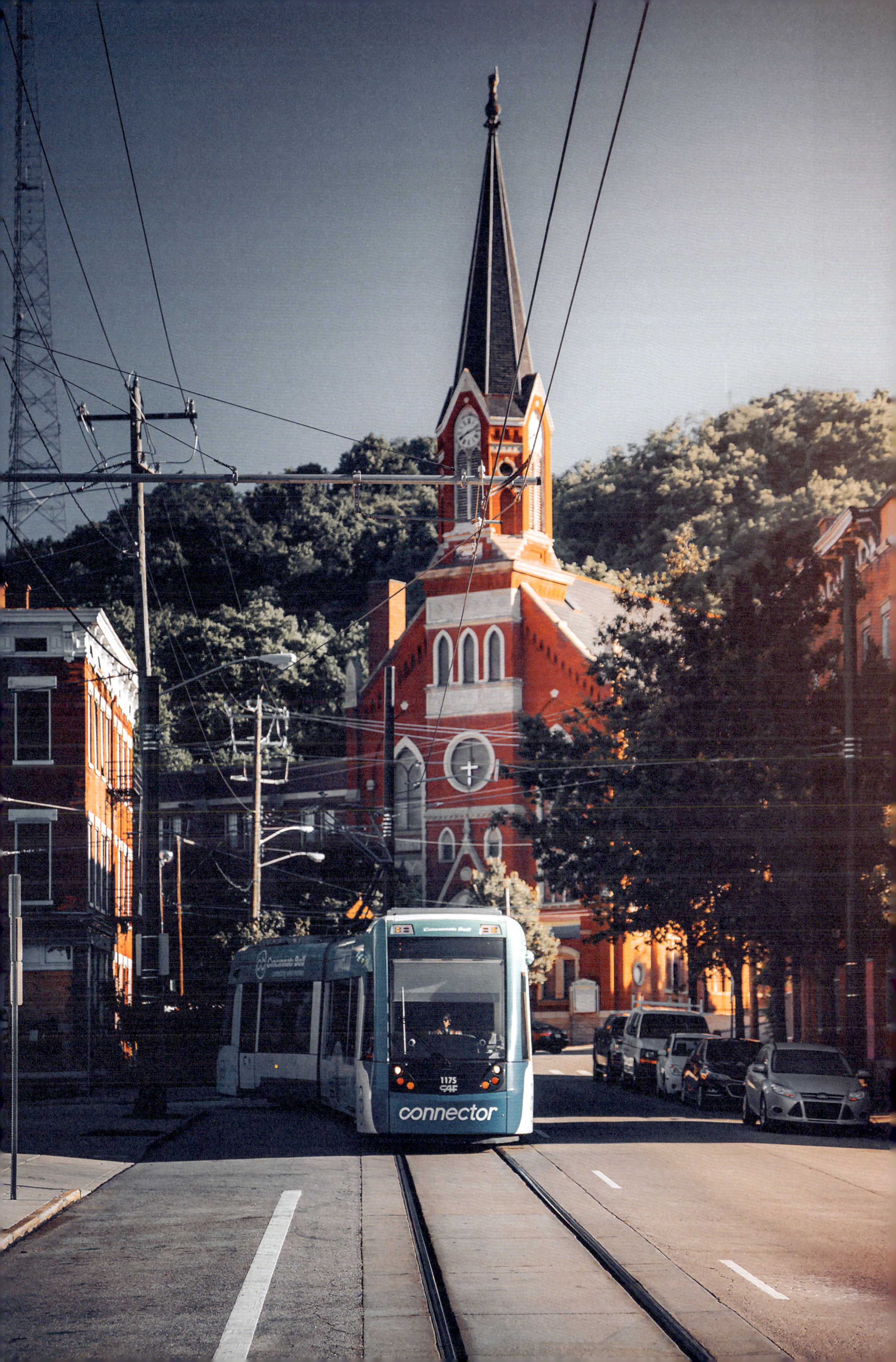
connector
1175

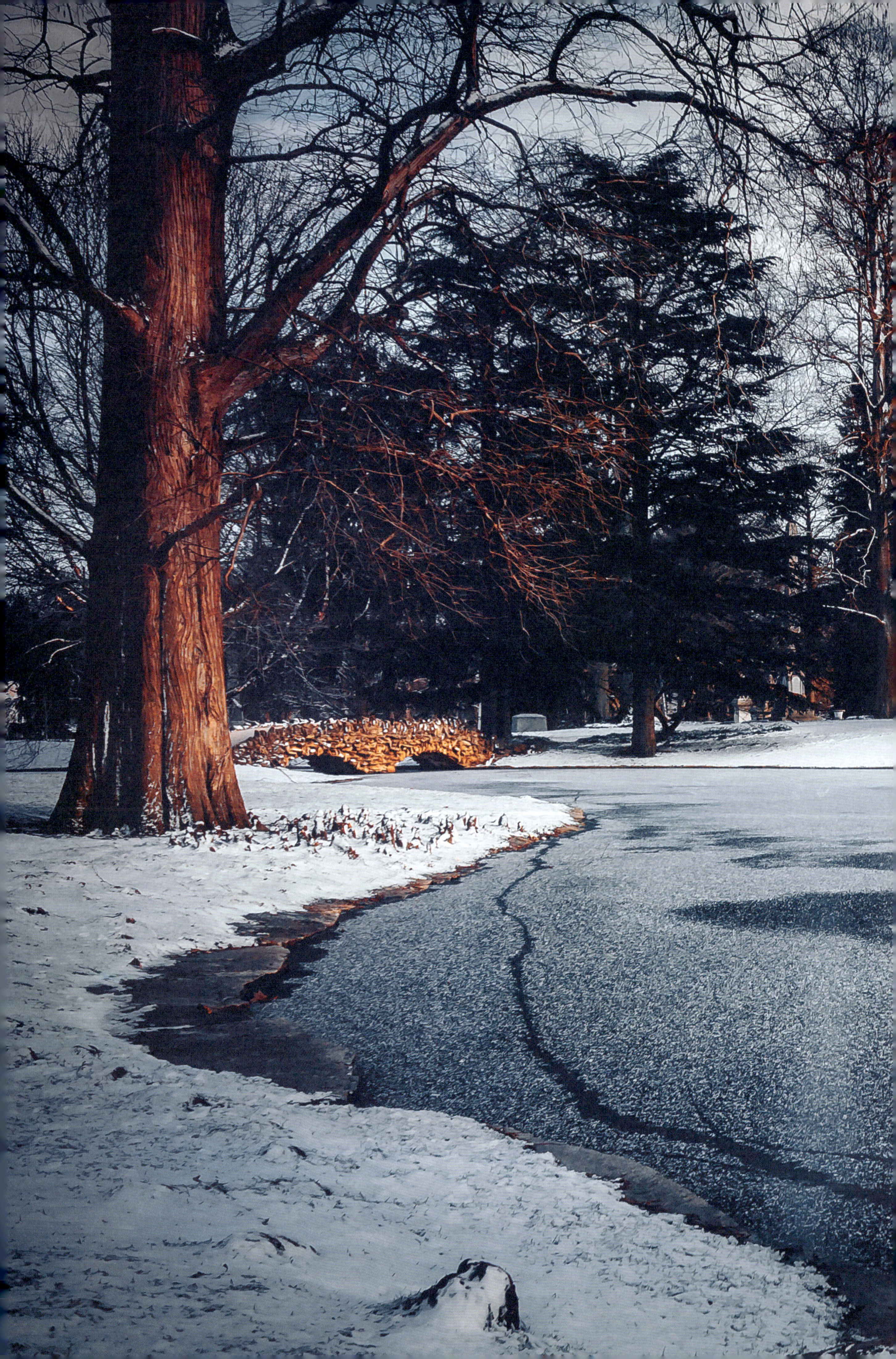

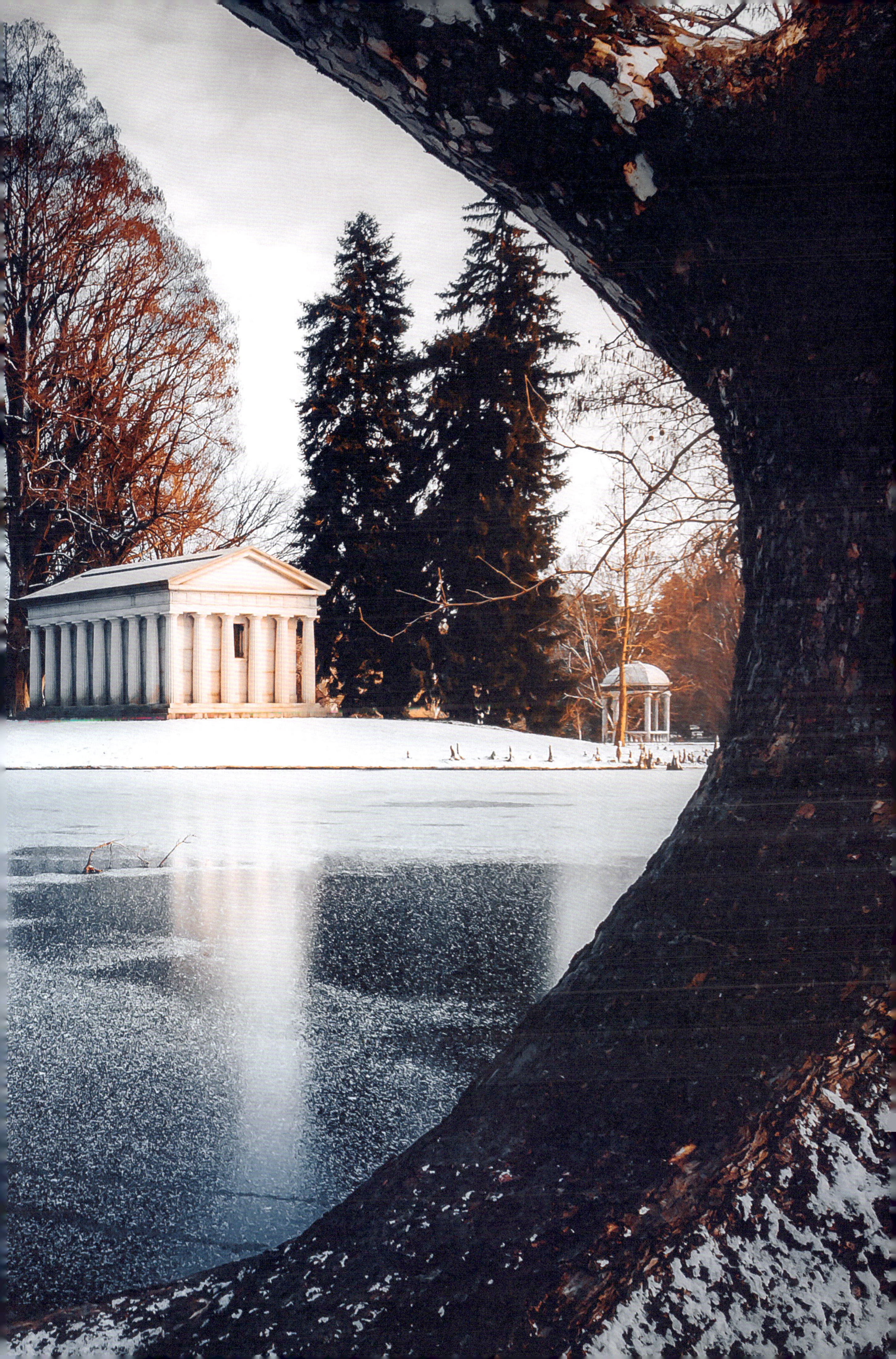

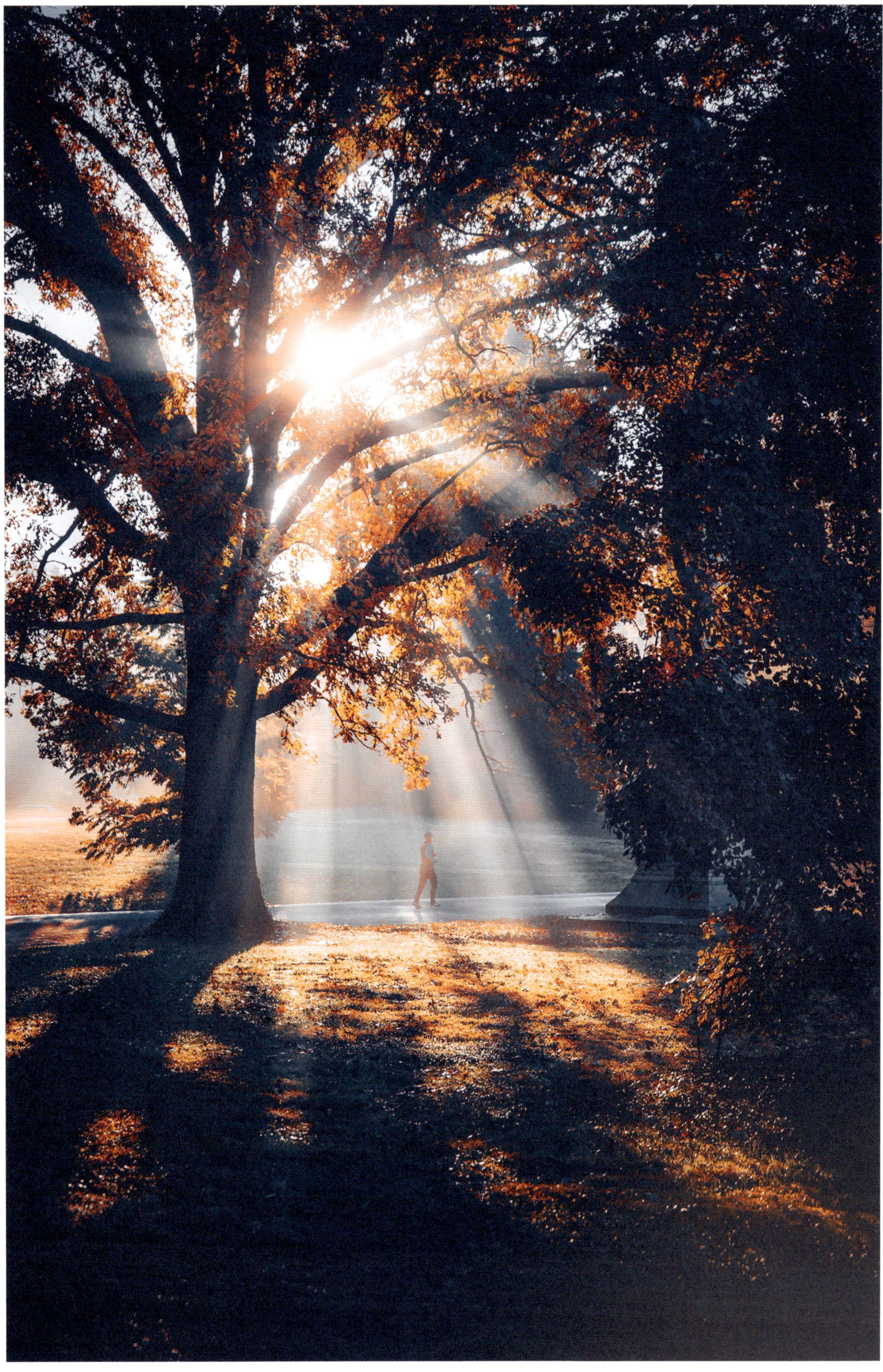

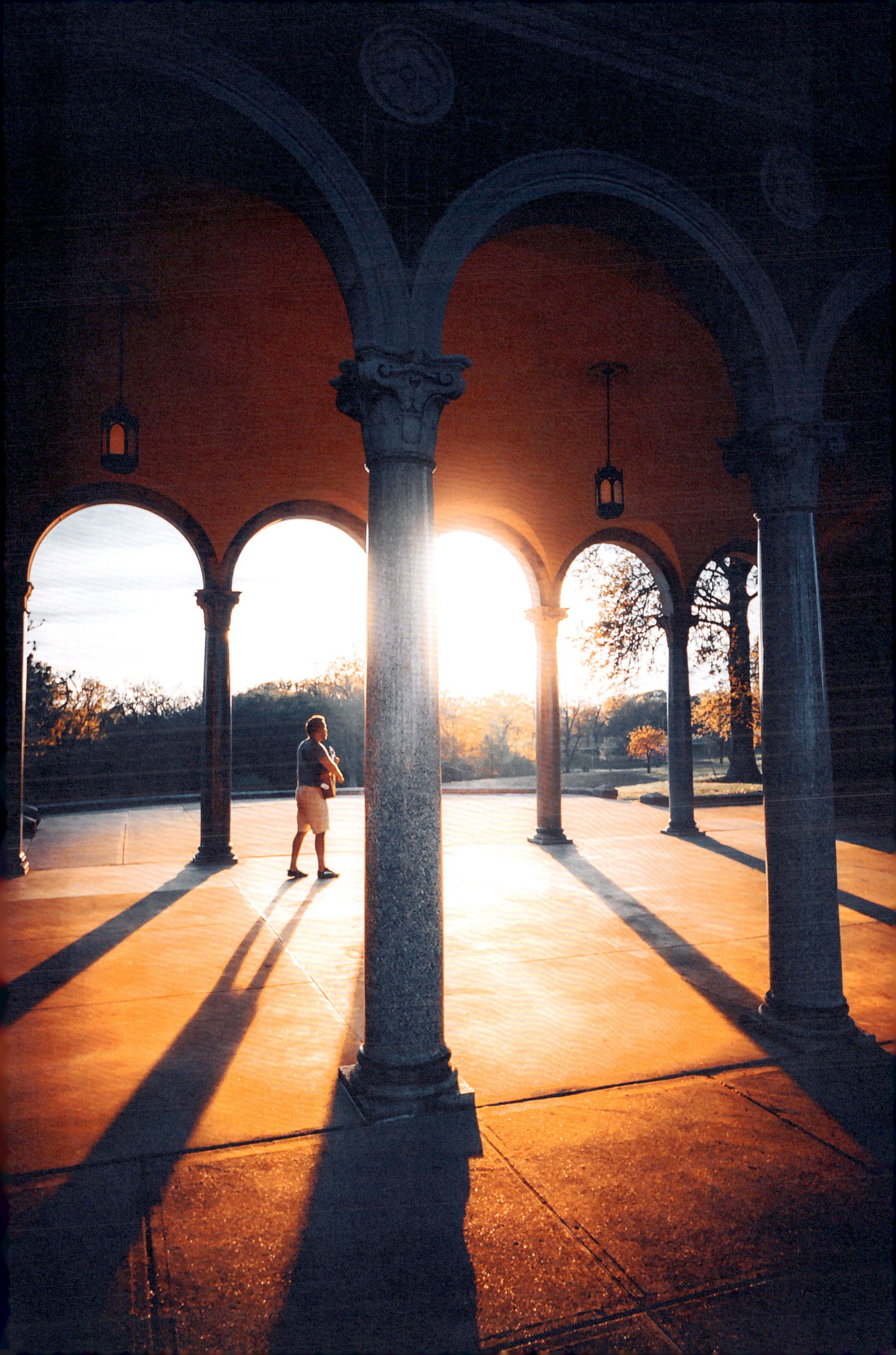

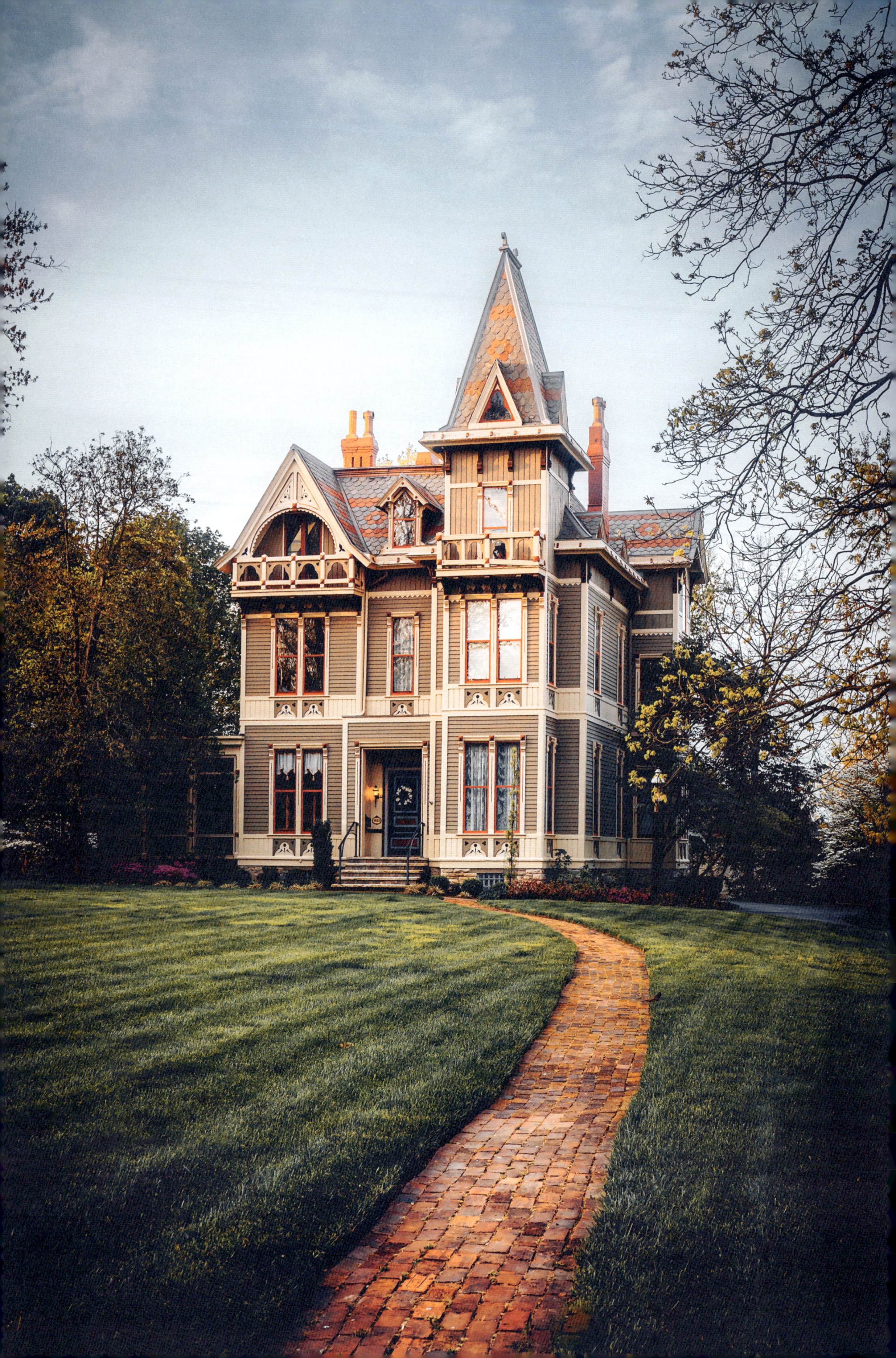

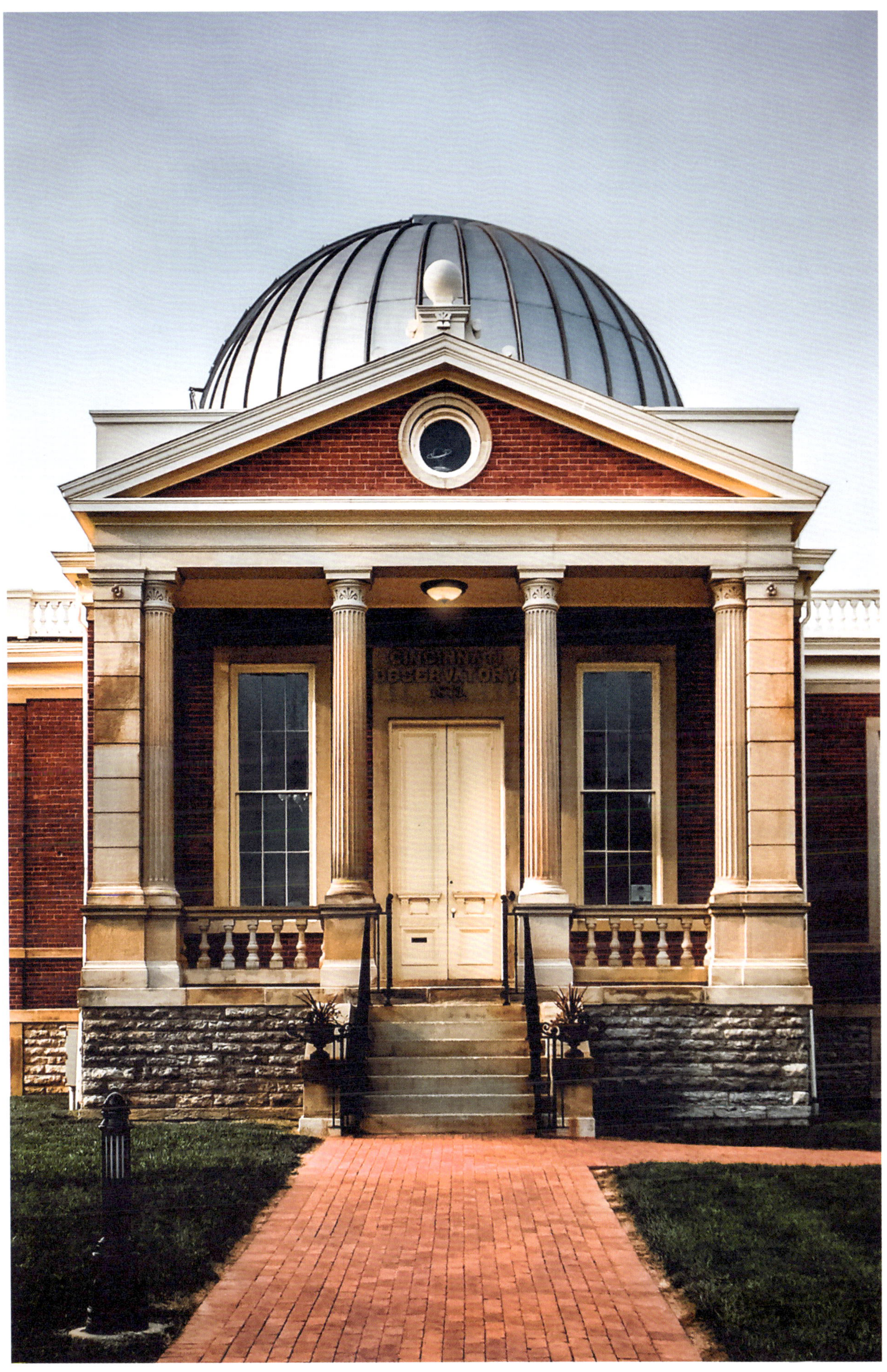
OBSERVATORY

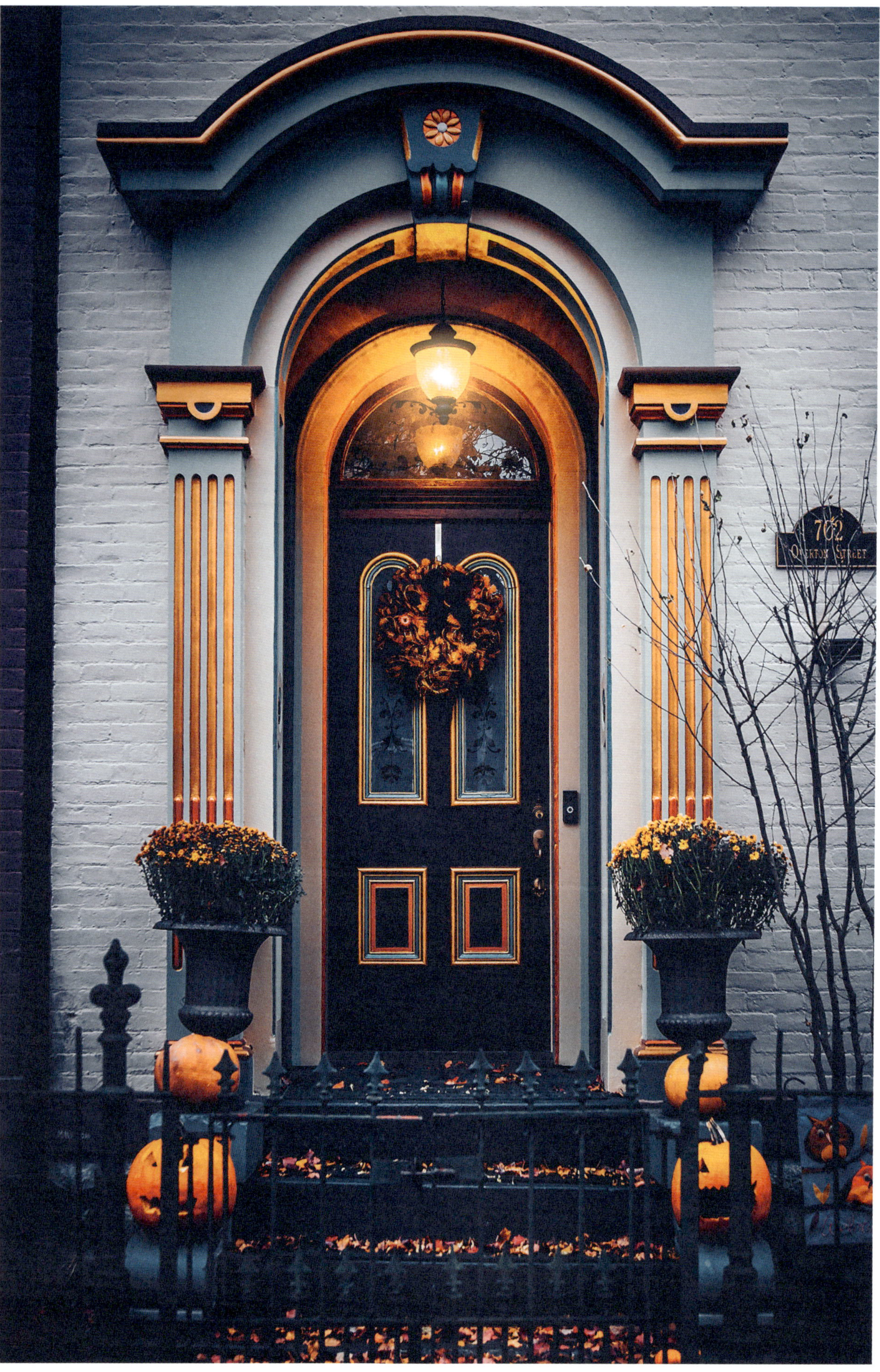
702
Street

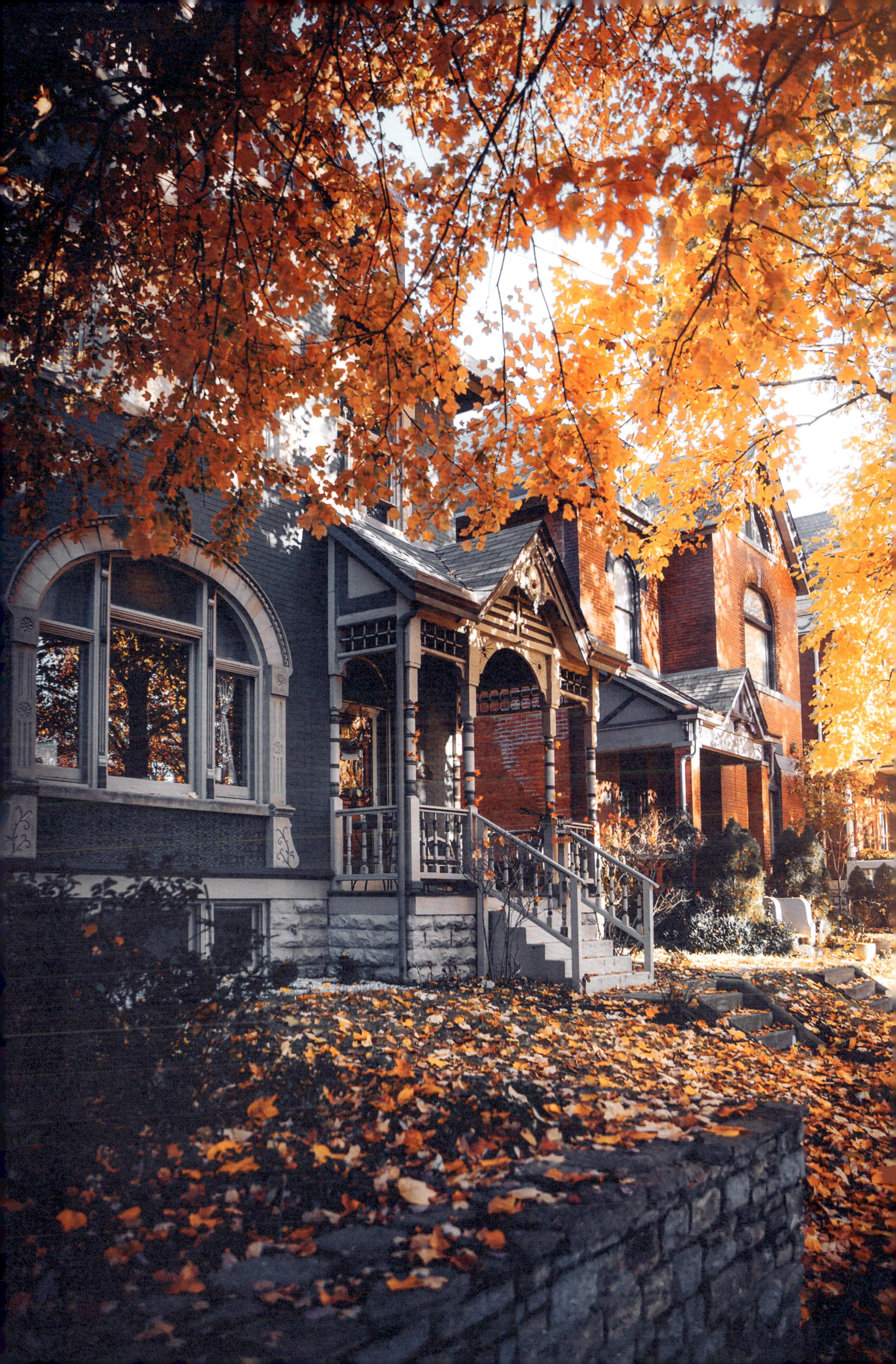

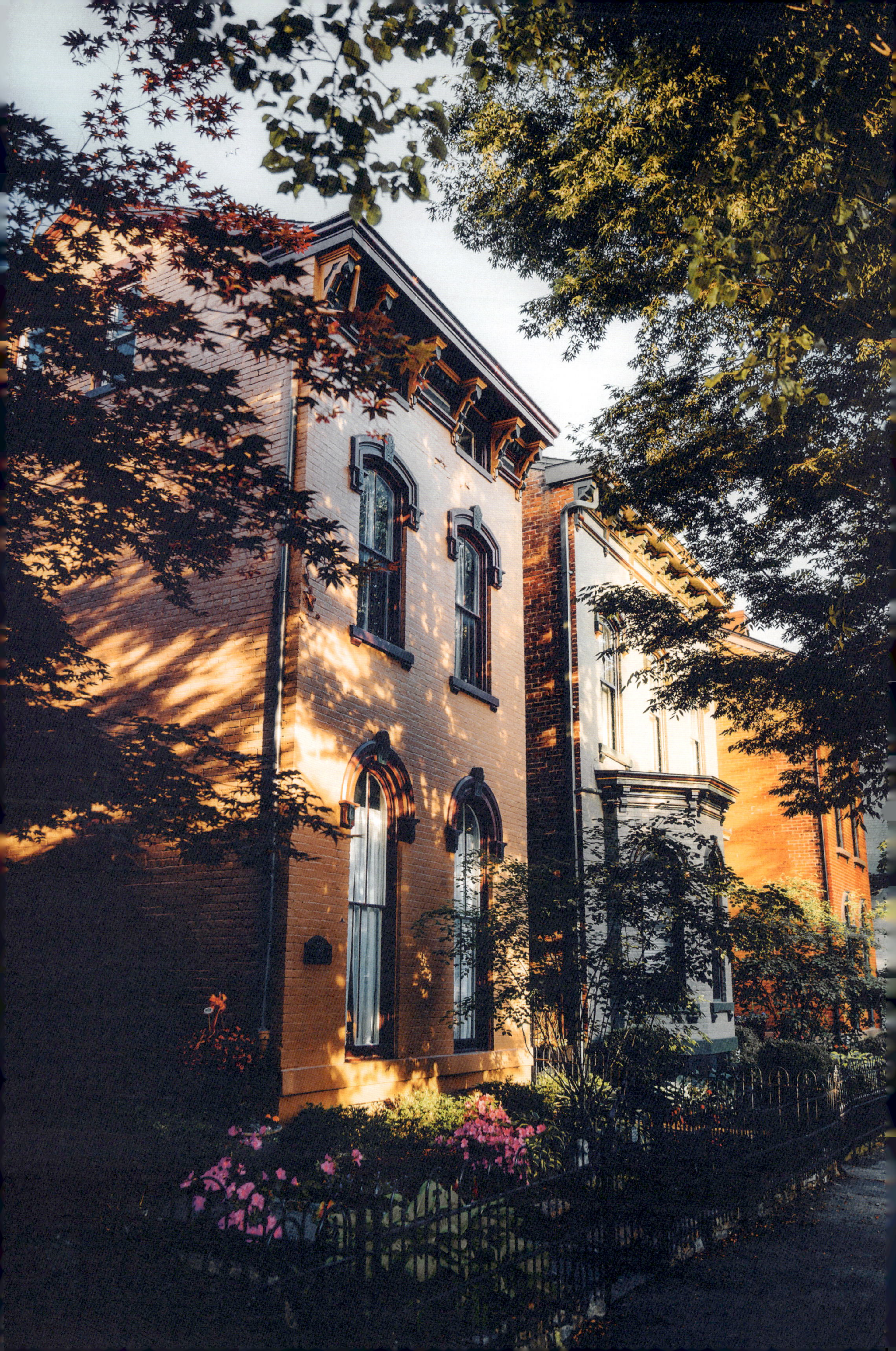

I find beauty everywhere.
I find beauty in my garden.

DORIS DAY

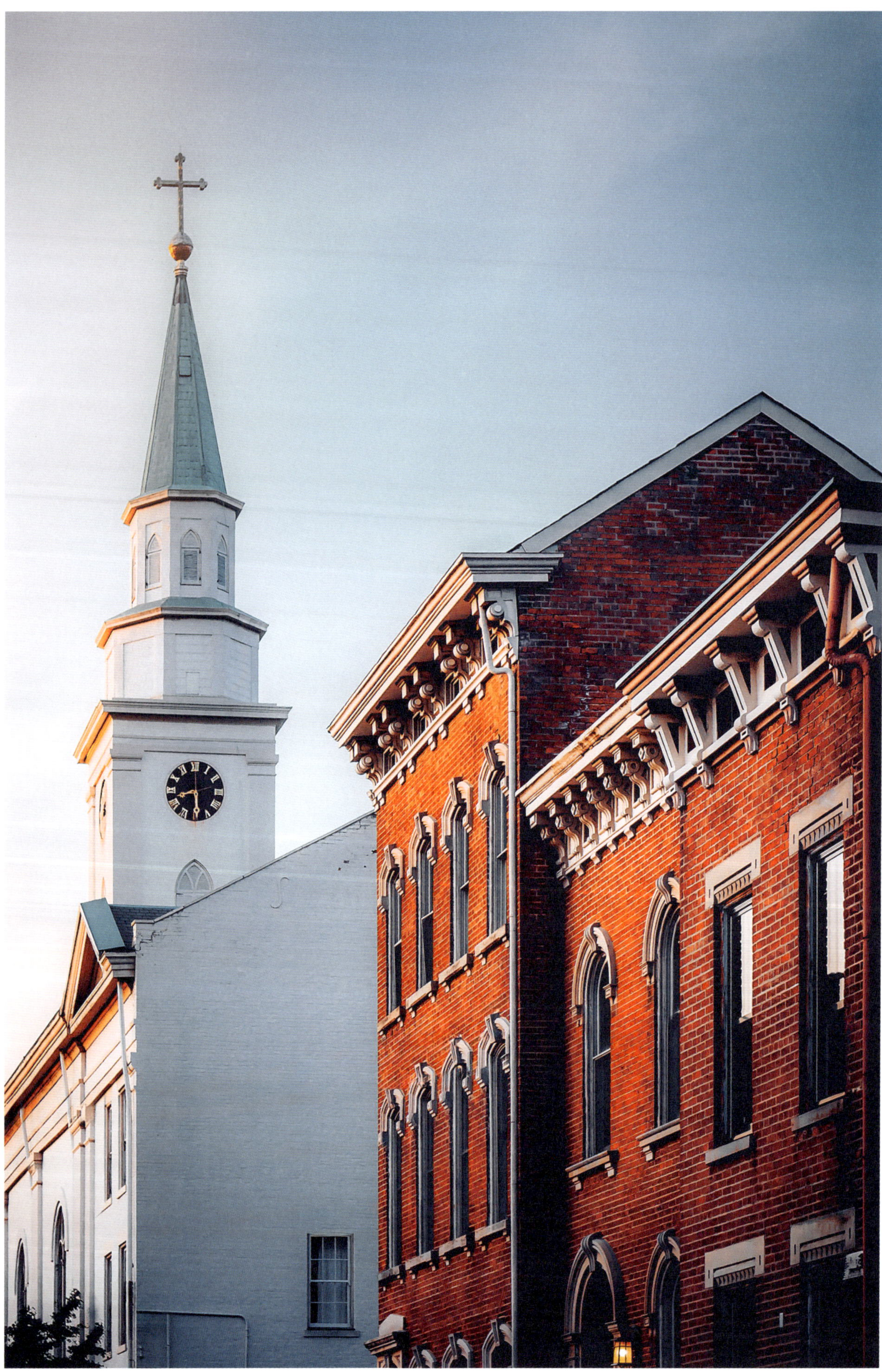

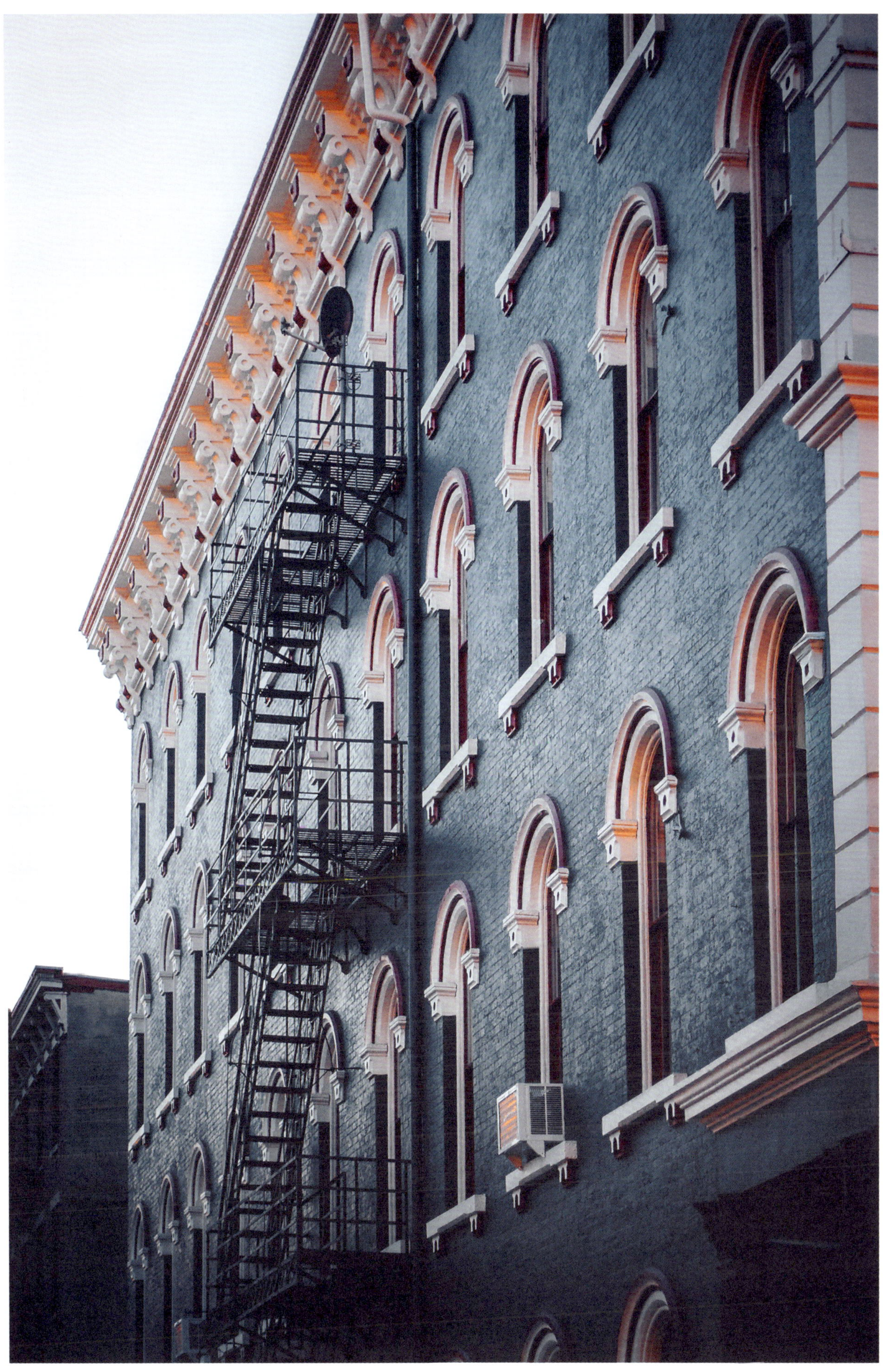

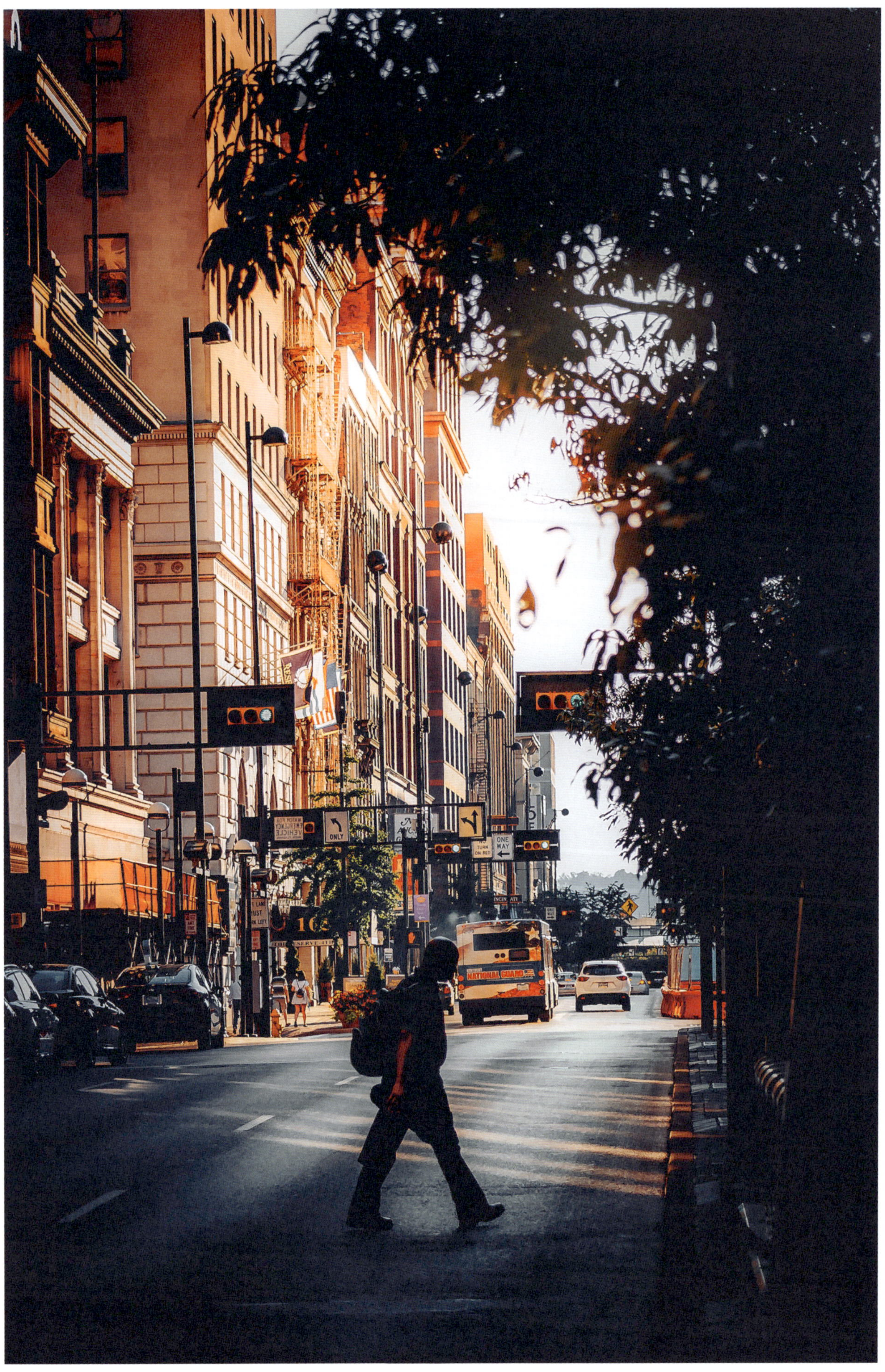
WATCH FOR
EMERGENCY
VEHICLE
ONLY
NO
TURN
ON RED
ONE
WAY
NATIONAL GUARD

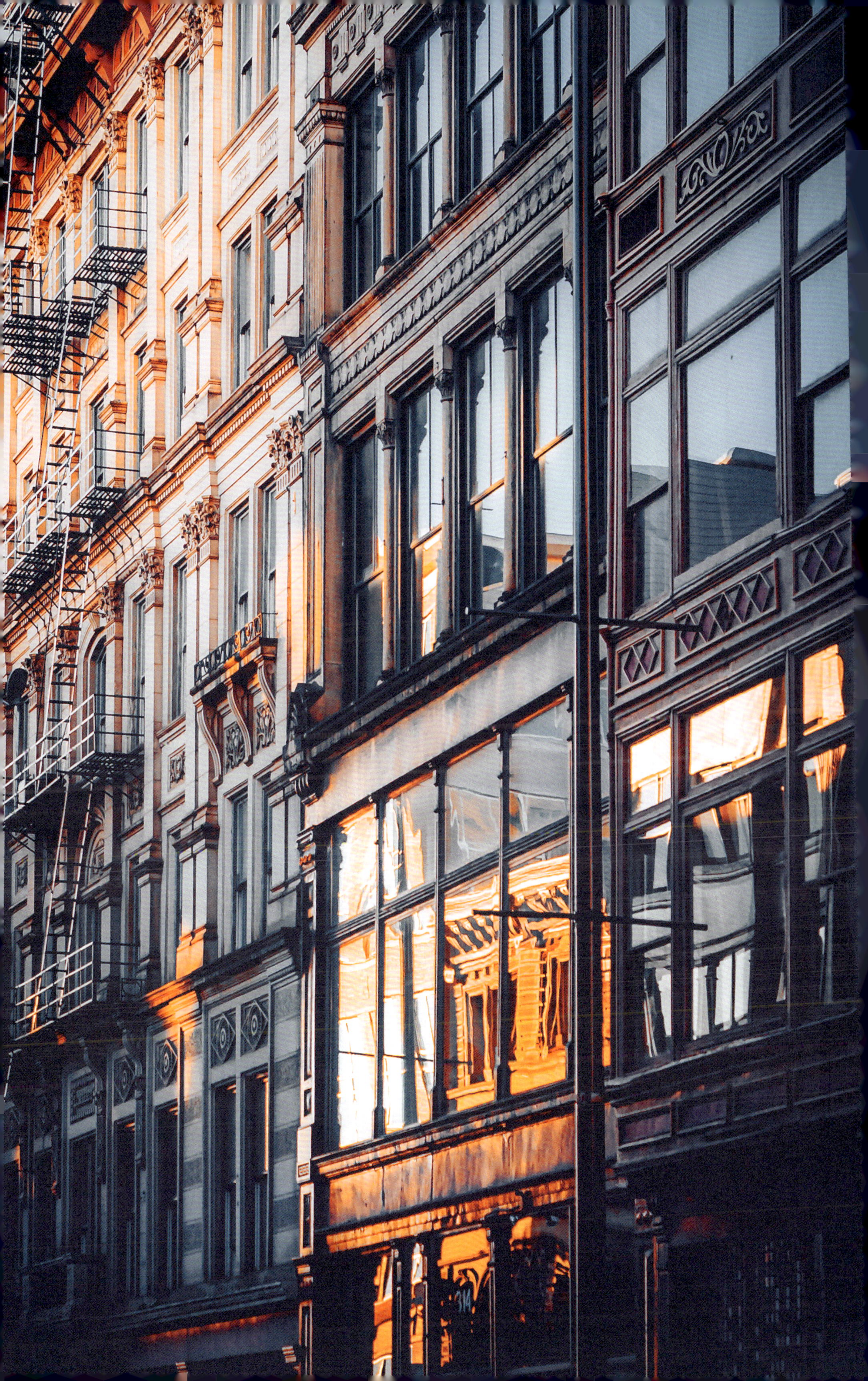

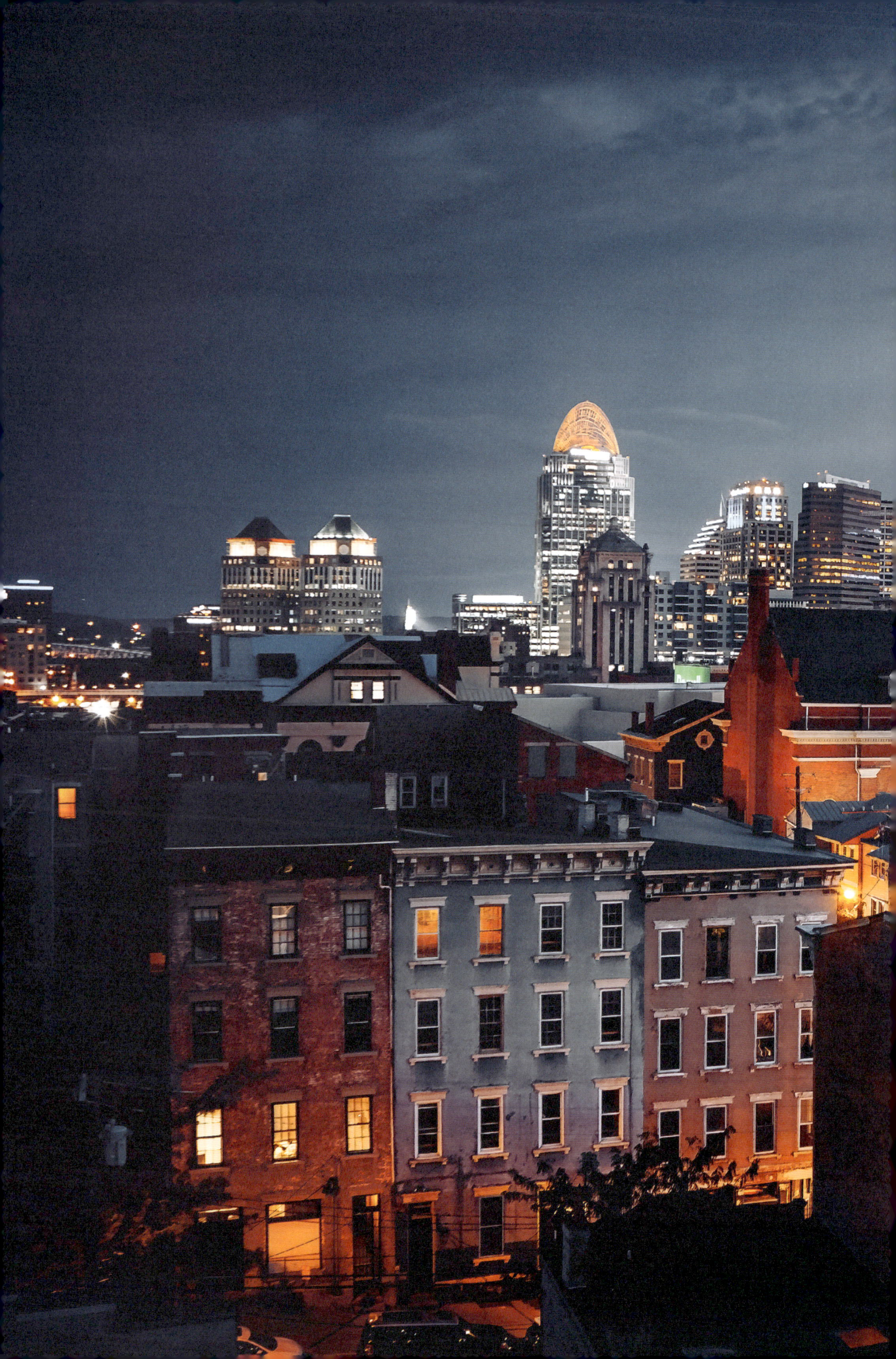

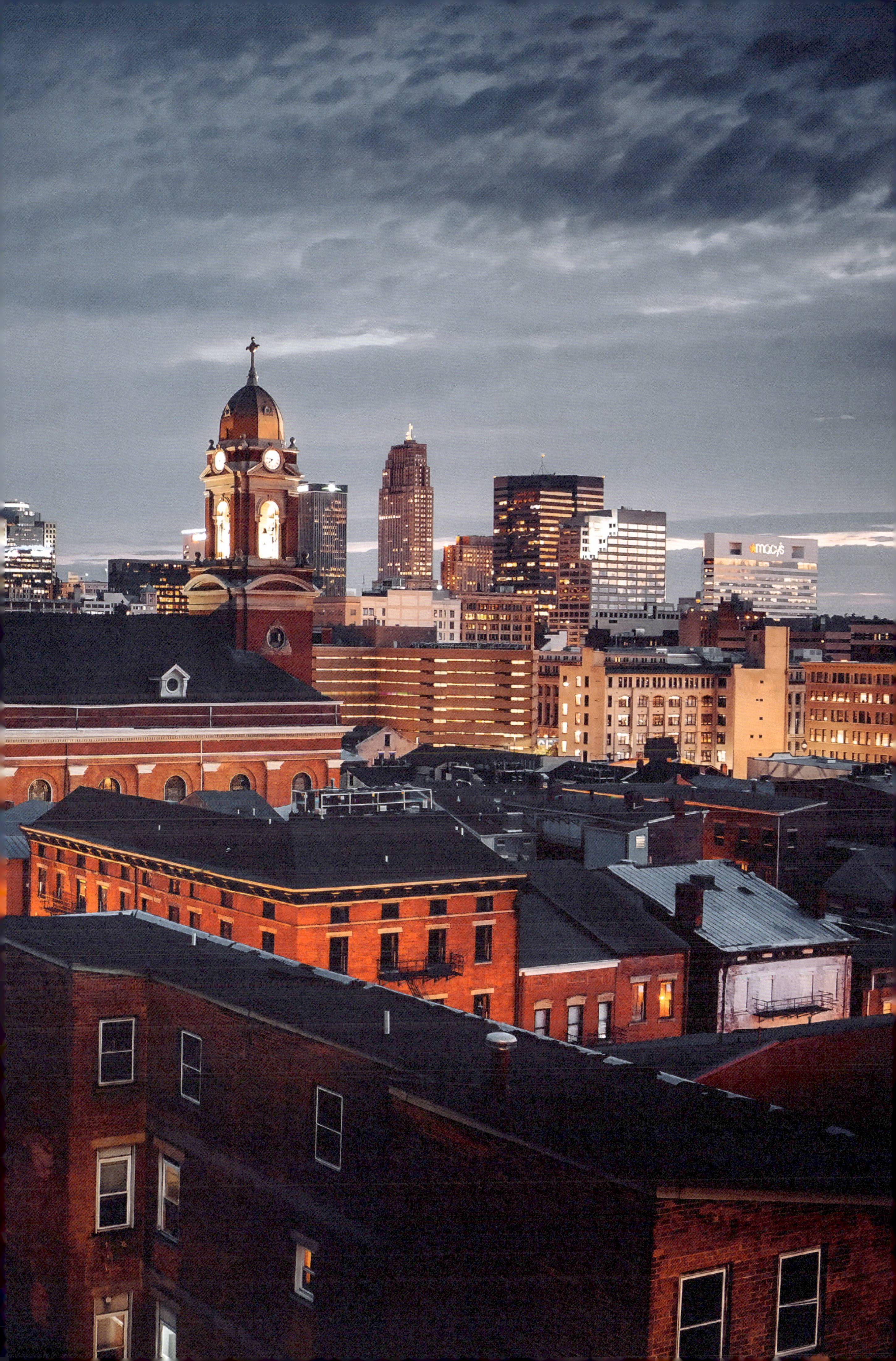
macy's

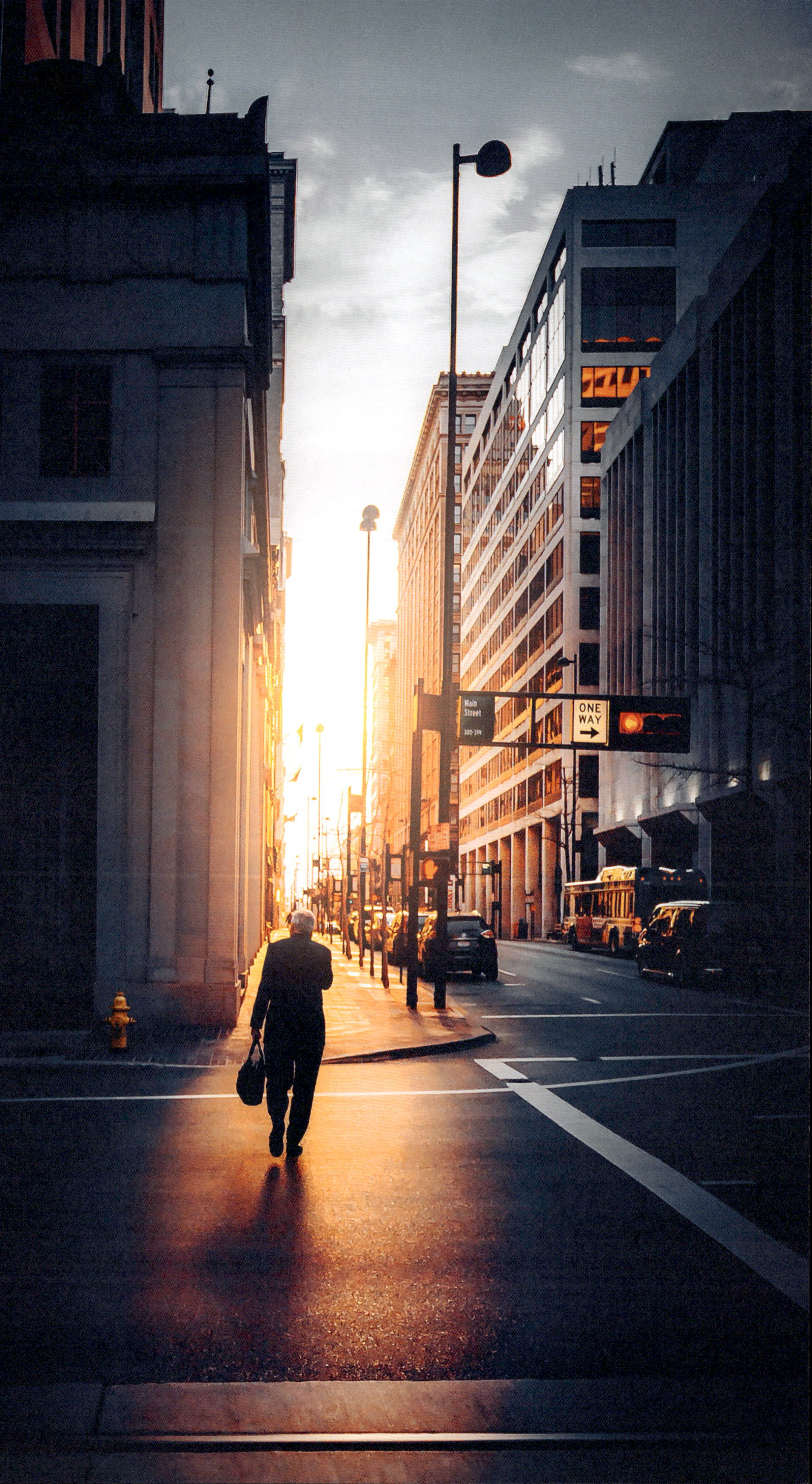
Main Street
ONE WAY

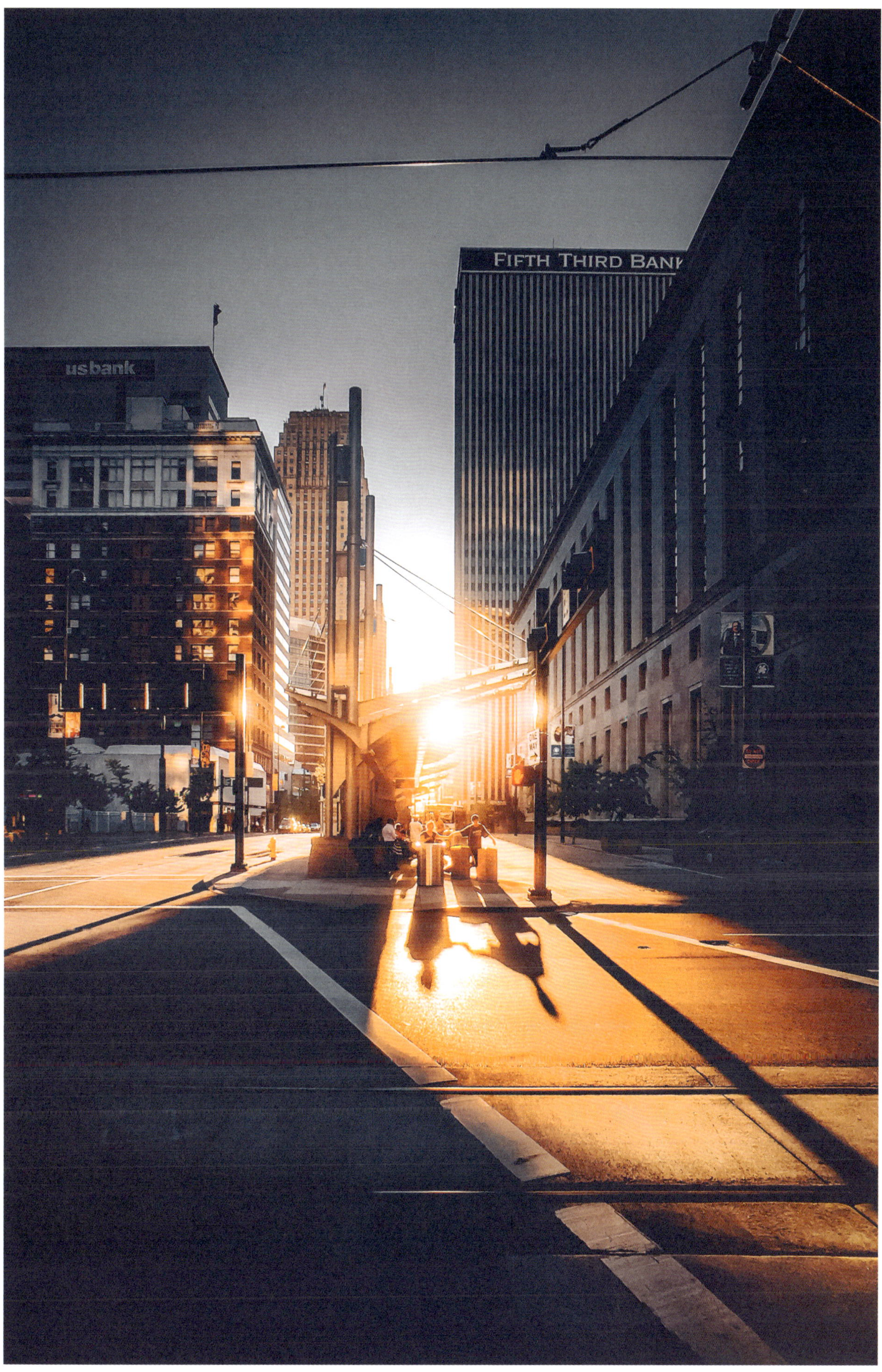
FIFTH THIRD BANK
usbank

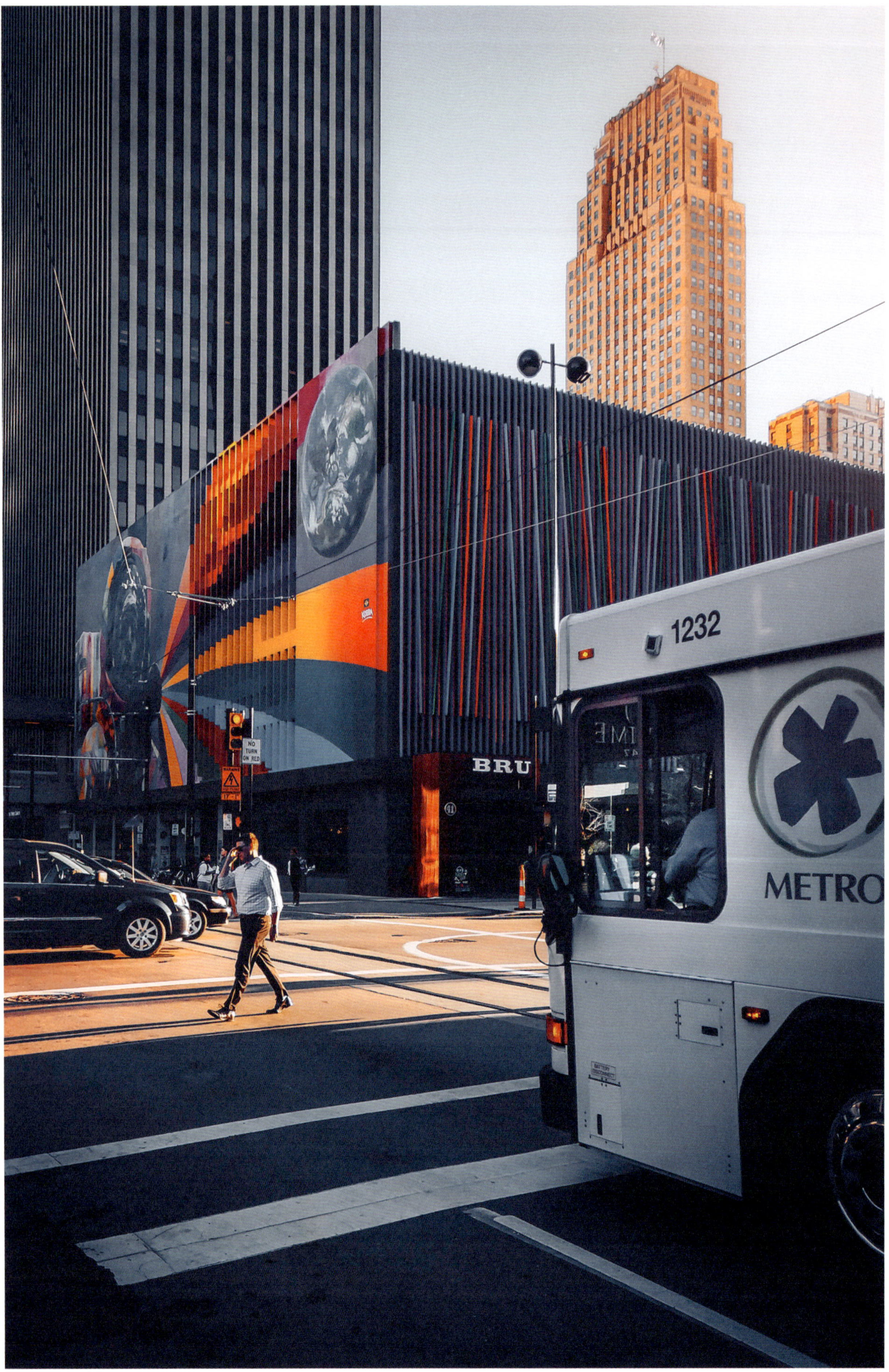
NO TURN ON RED
BRU
1232
METRO

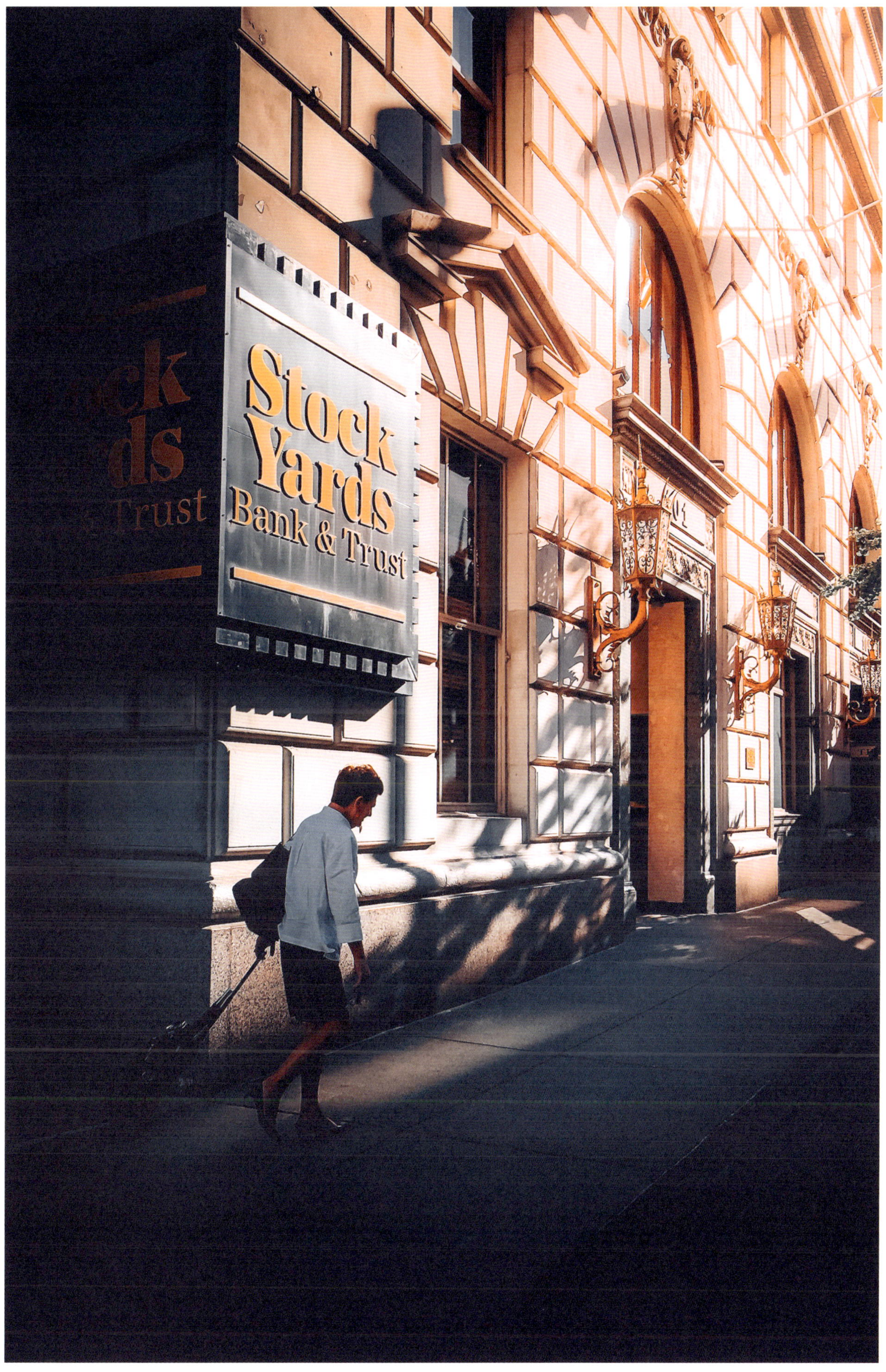
Stock
Yards
Bank & Trust

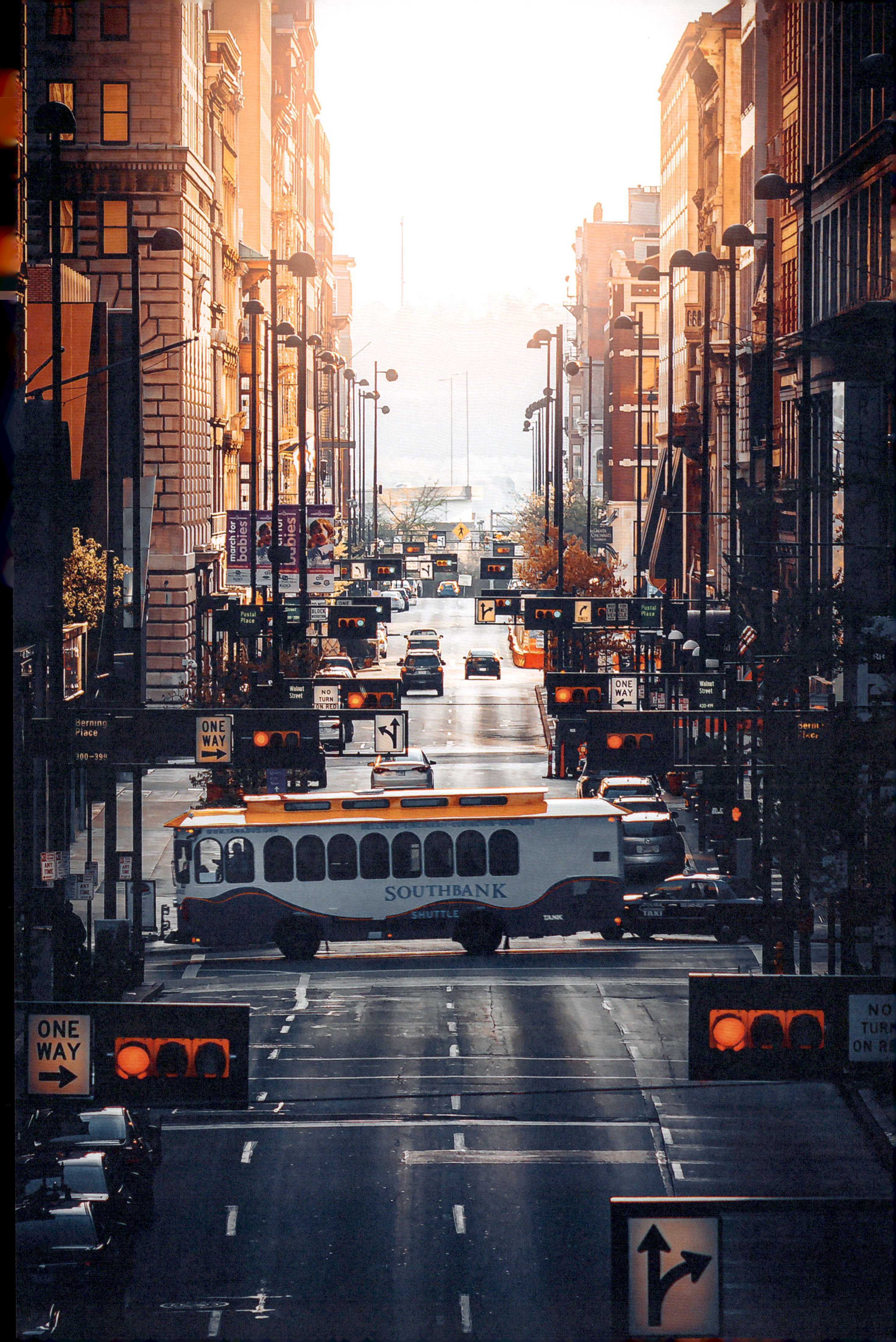
ONE WAY
ONE WAY
Berning Place
300-399
SOUTHBANK
SHUTTLE
march for babies

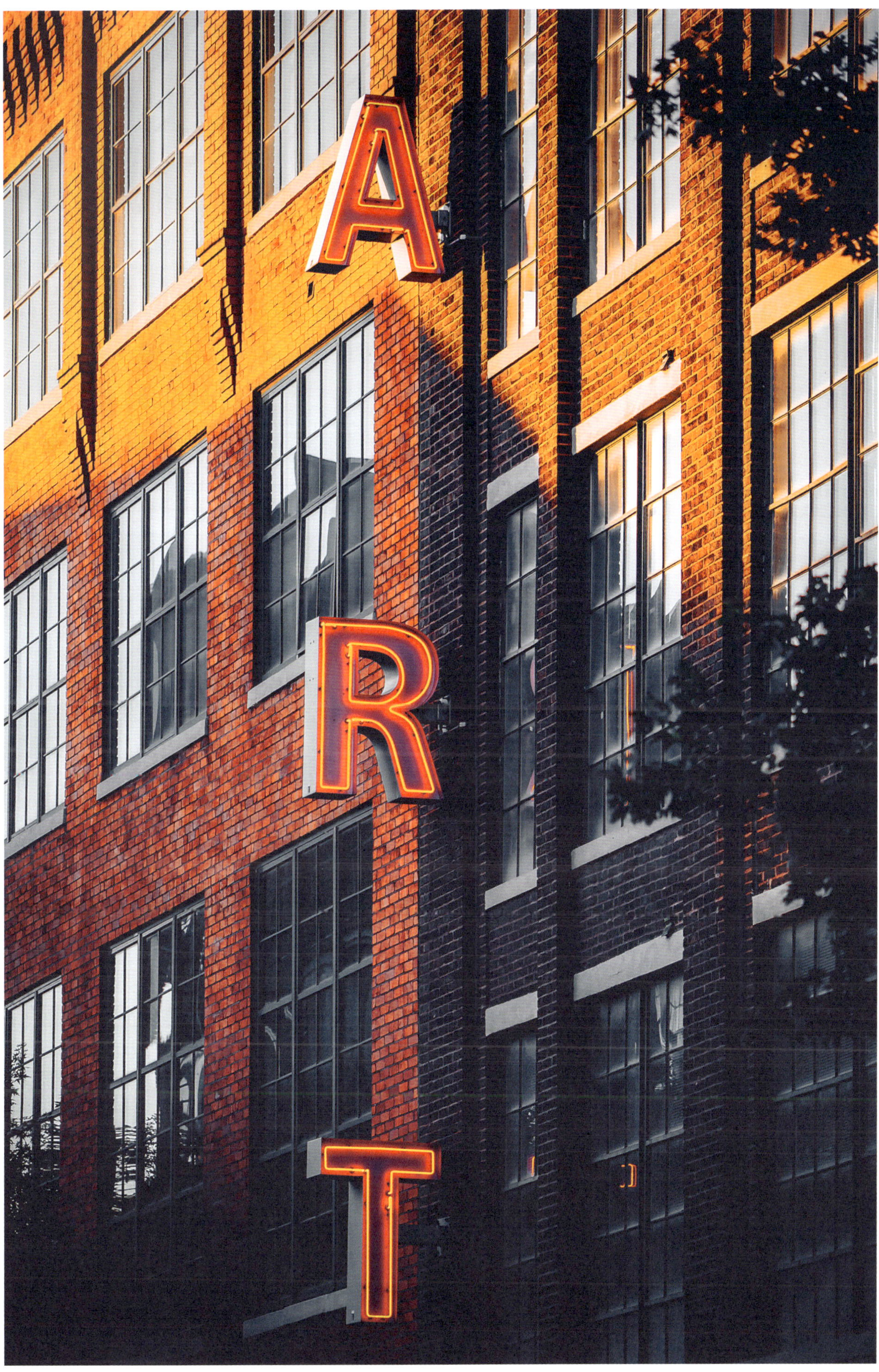
A
R
T

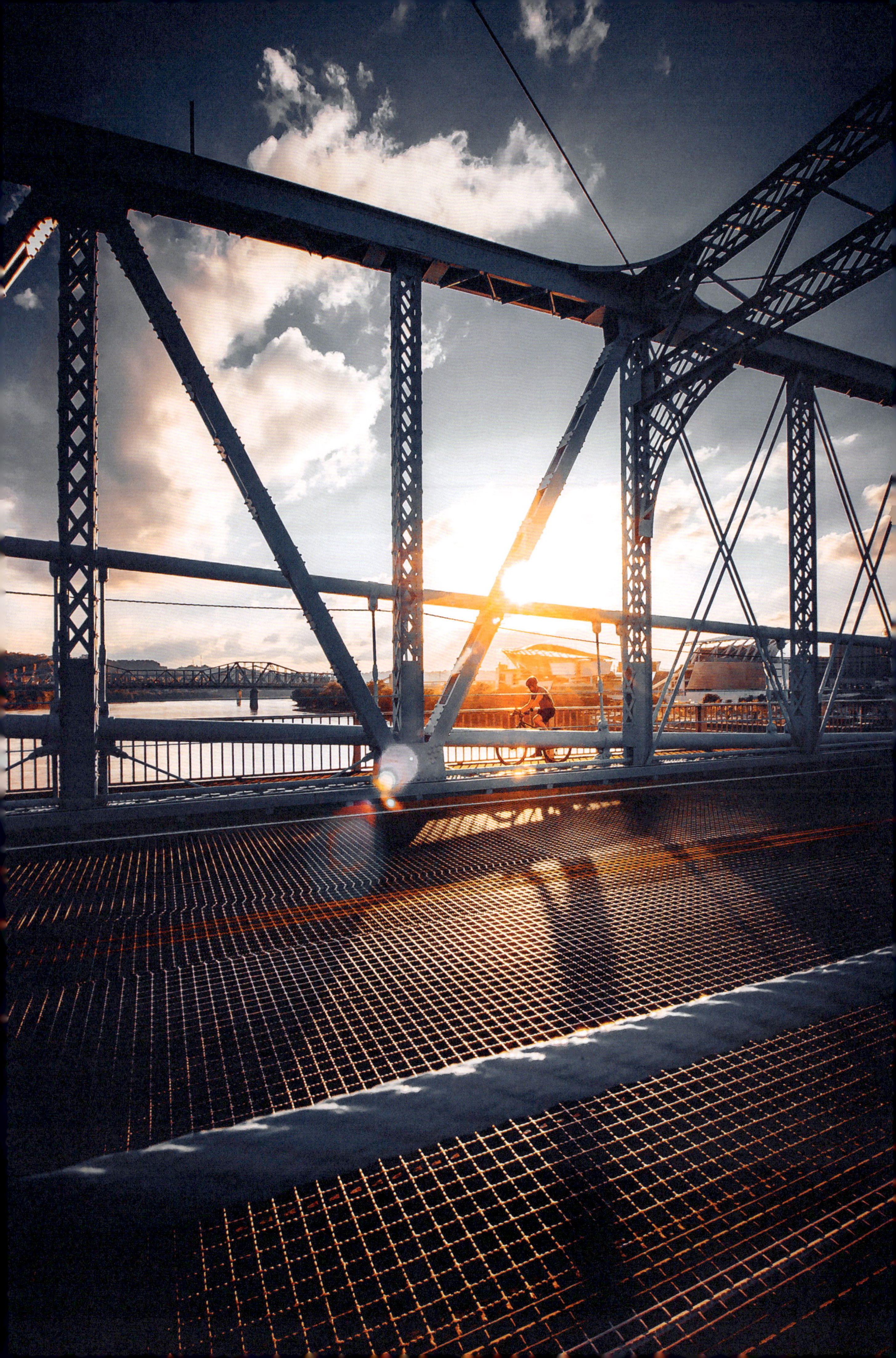

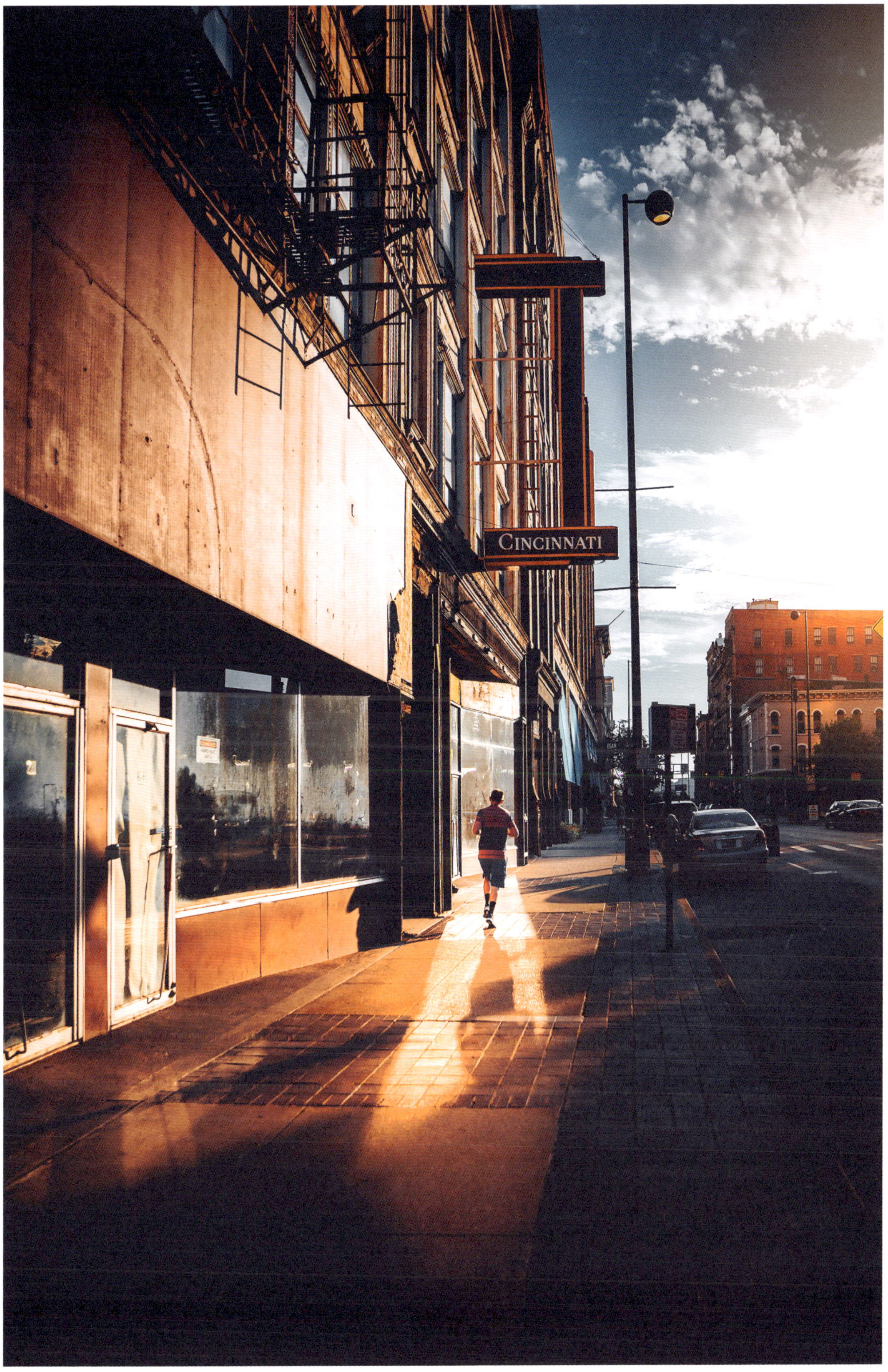
CINCINNATI

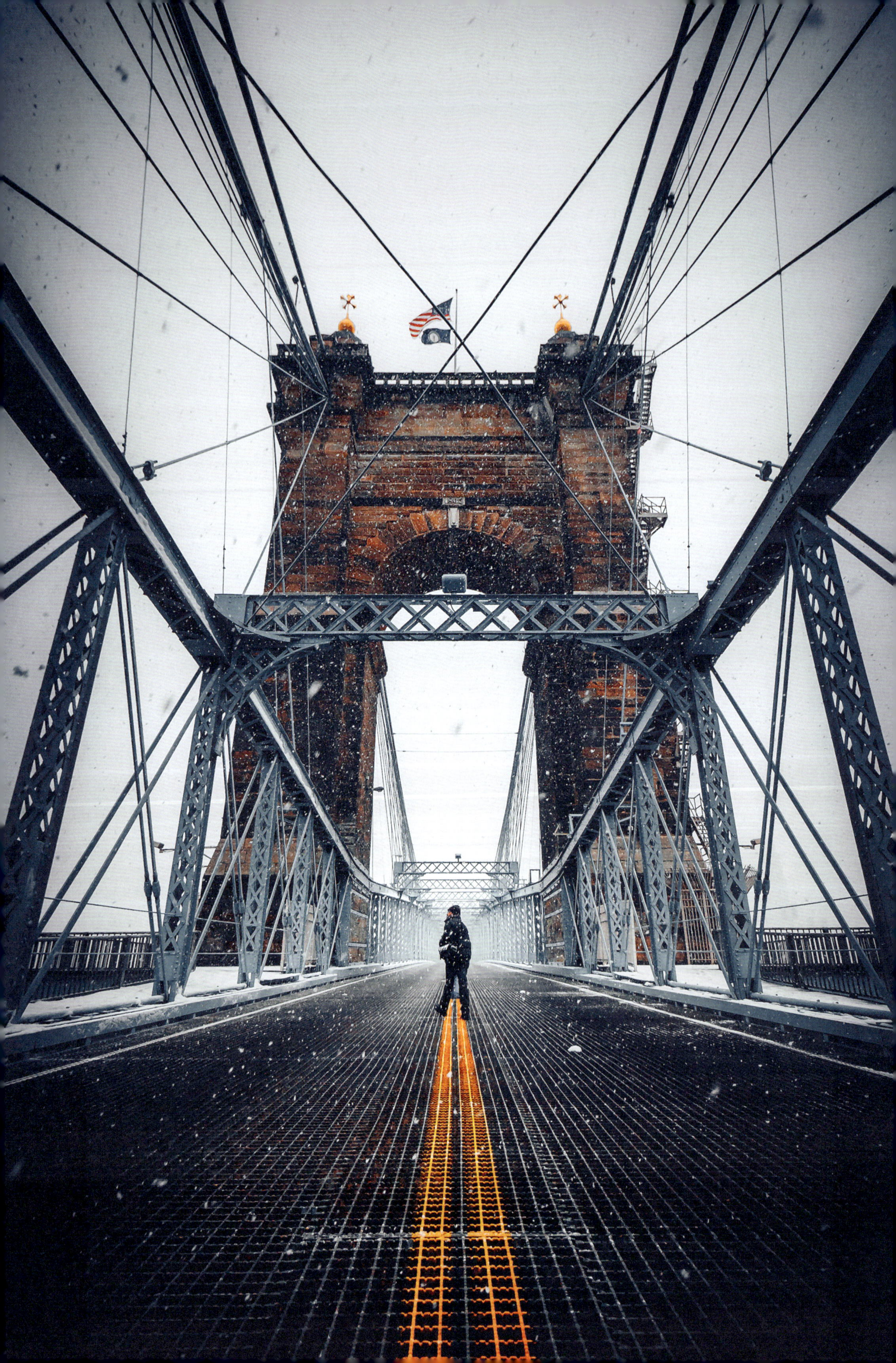

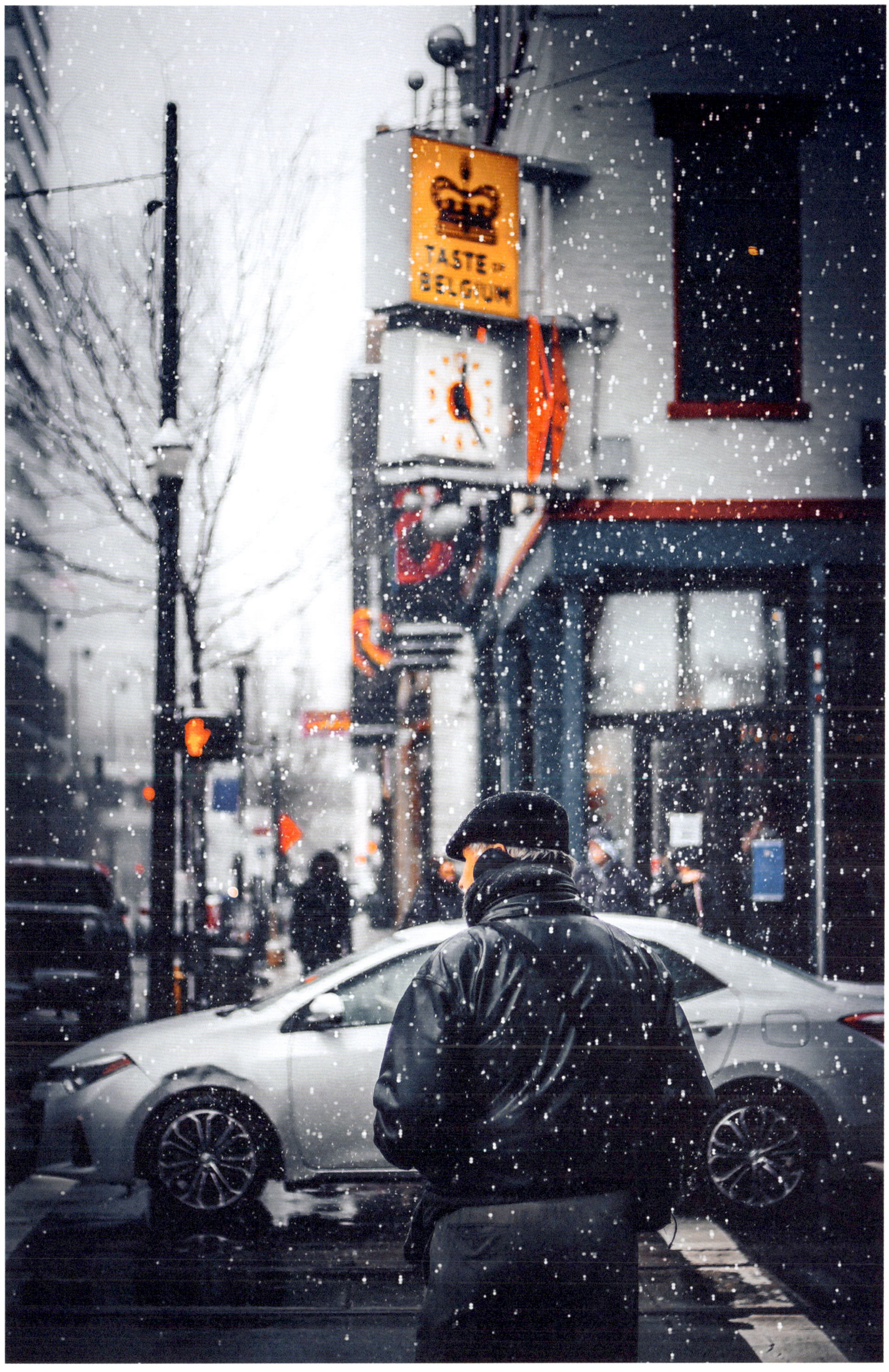
TASTE OF
BELGIUM

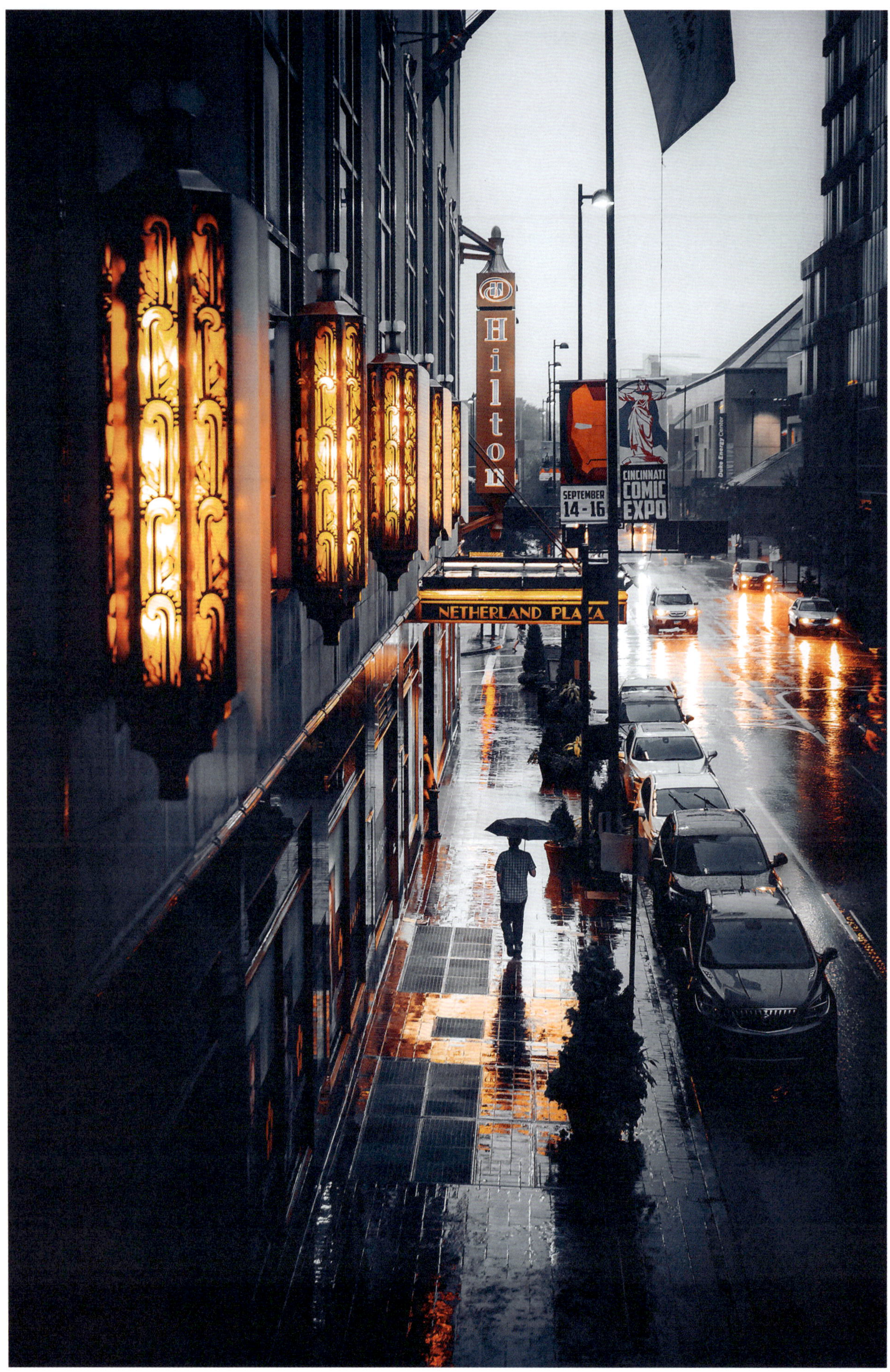
Hilton
NETHERLAND
SEPTEMBER
14-16
CINCINNATI
COMIC
EXPO

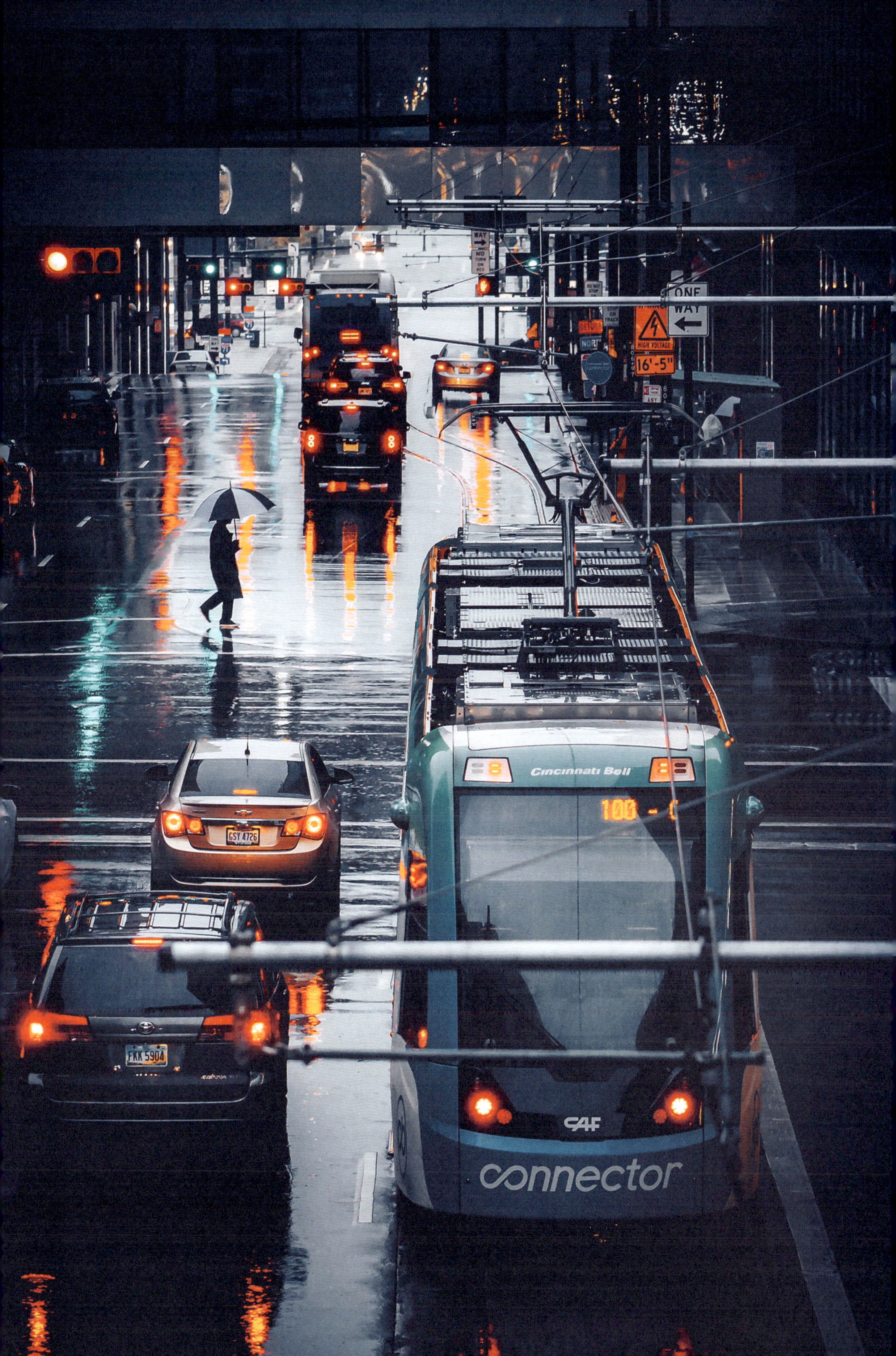
ONE WAY
HIGH VOLTAGE
16'-5"
Cincinnati Bell
CAF
connector

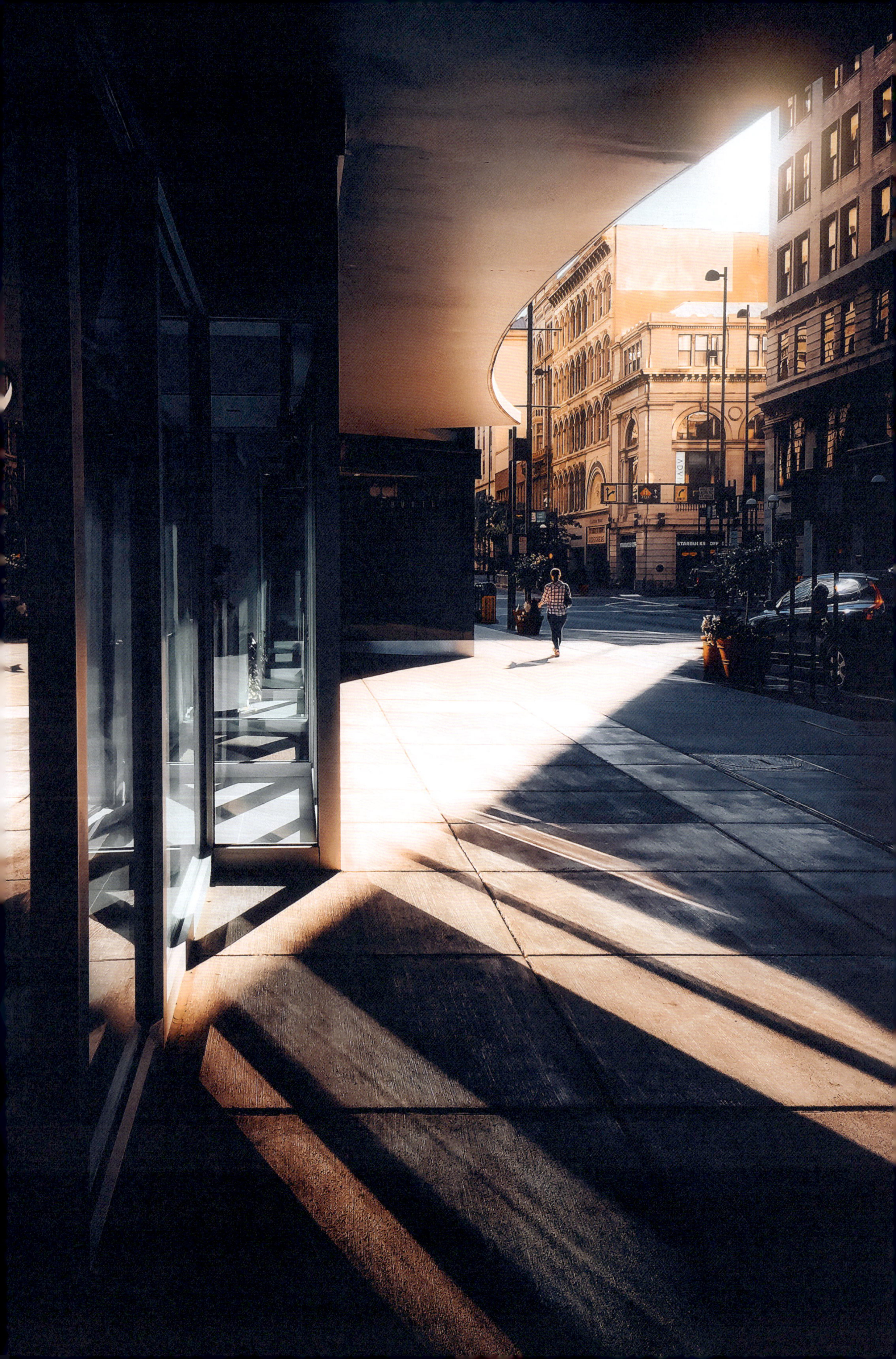
STARBUCKS

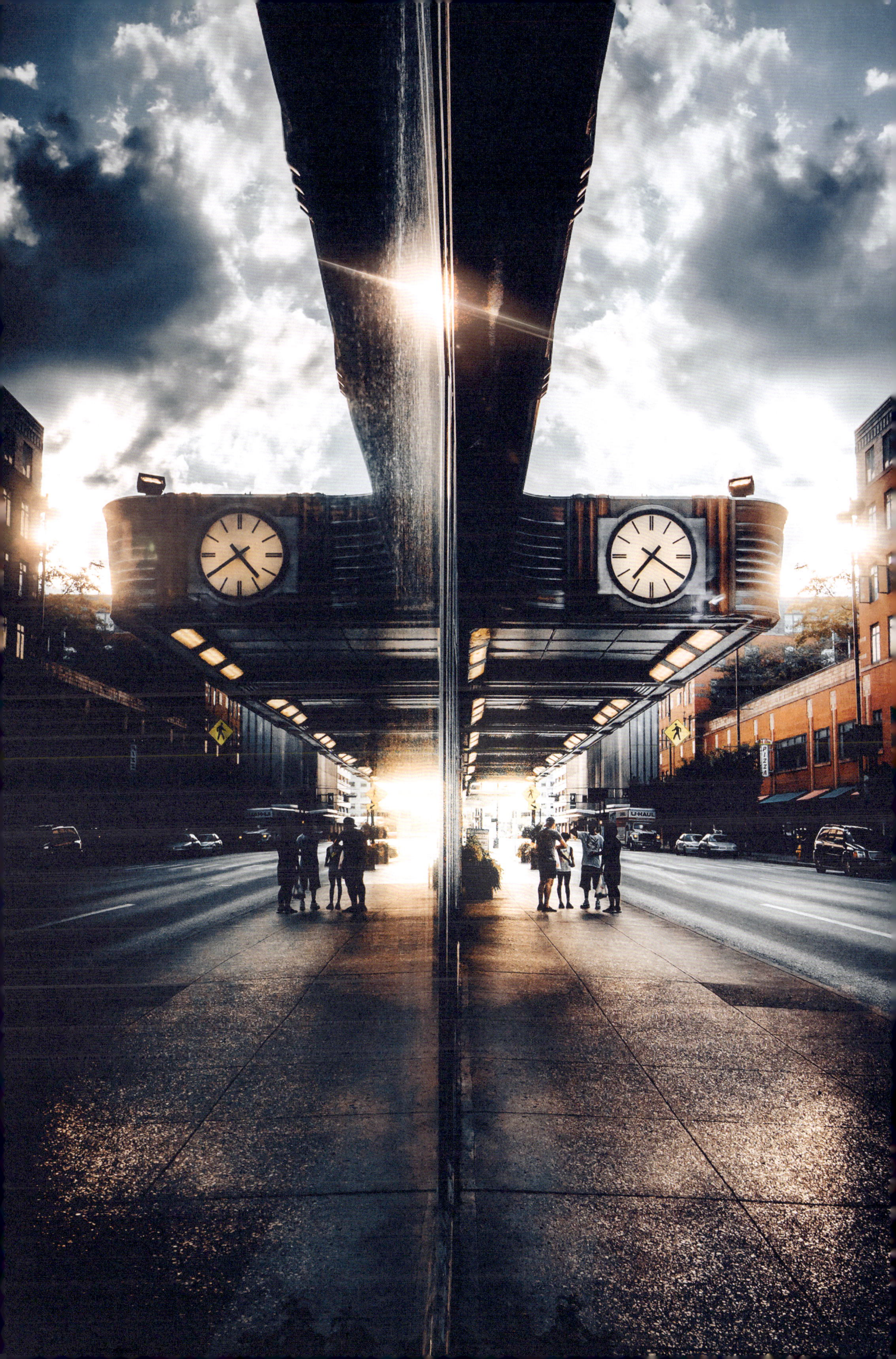
U-HAUL
PIZZA

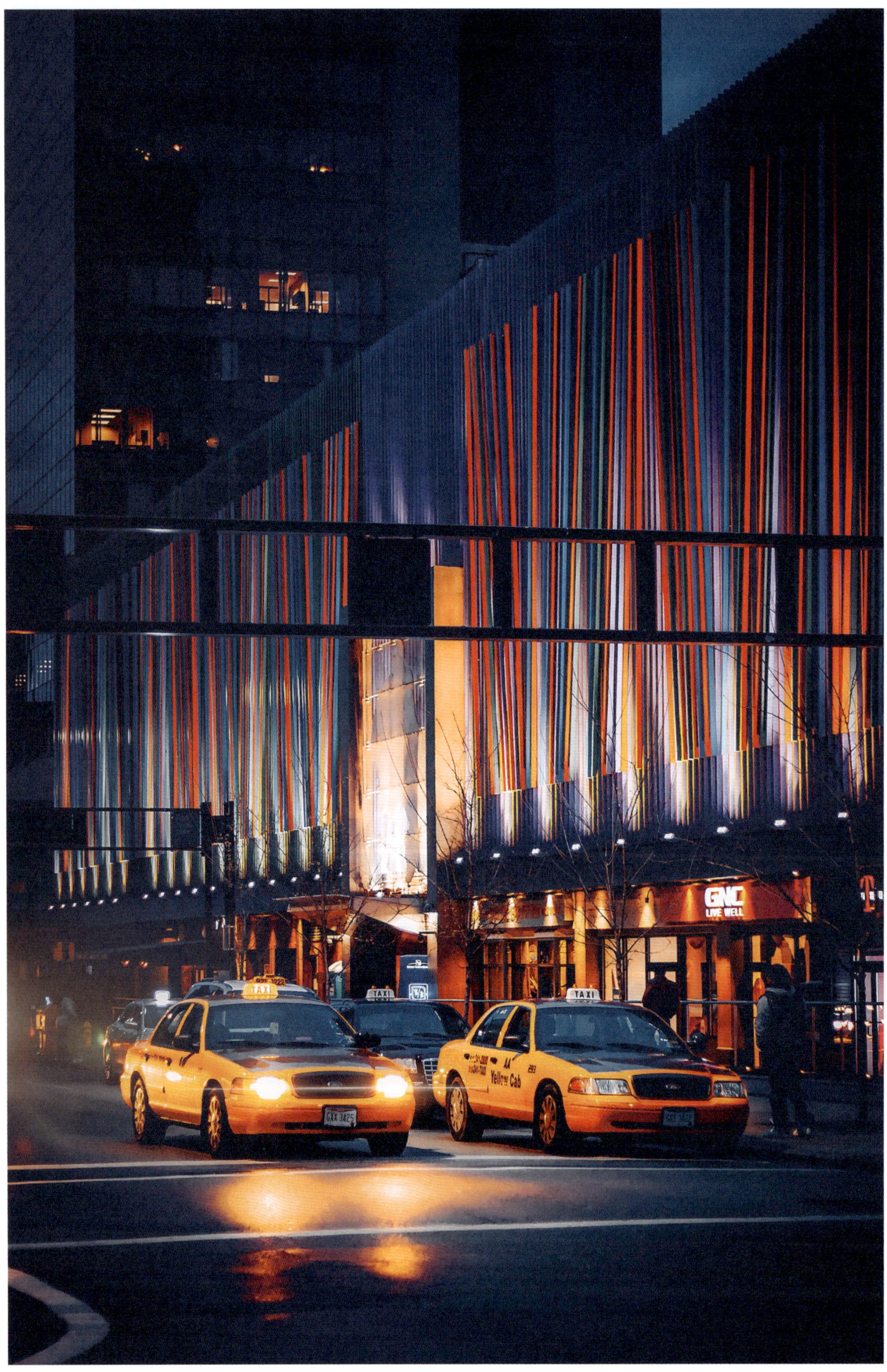
GNC
LIVE WELL
TAXI
TAXI
TAXI
Yellow Cab

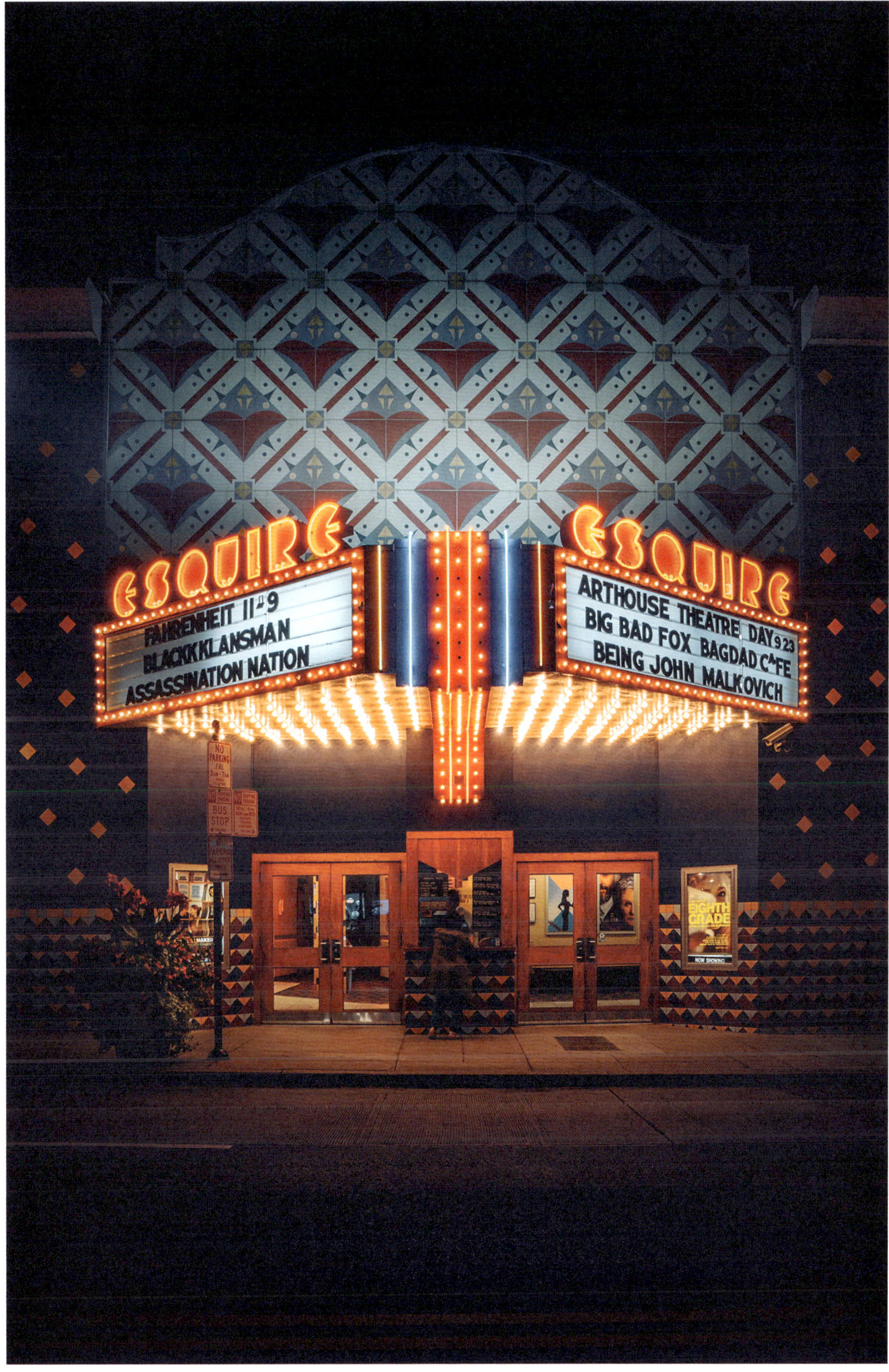
ESQUIRE
FAHRENHEIT 11/9
BLACKKKLANSMAN
ASSASSINATION NATION
ESQUIRE
ARTHOUSE THEATRE DAY 9 23
BIG BAD FOX BAGDAD CAFE
BEING JOHN MALKOVICH
NO PARKING
BUS STOP
EIGHTH GRADE
NOW SHOWING

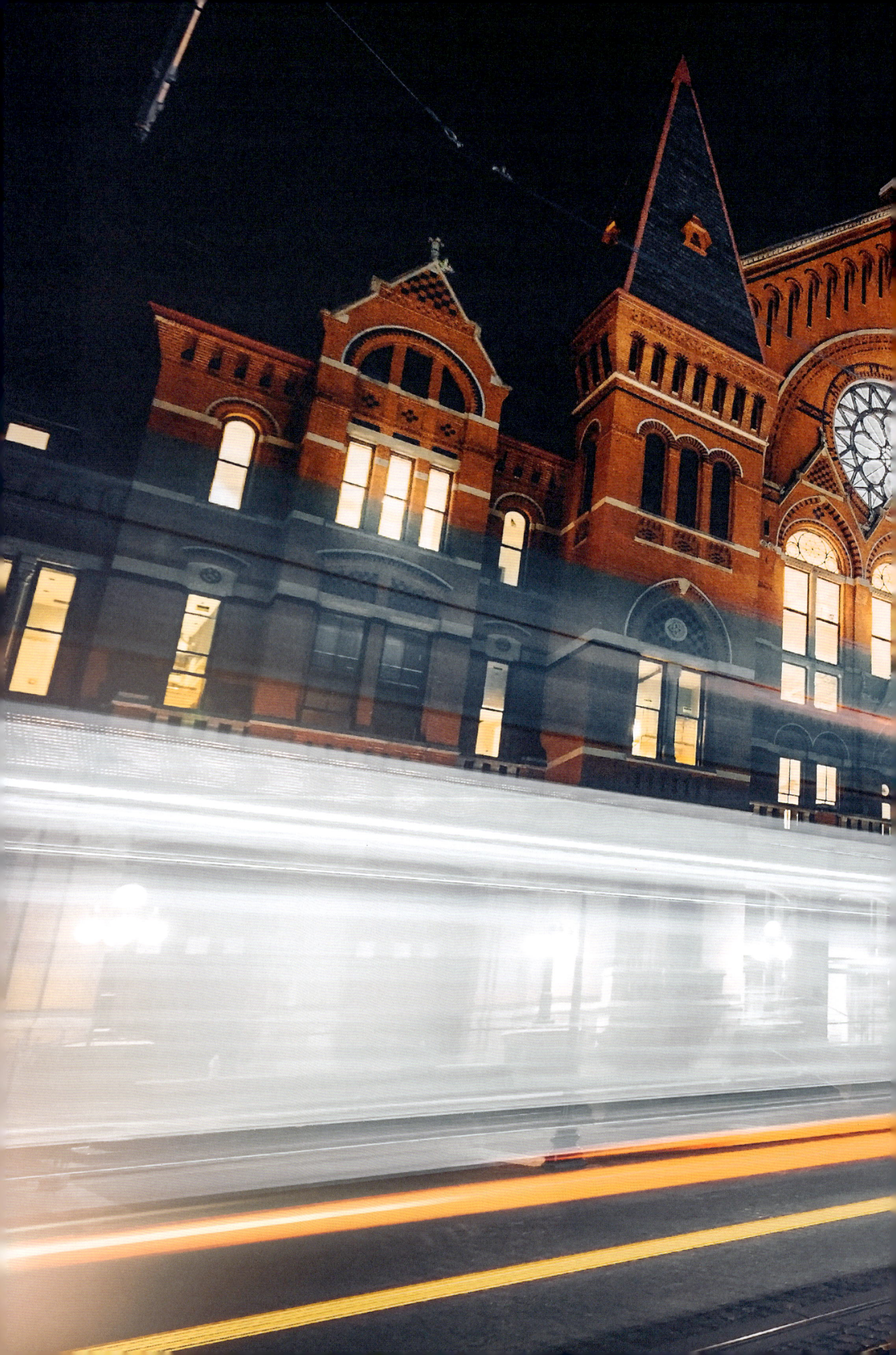

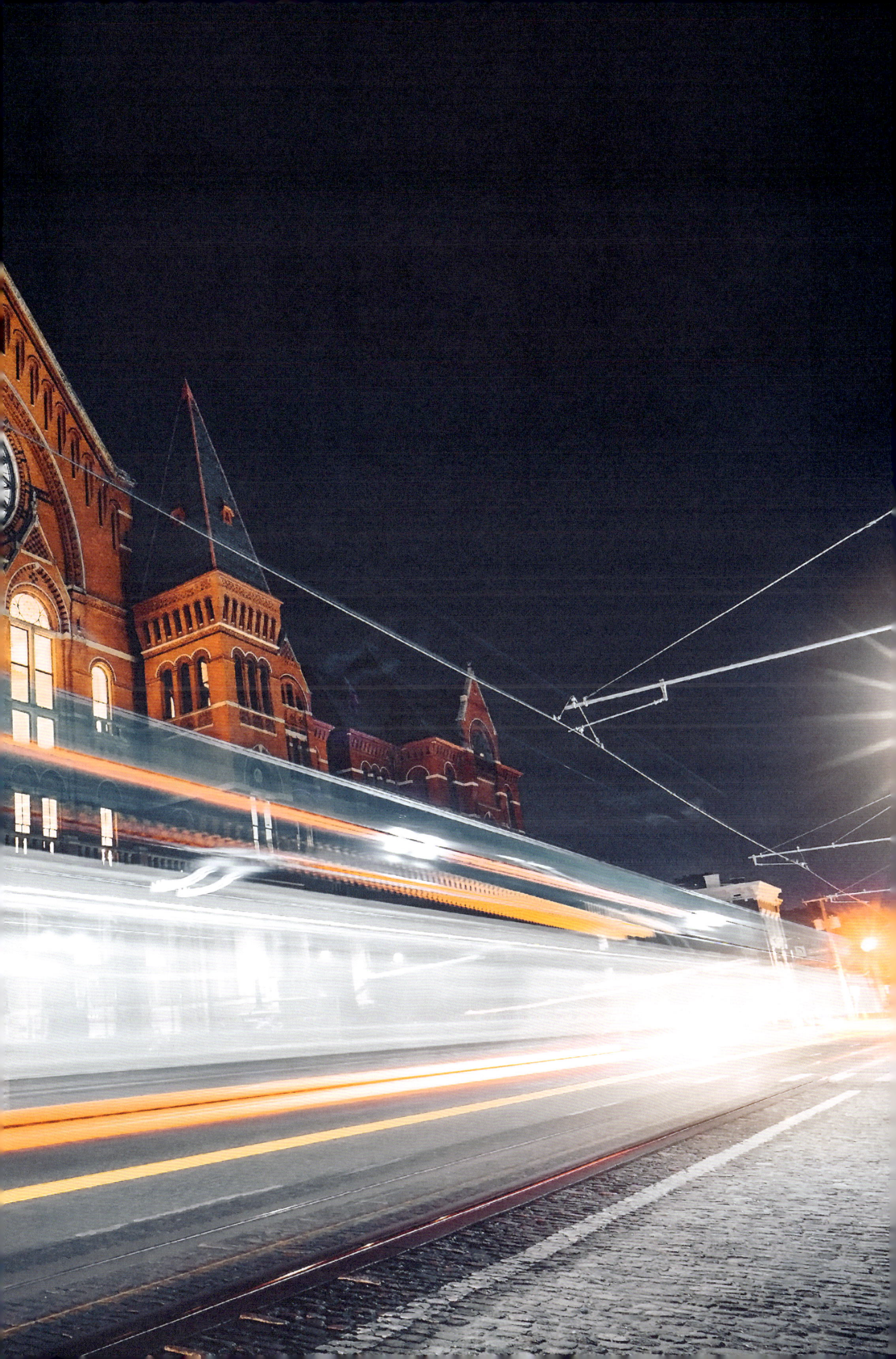

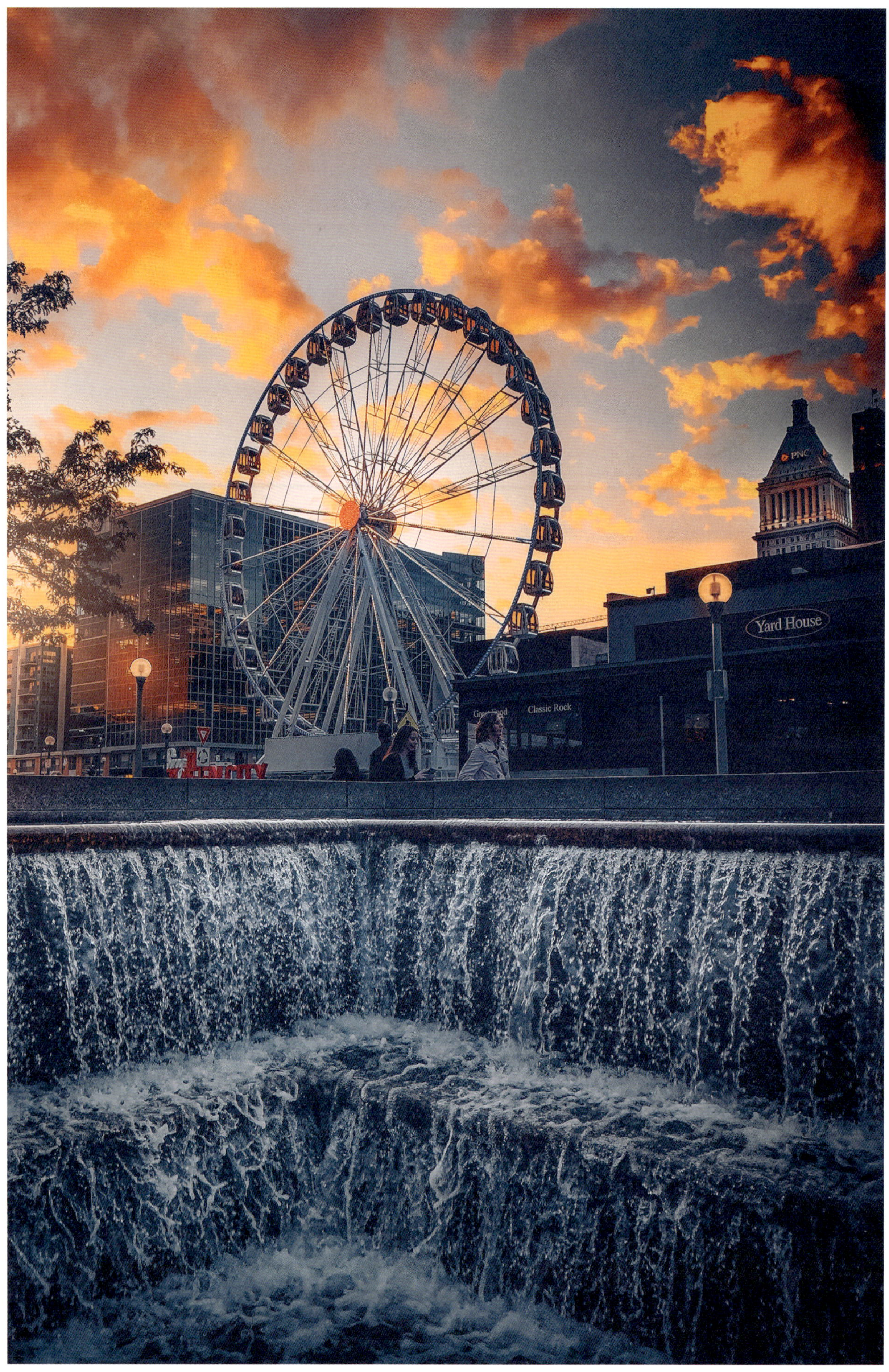
PNC
Yard House
Classic Rock

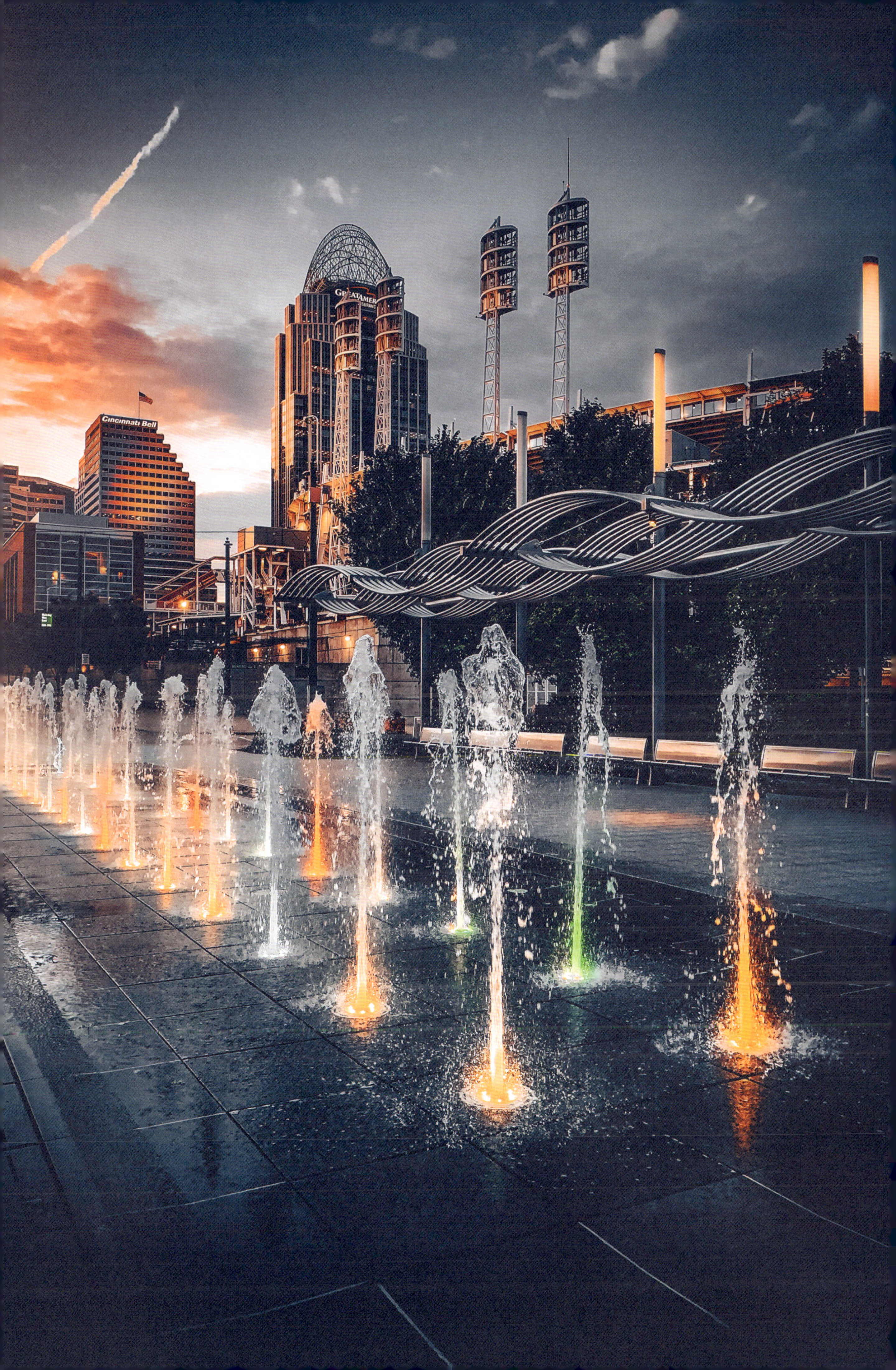
Cincinnati Bell

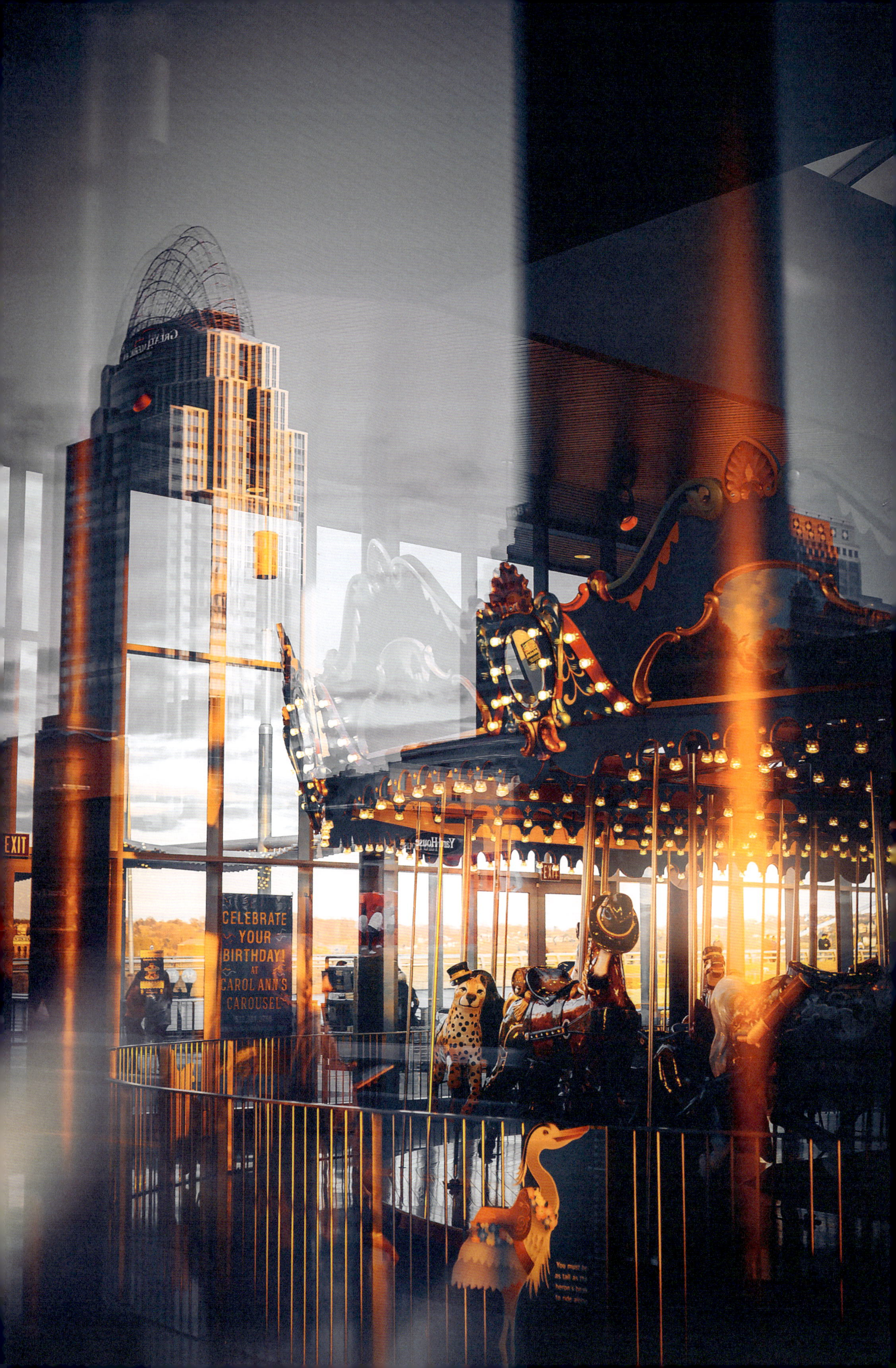
EXIT
CELEBRATE
YOUR
BIRTHDAY!
AT
CAROL ANN'S
CAROUSEL

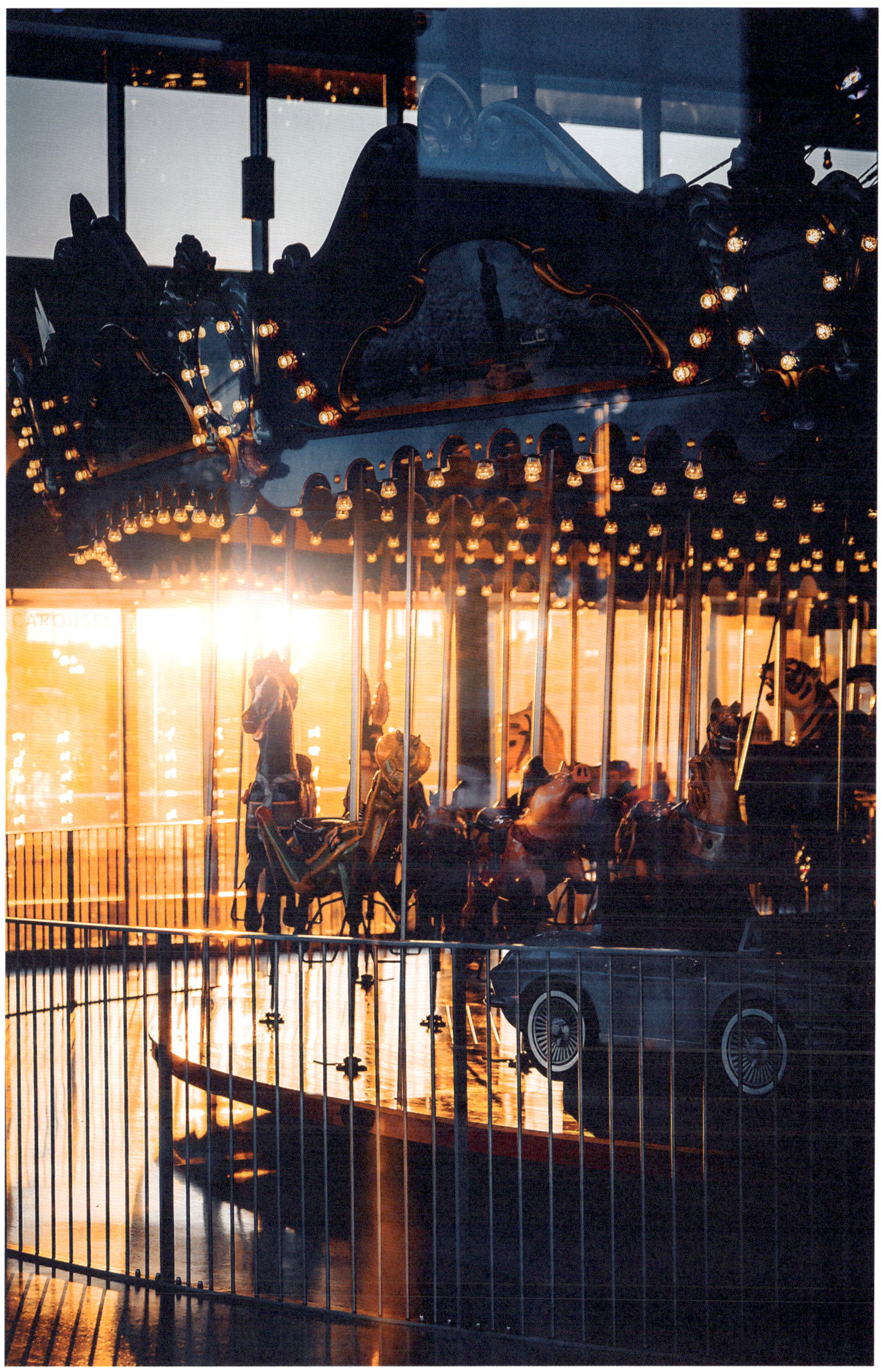

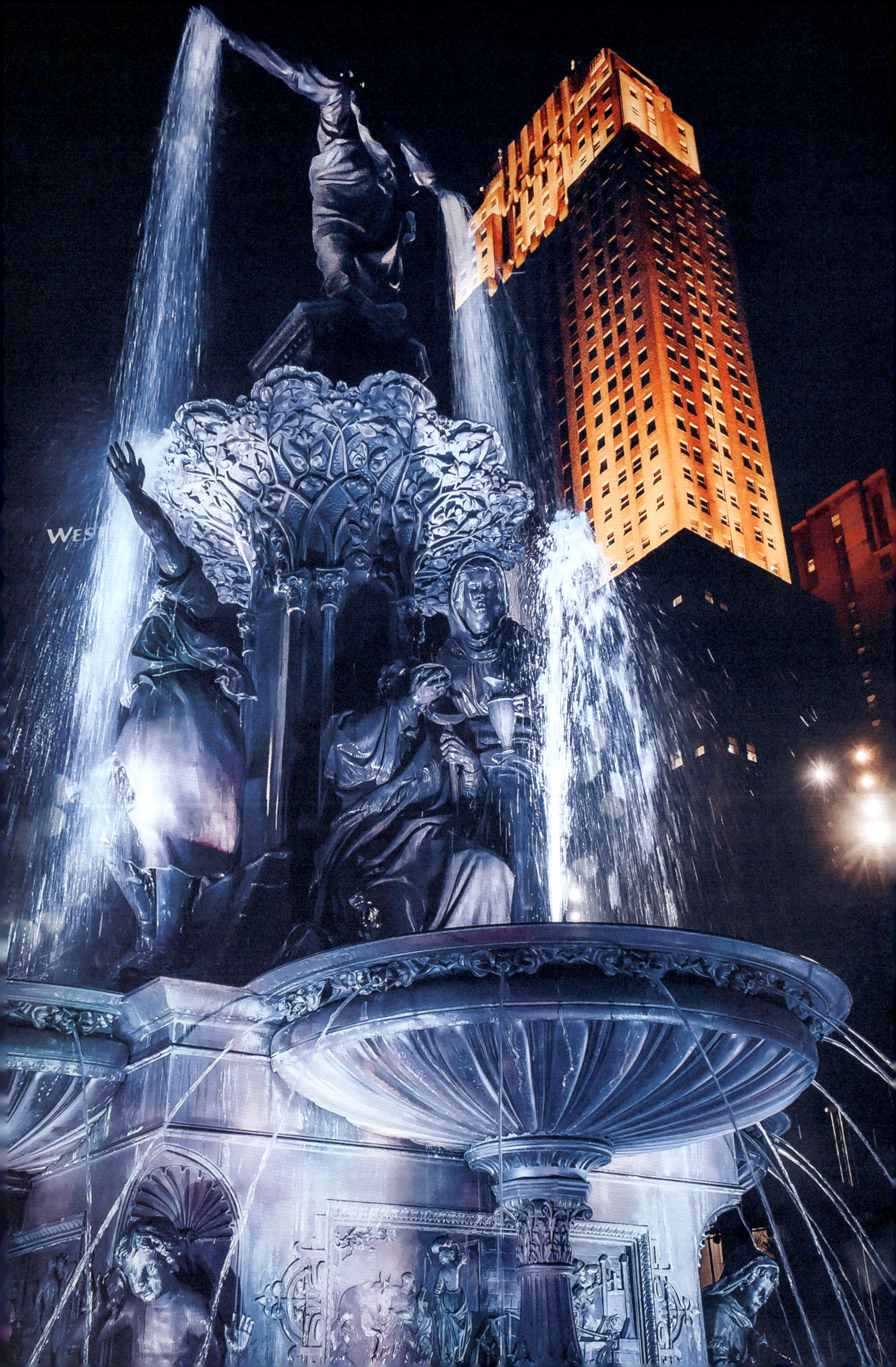

The Tyler Davidson Fountain is at once realistic and idealistic, practical and poetic.

JOHN CLUBBE

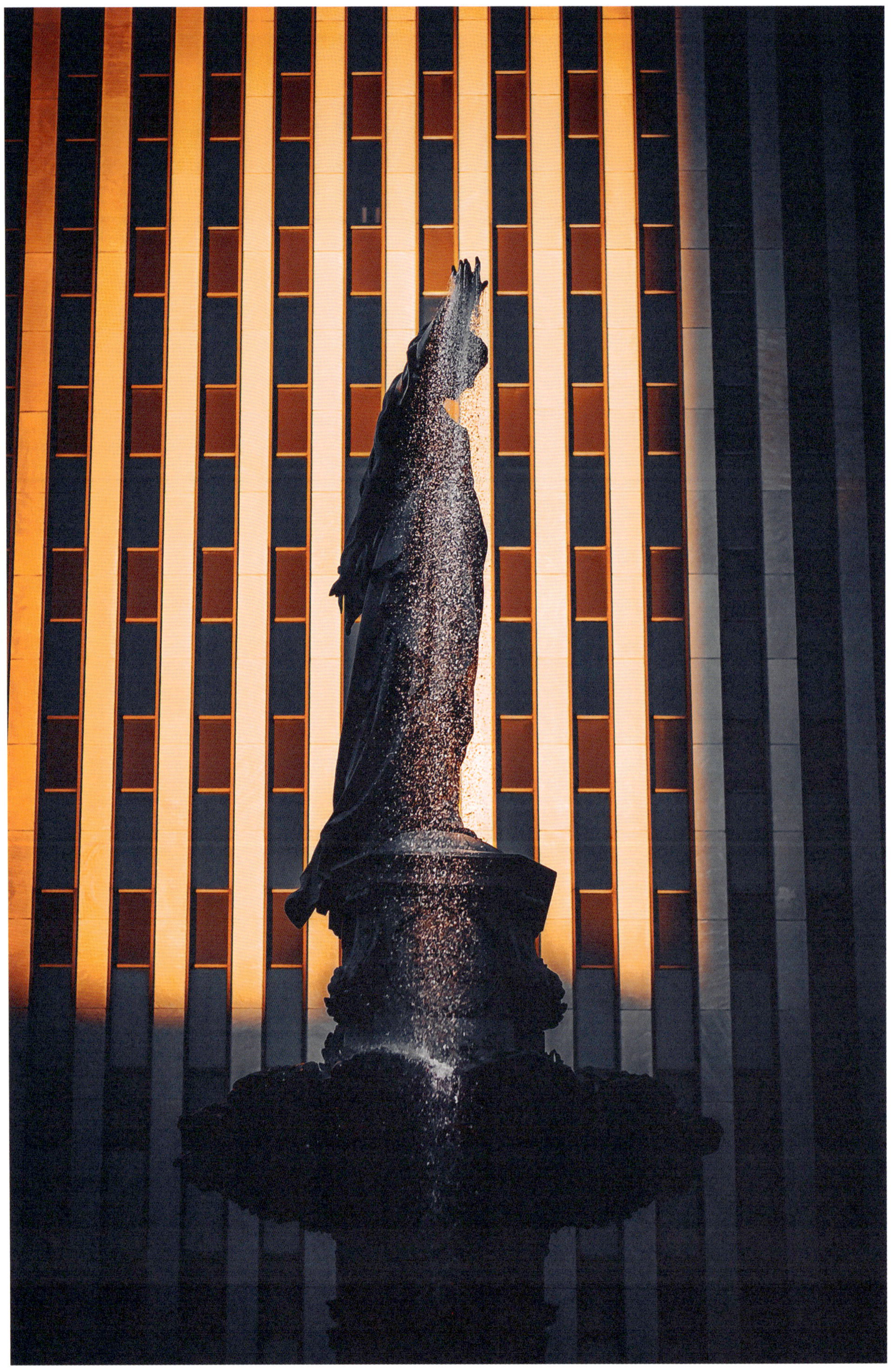

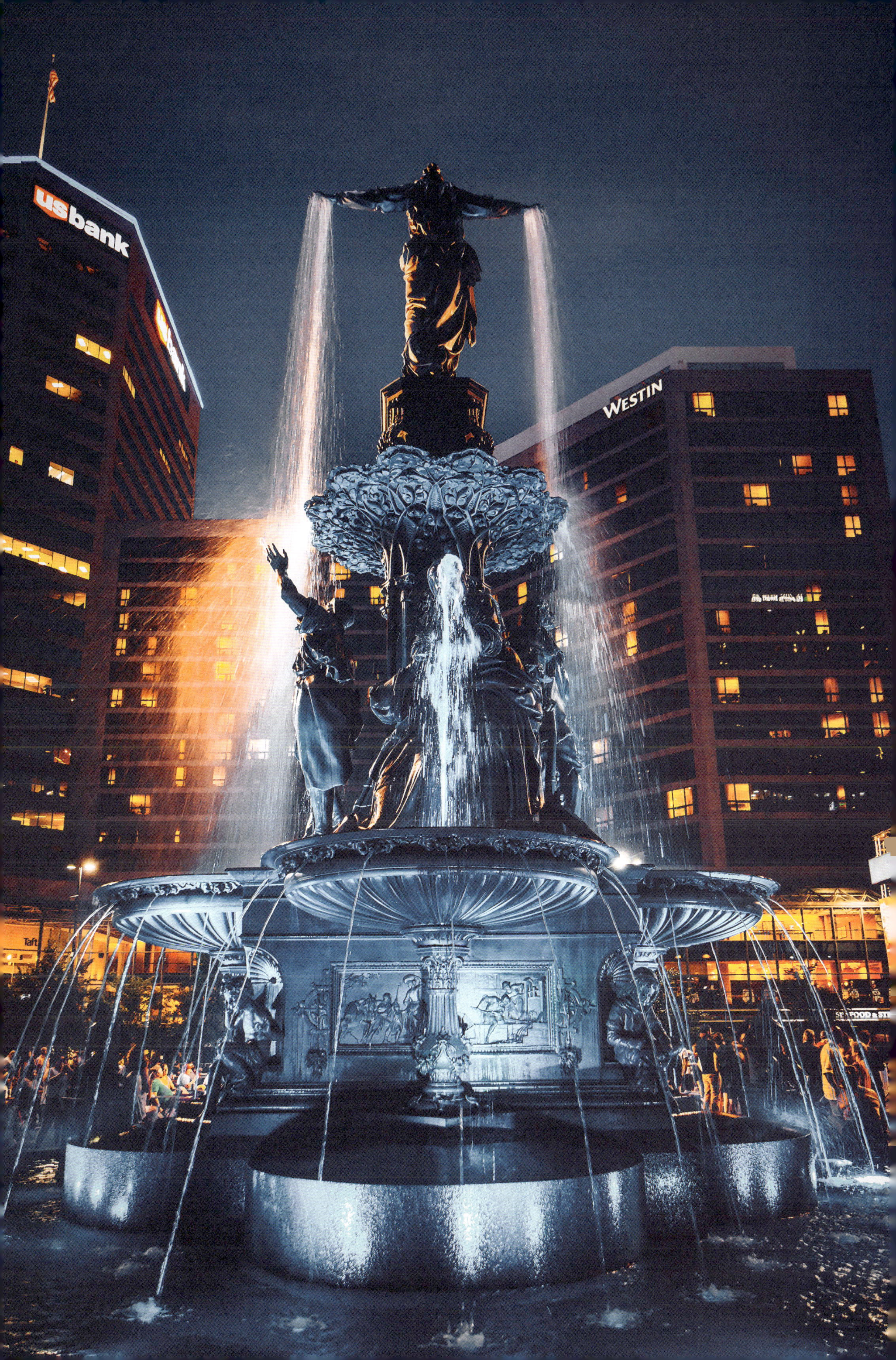
usbank
WESTIN

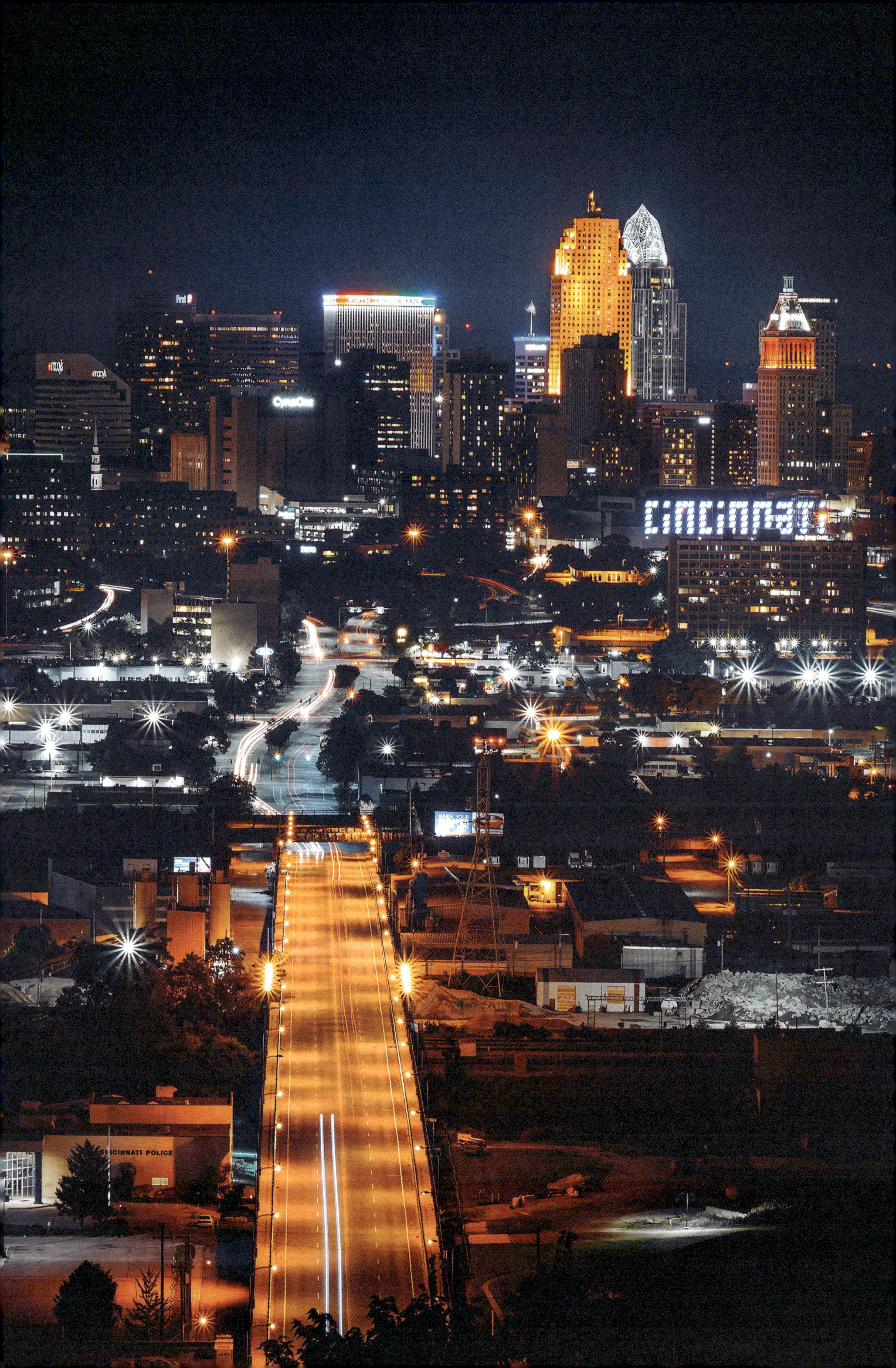
CINCINNATI
CINCINNATI POLICE

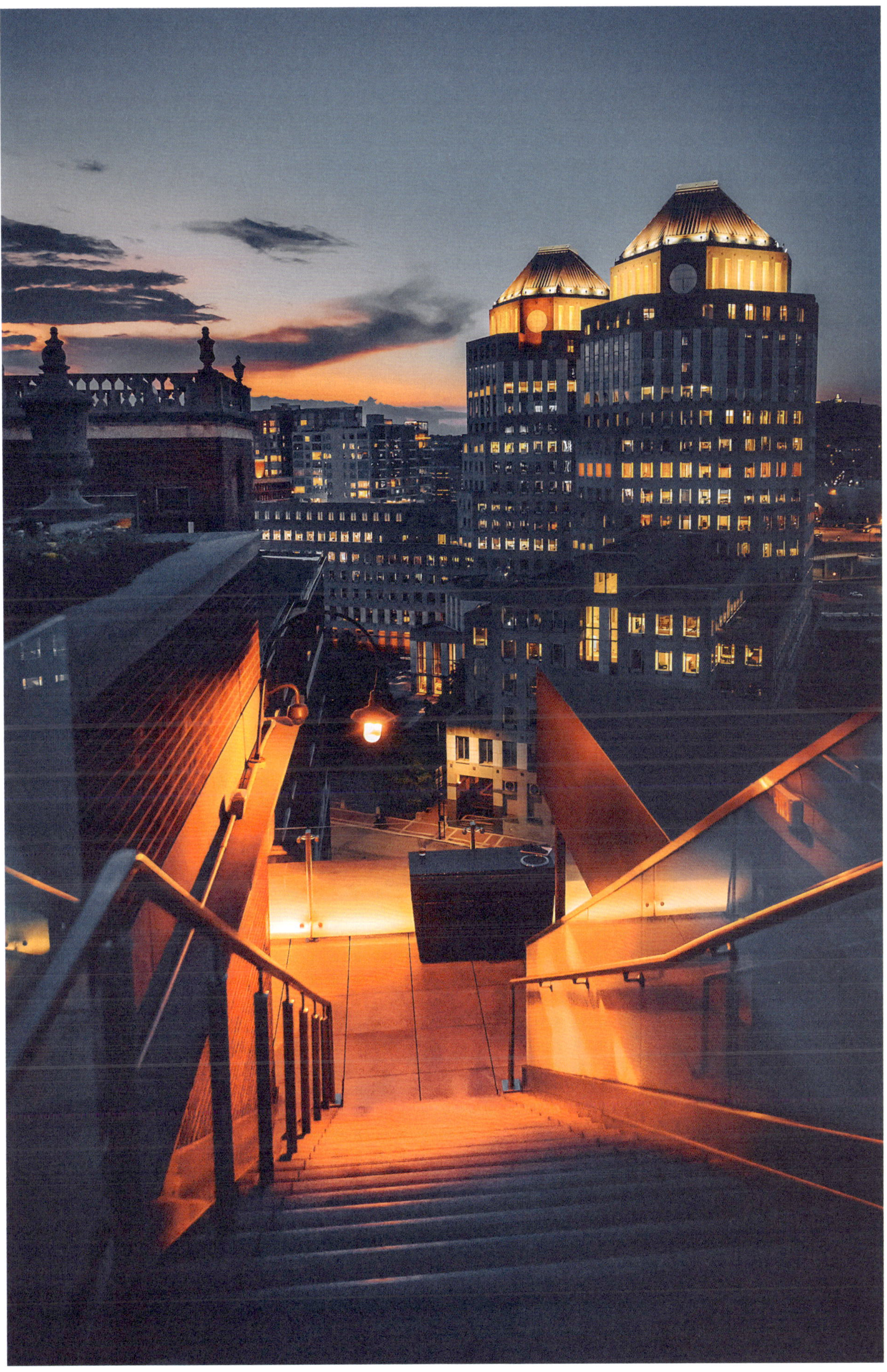

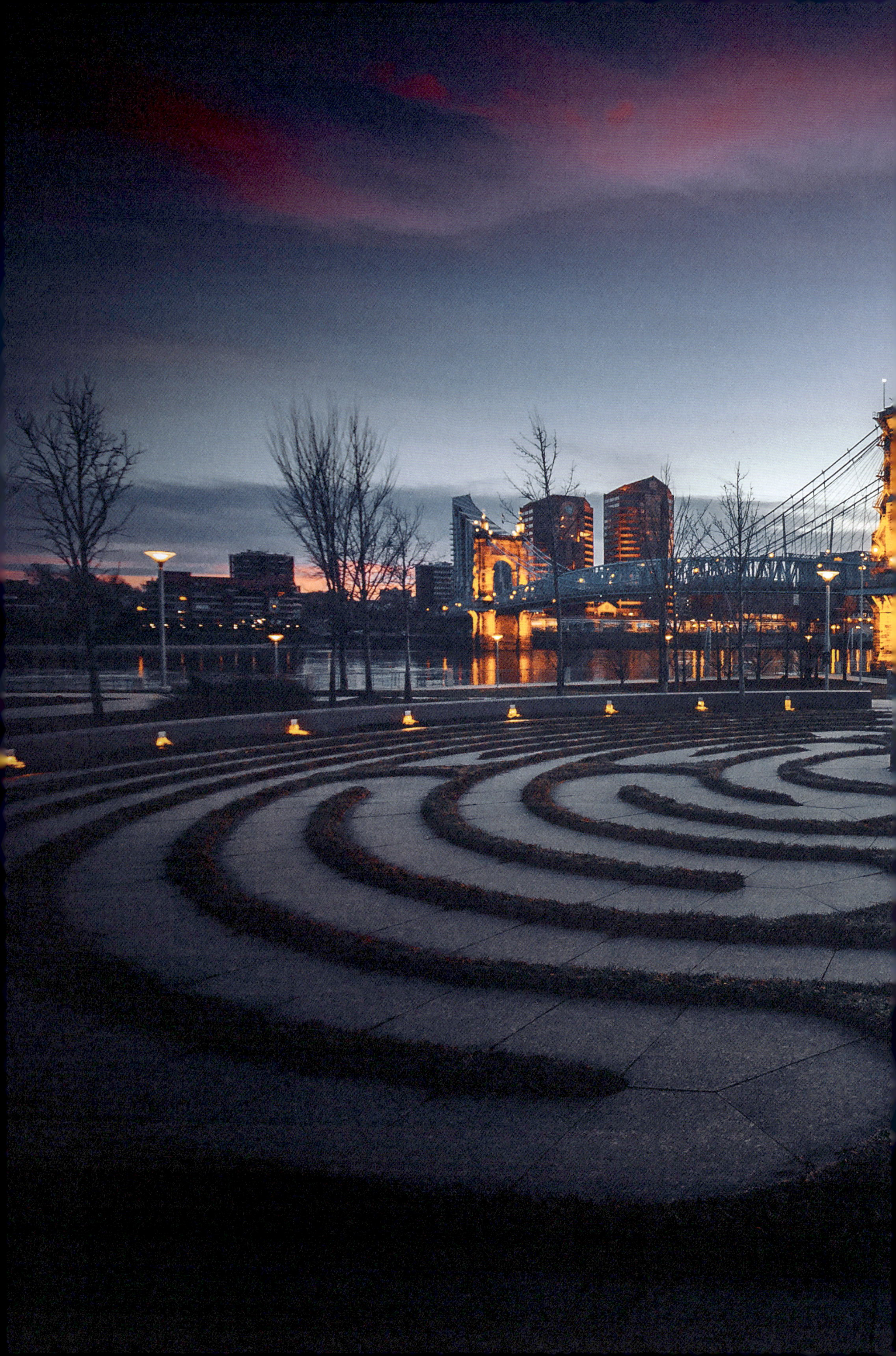

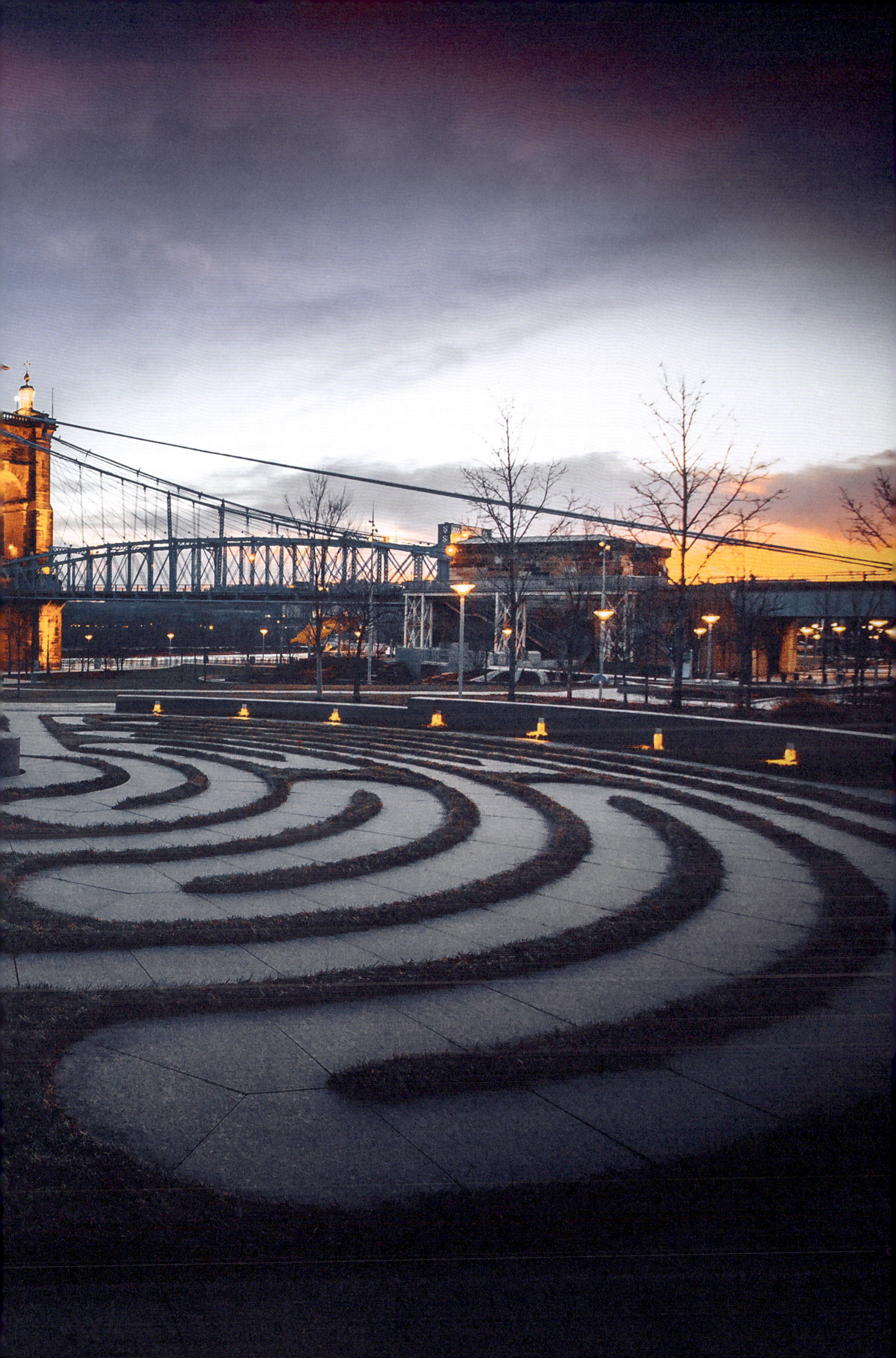

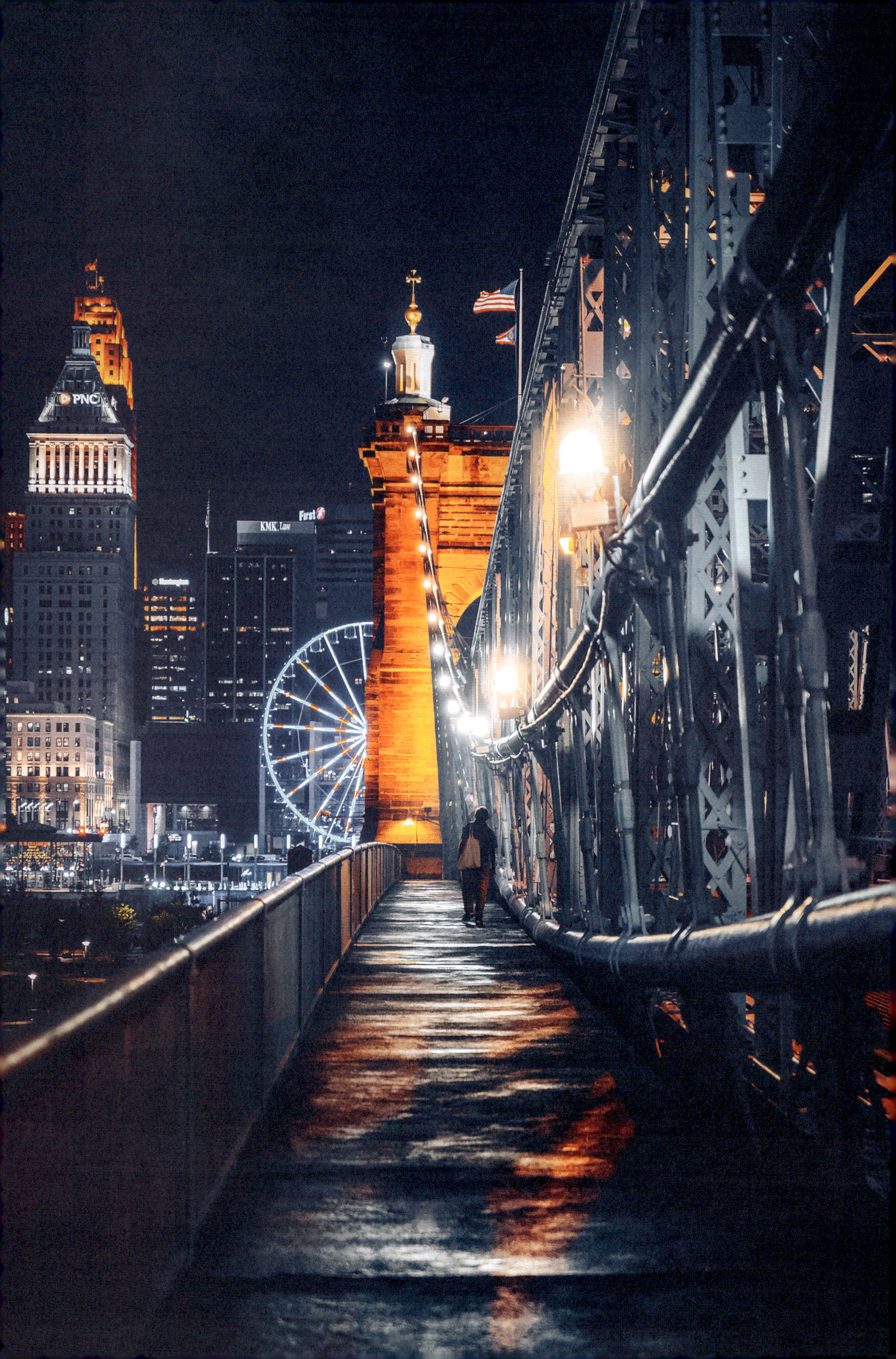

PNC
KMK Law
First

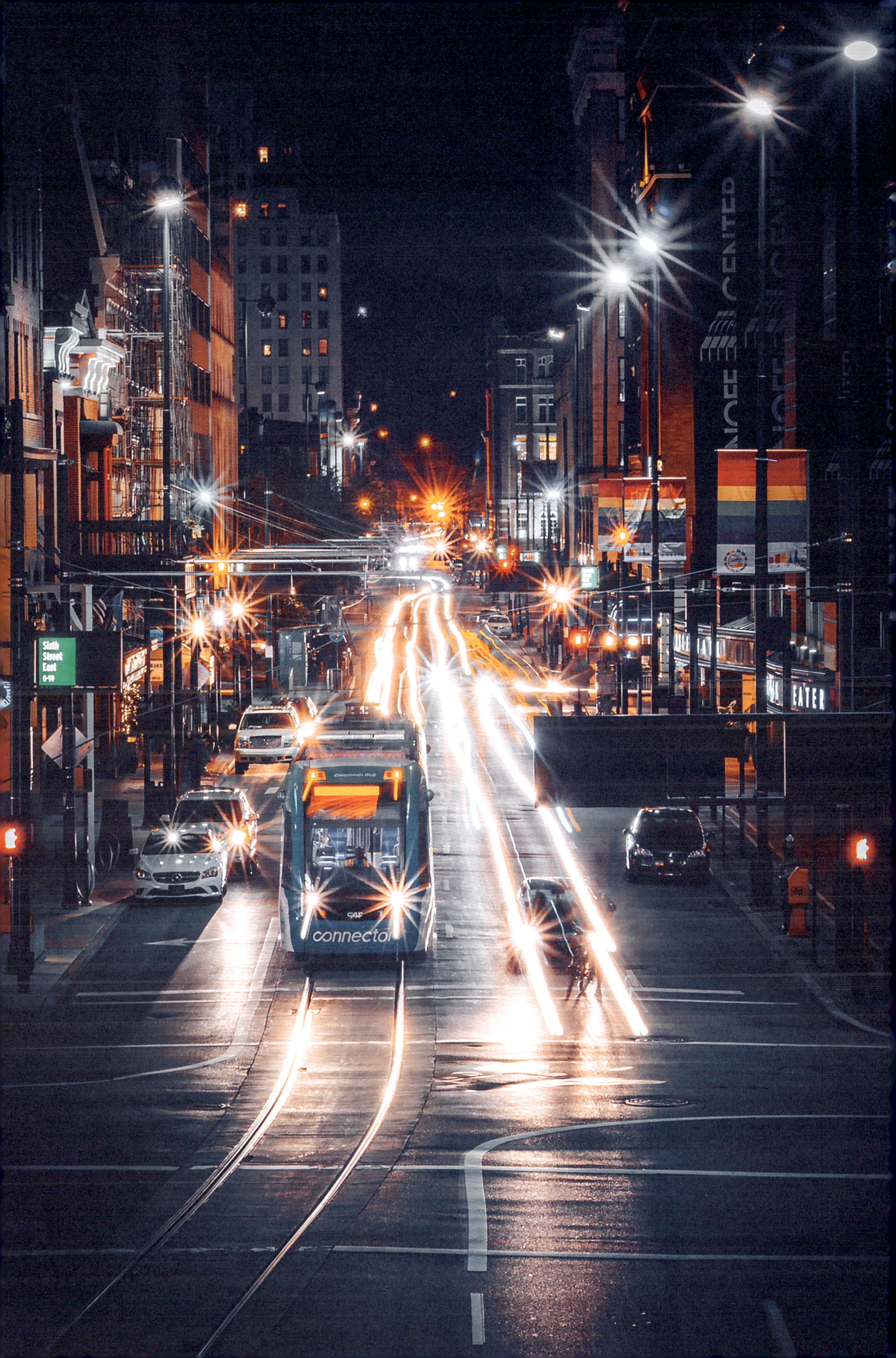
Sixth
Street
East
0-99
connector

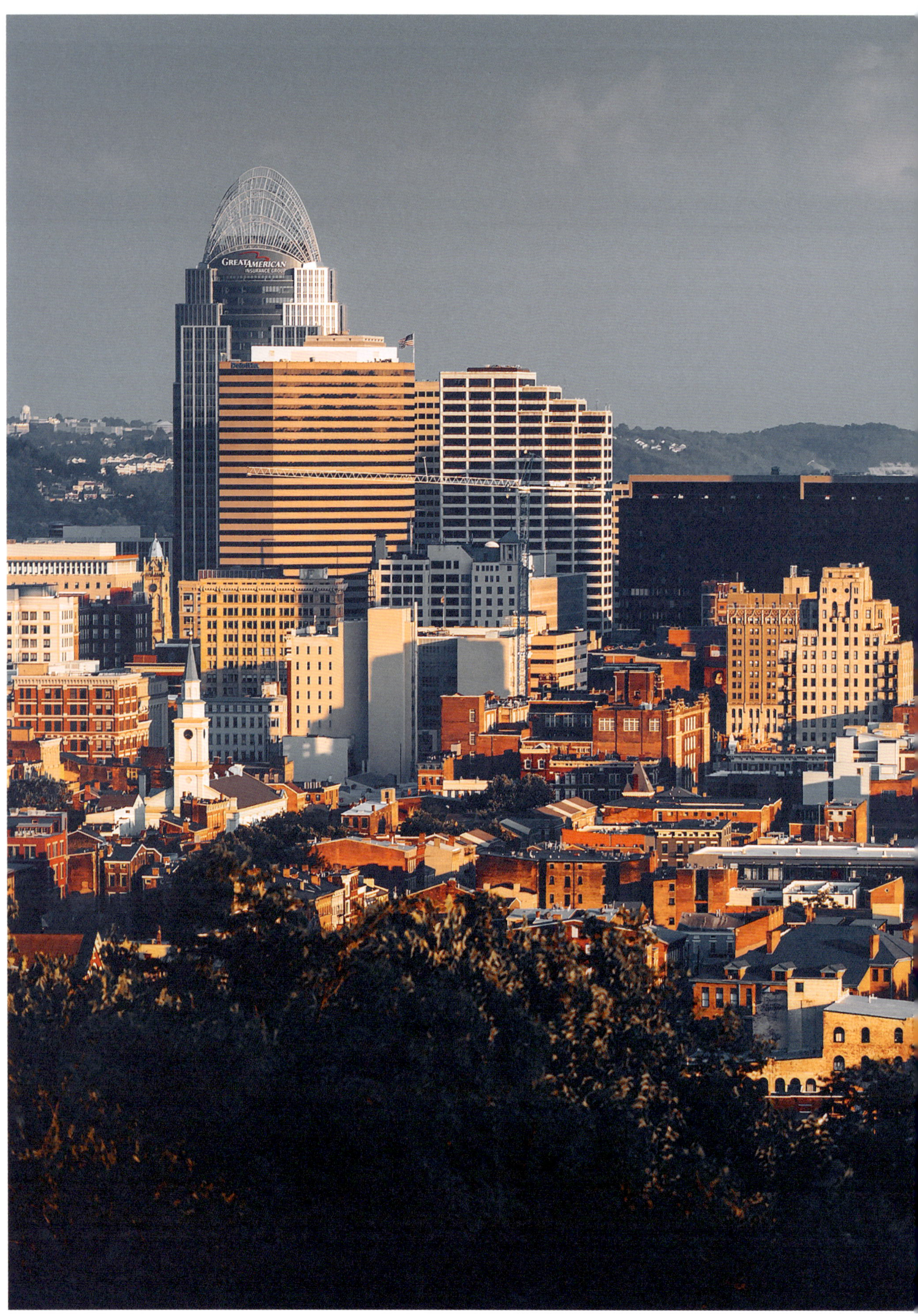
GREAT AMERICAN
INSURANCE GROUP

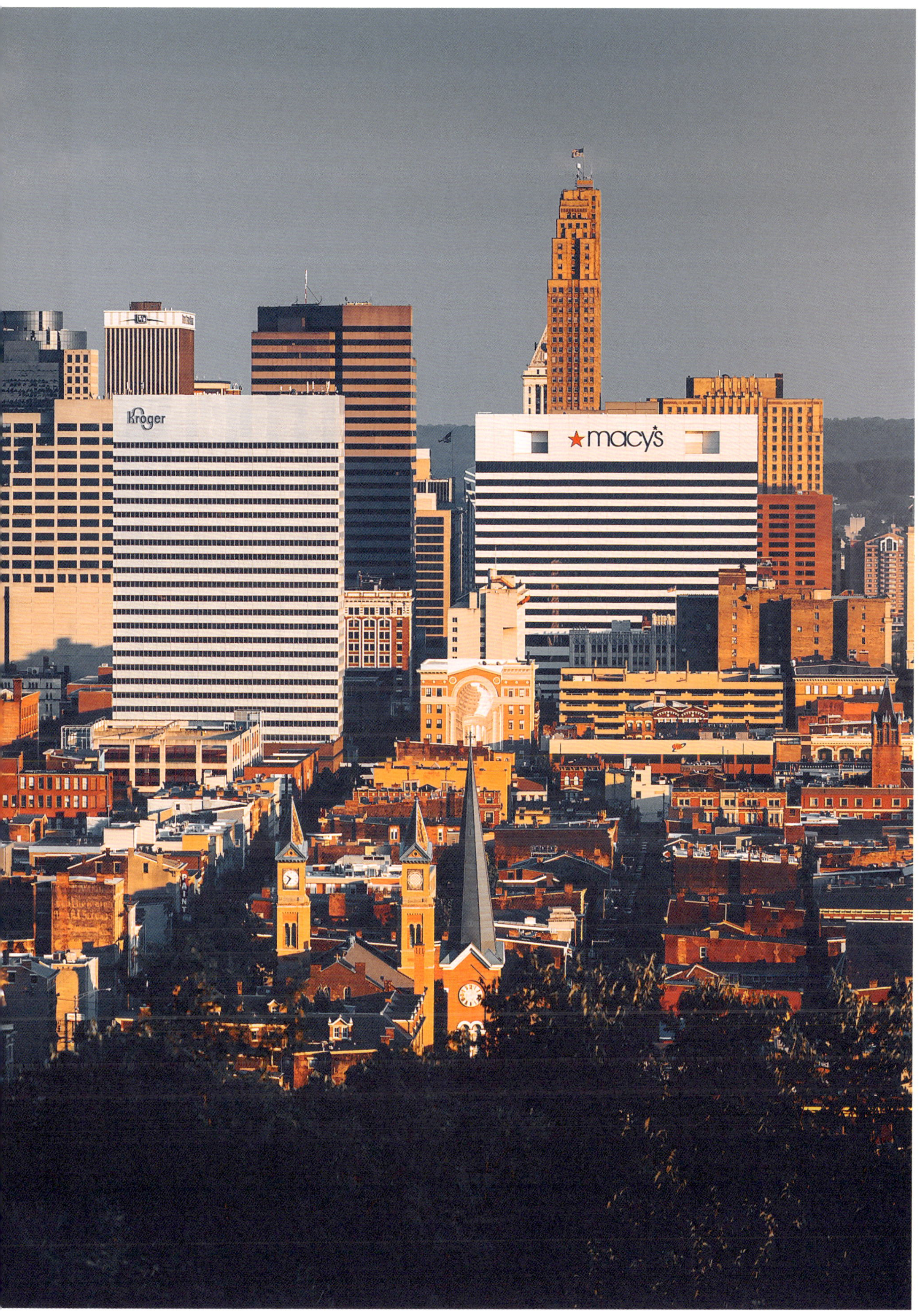
Kroger
macy's

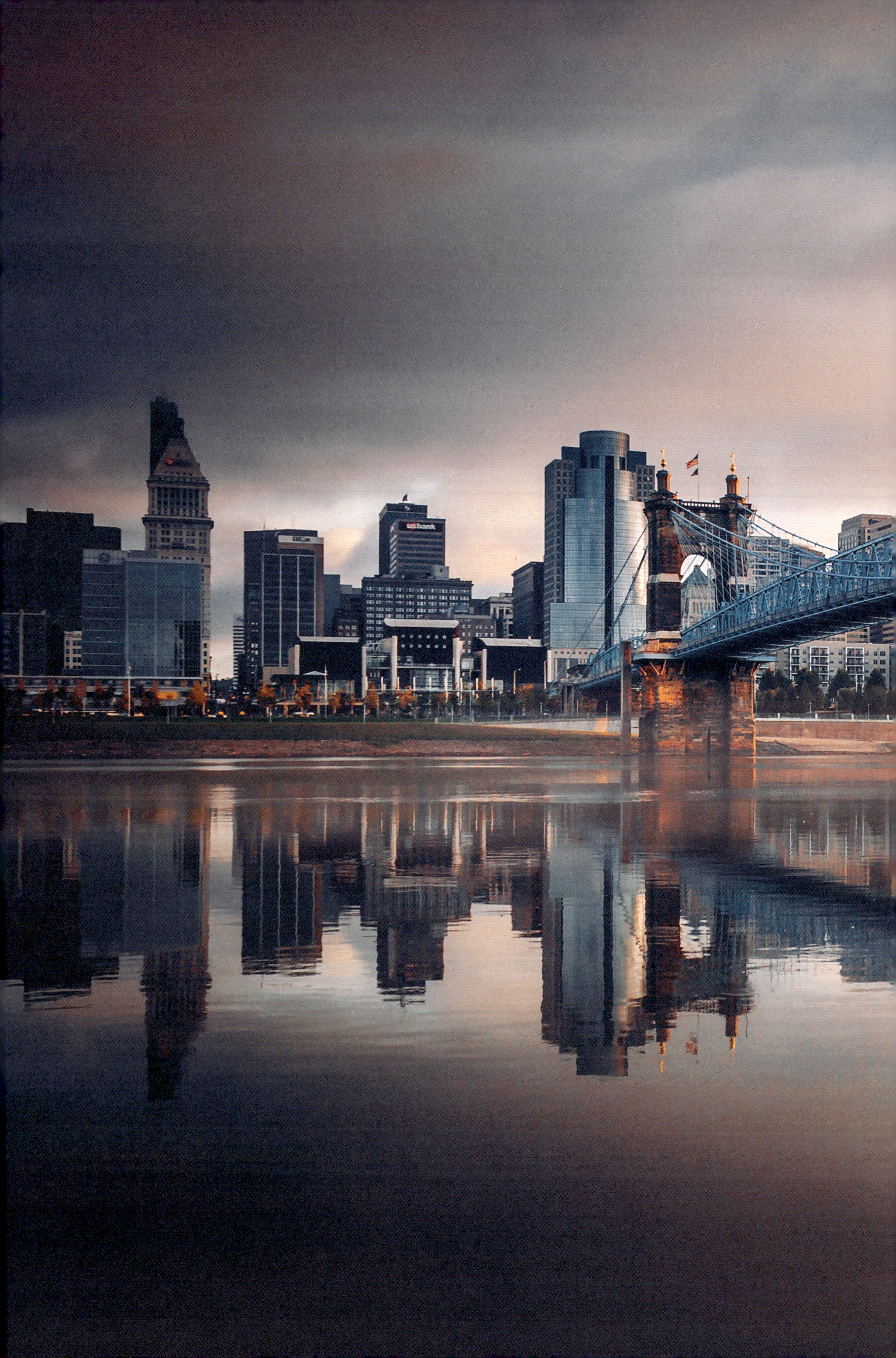
usbank

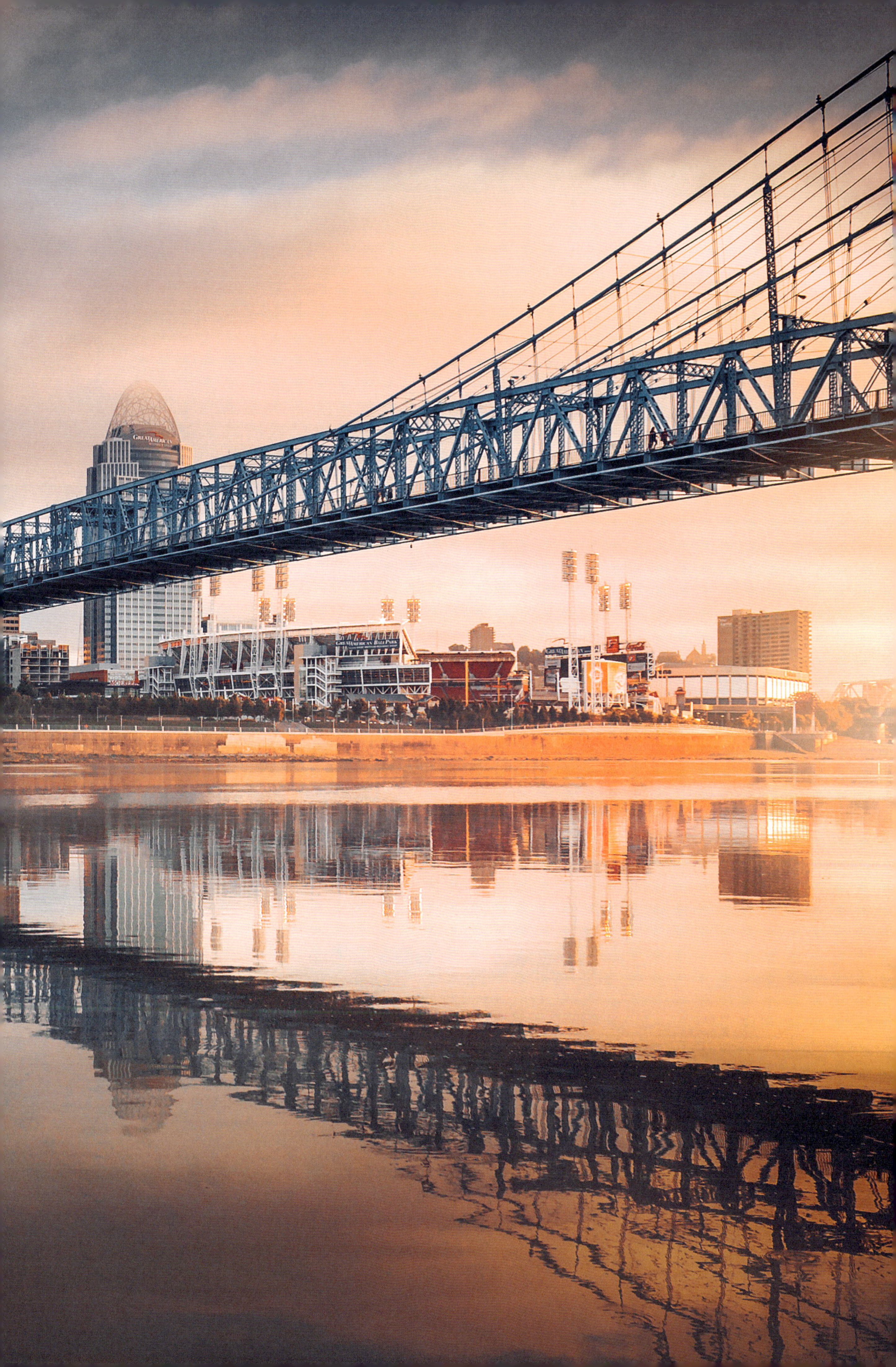
GREAT AMERICAN
GREAT AMERICAN BALL PARK

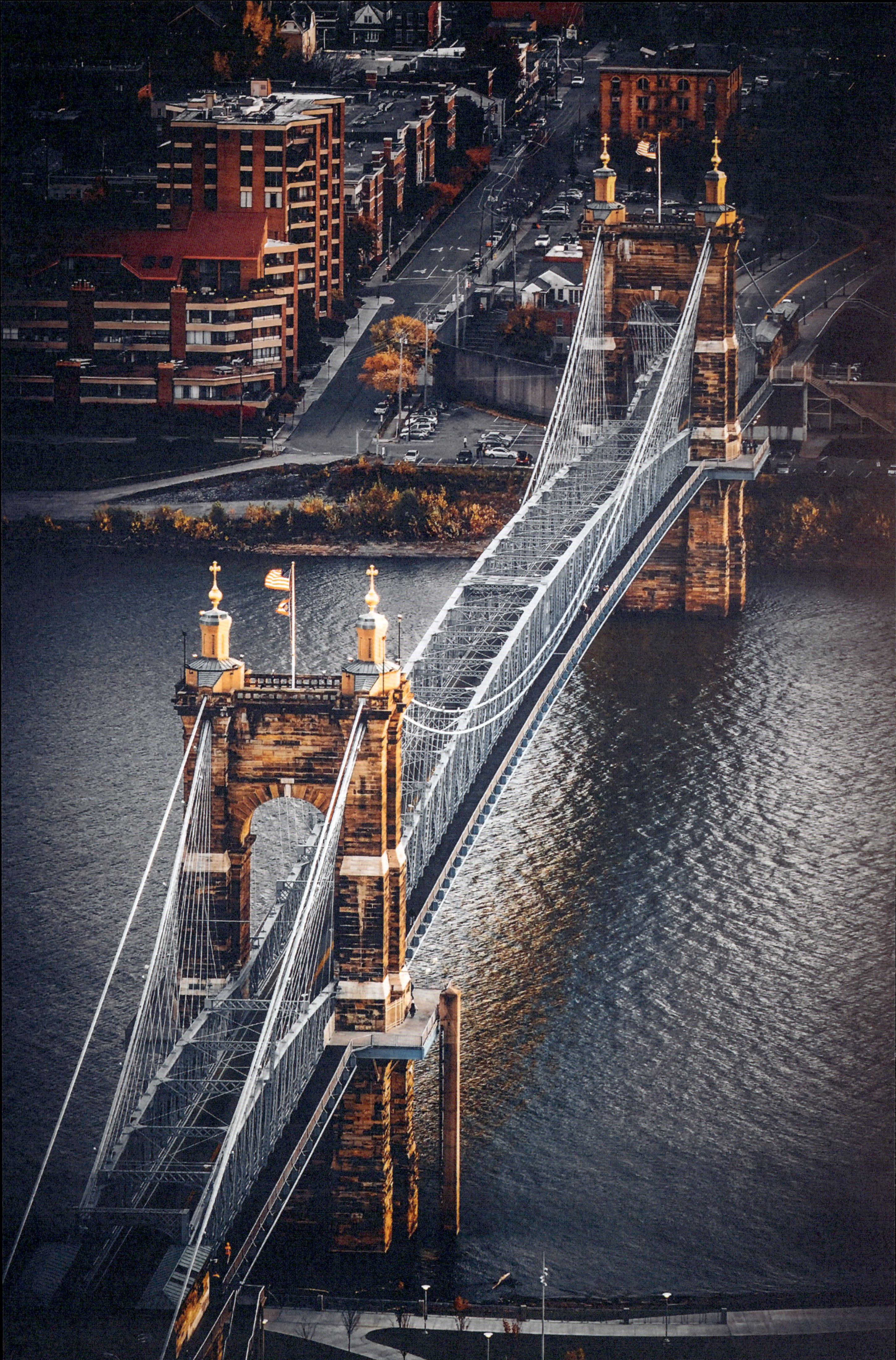

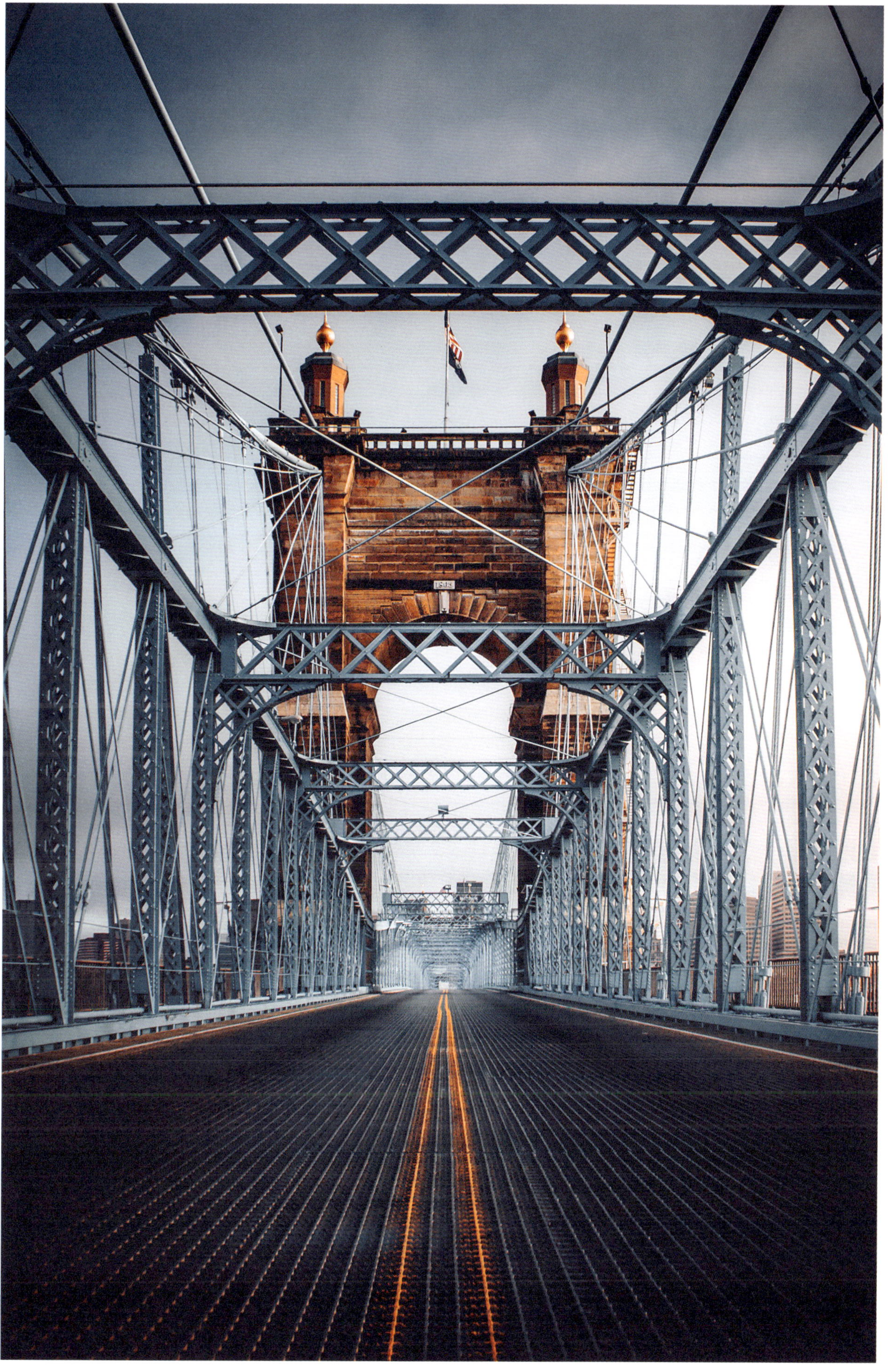

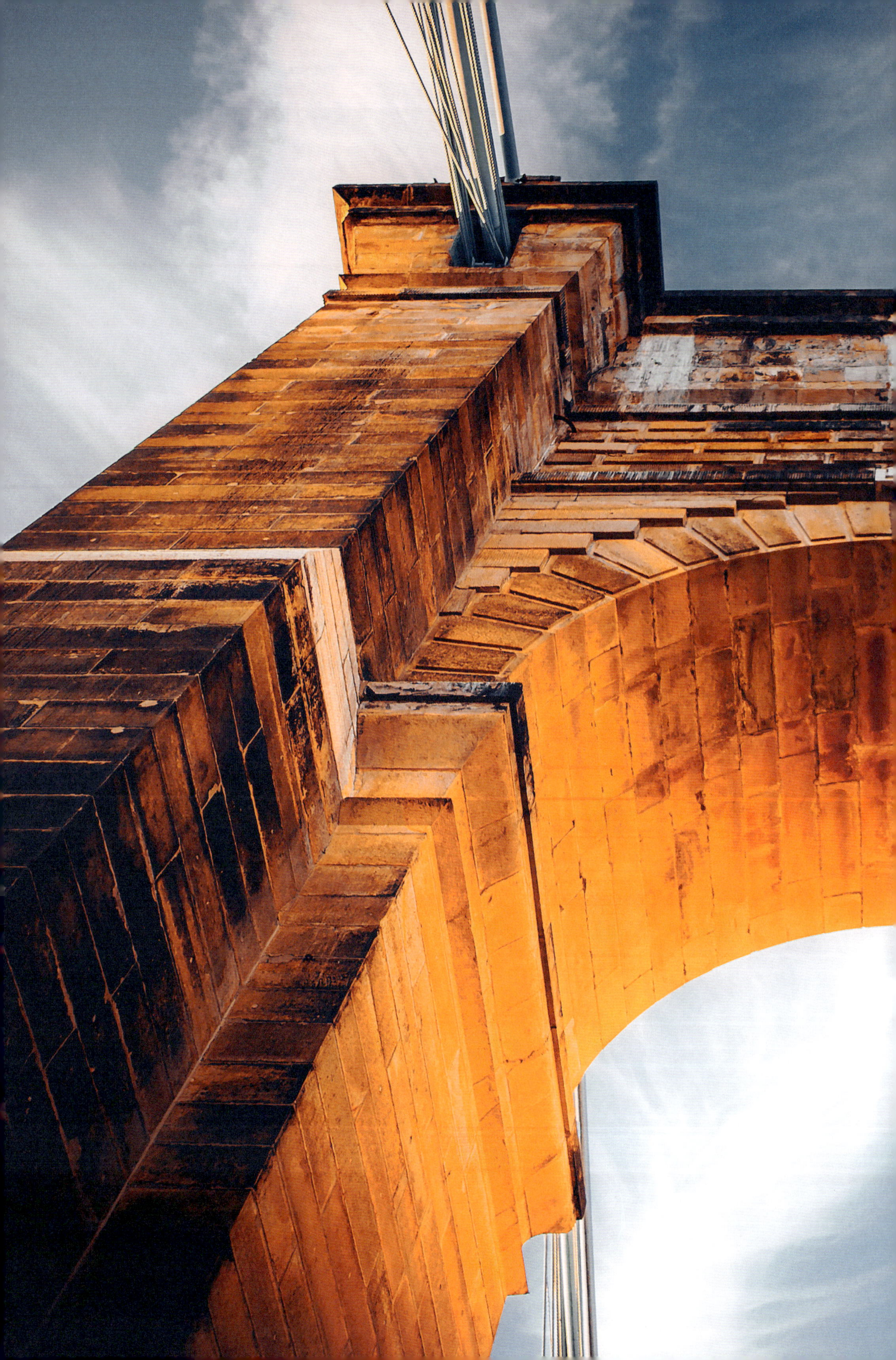

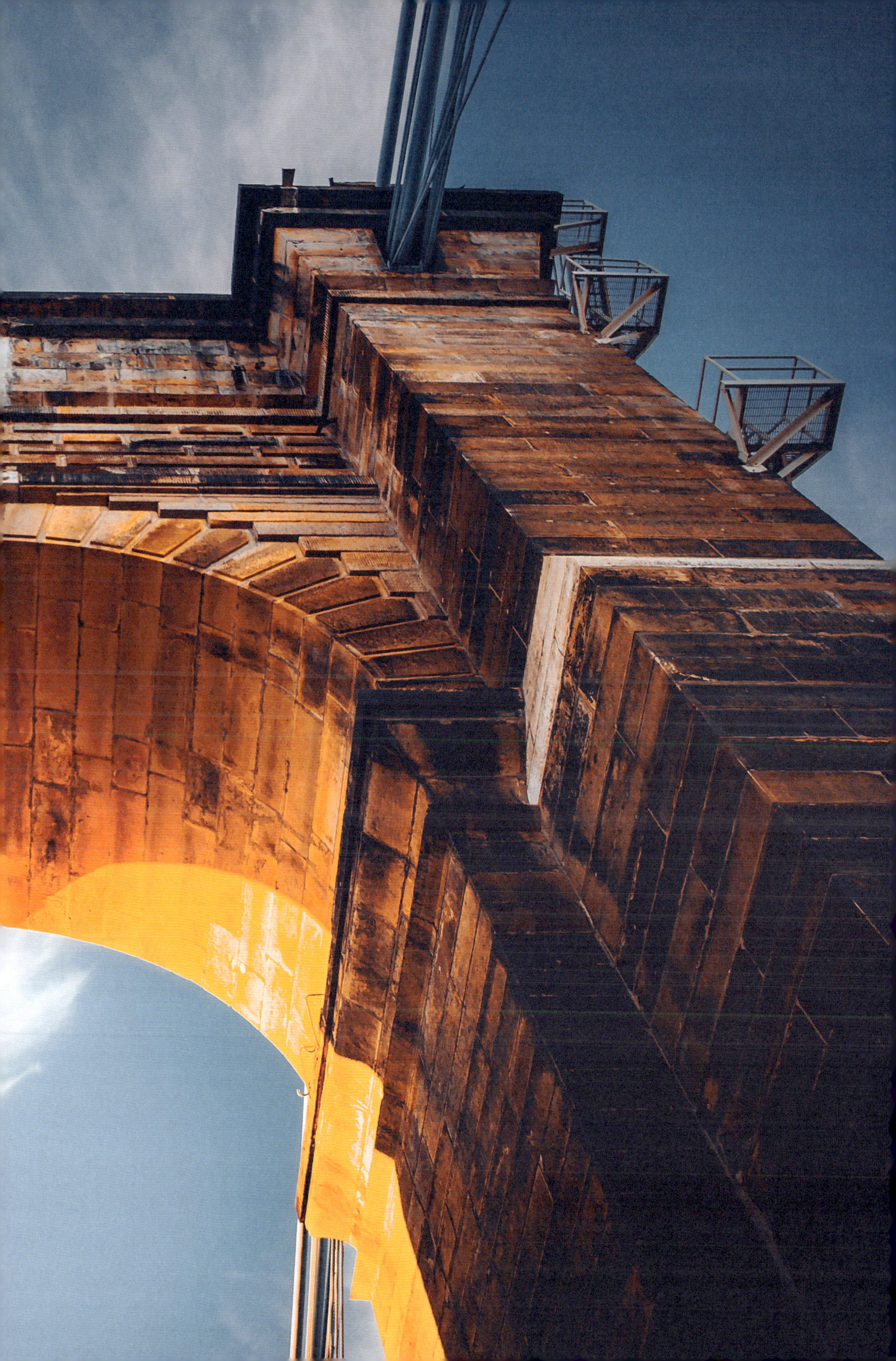

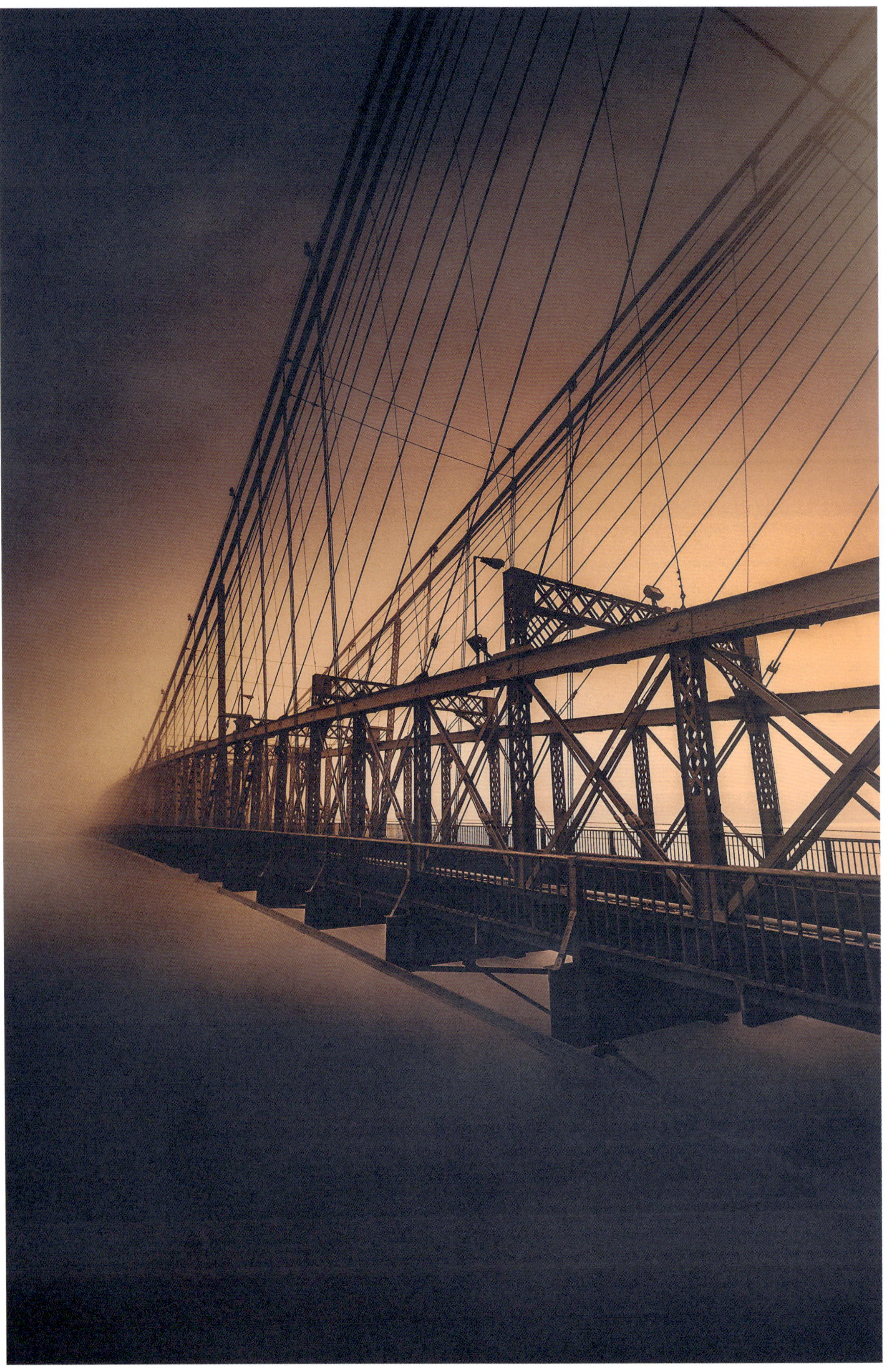

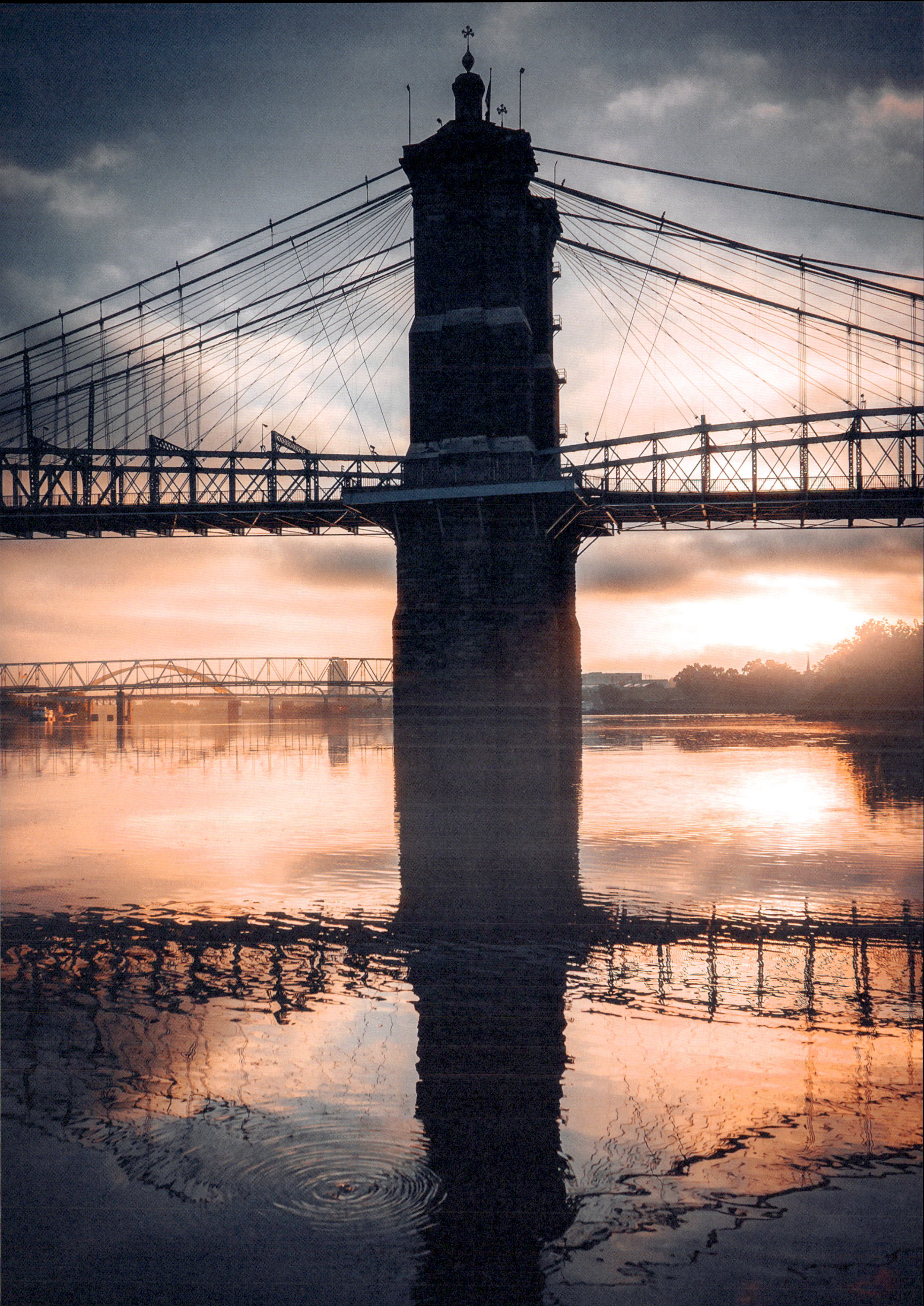

… this bridge, when constructed, will possess great claims as a national monument. As a splendid work of art and as a remarkable specimen of the modern engineering and construction, it will stand unrivaled upon the continent.

JOHN A. ROEBLING

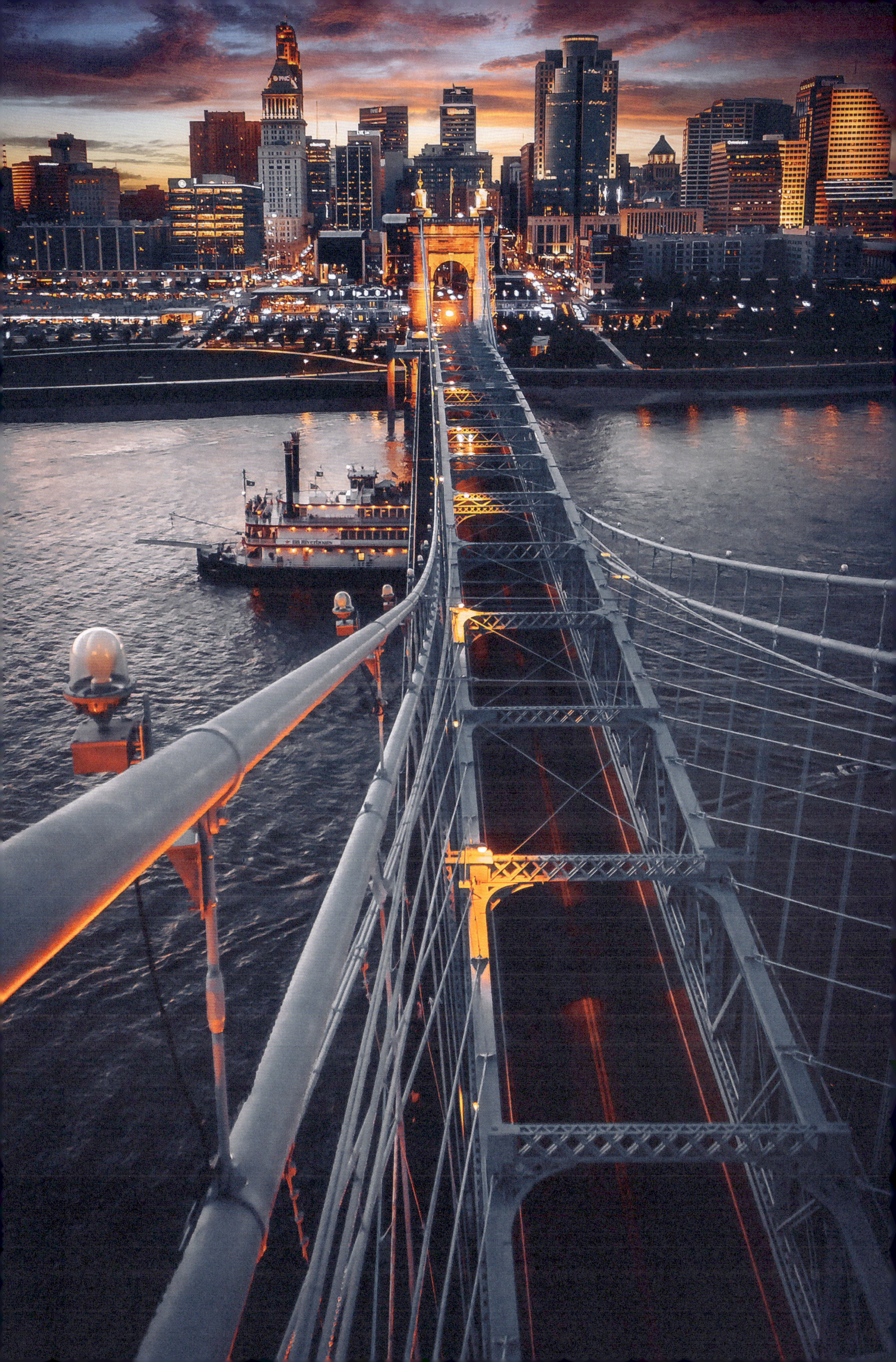
PNC

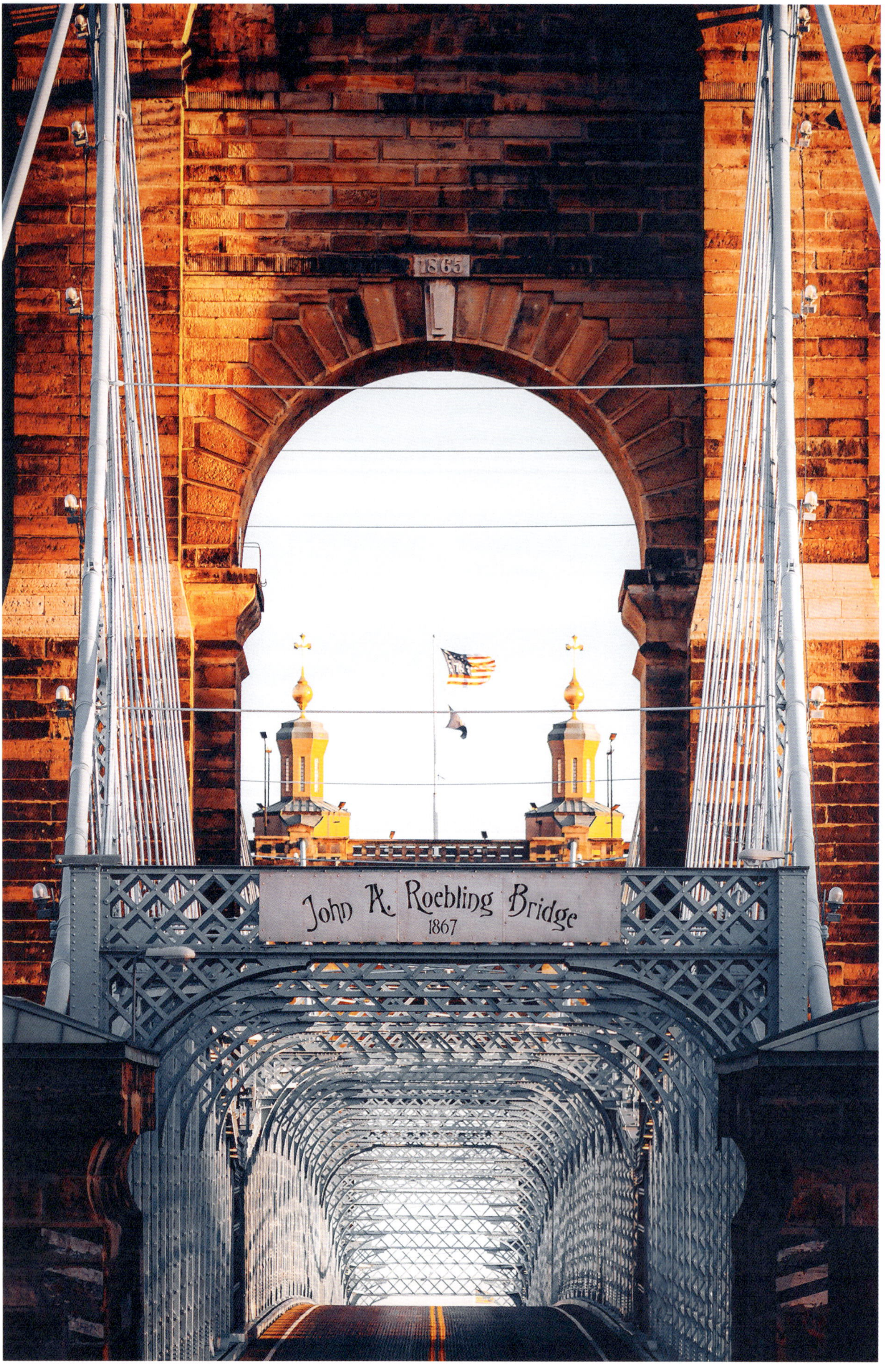
1865
John A. Roebling Bridge
1867

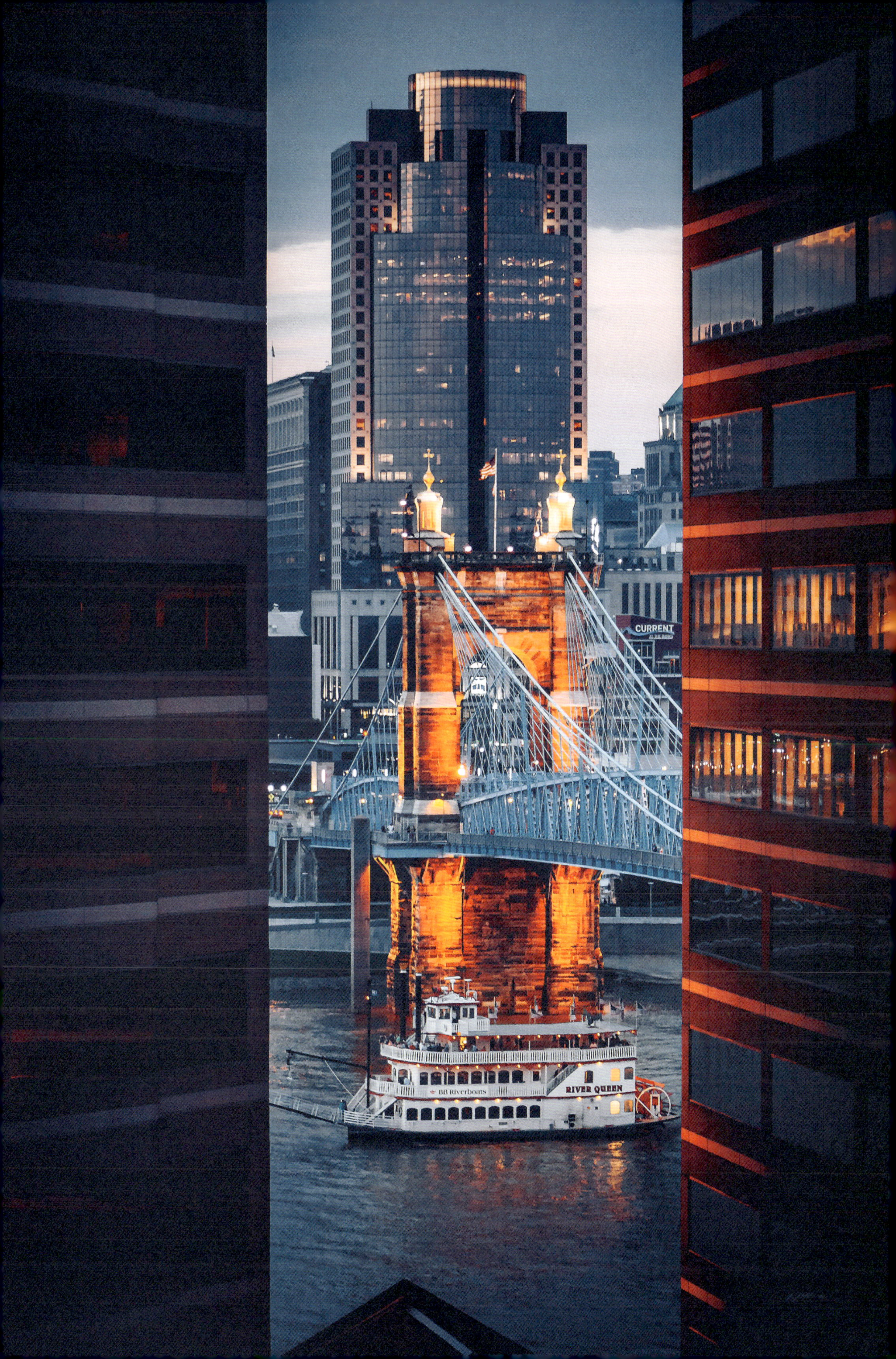
CURRENT
BB Riverboats
RIVER QUEEN

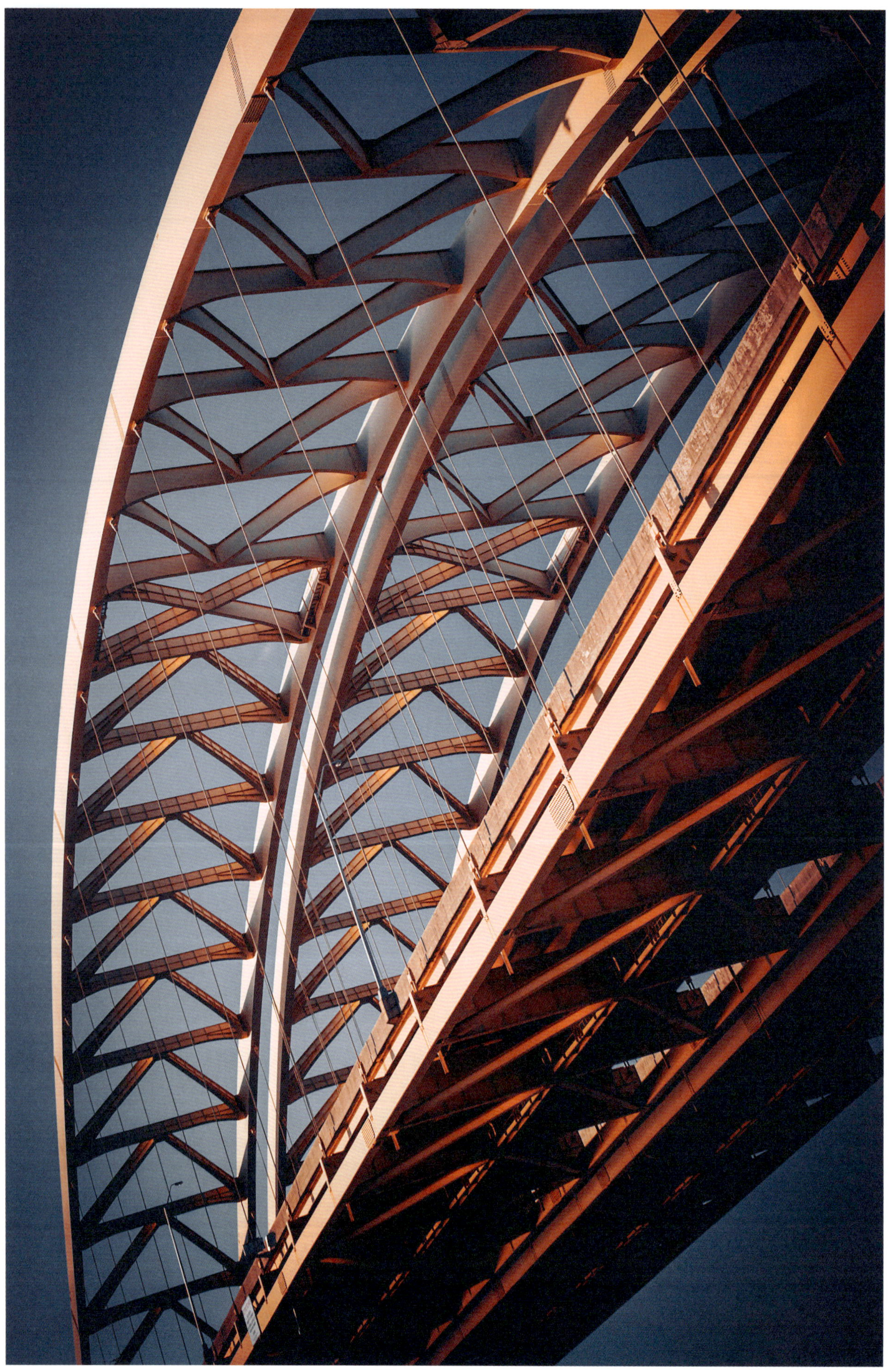

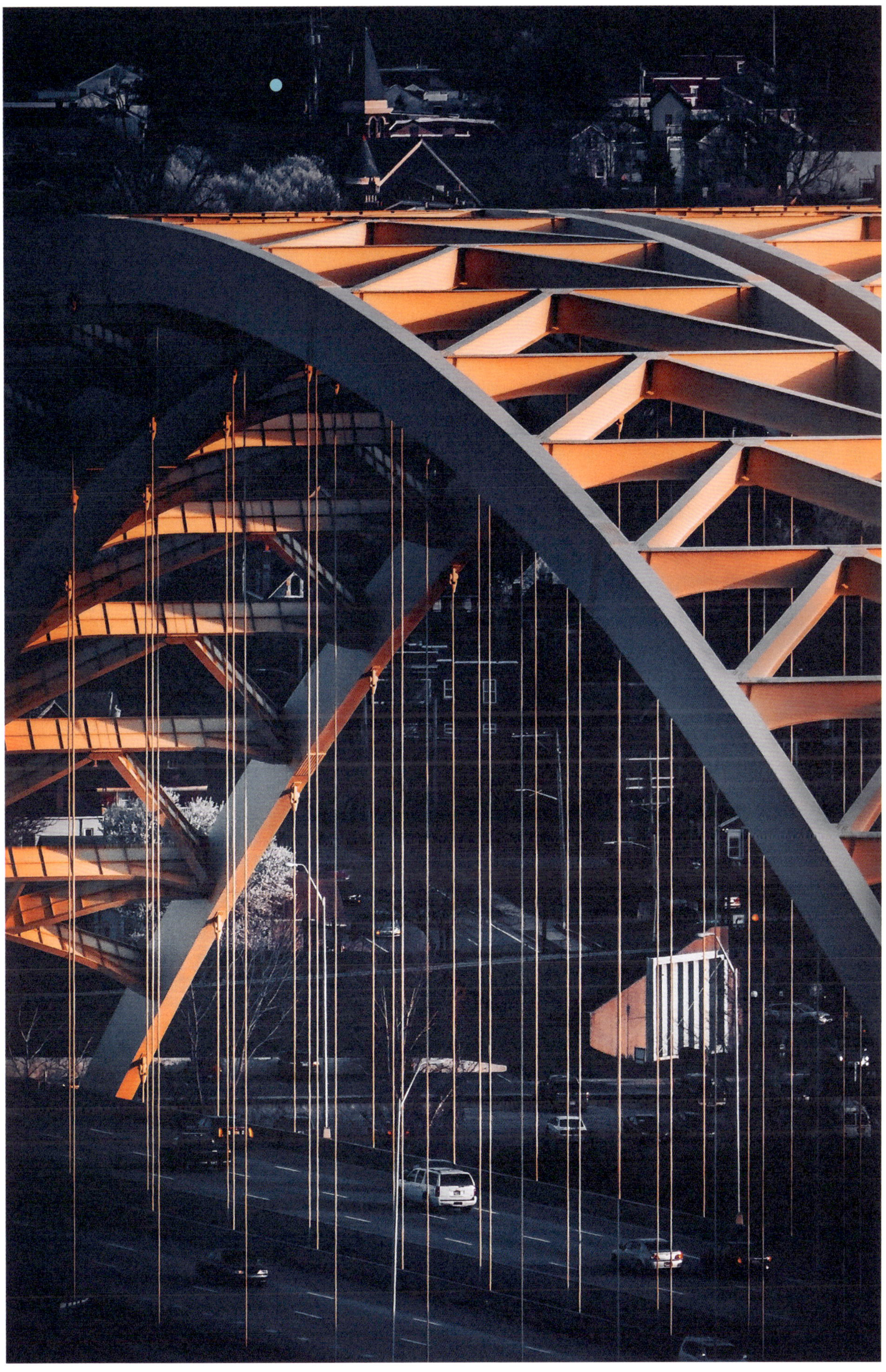

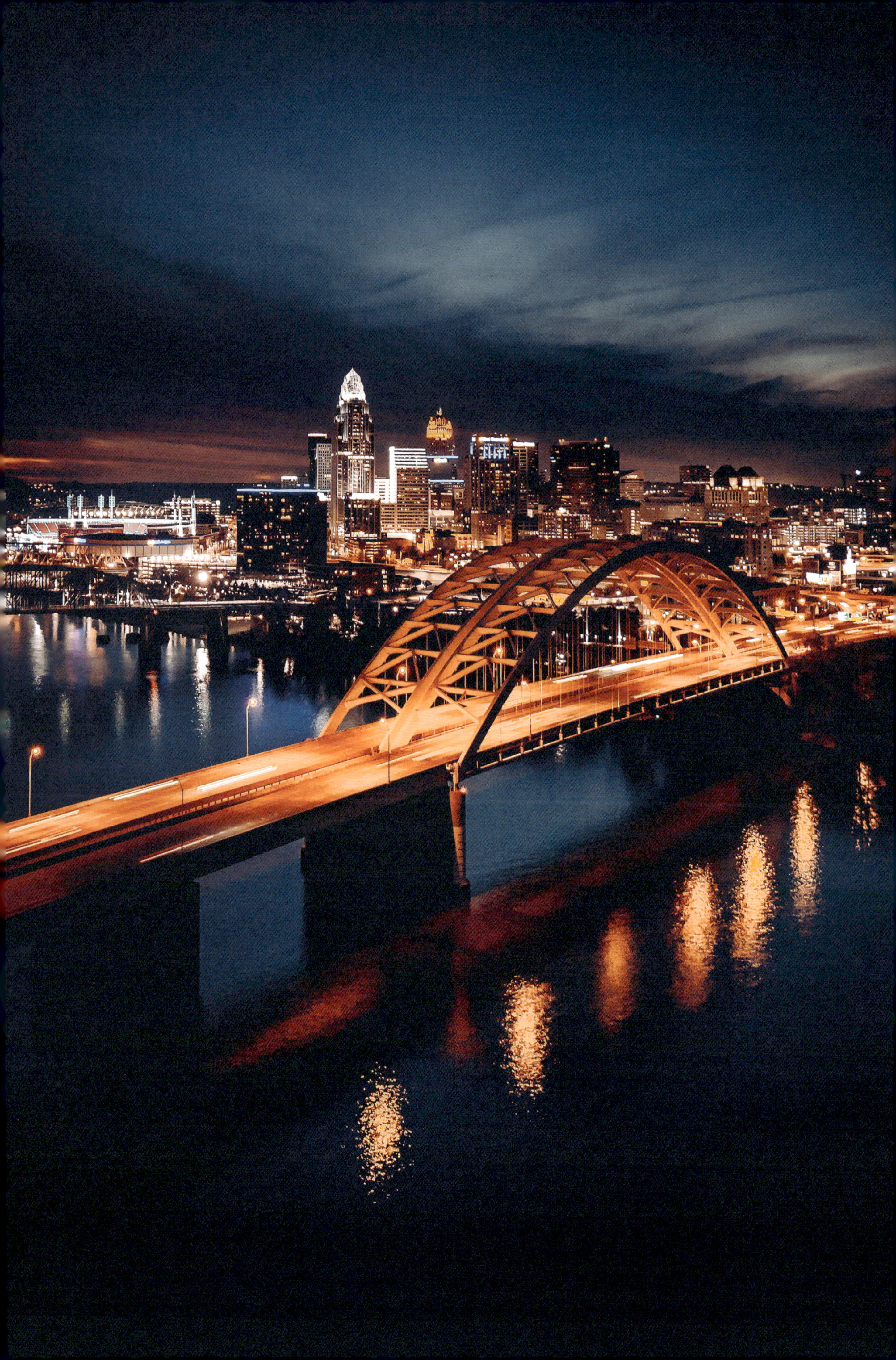

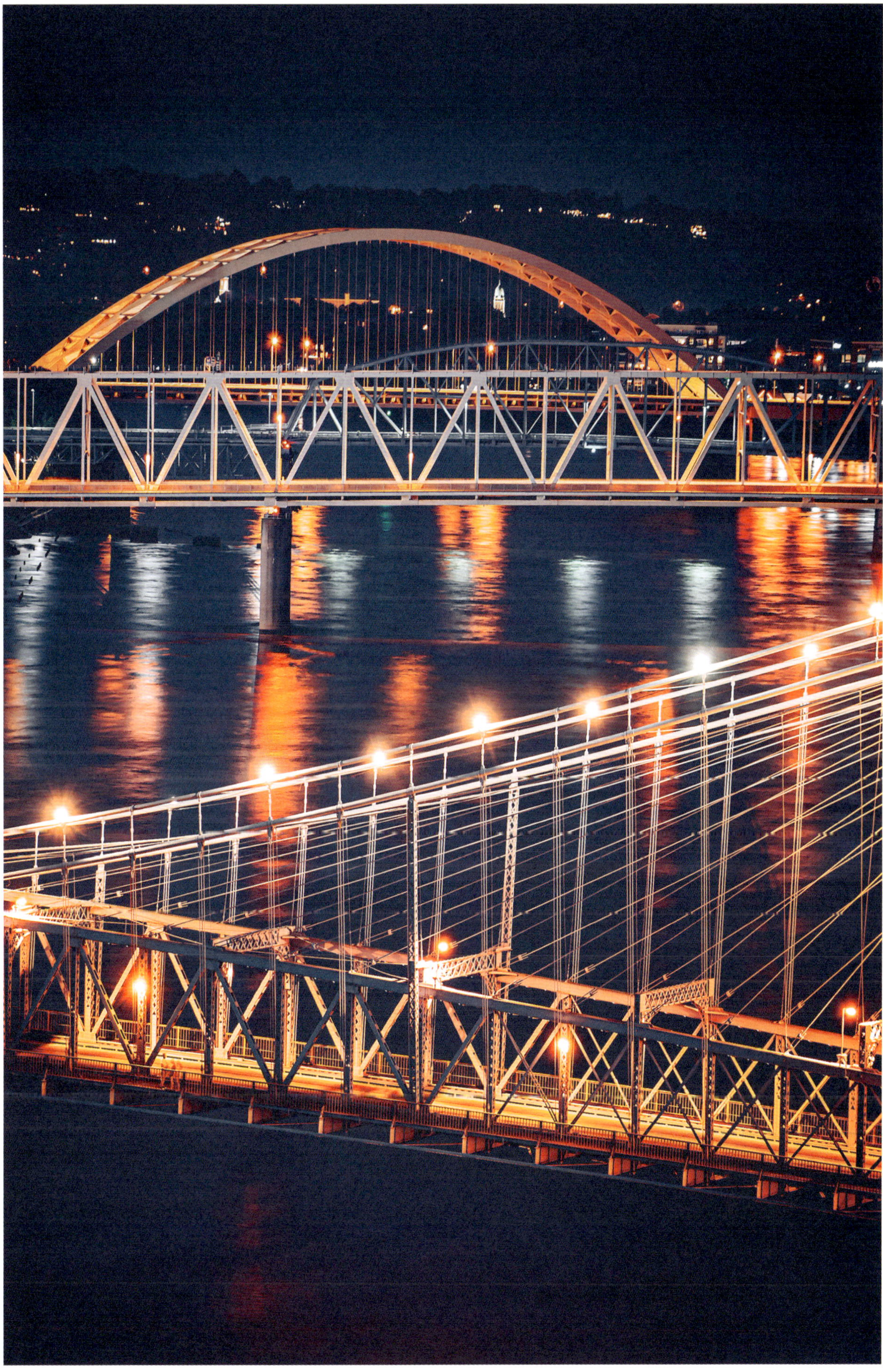

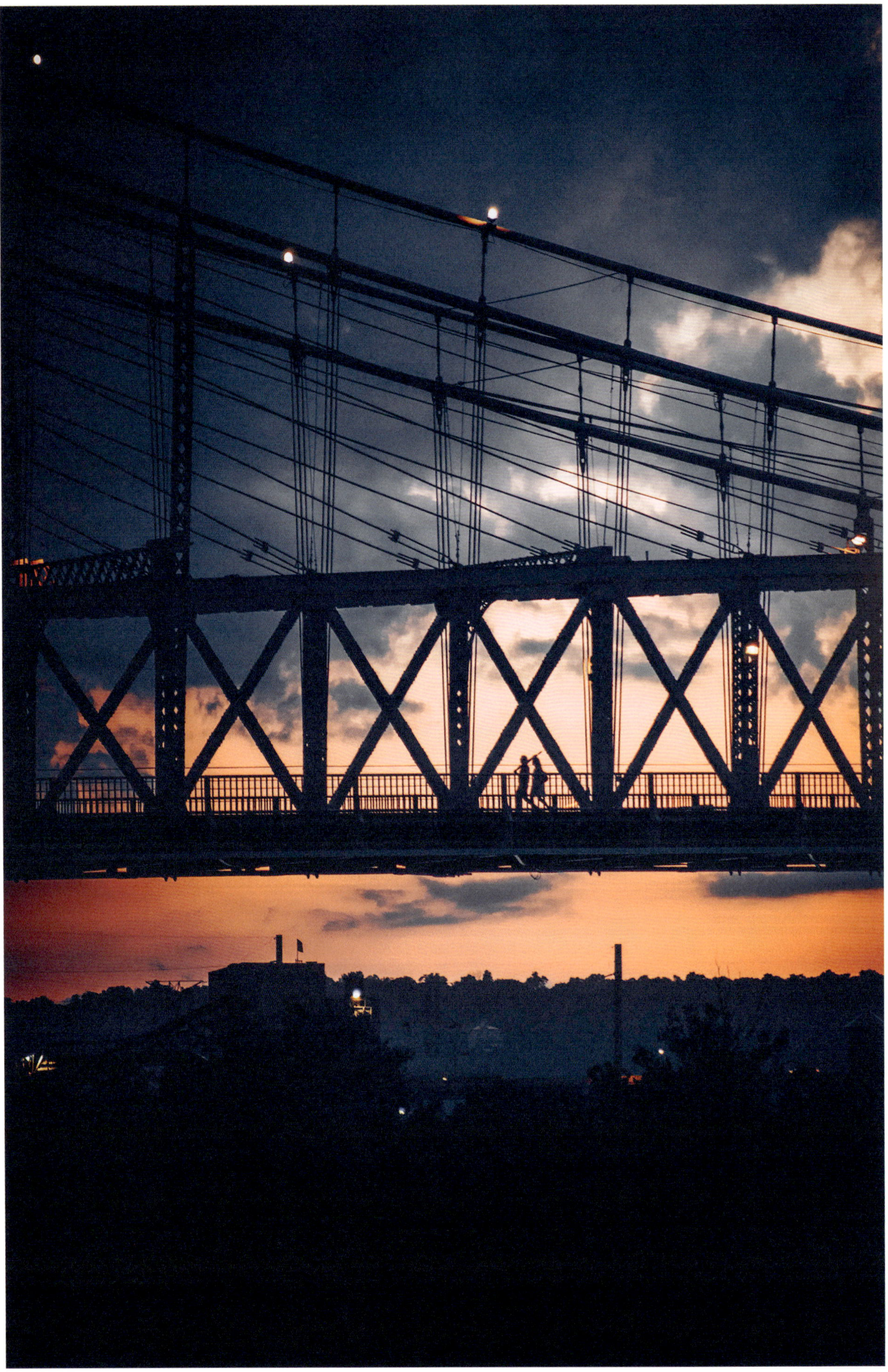

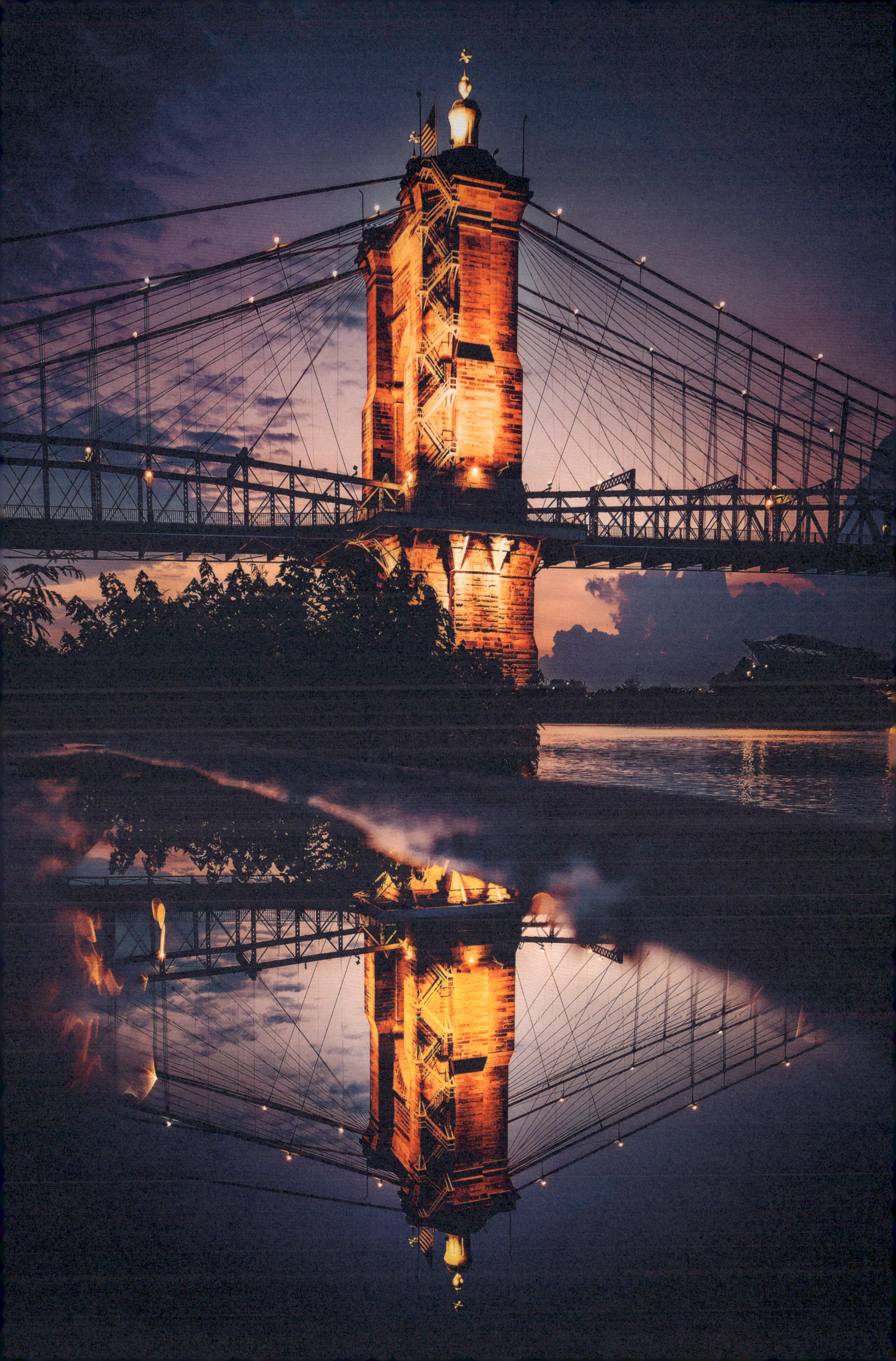

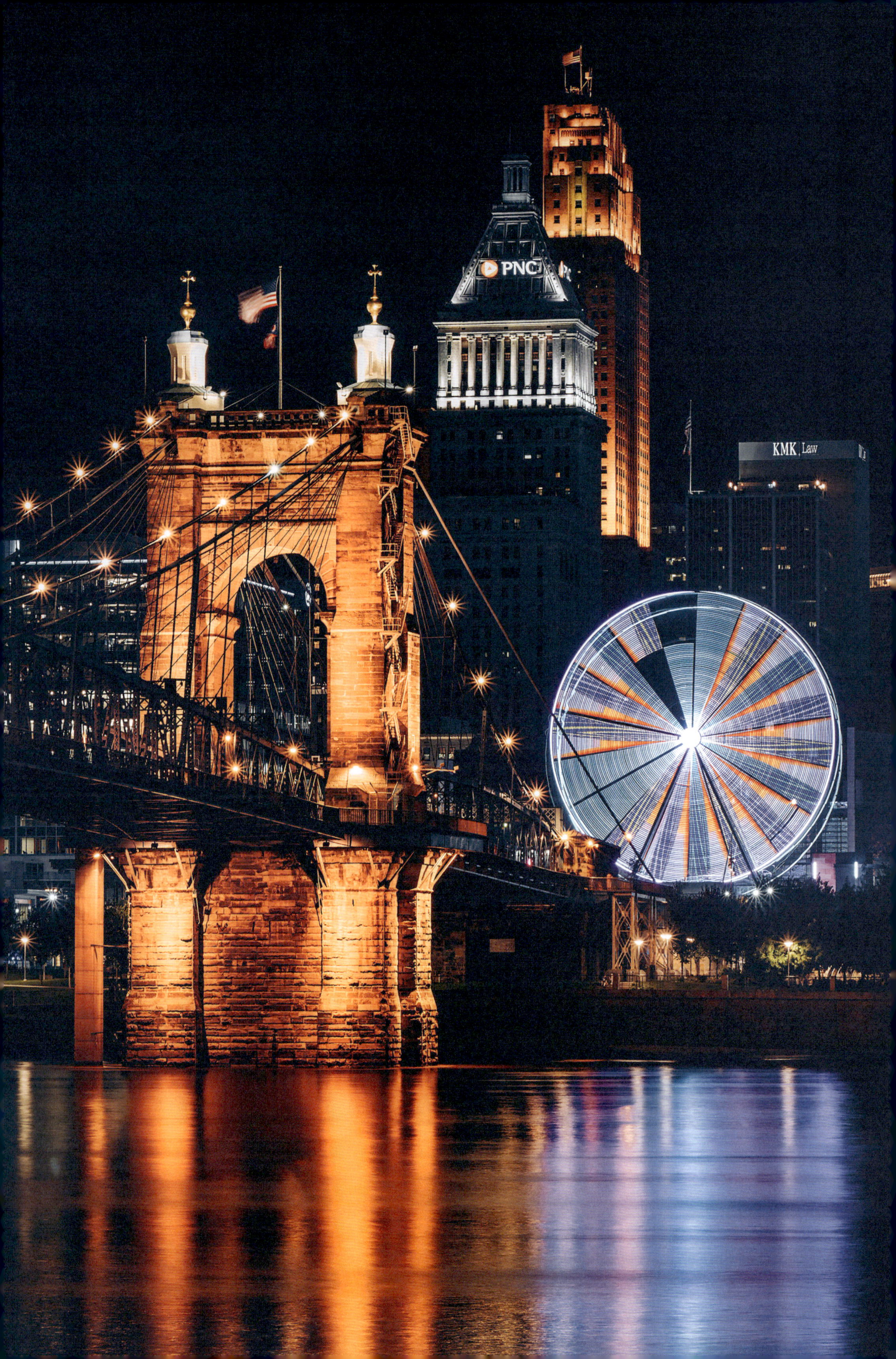
PNC
KMK Law

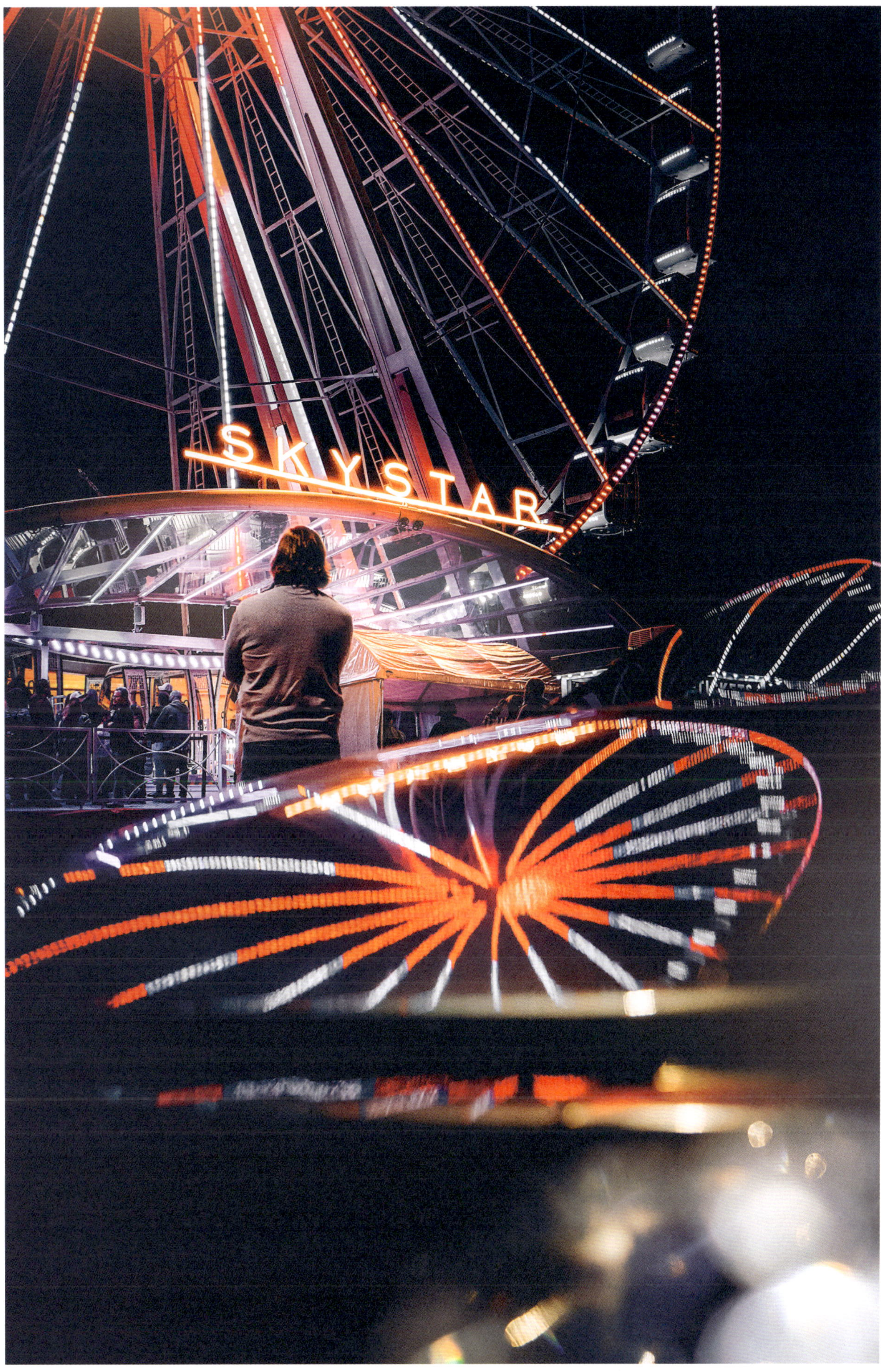
SKYSTAR

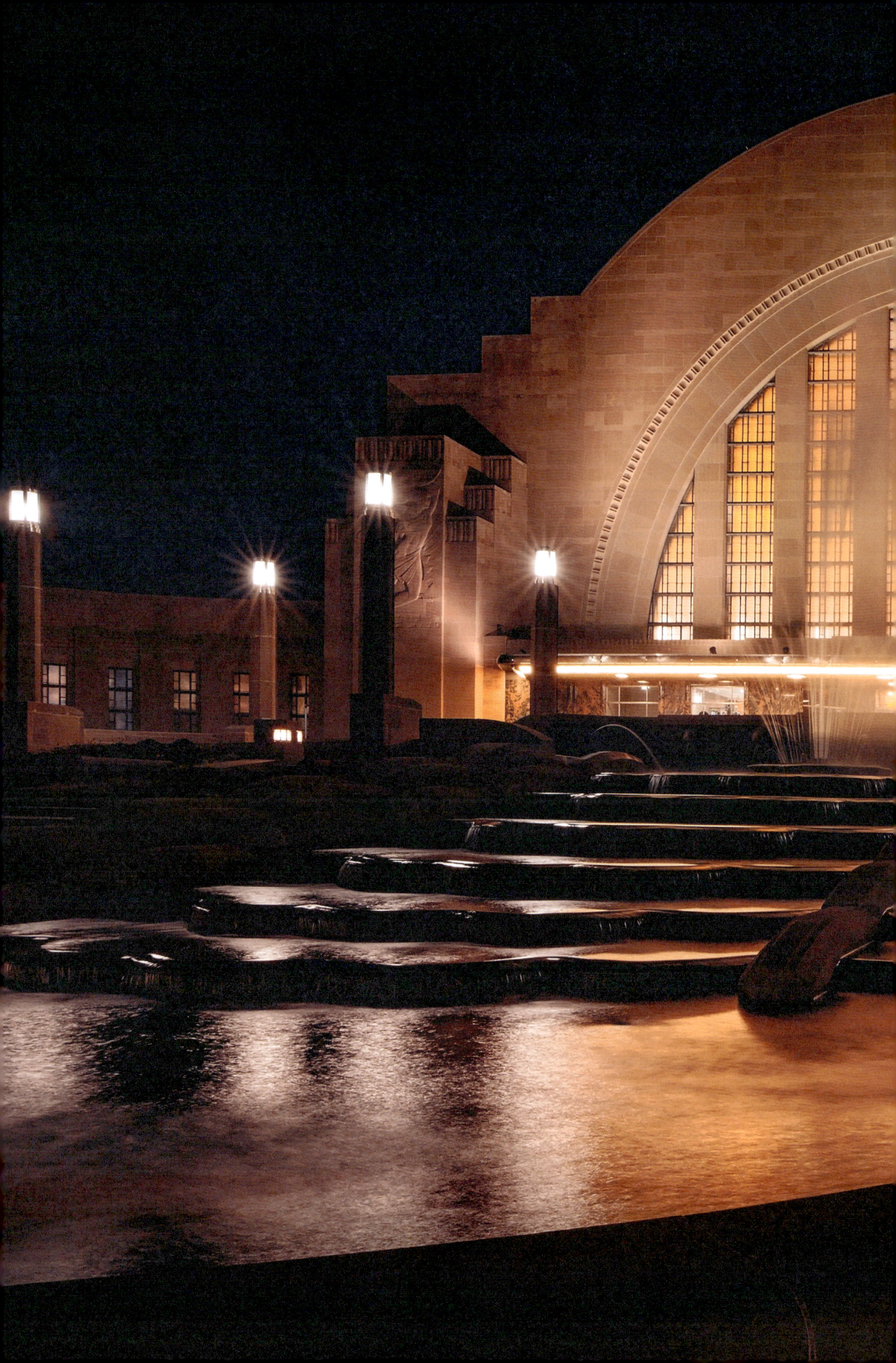

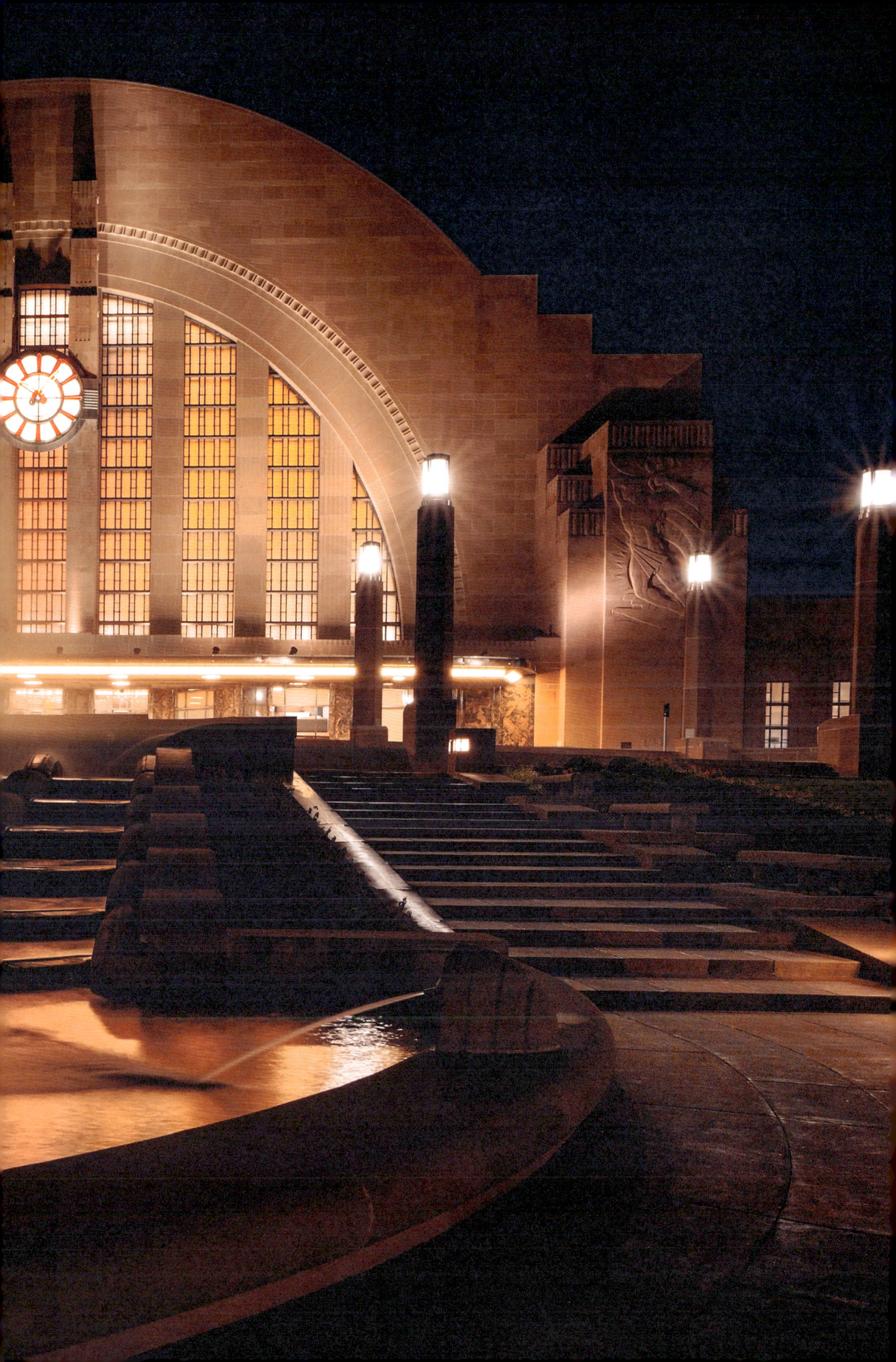

Cincinnati Union Terminal was not so much architecture as a work of art that happened to house human activity. It is considered an Art Deco masterpiece.

JEFFREY T. DARBEE

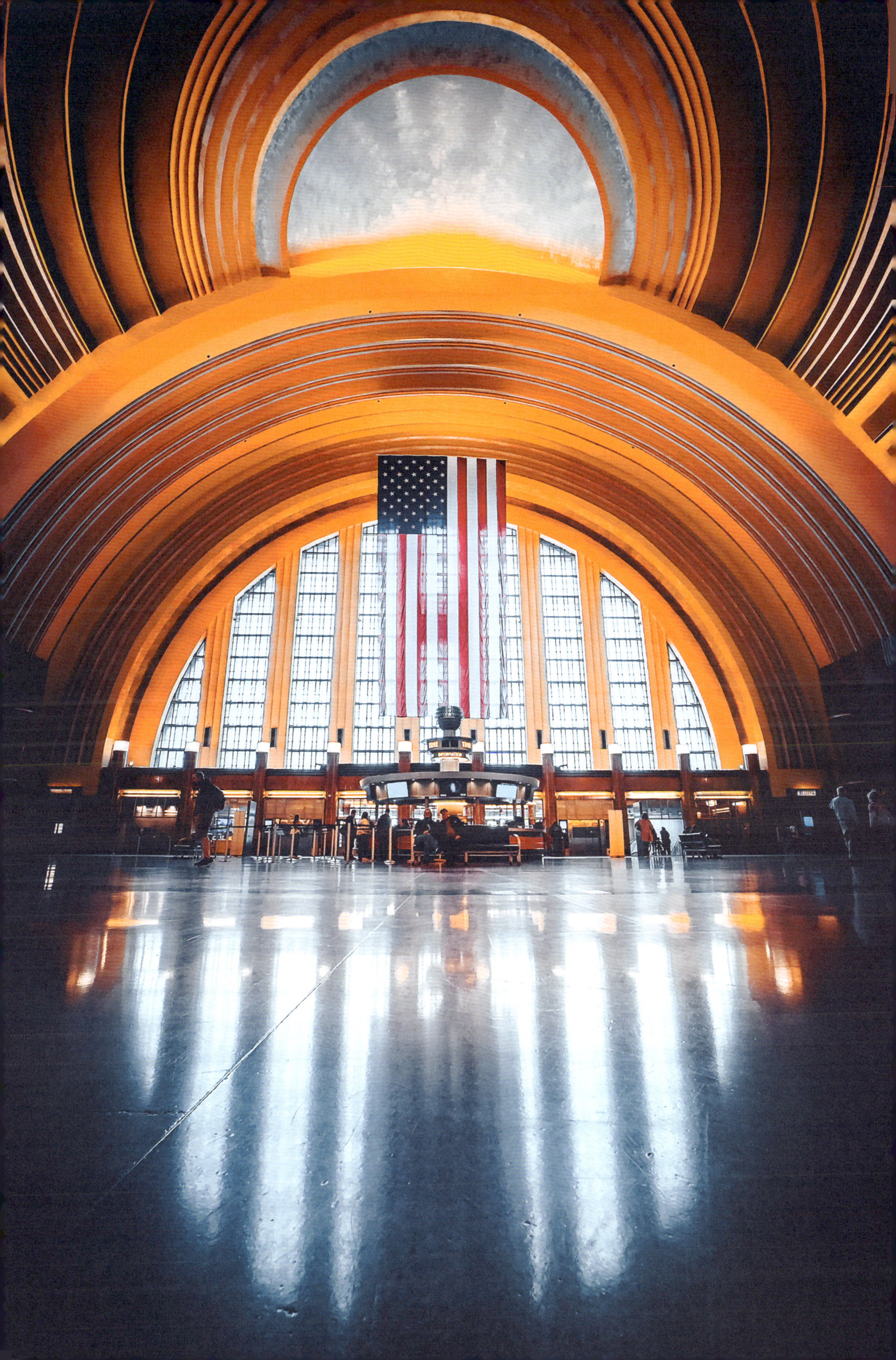

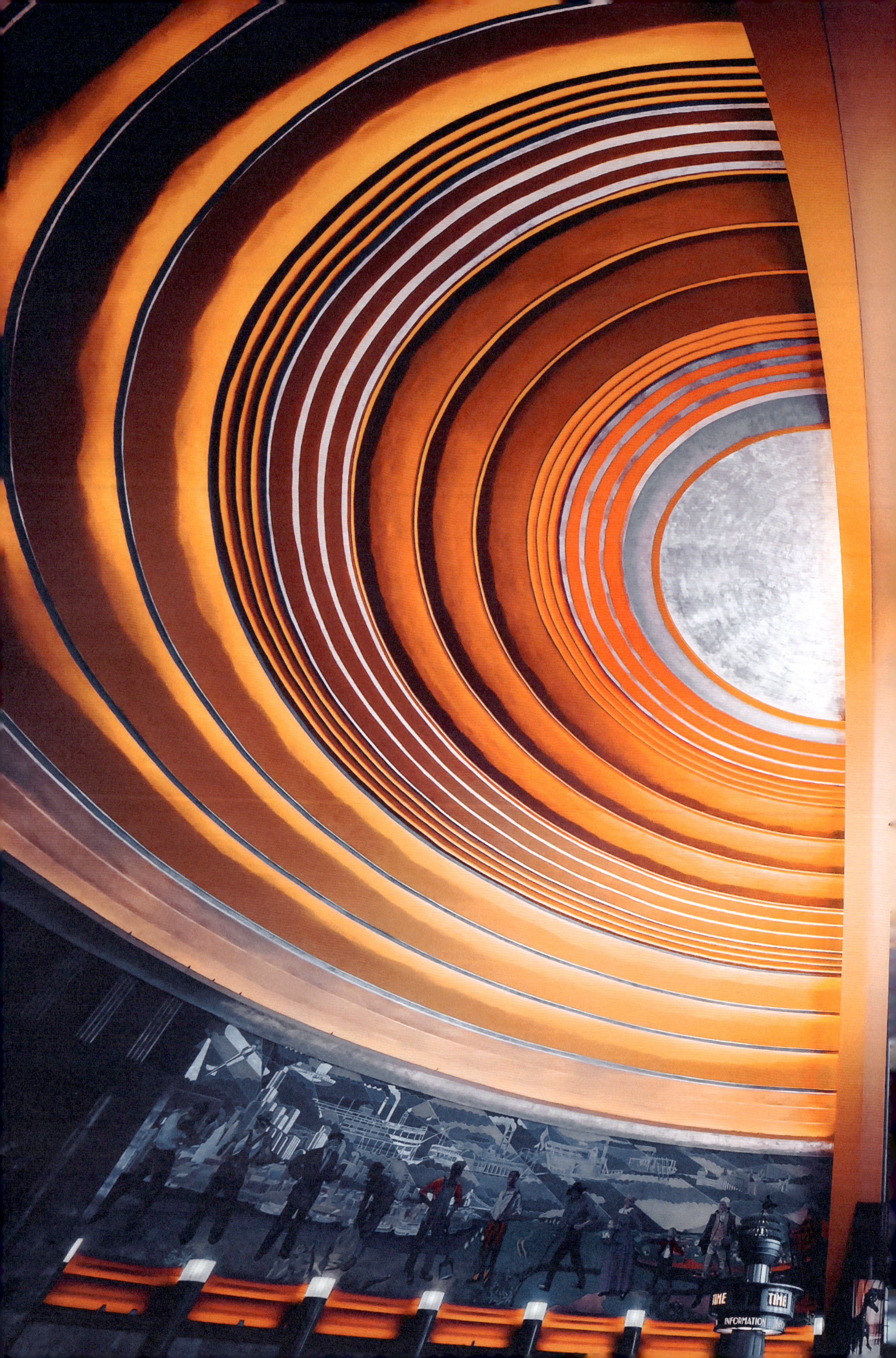
TIME
TIME
INFORMATION

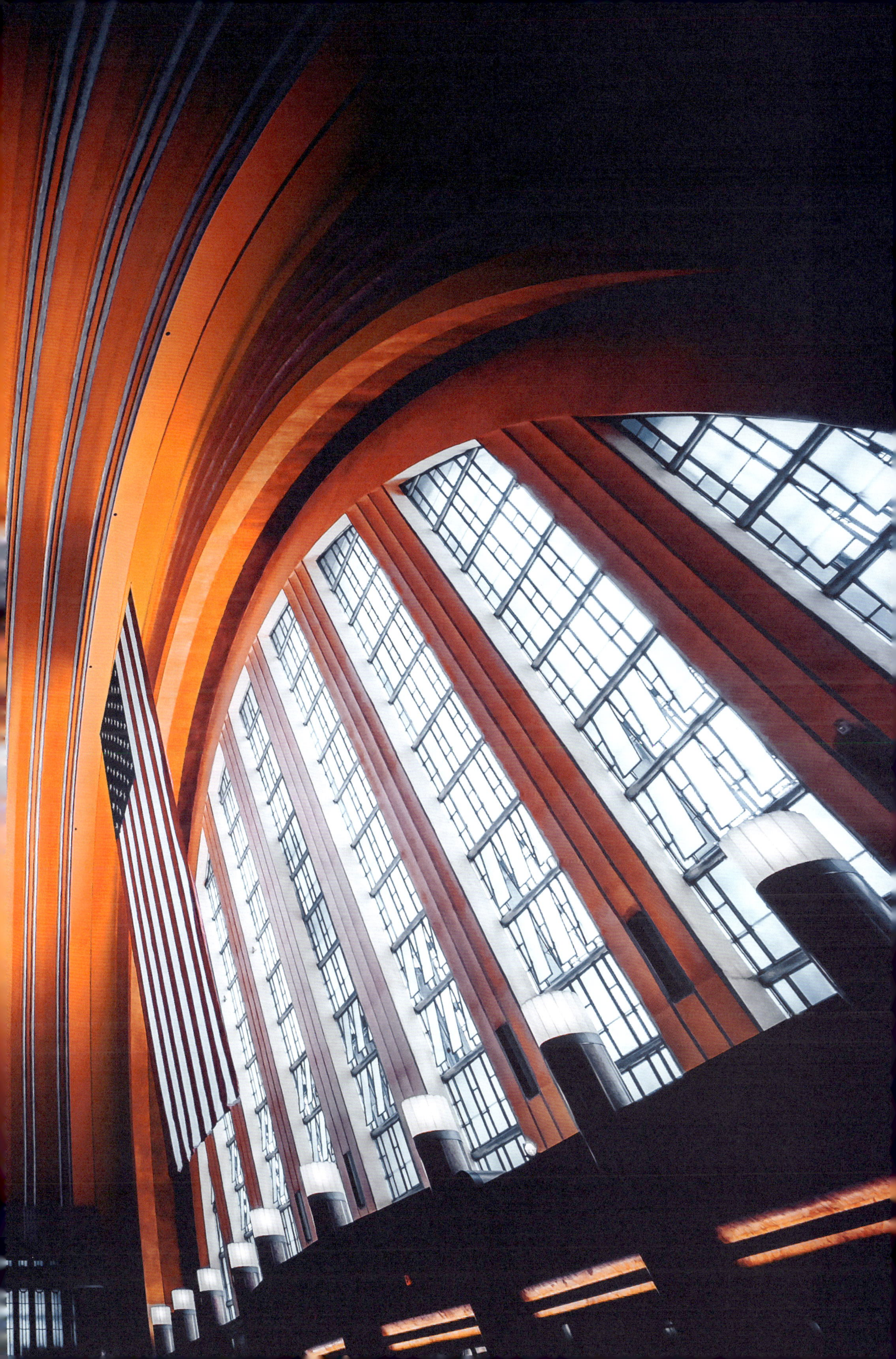

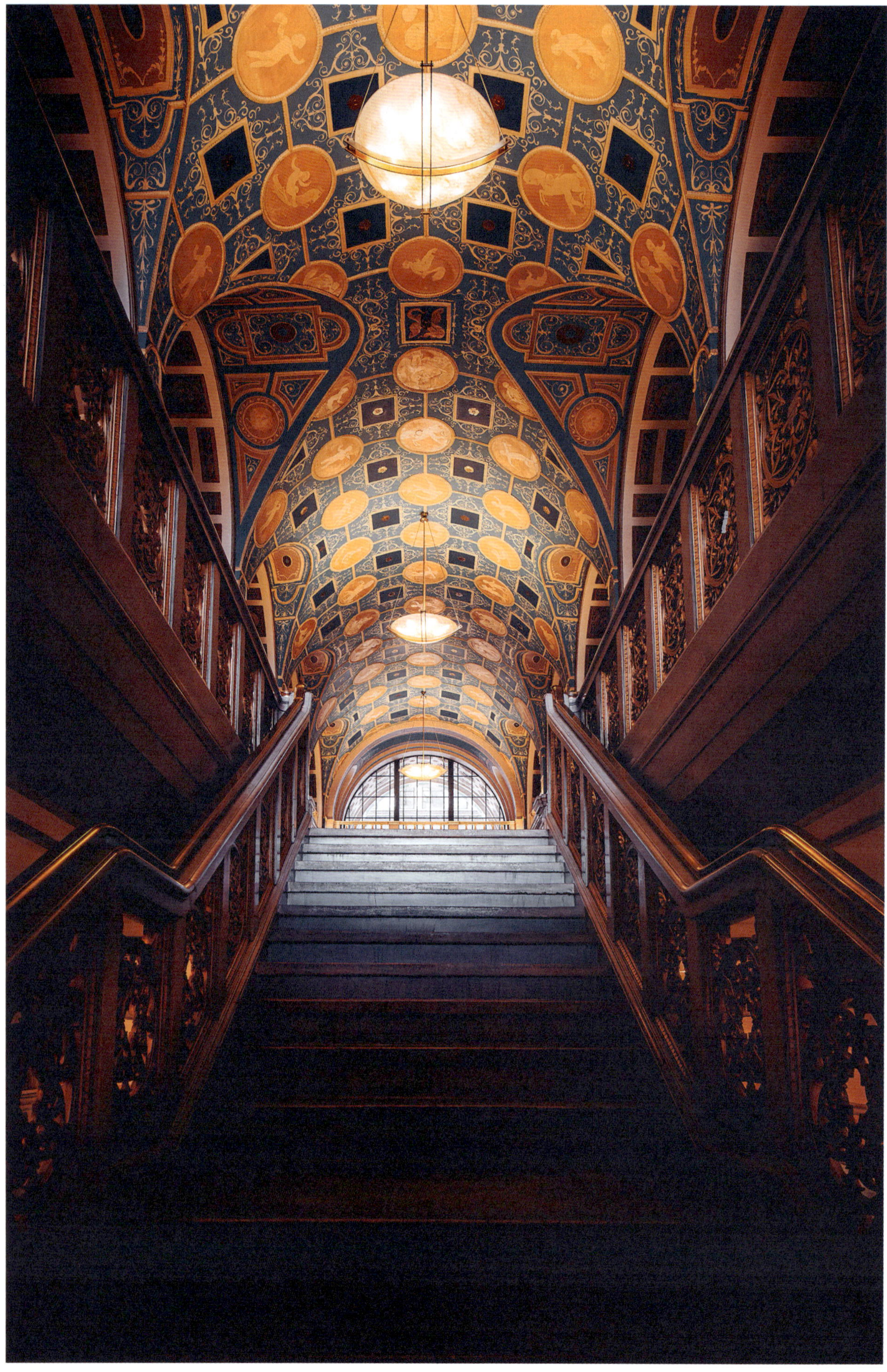

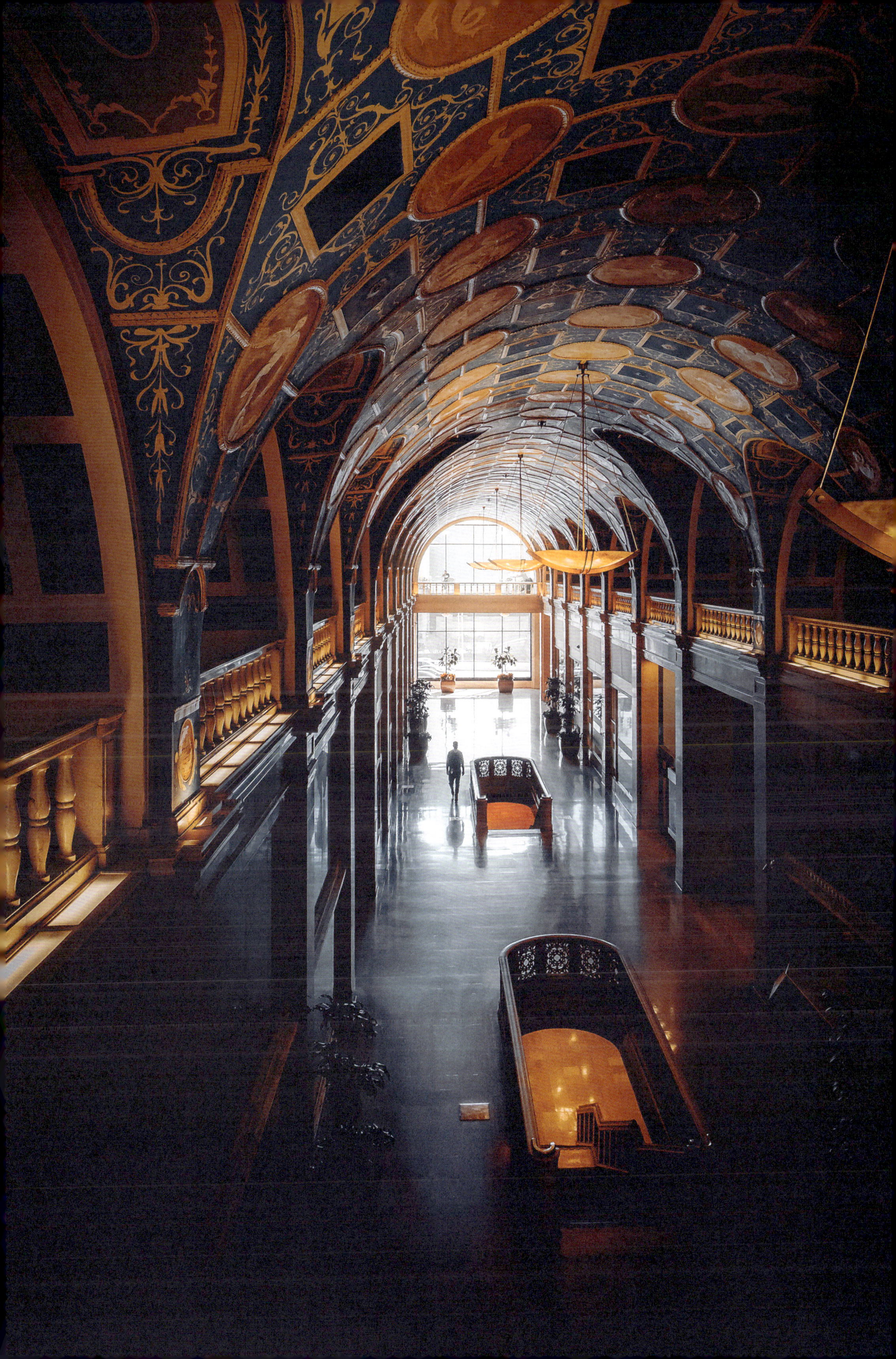

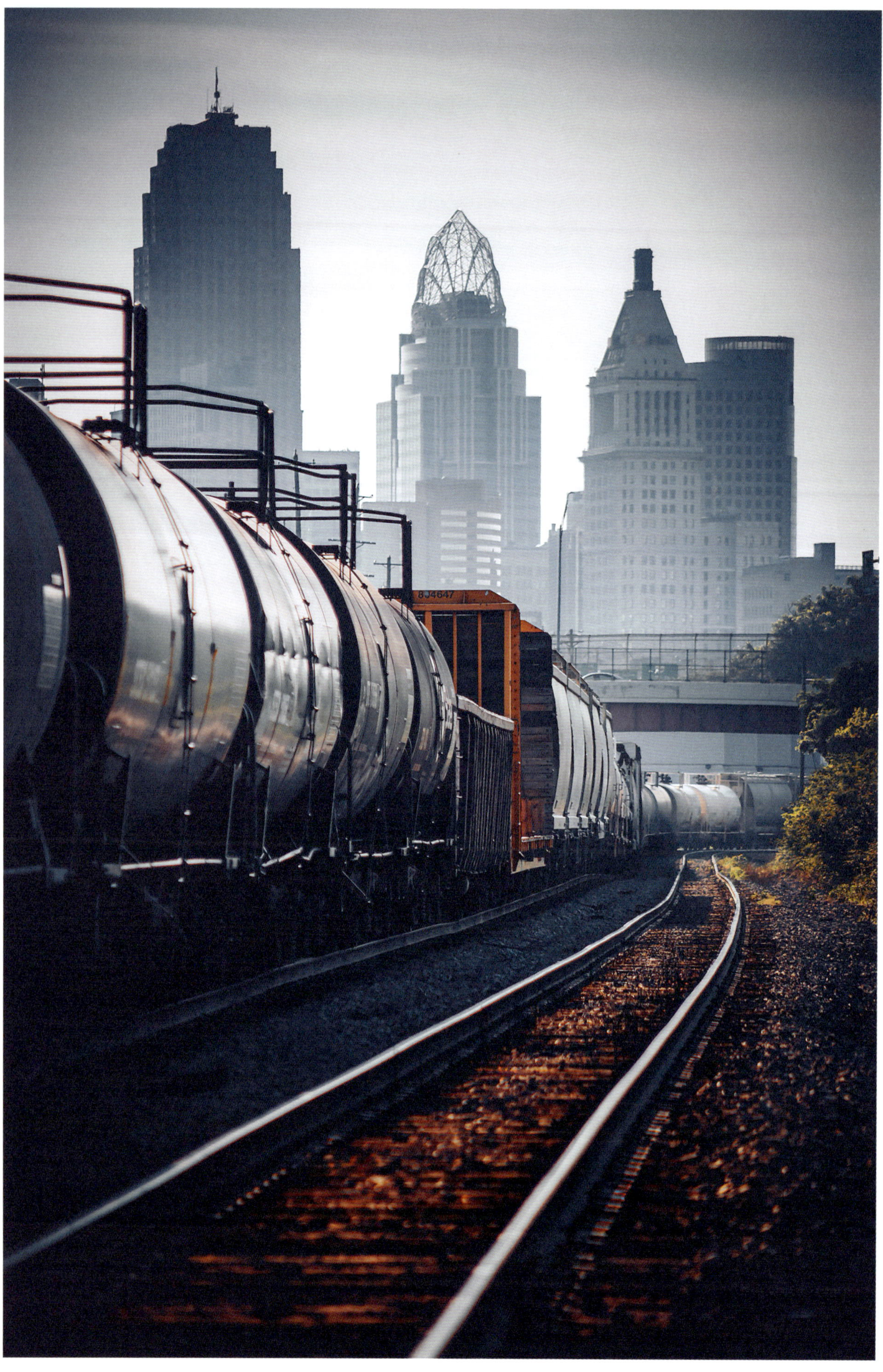

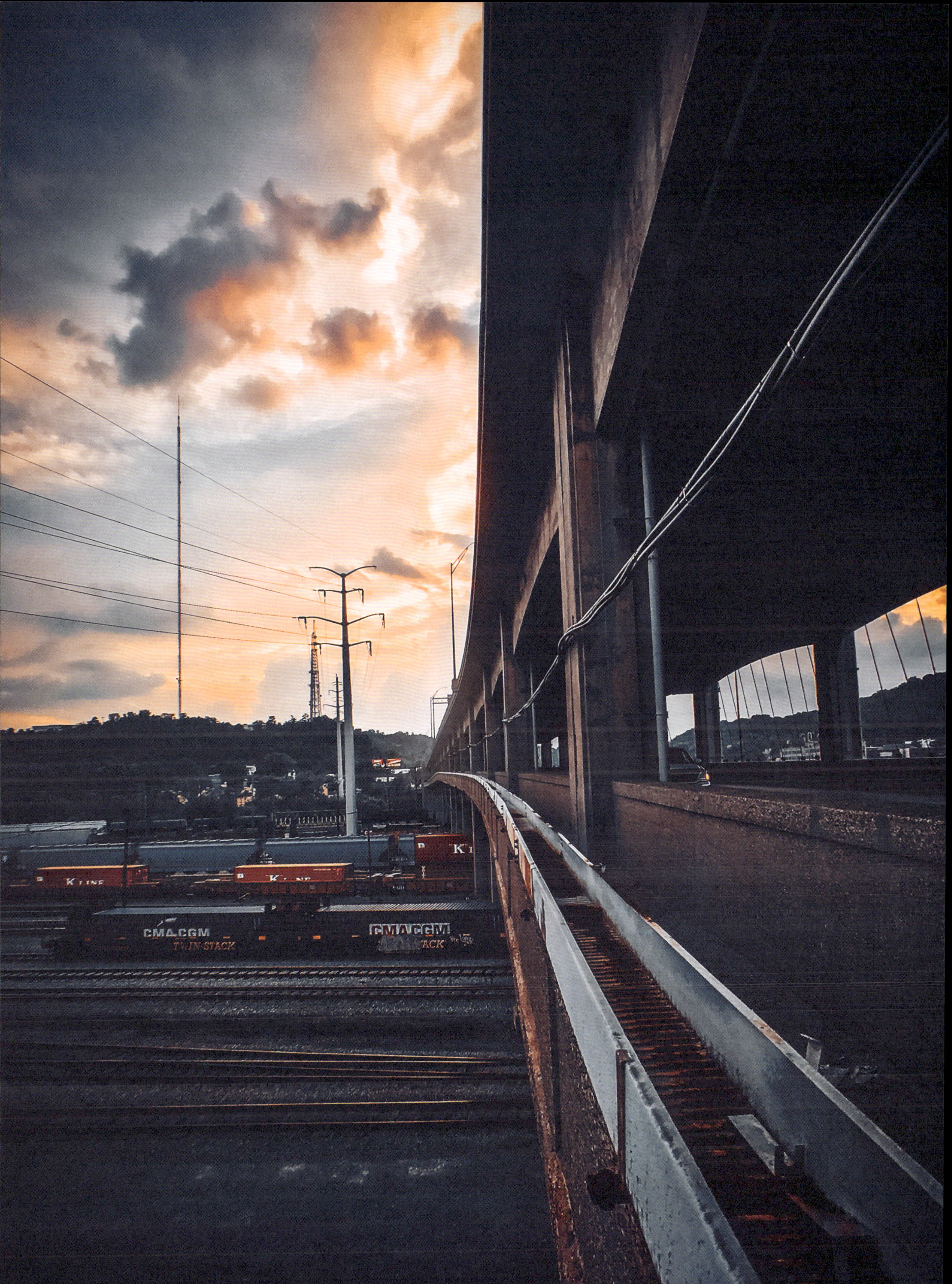
K LINE
CMA CGM
TWIN-STACK
CMA CGM

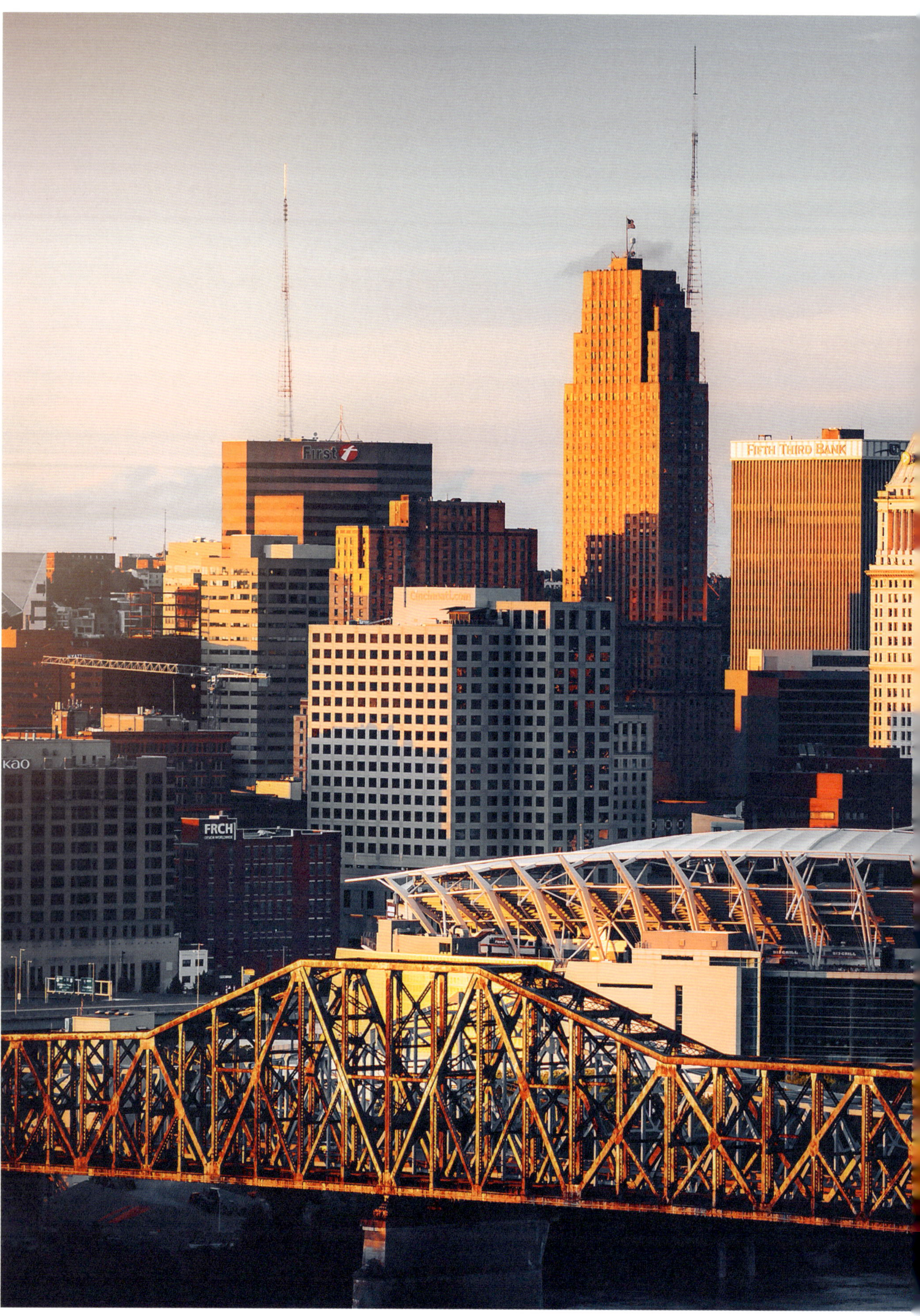
First
FIFTH THIRD BANK
FRCH

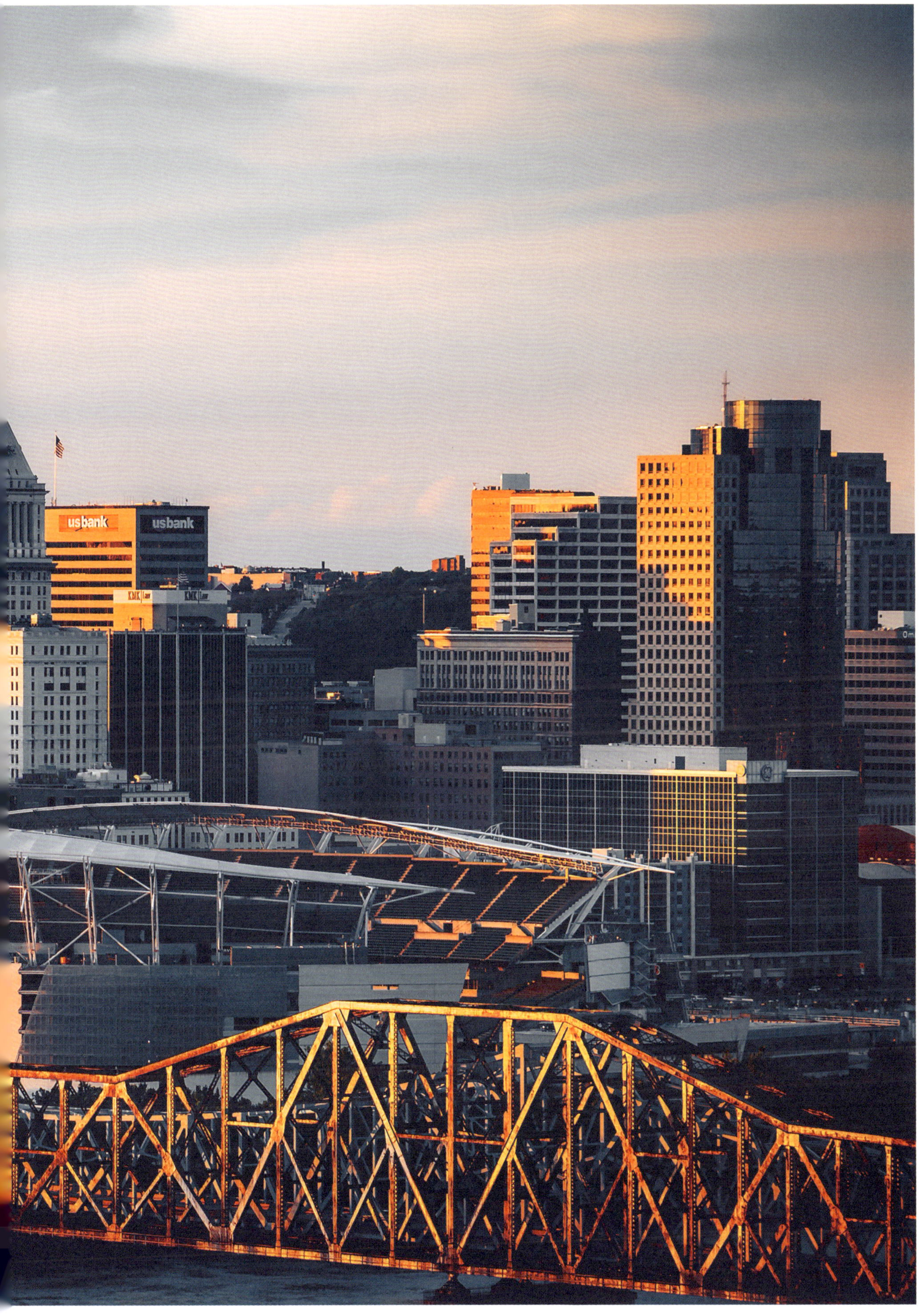
usbank
usbank

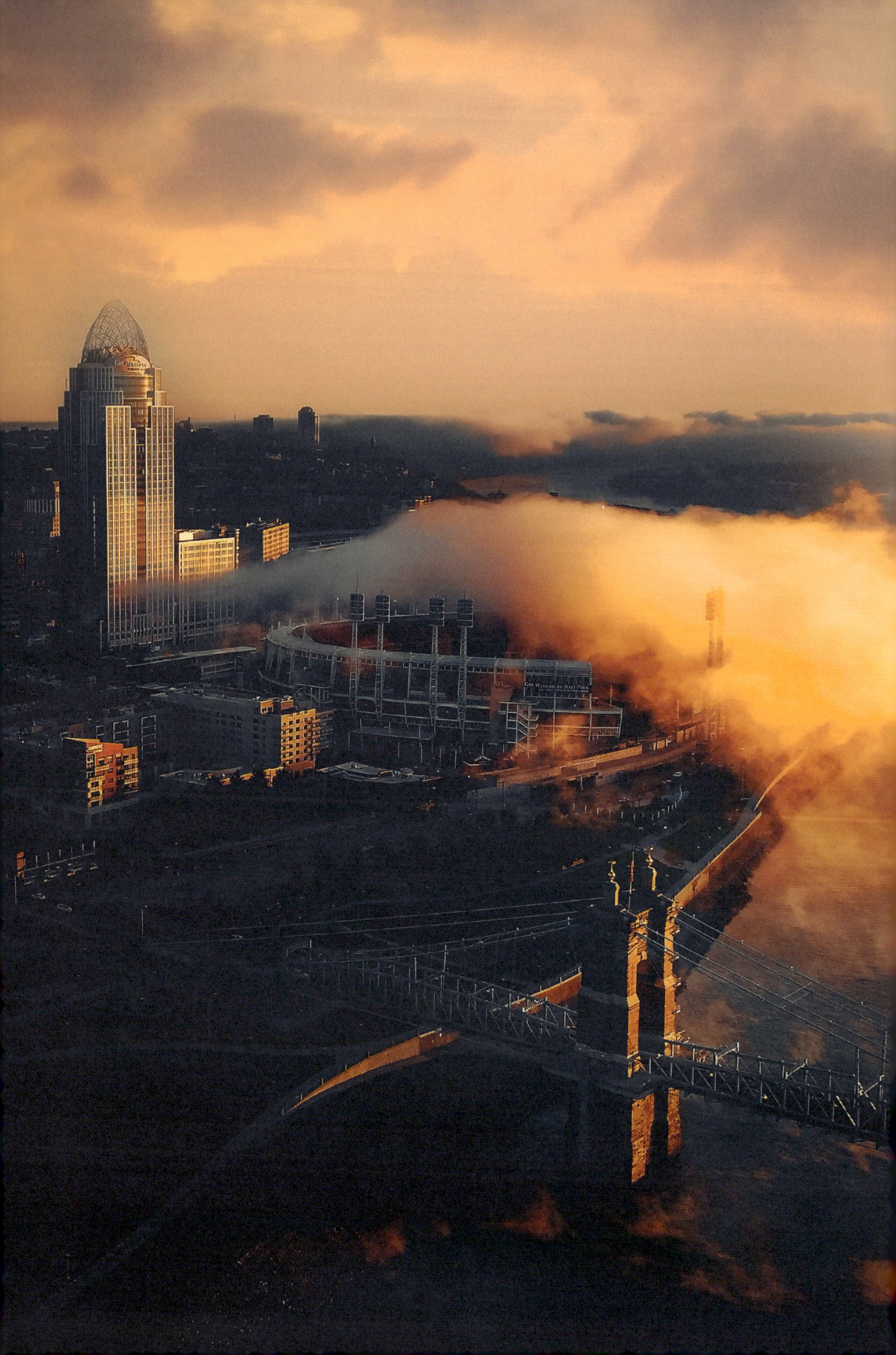

In the Cincinnati of my childhood, baseball was a religion.

BRANDON HARRIS

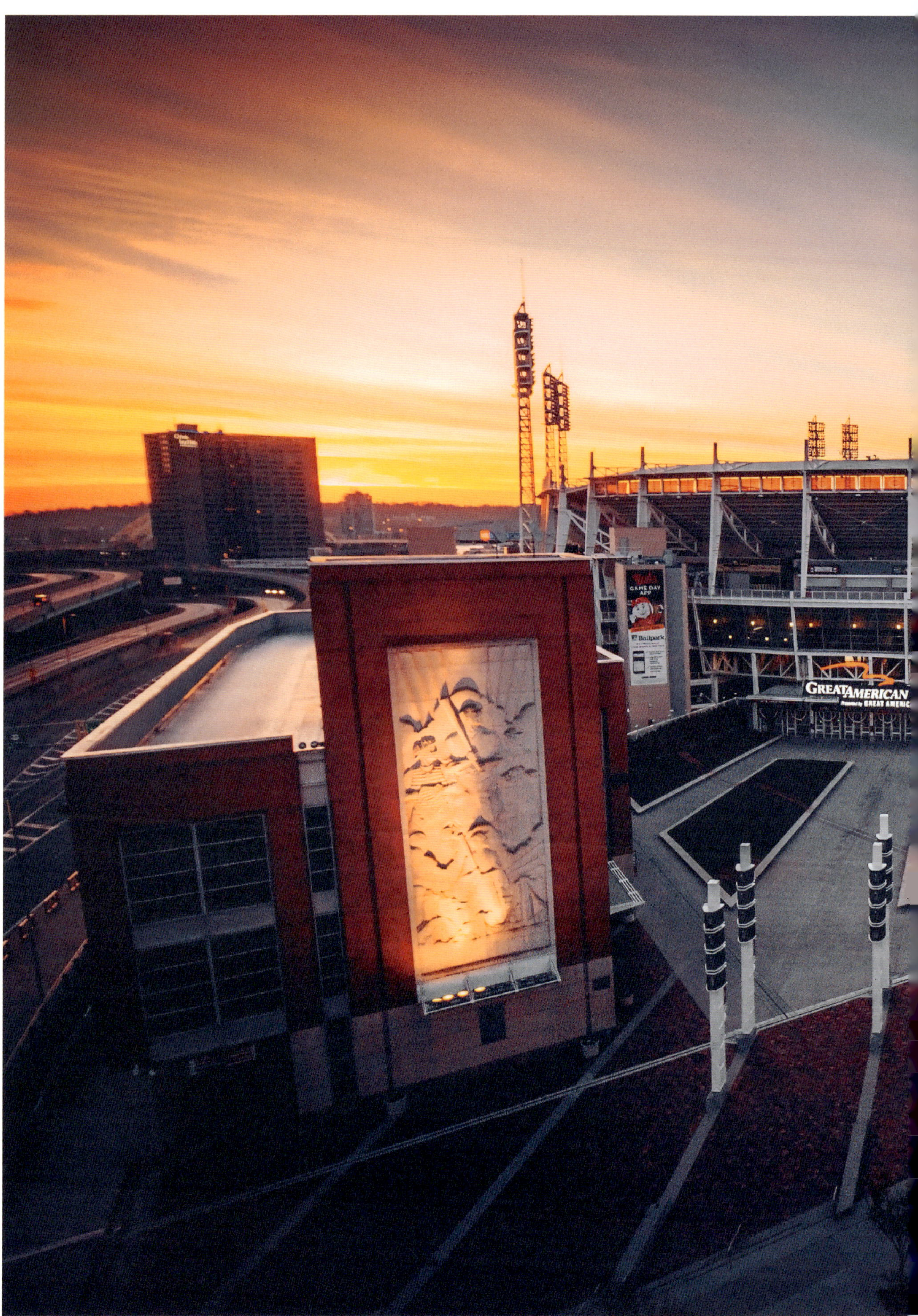
GAME DAY APP
Ballpark
GREAT AMERICAN

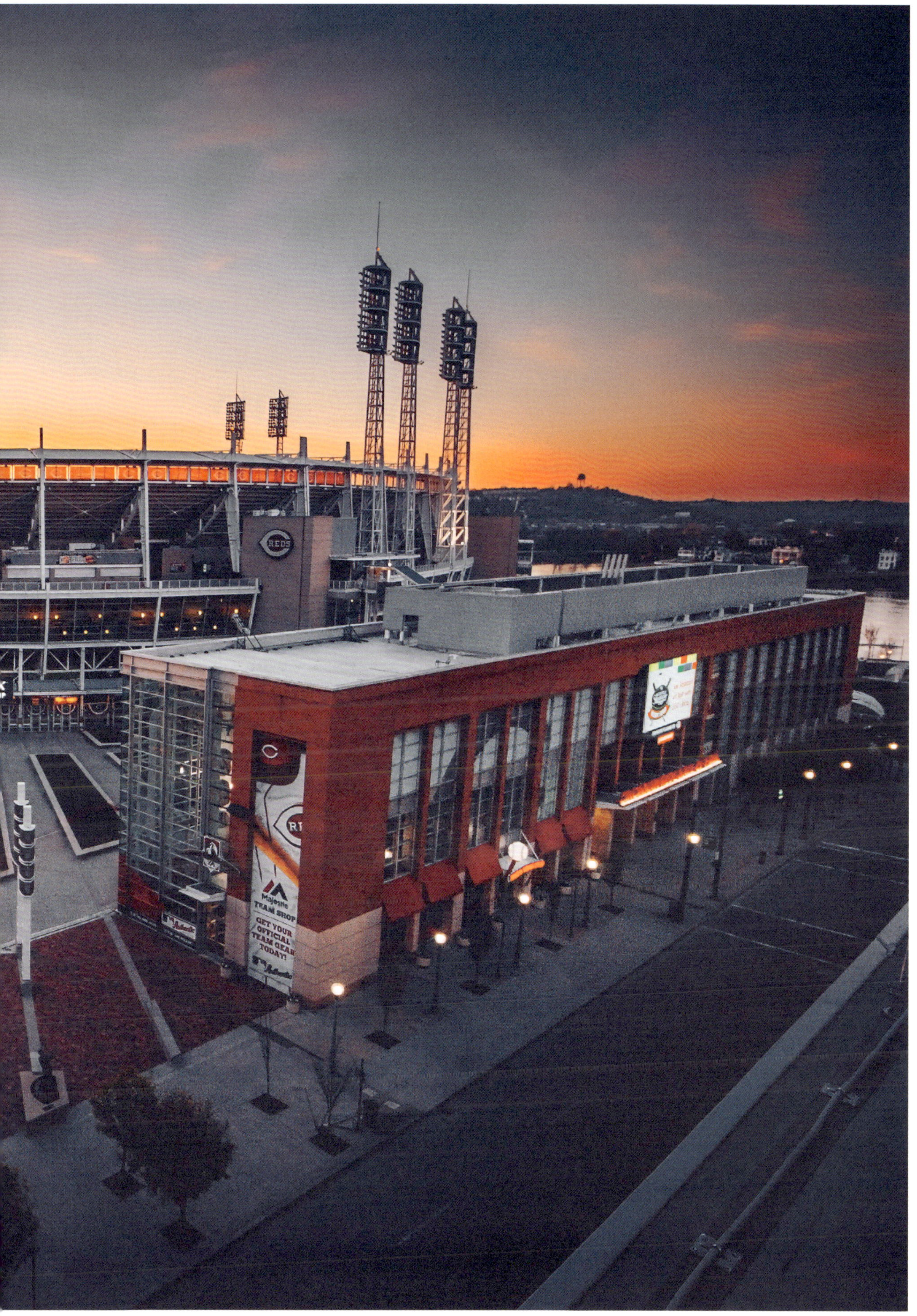
REDS
Majestic
TEAM SHOP
GET YOUR
OFFICIAL
TEAM GEAR
TODAY!

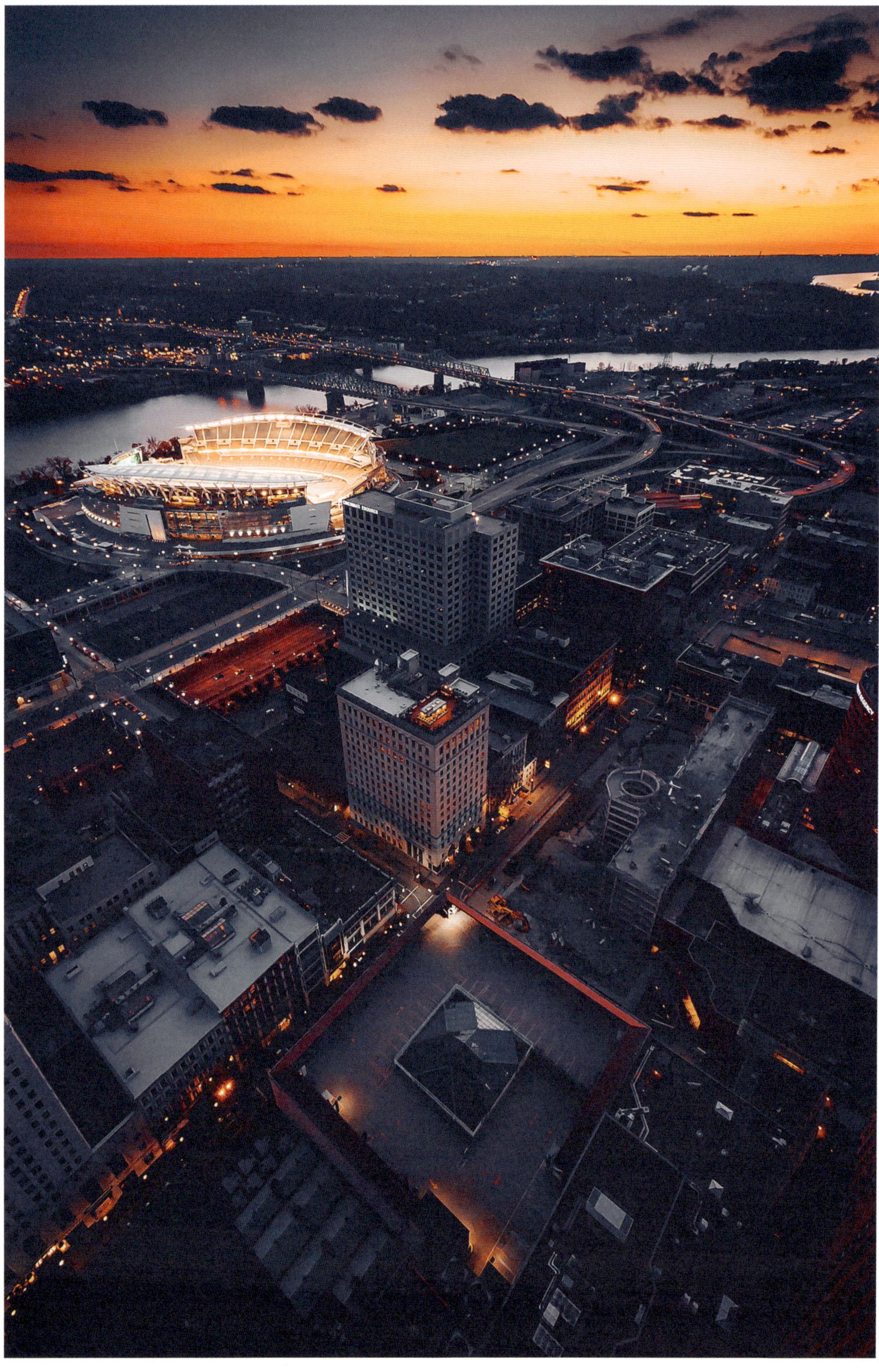

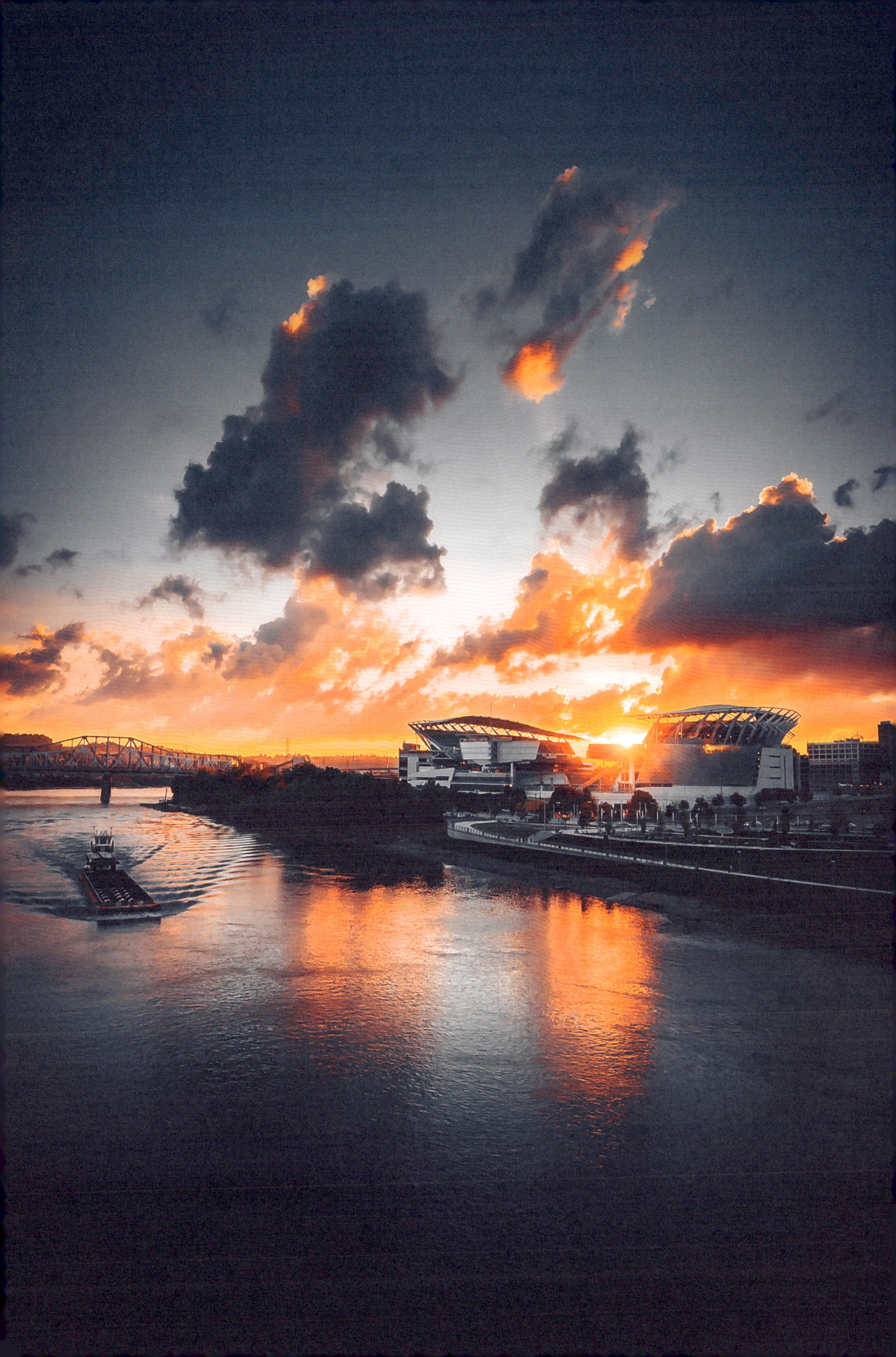

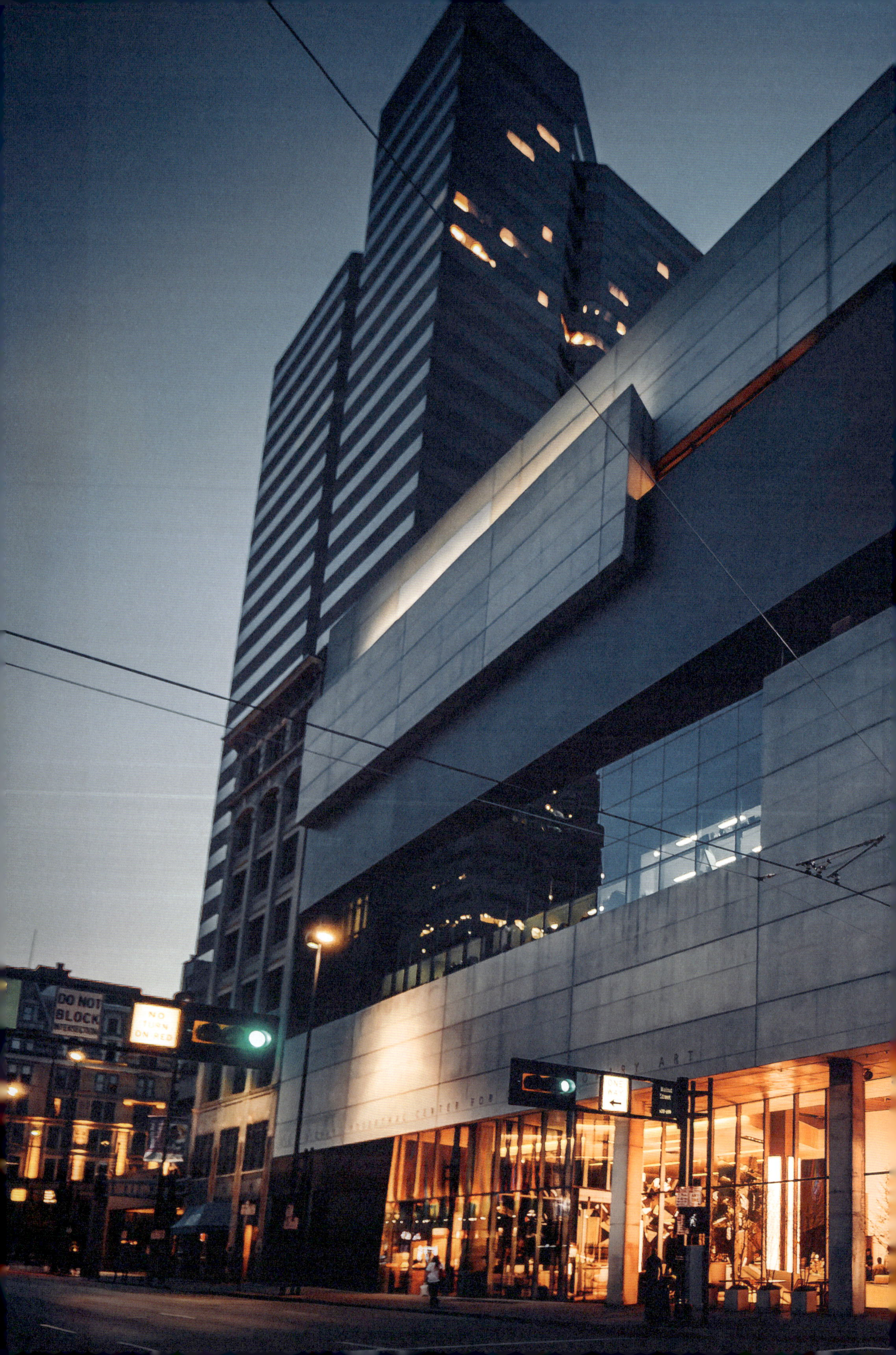
DO NOT BLOCK
NO TURN ON RED
ONE WAY

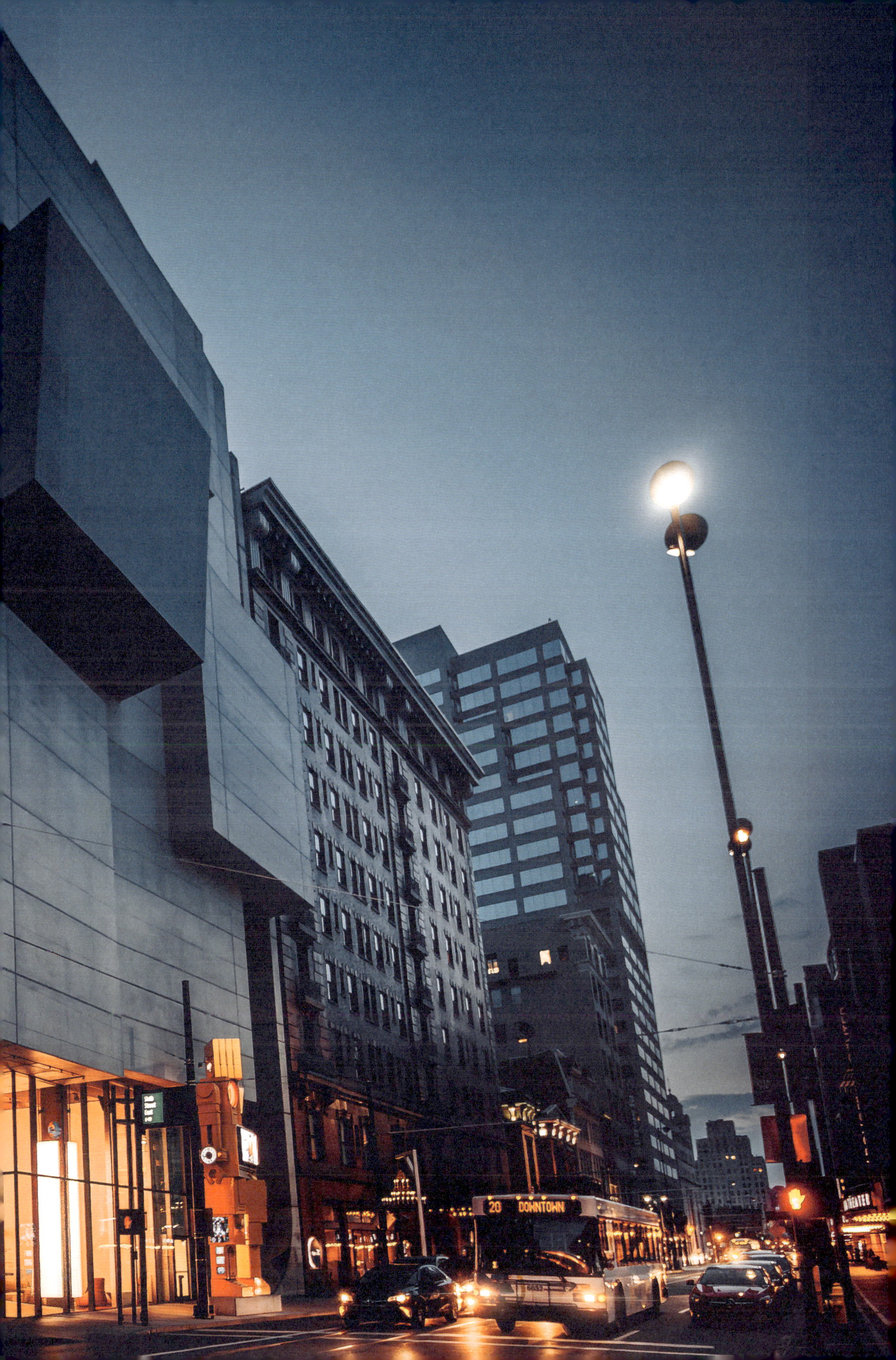
20 DOWNTOWN

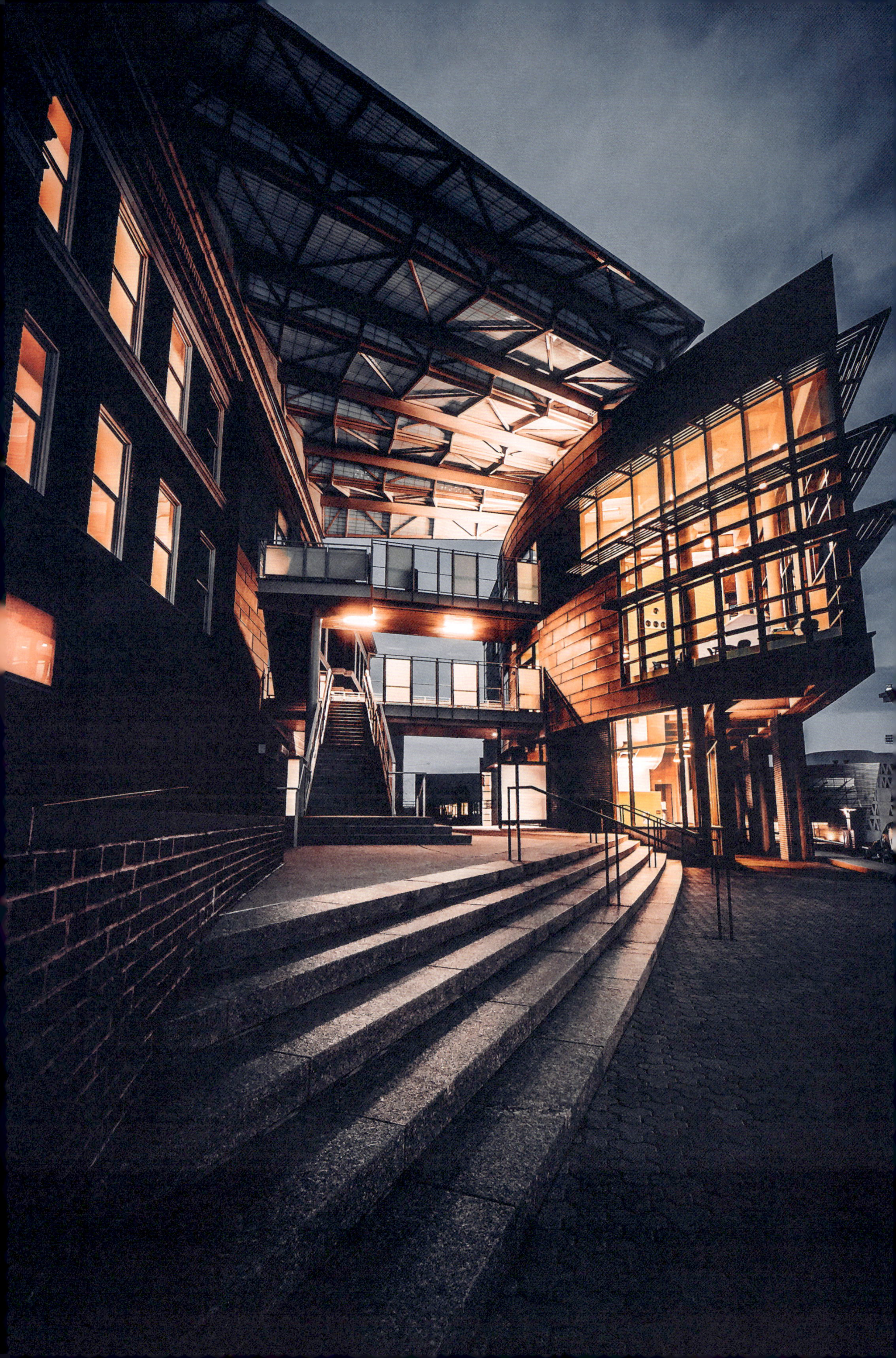

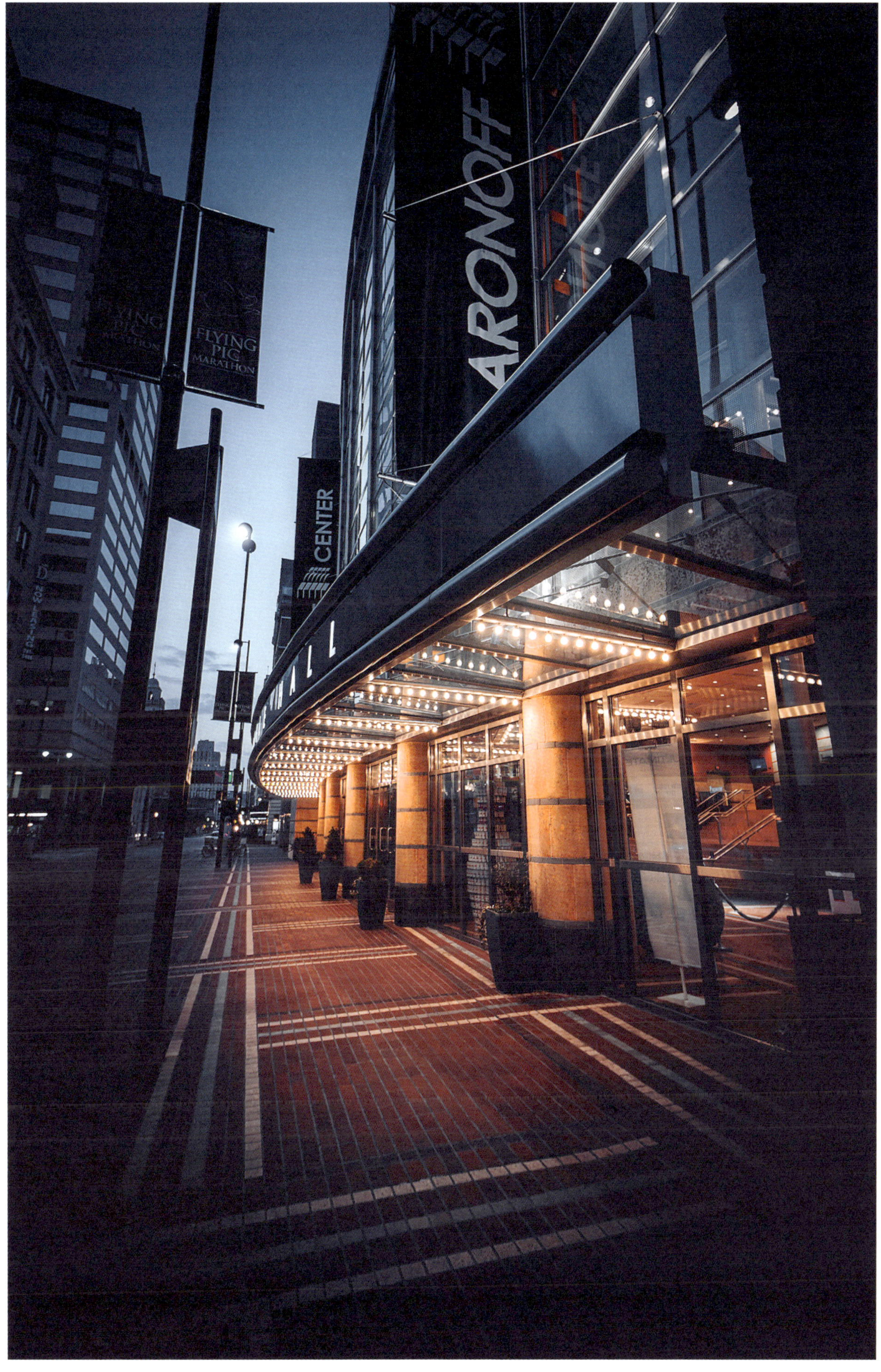
ARONOFF
CENTER
FLYING PIG MARATHON

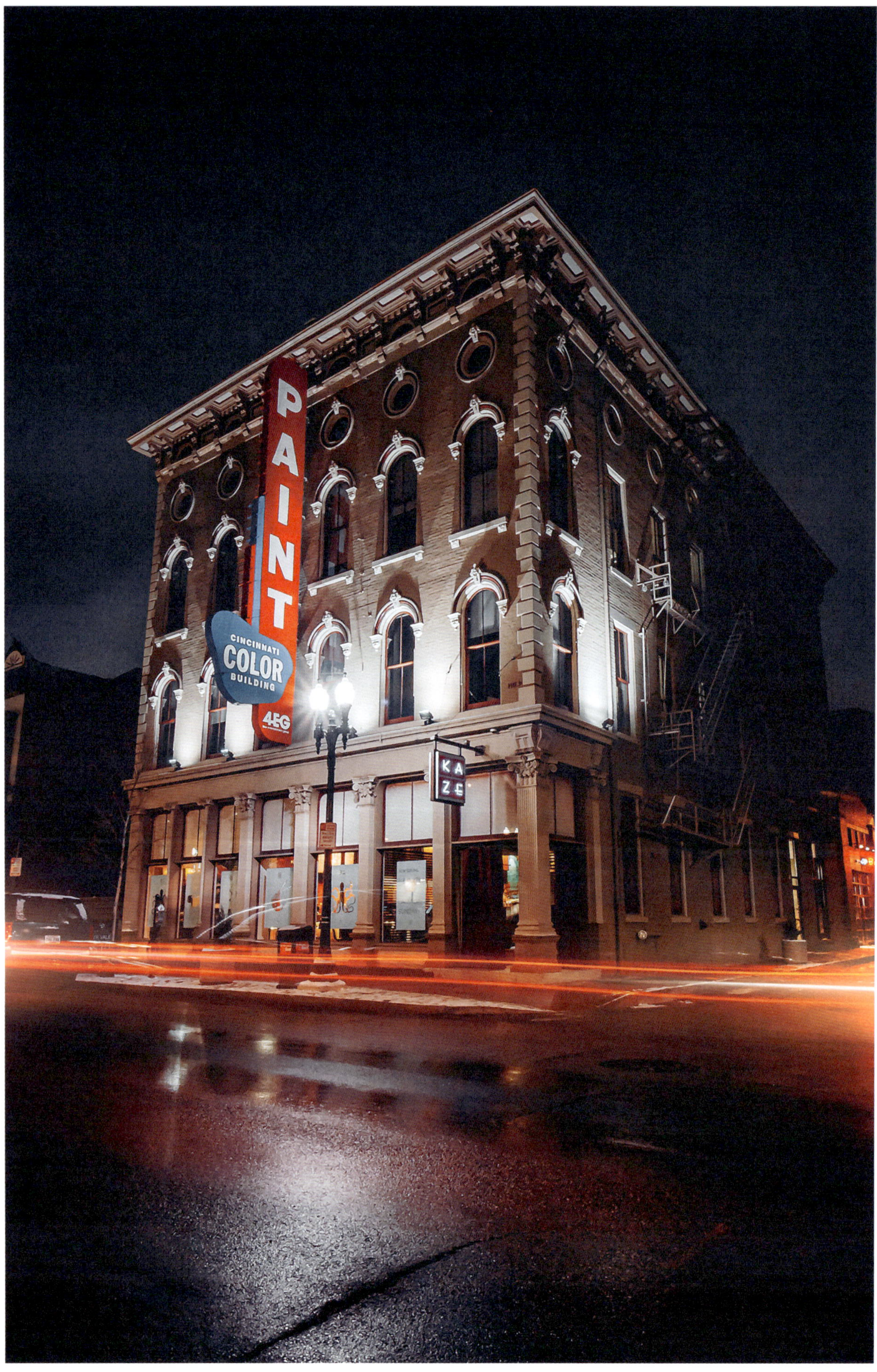
PAINT
CINCINNATI
COLOR
BUILDING
4EG
KAZE

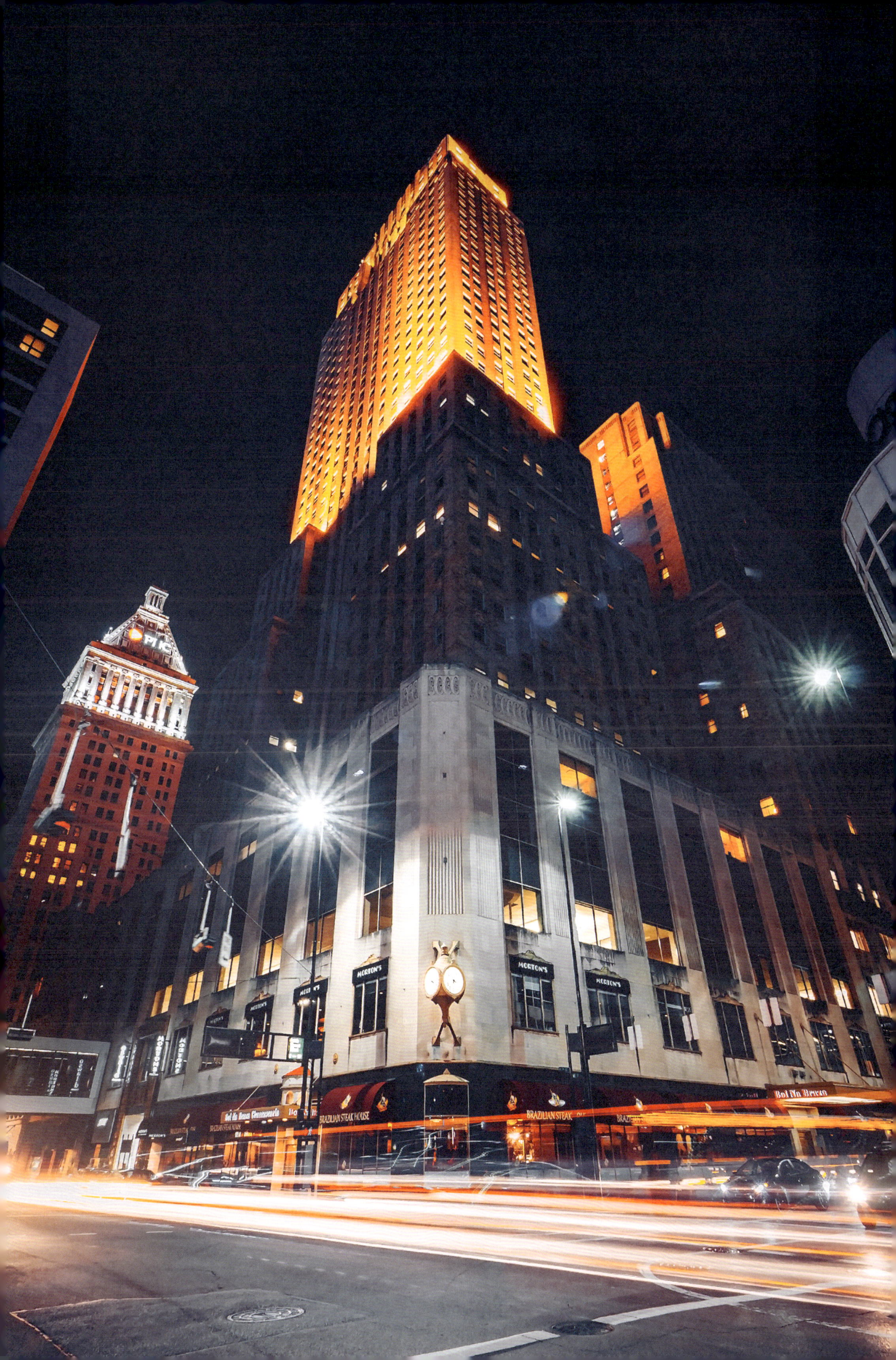
MORTON'S
MORTON'S
MORTON'S
BRAZILIAN STEAK HOUSE
BRAZILIAN STEAK HOUSE

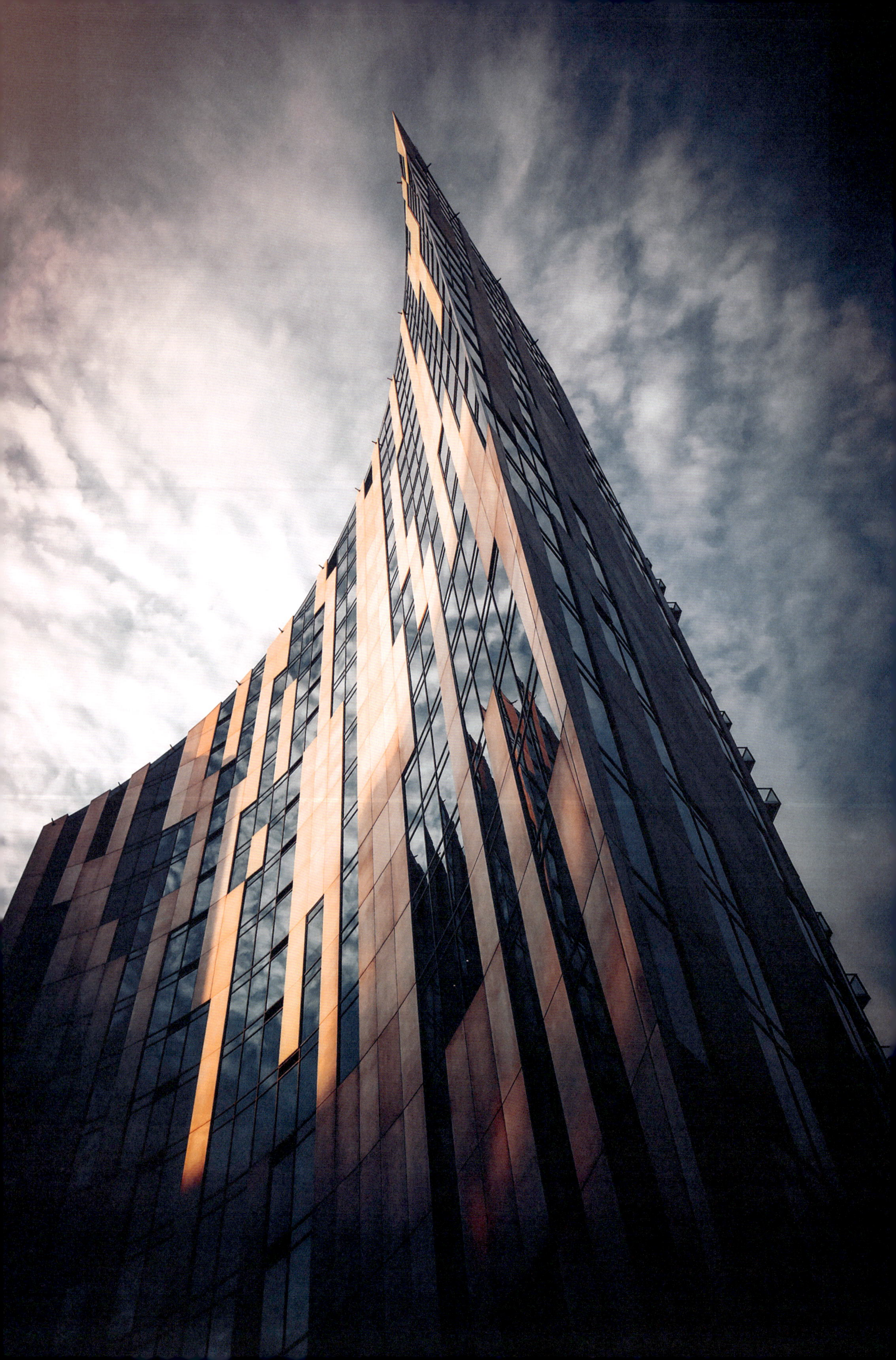

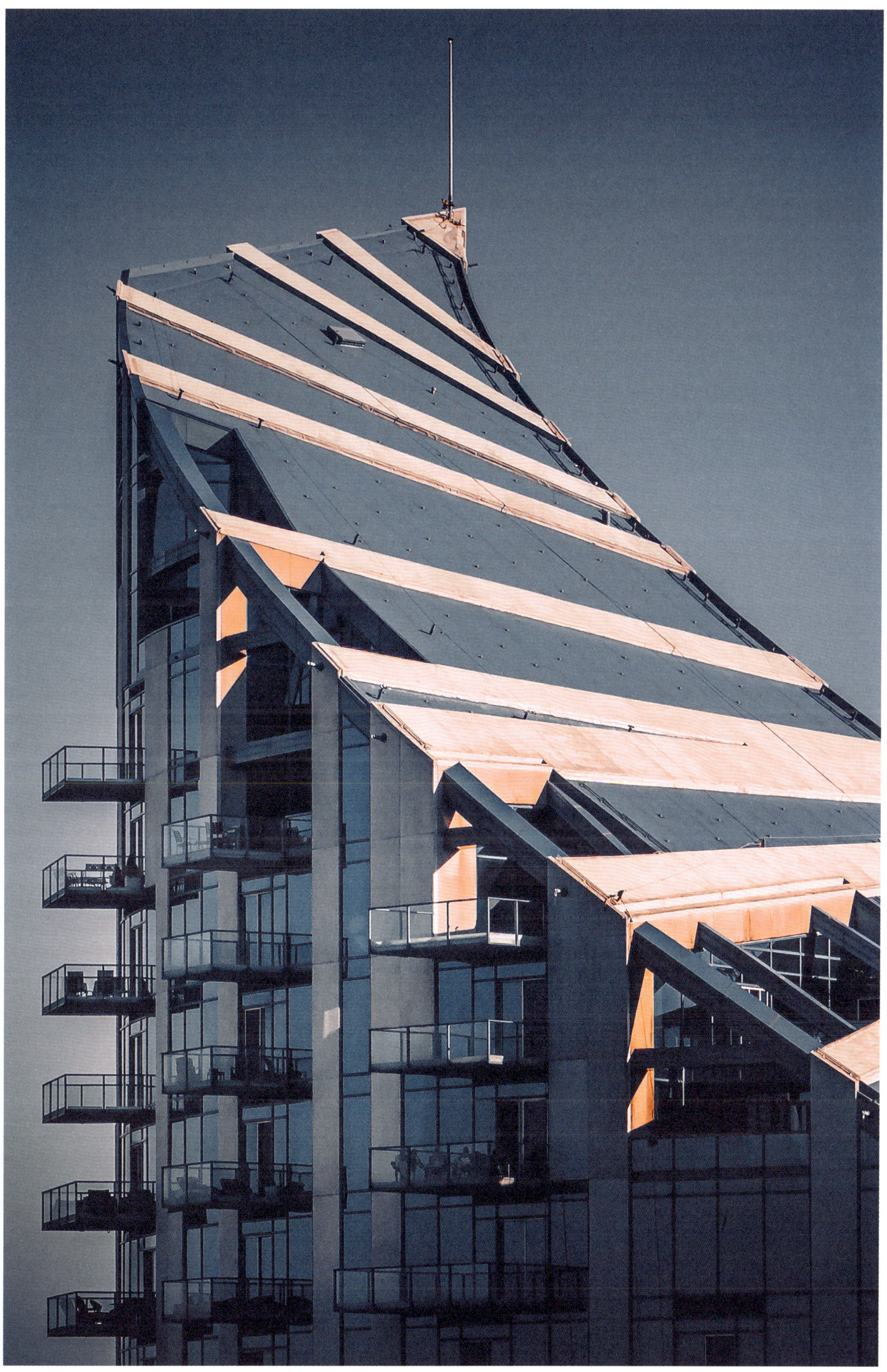

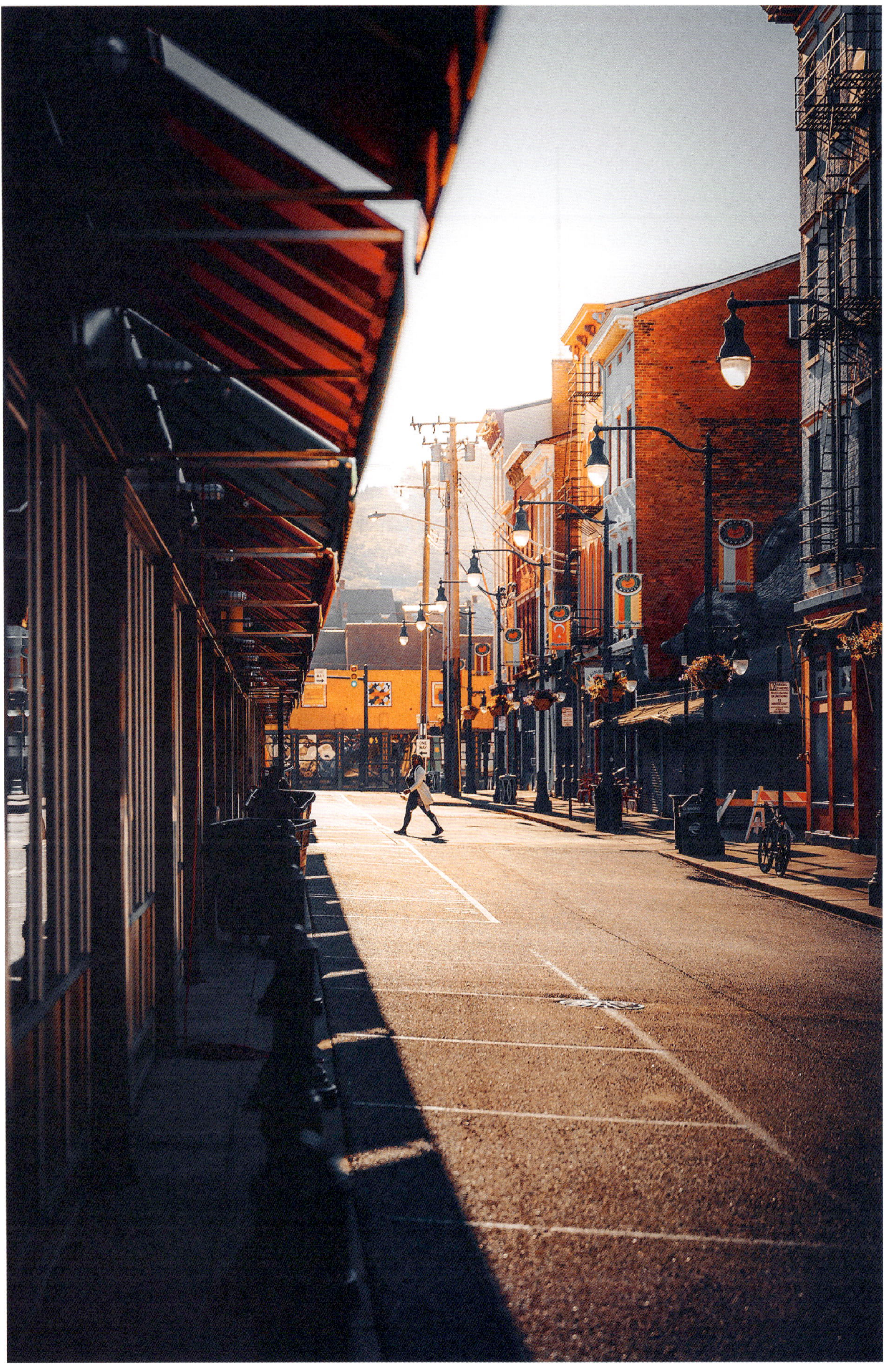

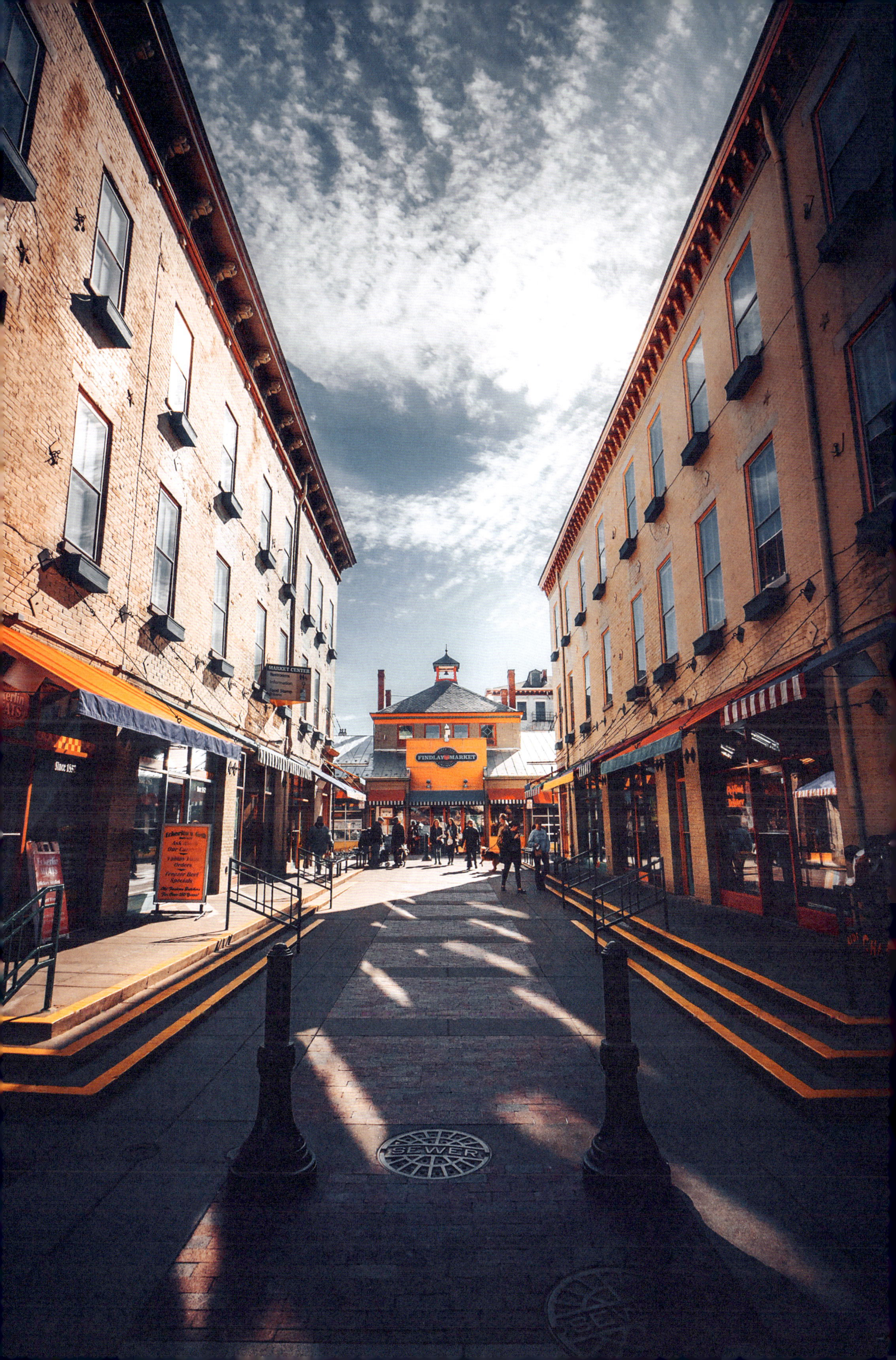
MARKET CENTER
Restrooms
Information
Since 1857
Ask About
Our Cuts
Freezer Beef
Specials
FINDLAY MARKET
SEWER

Art takes different forms…
But it represents something
that is basic in all of us –
our history.

GEORGE CLOONEY

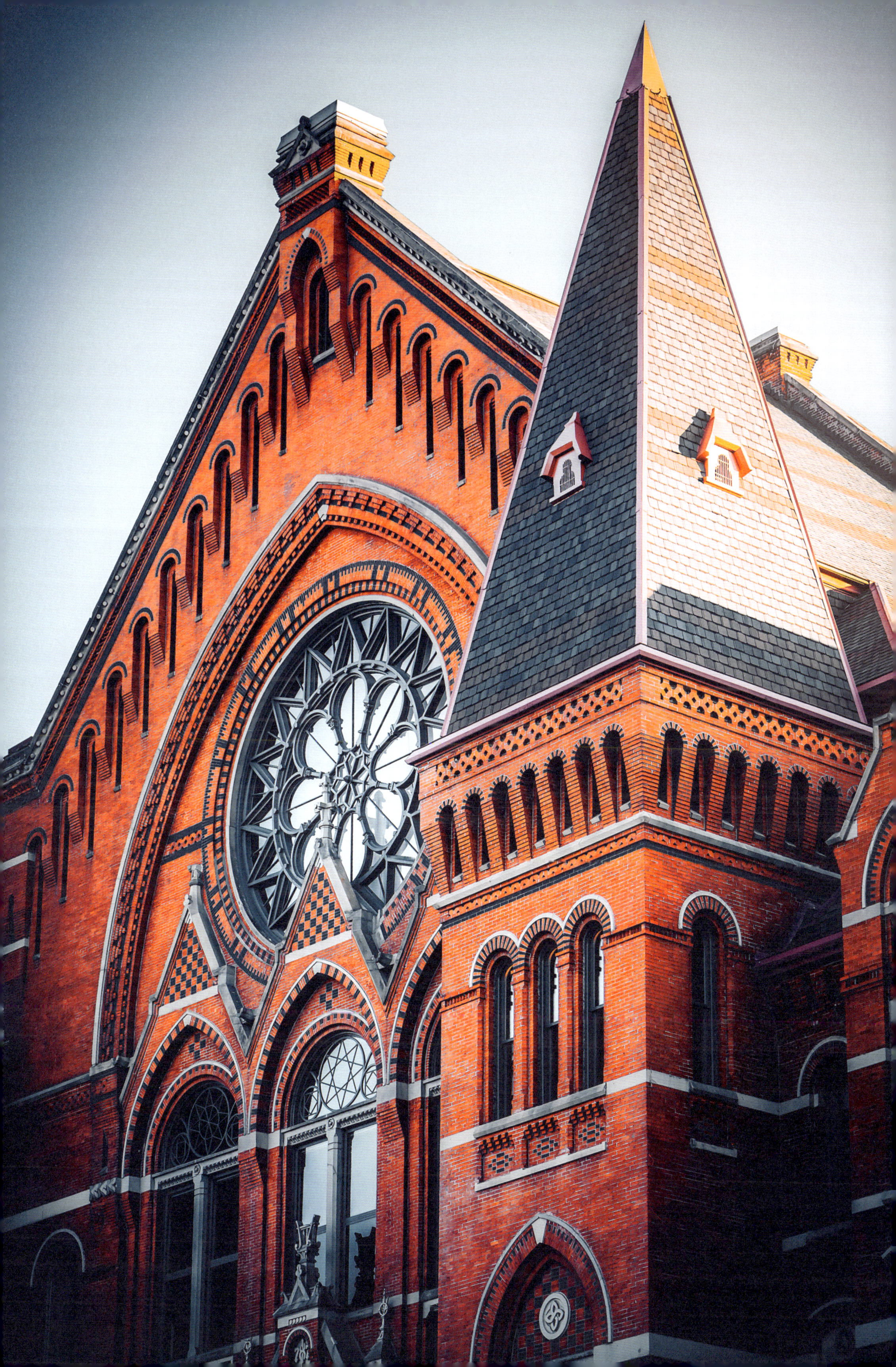

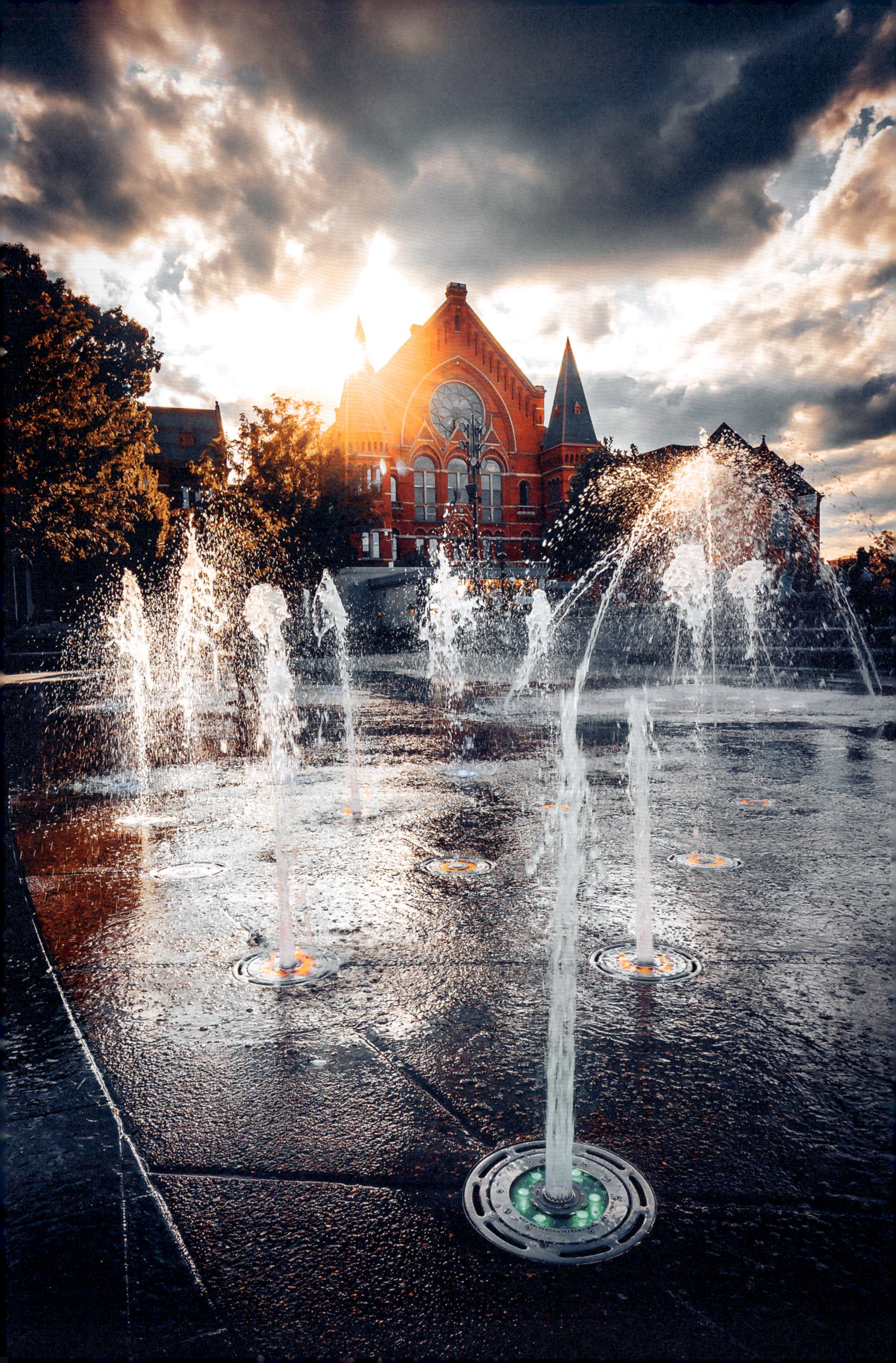

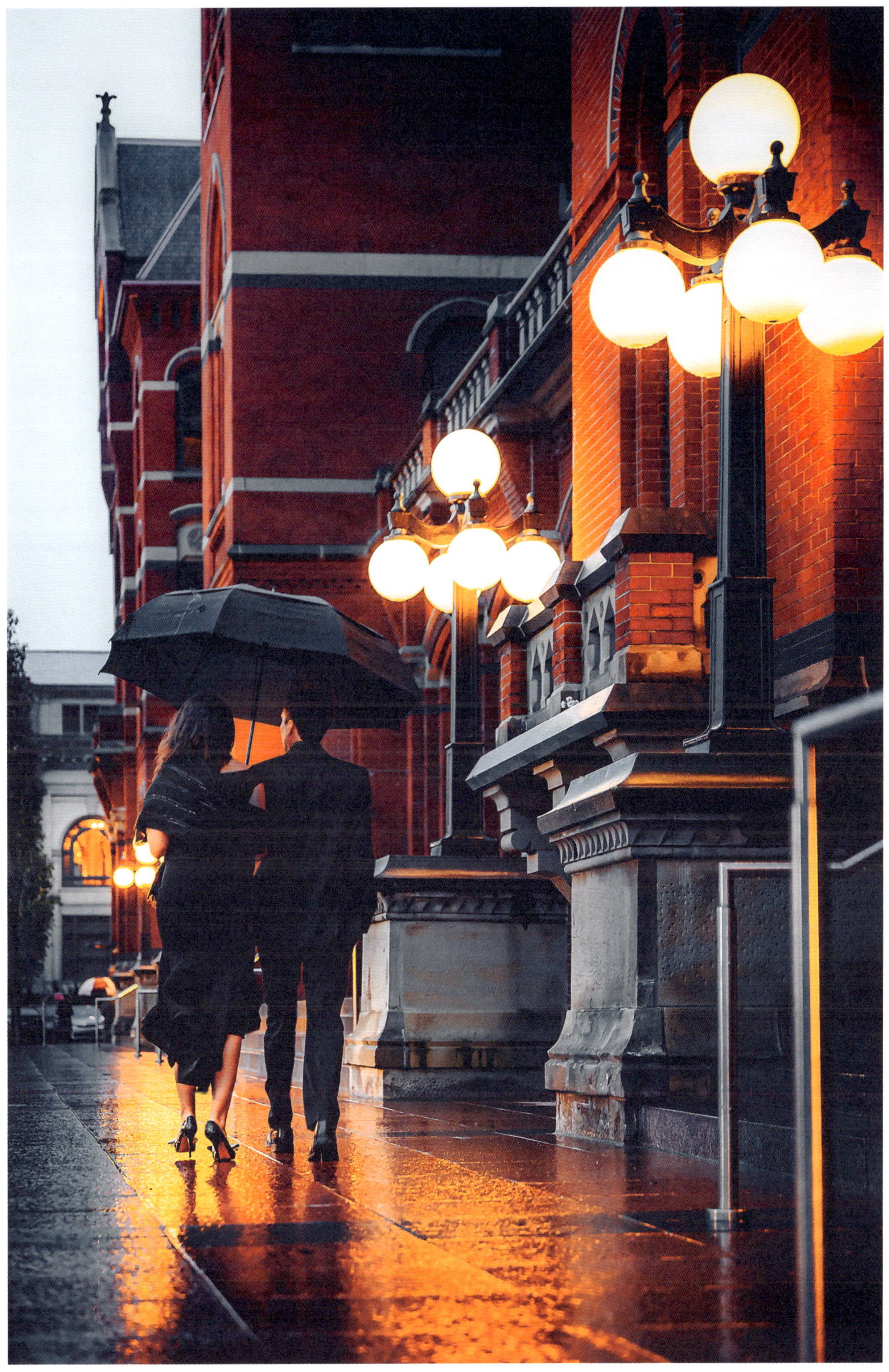

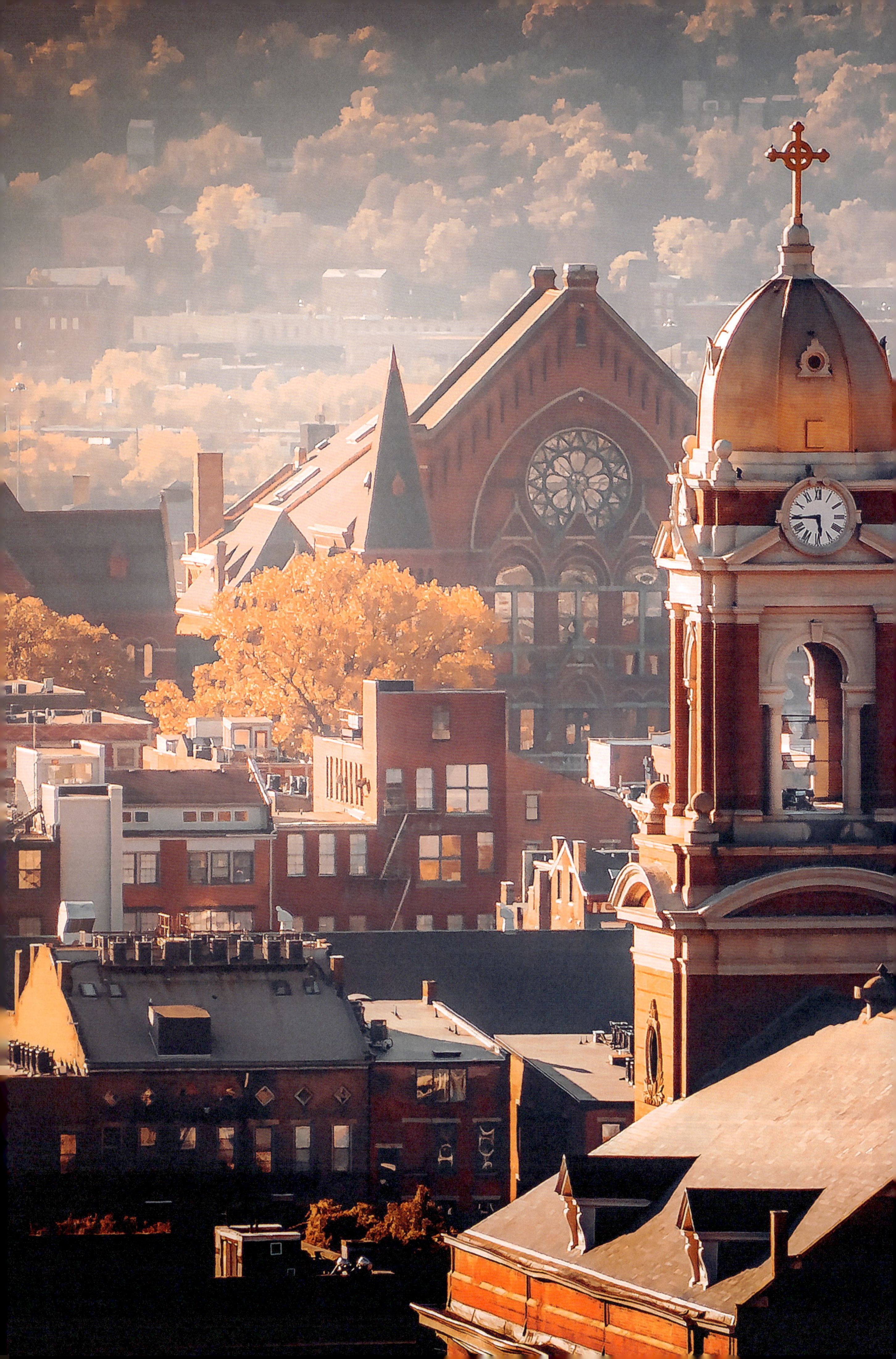

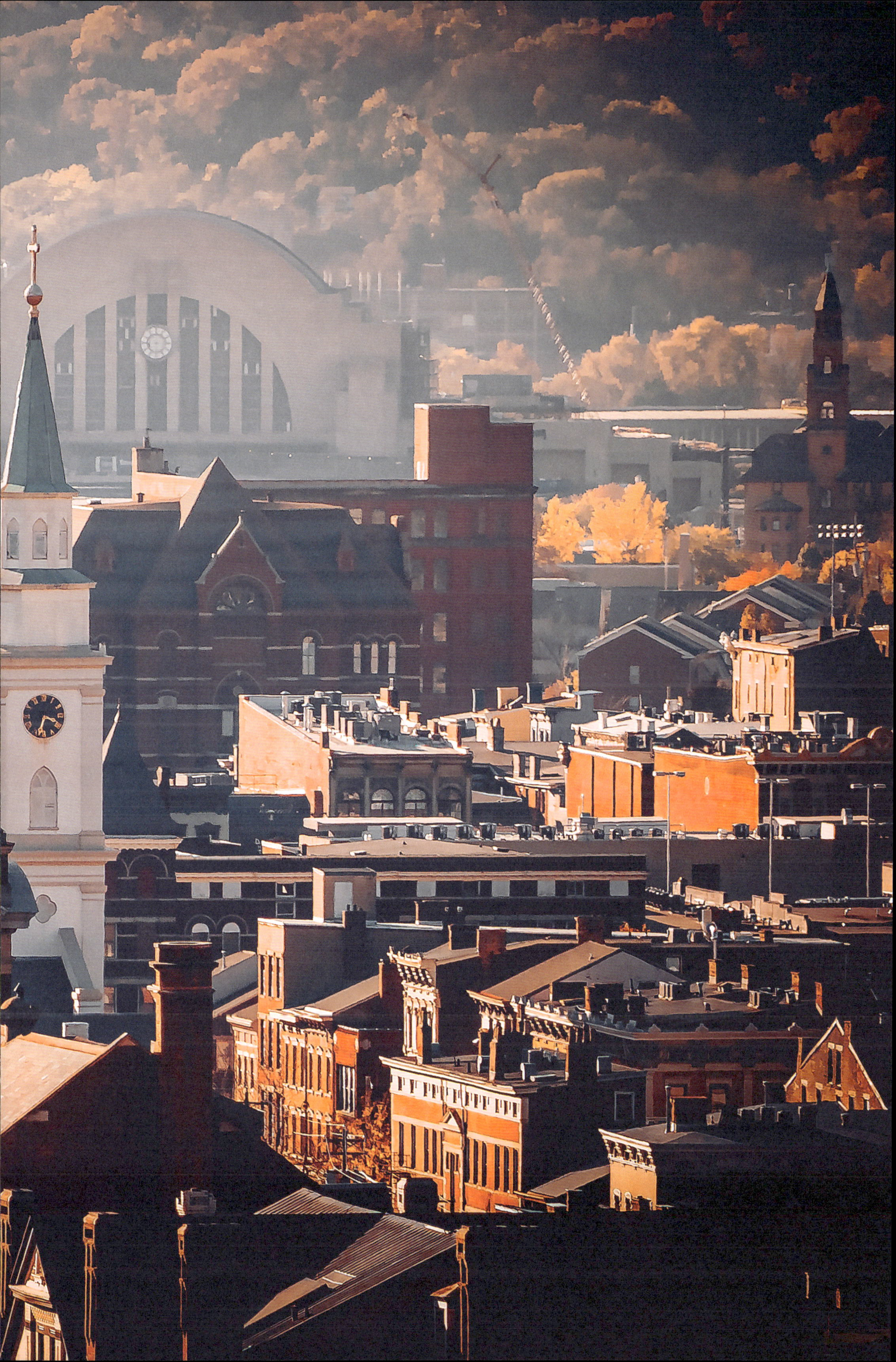

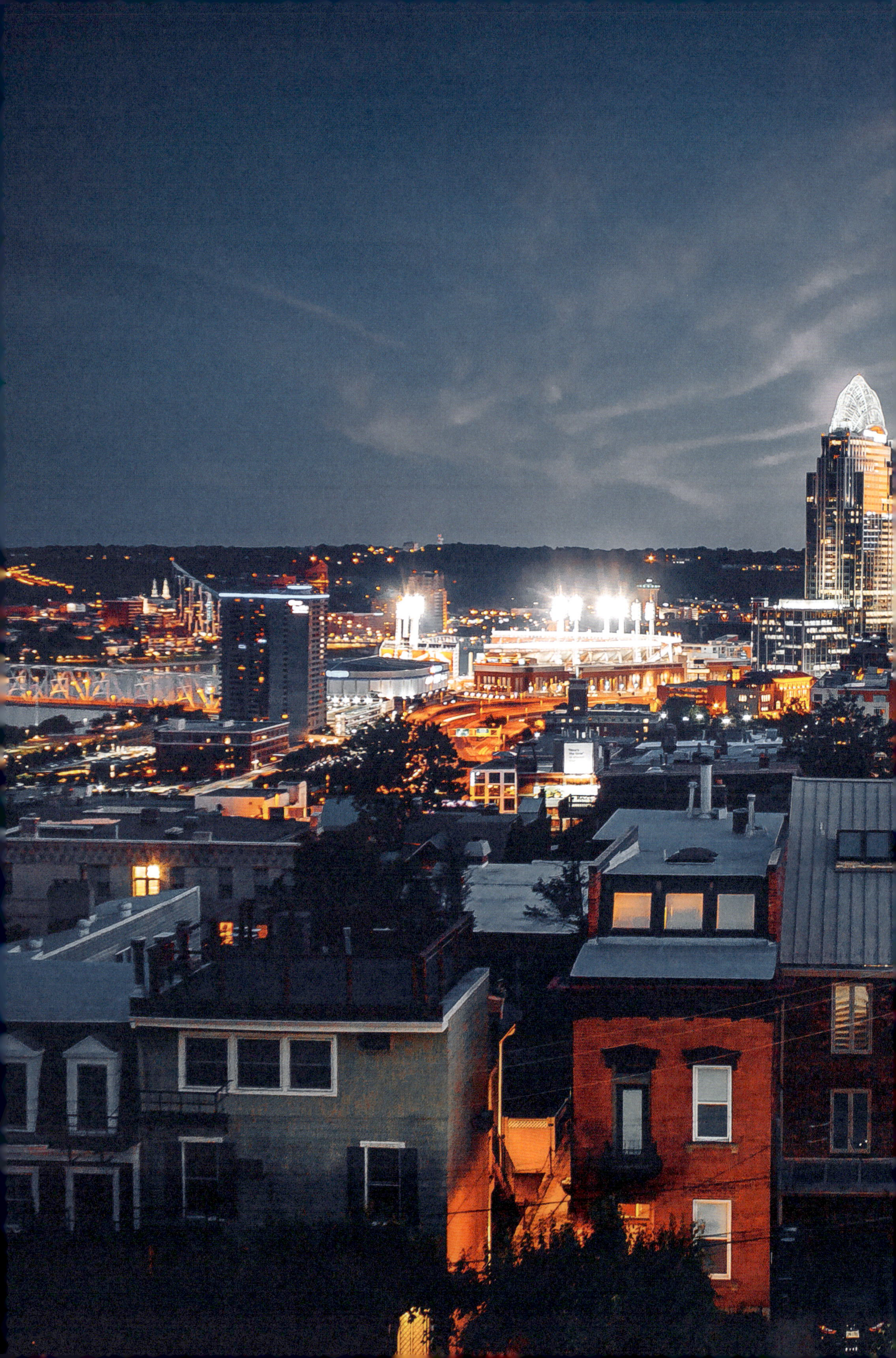

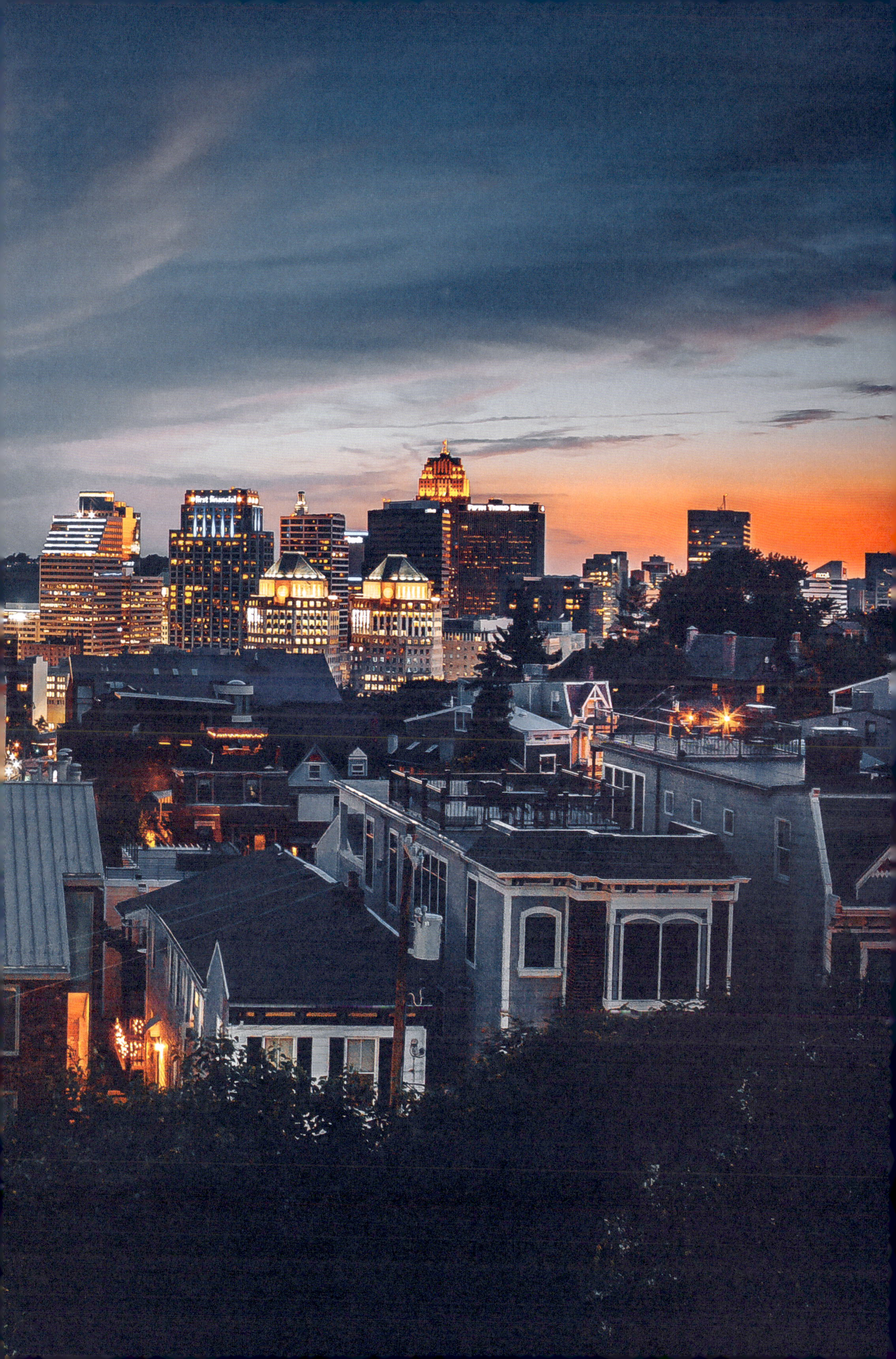
first financial
FIFTH THIRD BANK

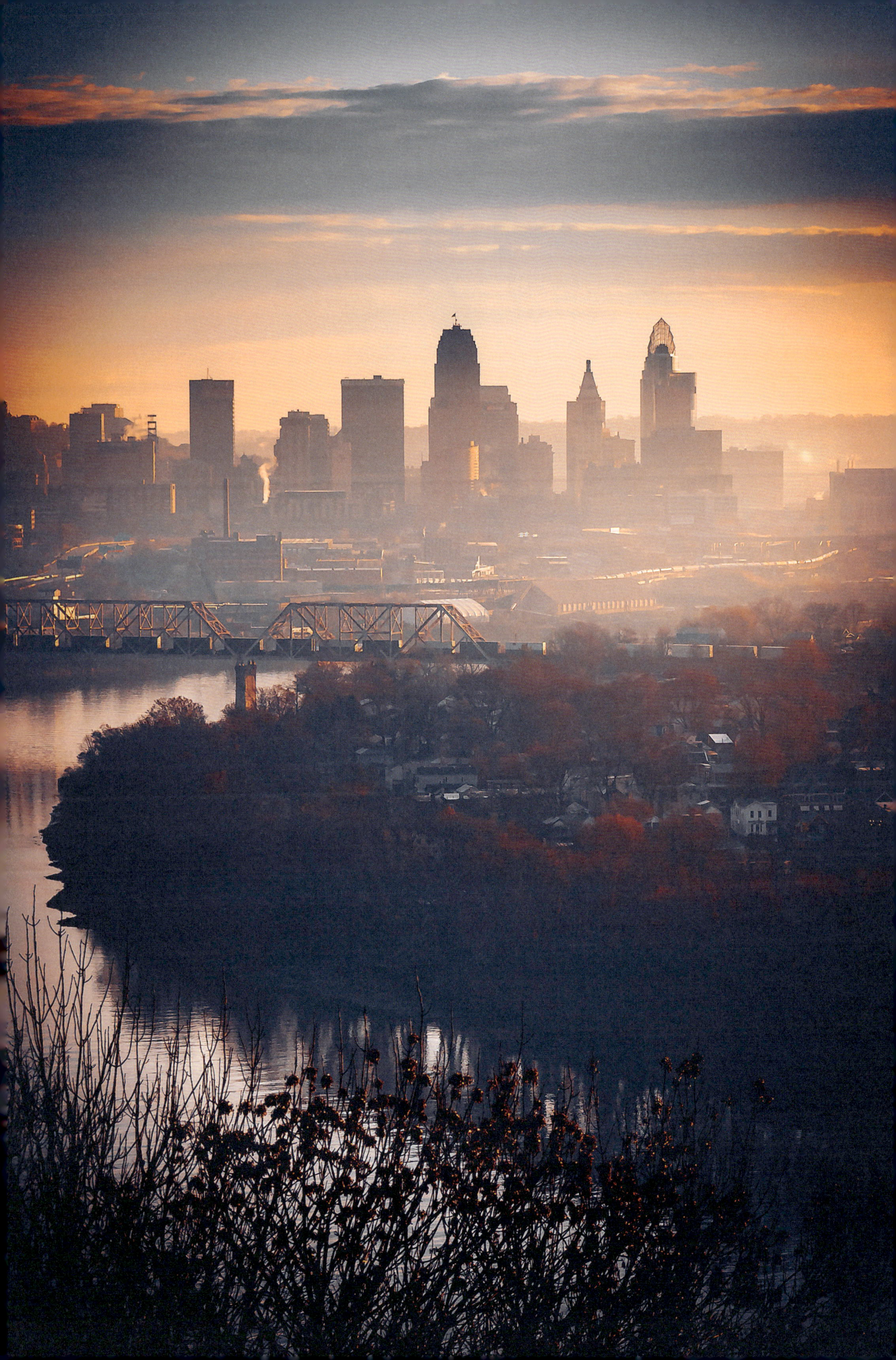

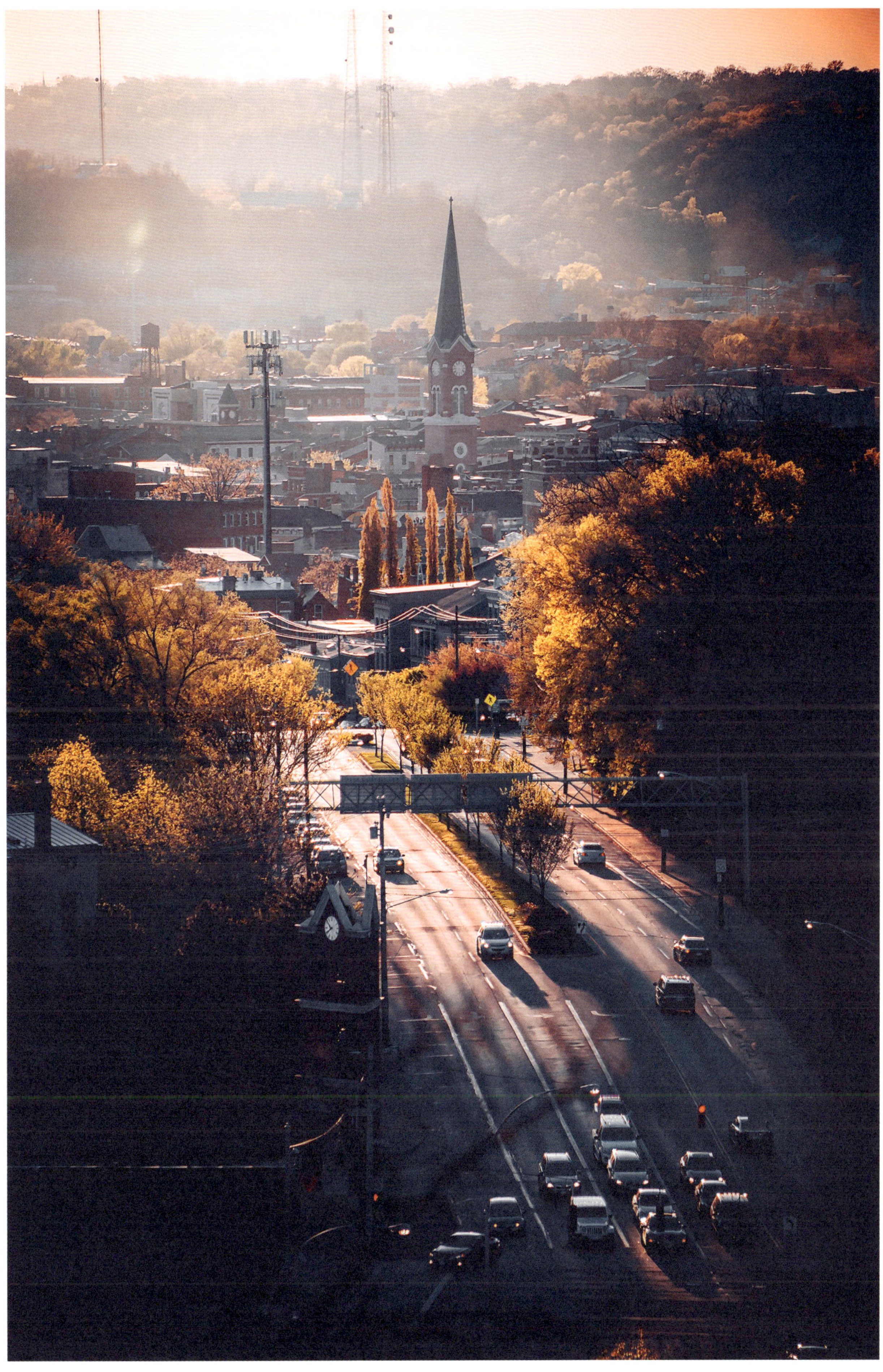

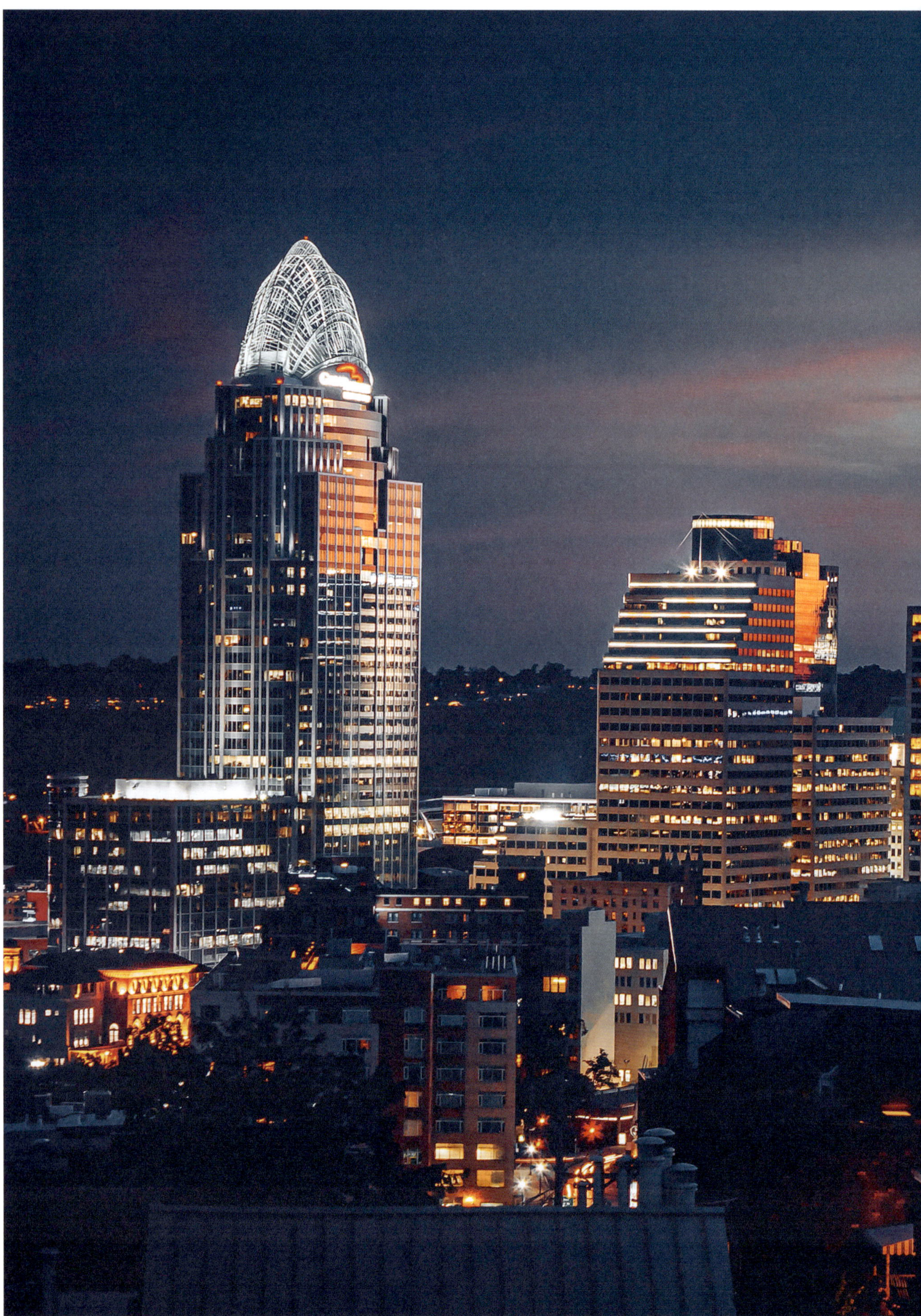

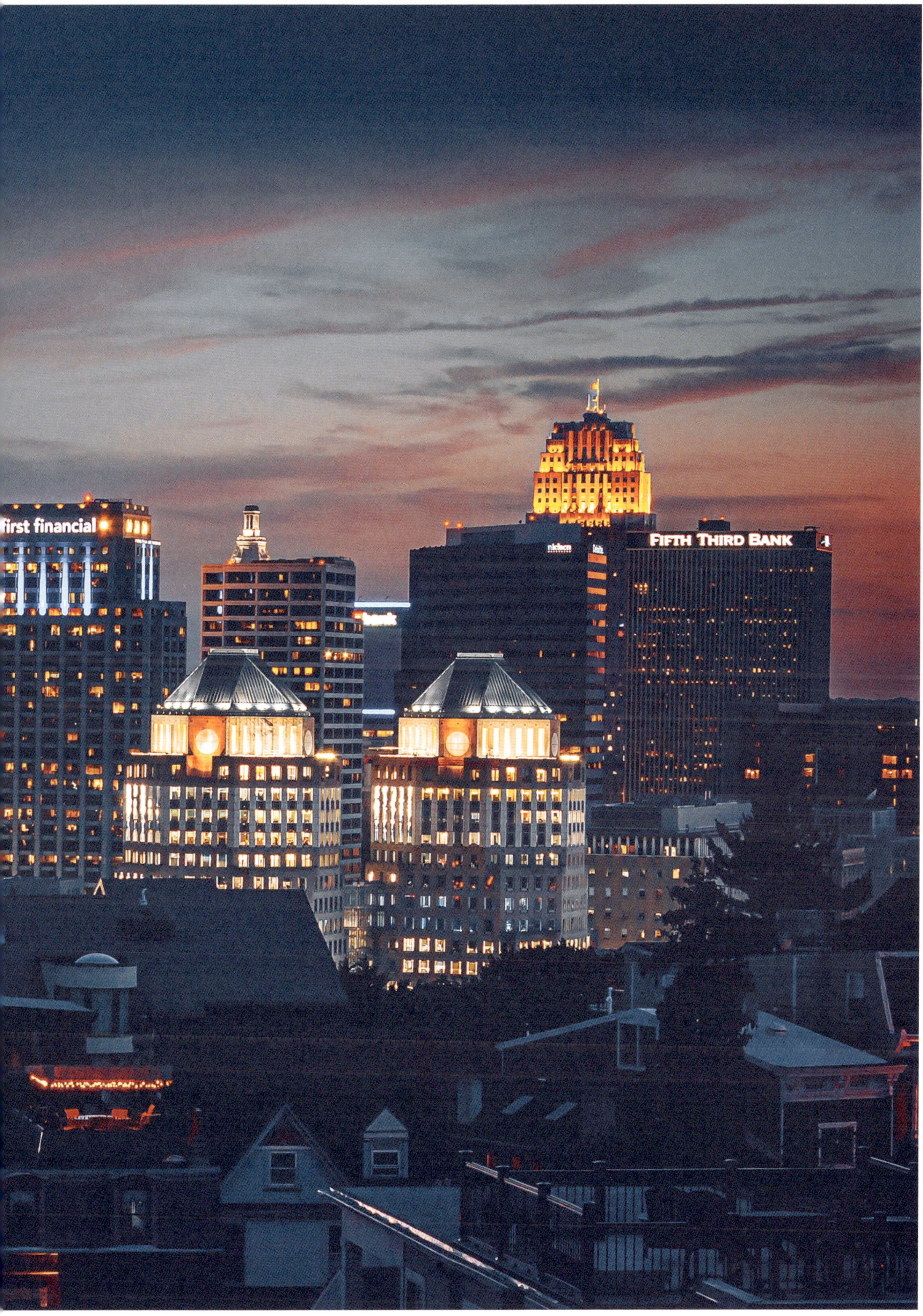
first financial
FIFTH THIRD BANK

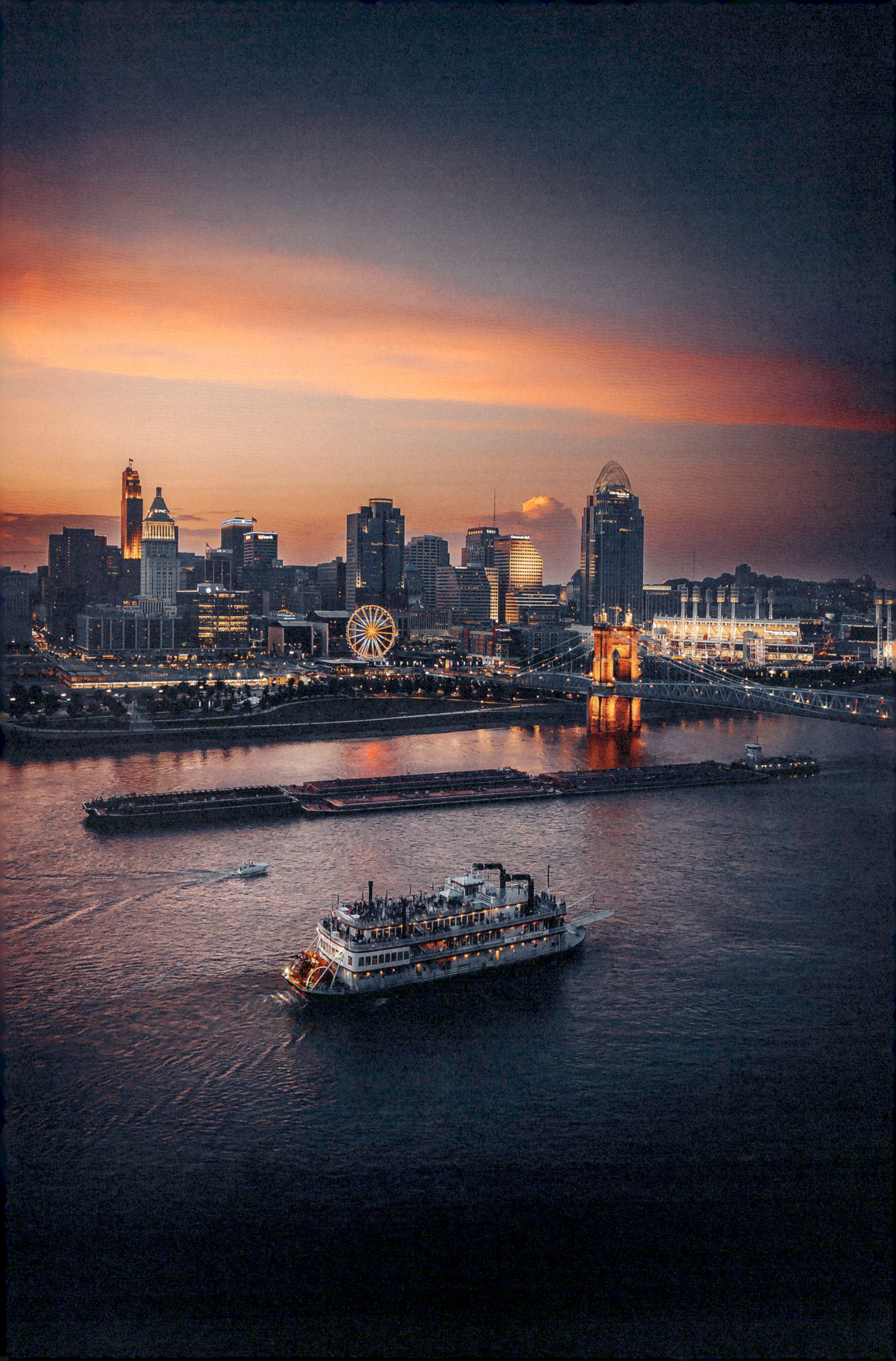

The Ohio is the most beautiful river on earth.

THOMAS JEFFERSON

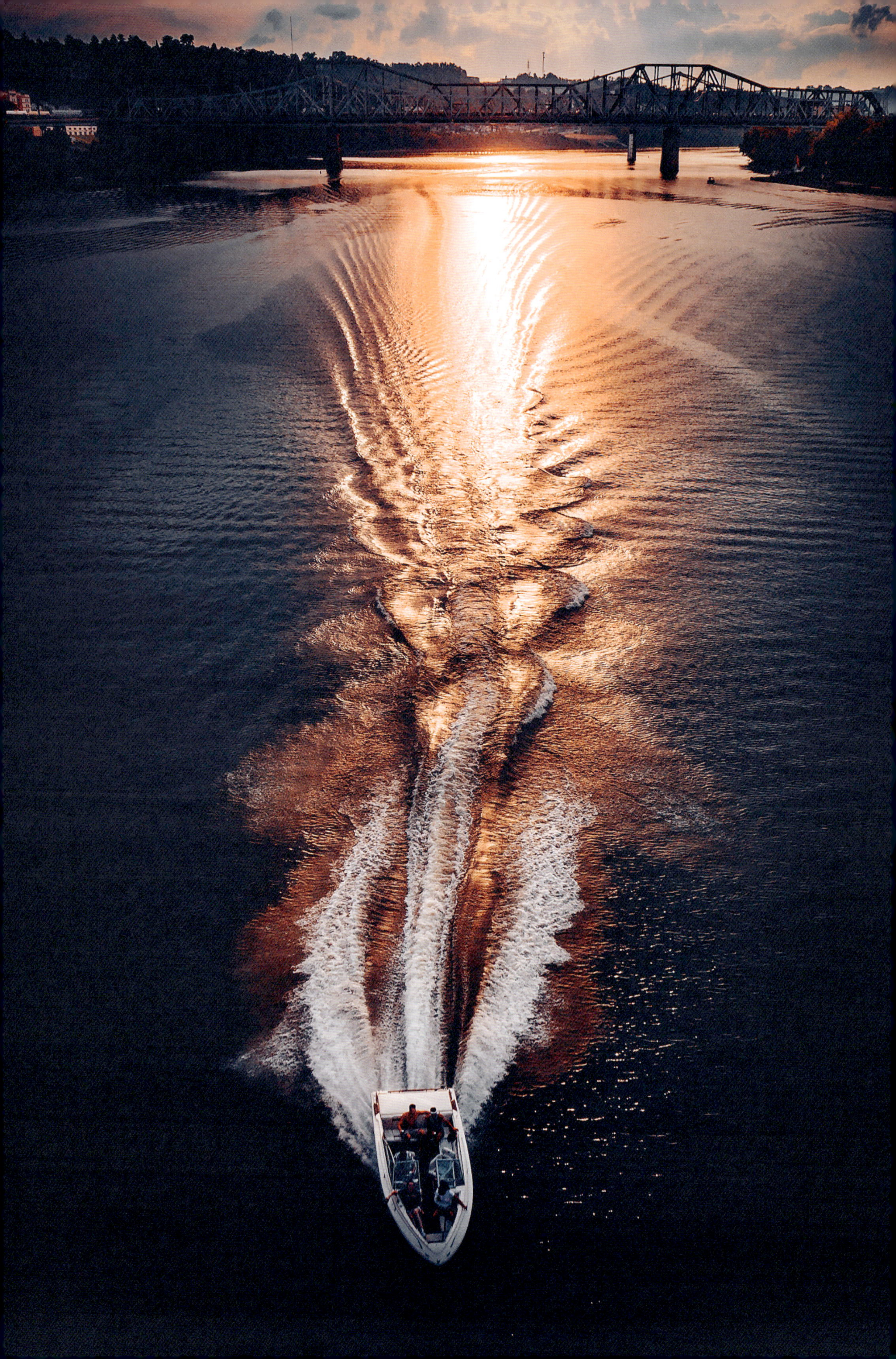

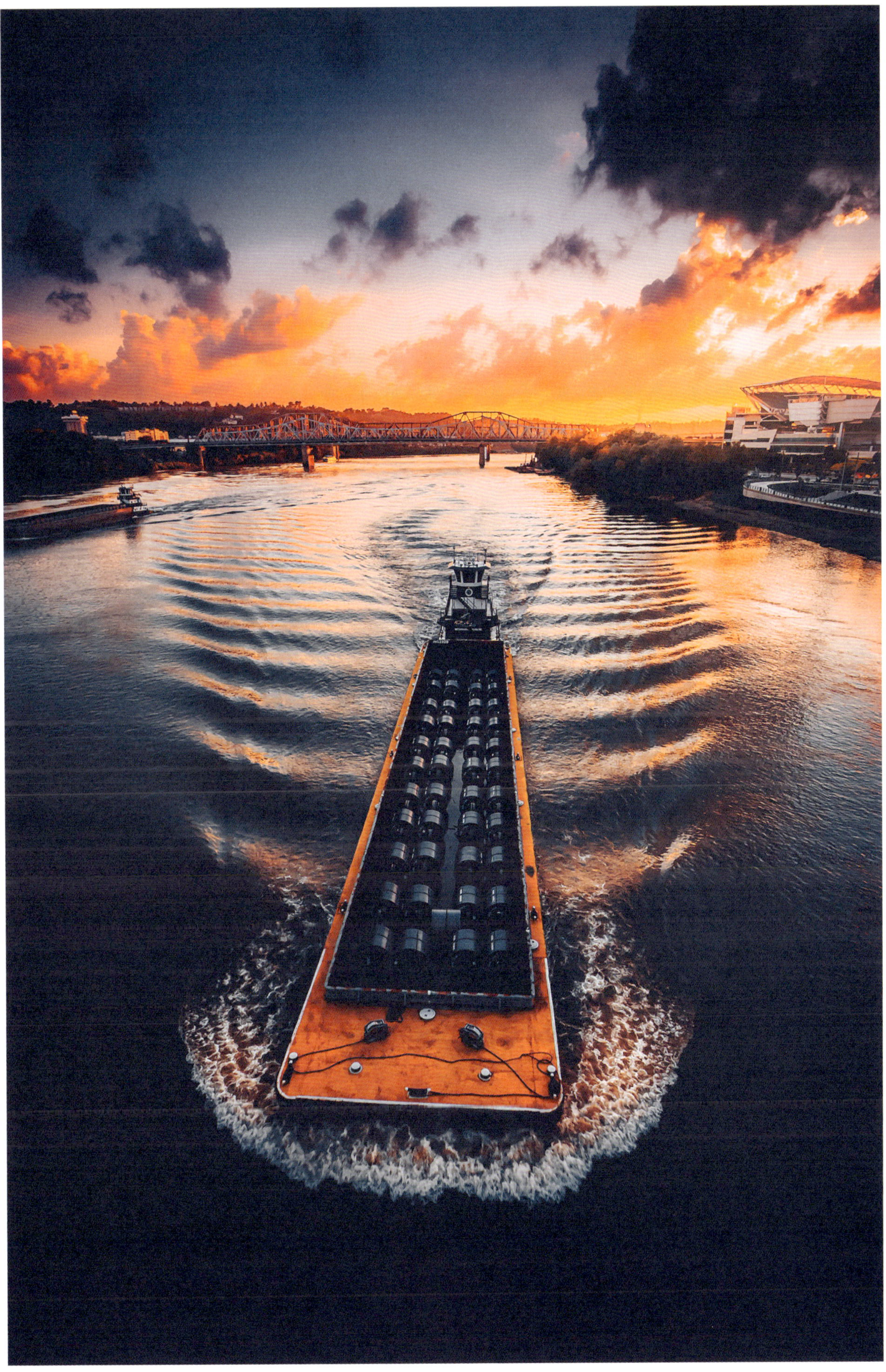

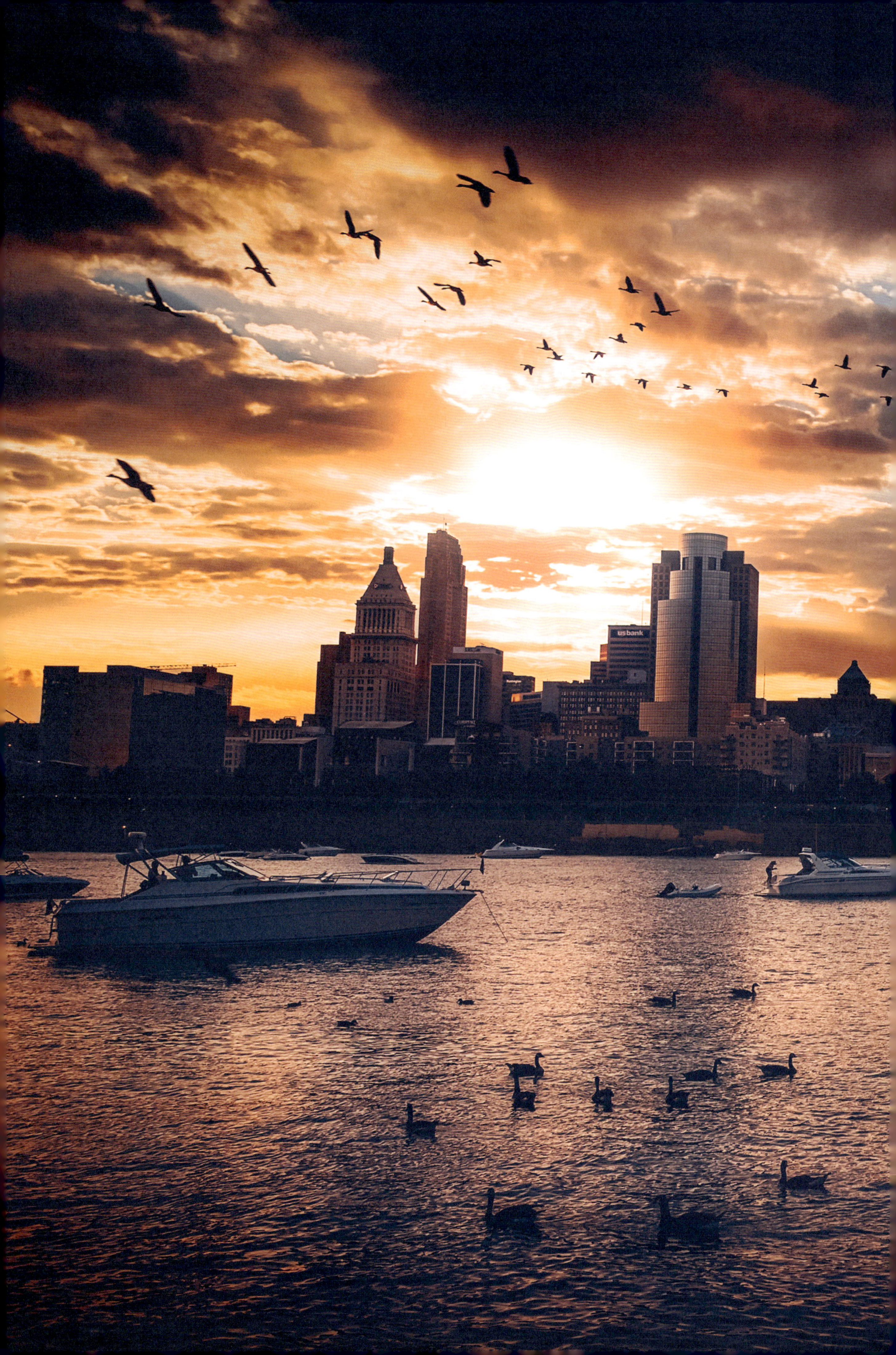
usbank

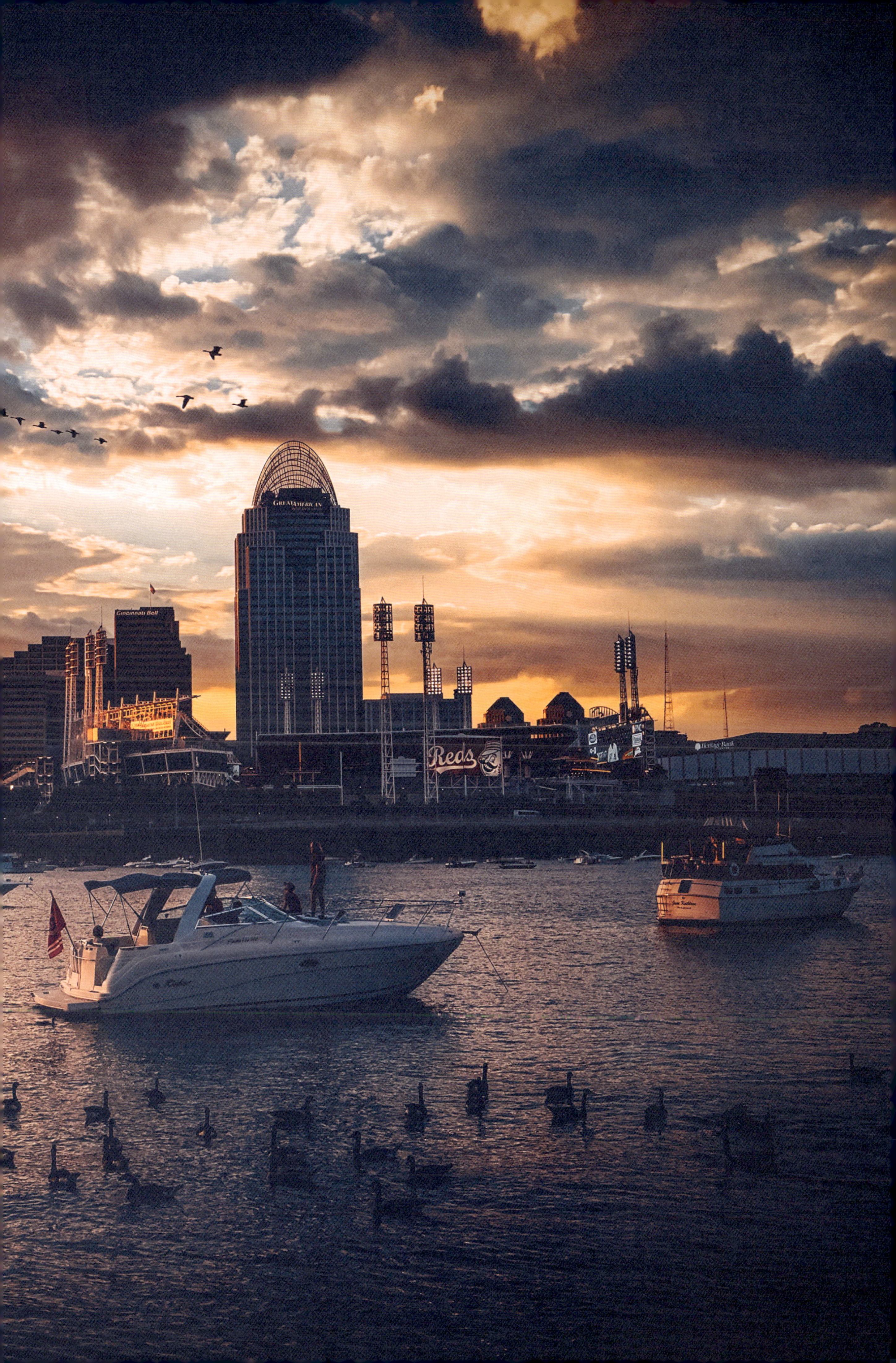
Cincinnati Bell
Reds

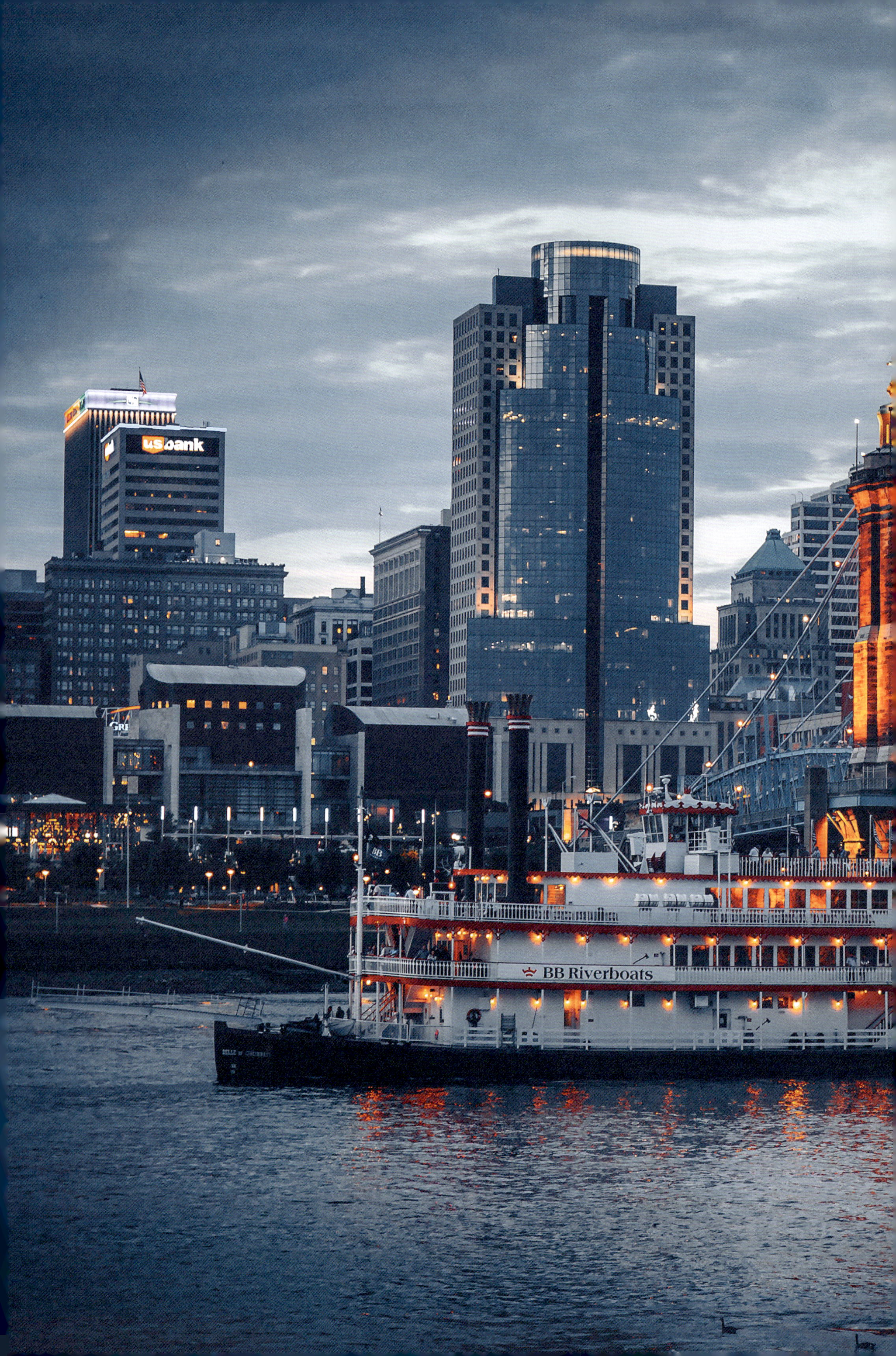
usbank
BB Riverboats

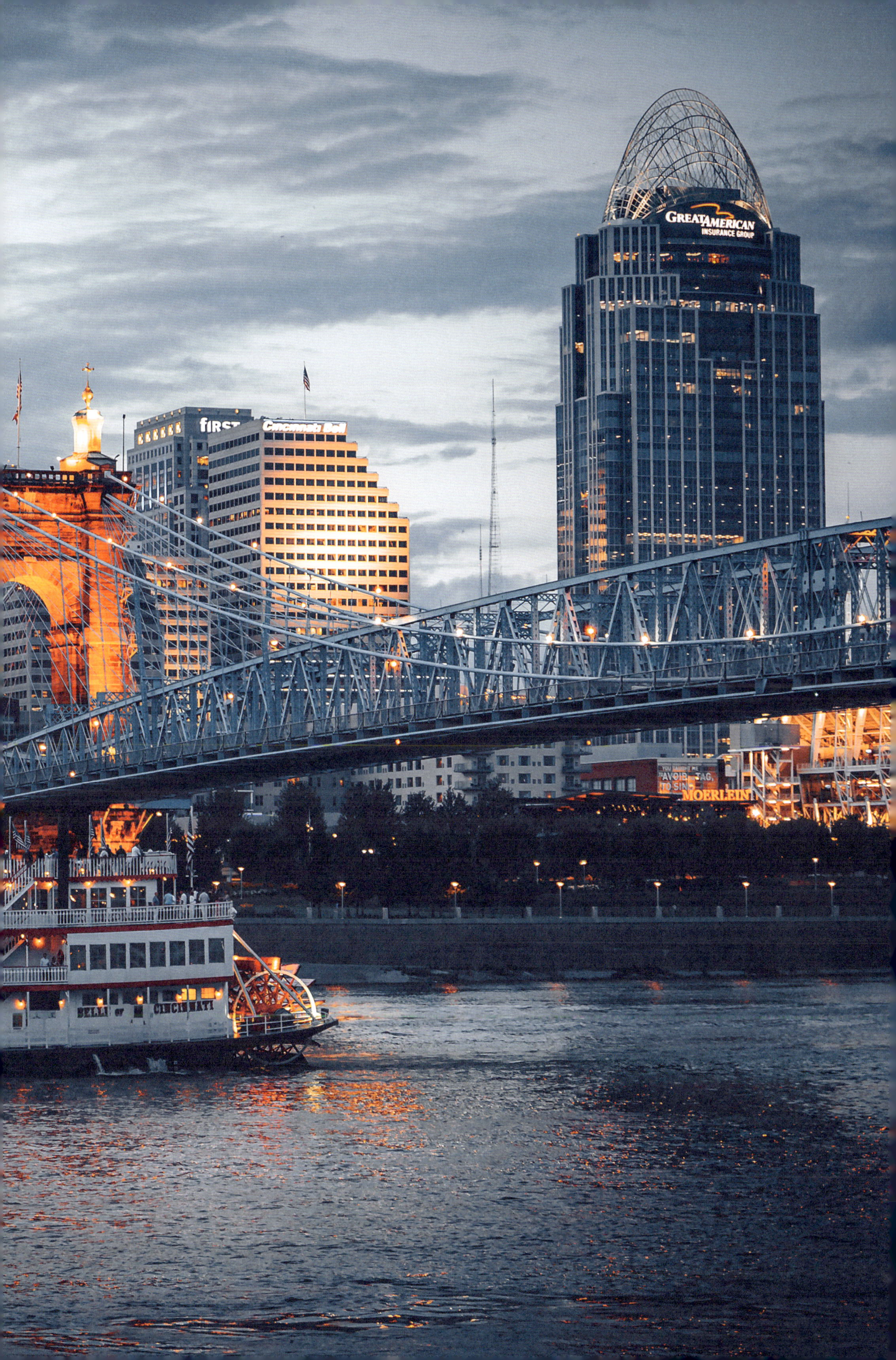
GREAT AMERICAN
INSURANCE GROUP
FIRST
Cincinnati Bell
MOERLEIN
CINCINNATI

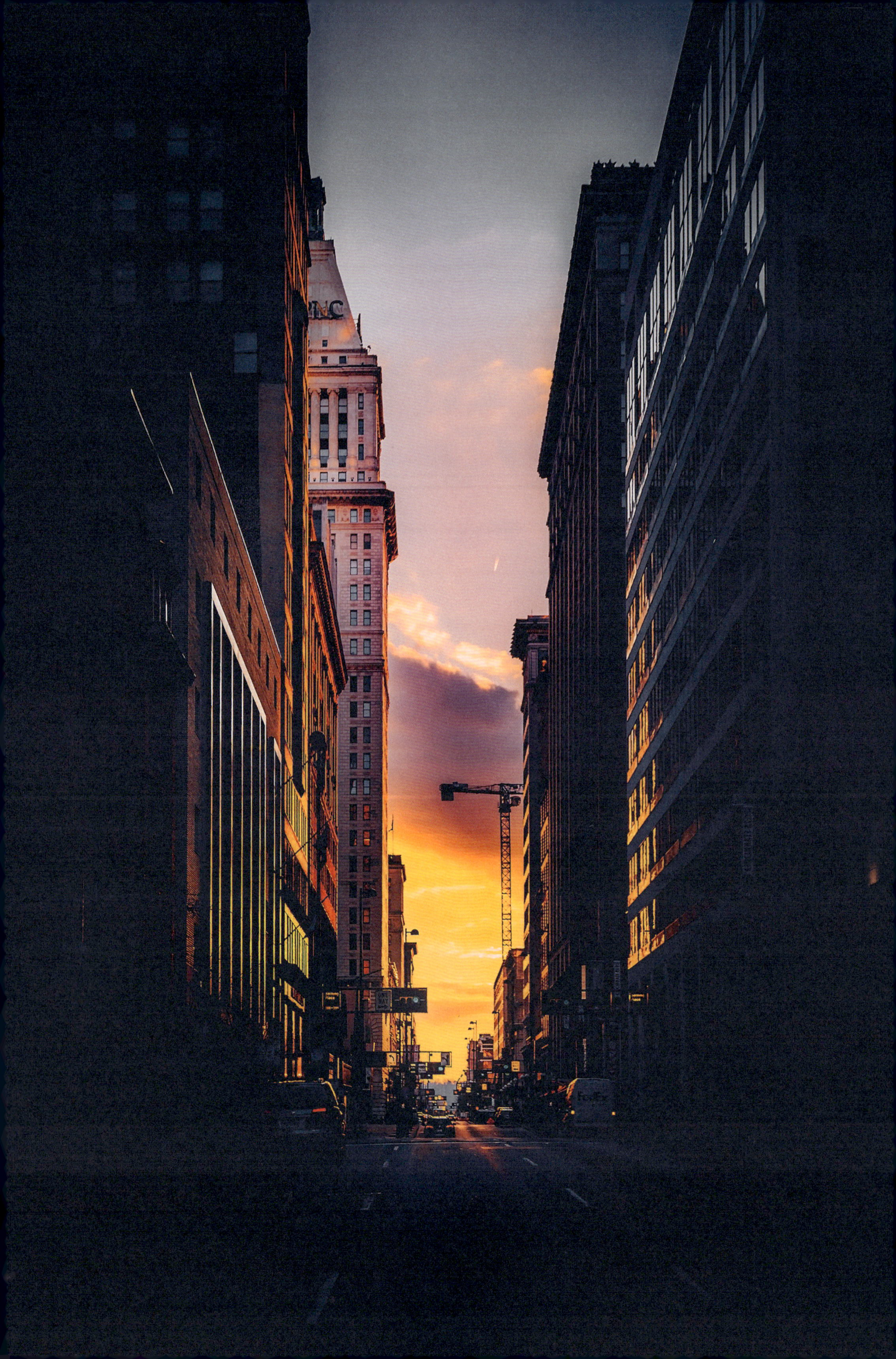

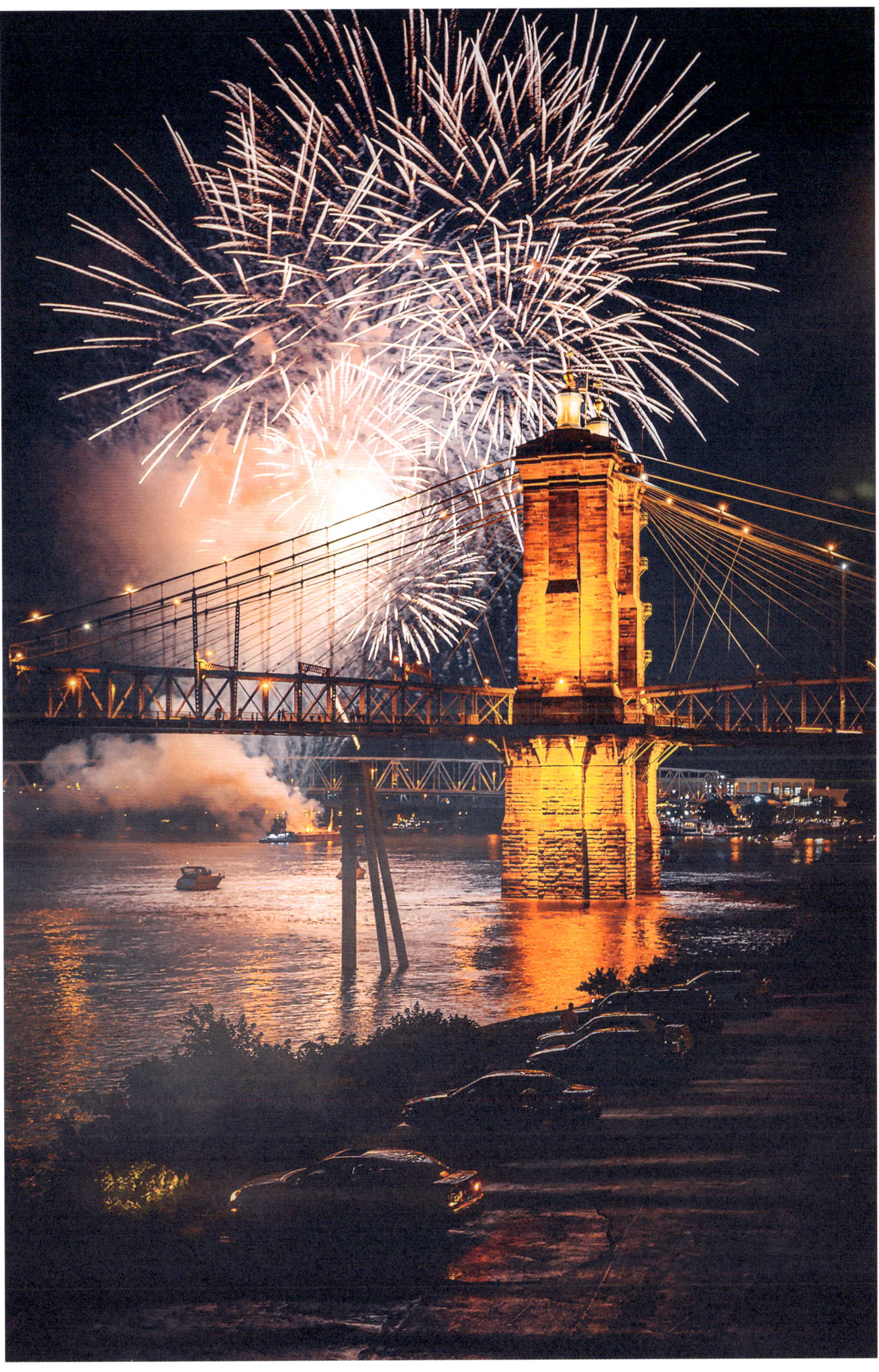

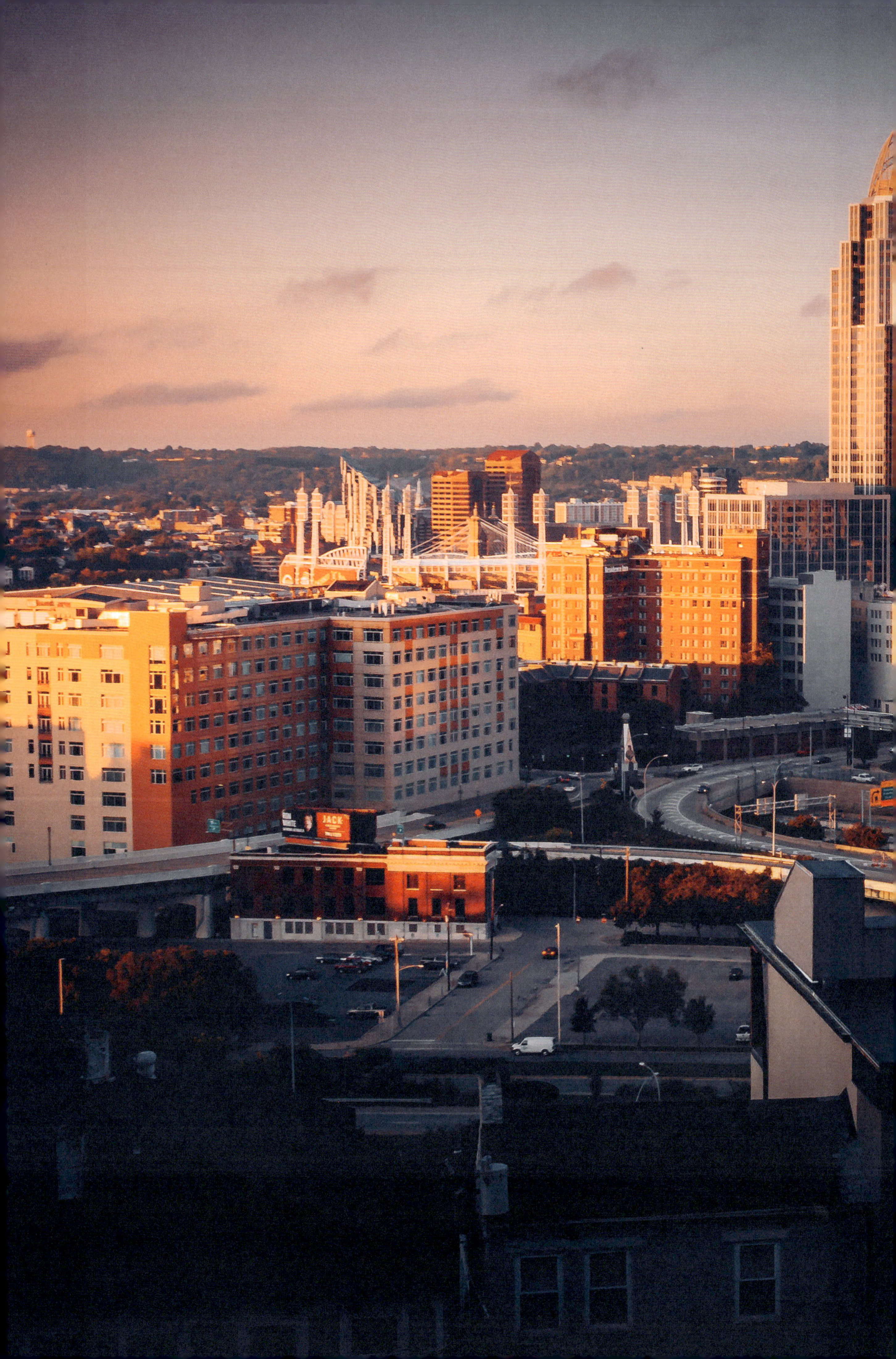
JACK

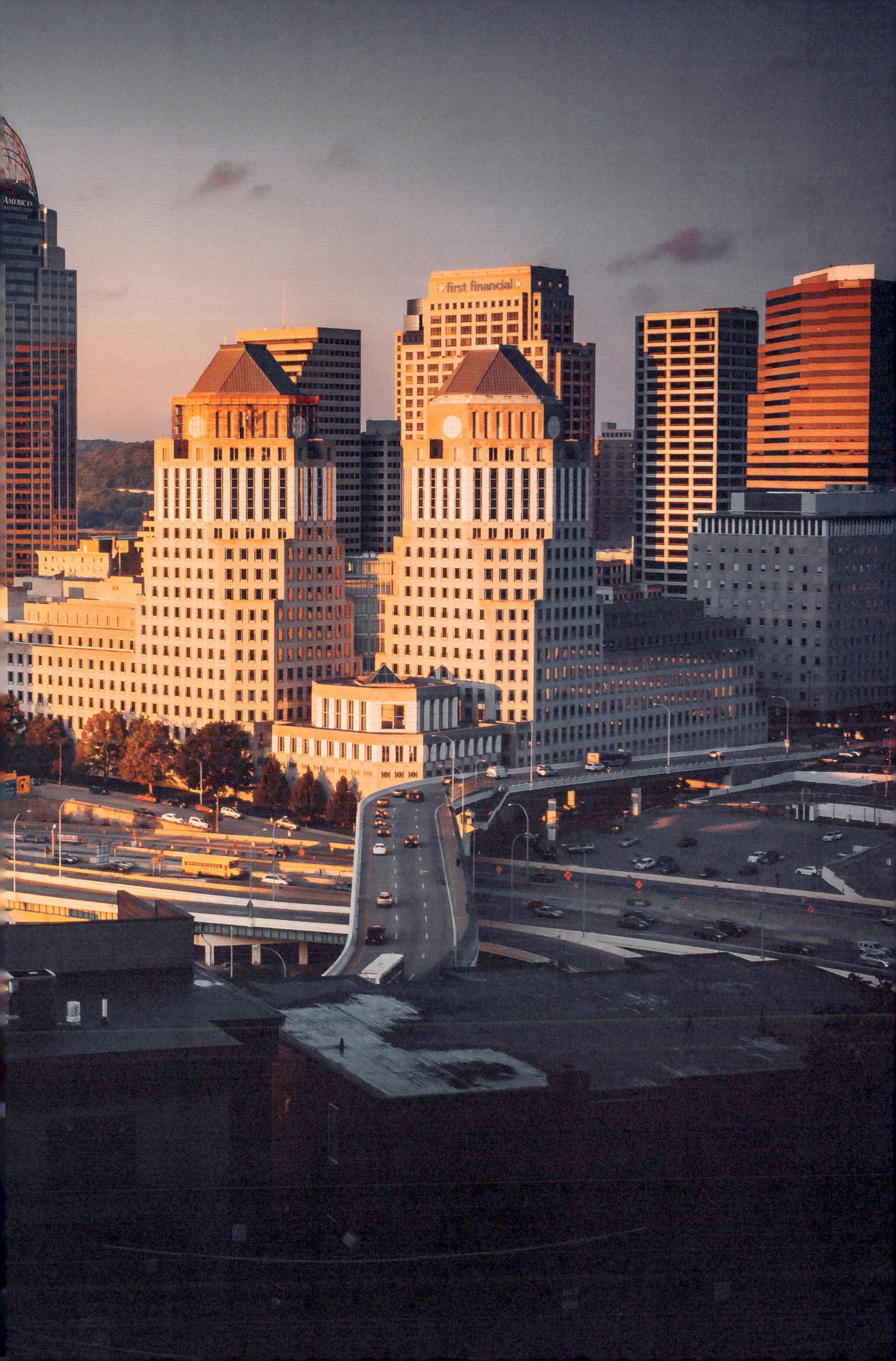
AMERICAN
first financial

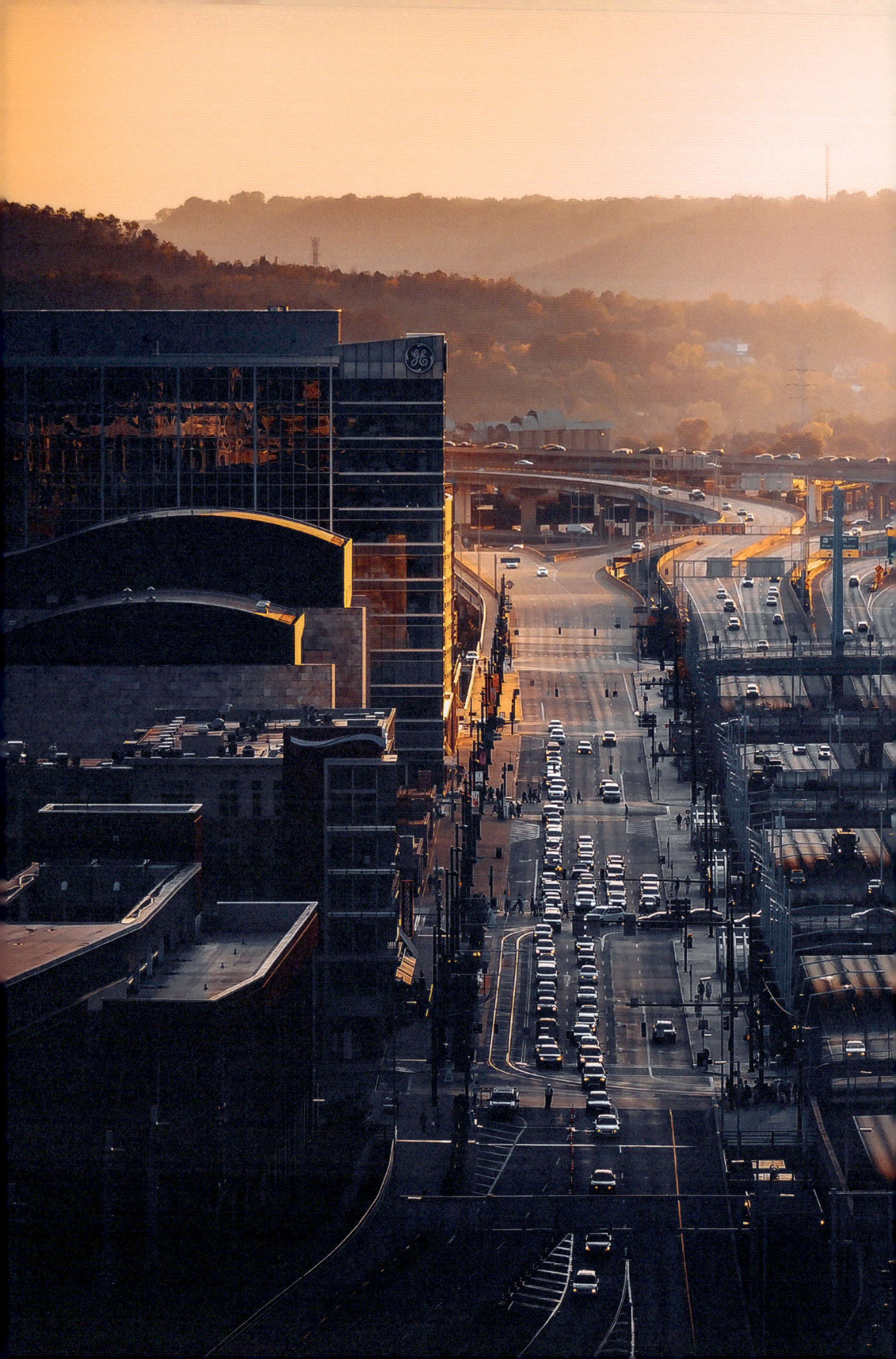

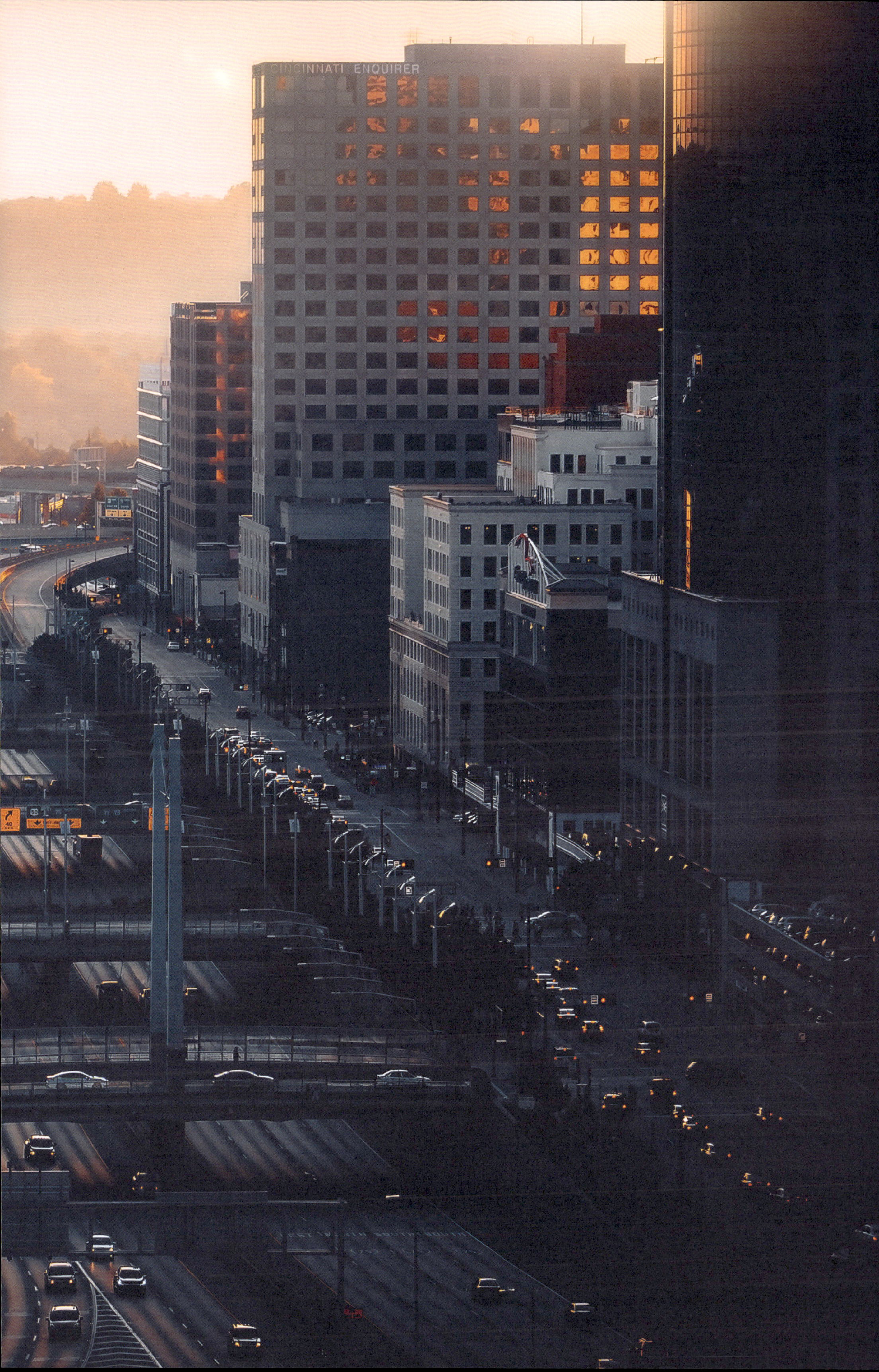
CINCINNATI ENQUIRER

ARTIST'S STATEMENT

When I first moved to Cincinnati in 2015, I had preconceived notions of a sleepy, post-industrial city. However, I quickly discovered a vibrant, historic, and culturally rich metropolis. I'll never forget the first time I looked up at the Roebling Bridge from Smale Park. As a New York native, it felt oddly familiar—a feeling that was confirmed after learning it was the prototype for the Brooklyn Bridge!

During my four years studying clinical psychology at Xavier University, photographing the Queen City became a mindfulness practice and crucial creative outlet. I discovered the majestic Music Hall, the Art Deco masterpieces of the Carew Tower, Union Terminal, and Dixie Terminal, and the Italianate facades of the mid-1800's houses in Over-the-Rhine and Historic Newport. As I walked through the Greater Cincinnati streets, it sometimes felt as if I was strolling through a quiet European town, and other times, as if I was transported back in time through old New York or London. Yet, there is also a stunning juxtaposition of modern architecture as seen in the Great American Tower and the Scripps Center. Their blocks echo with the ringing bells of the new Connector streetcar.

Photographing Cincinnati's bright skyline reflected over the Ohio River was also breathtaking. It was always a bonus to see a barge, tugboat, speedboat, or riverboat pass through, or to hear the roar of the crowds from the Reds' Great American Ball Park or the Bengals' Paycor Stadium from across the river. Zooming out, the city's seven hills offered plenty of breathtaking skyline views, including my favorites from Mount Adams and Mount Echo. It was not uncommon for me to photograph one location for sunset and return the next morning for sunrise at the exact same vantage point.

Even though Charles Dickens called Cincinnati thriving and animated when he visited in 1842, my hope is the photographs in this book convey that same beauty and energy the city still possesses today. I developed my stylized approach to photography attempting to cast this city in sunrise, sunset, and twilight hour light from as many angles as possible. *Cincinnati Dreaming* invites you to discover the Queen City's gems for yourself.

MIKE POGGIOLI

@mpthecomebackid

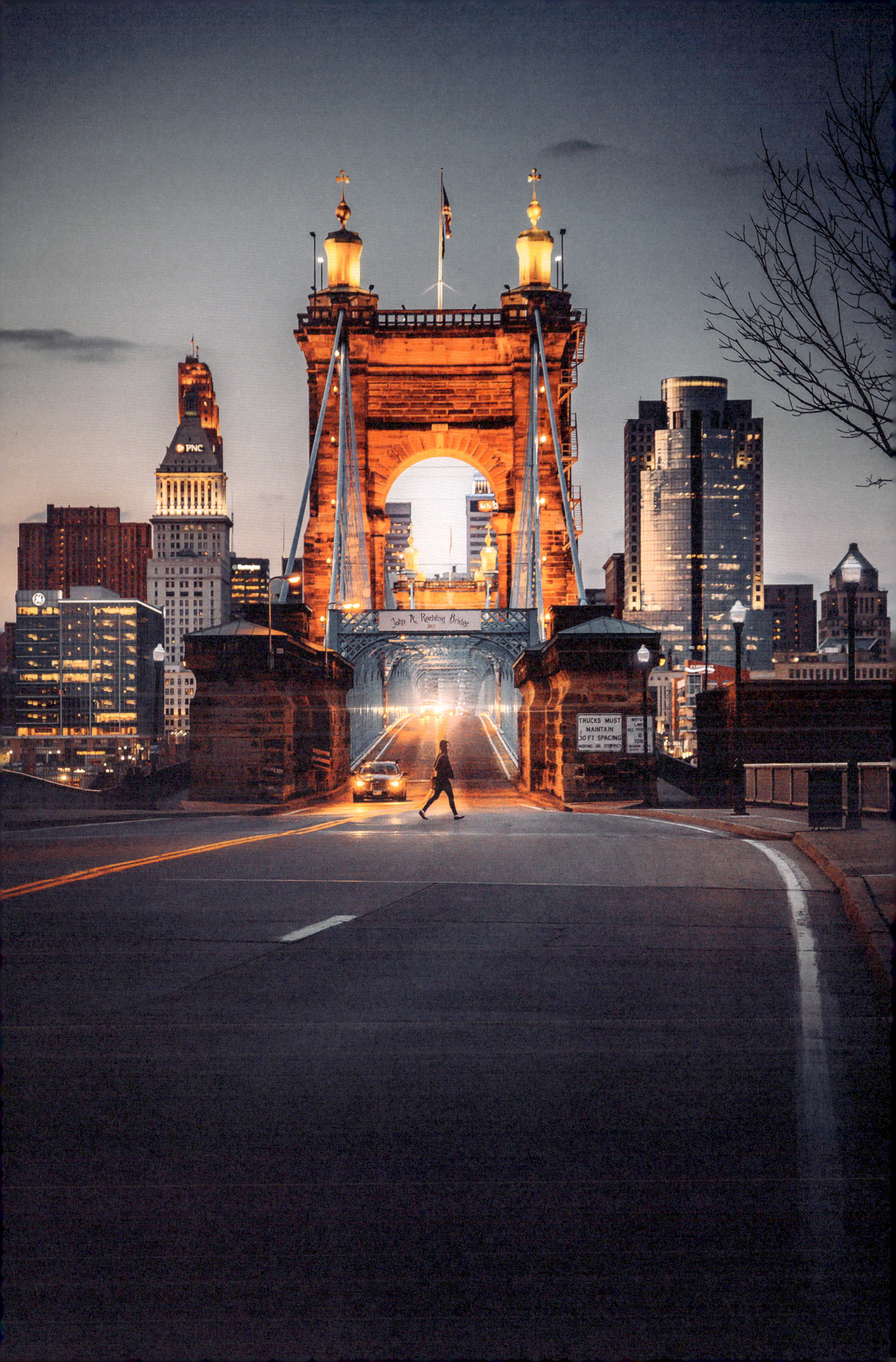
PNC
John A. Roebling Bridge
TRUCKS MUST
MAINTAIN
30 FT SPACING
MOVING OR STOPPED

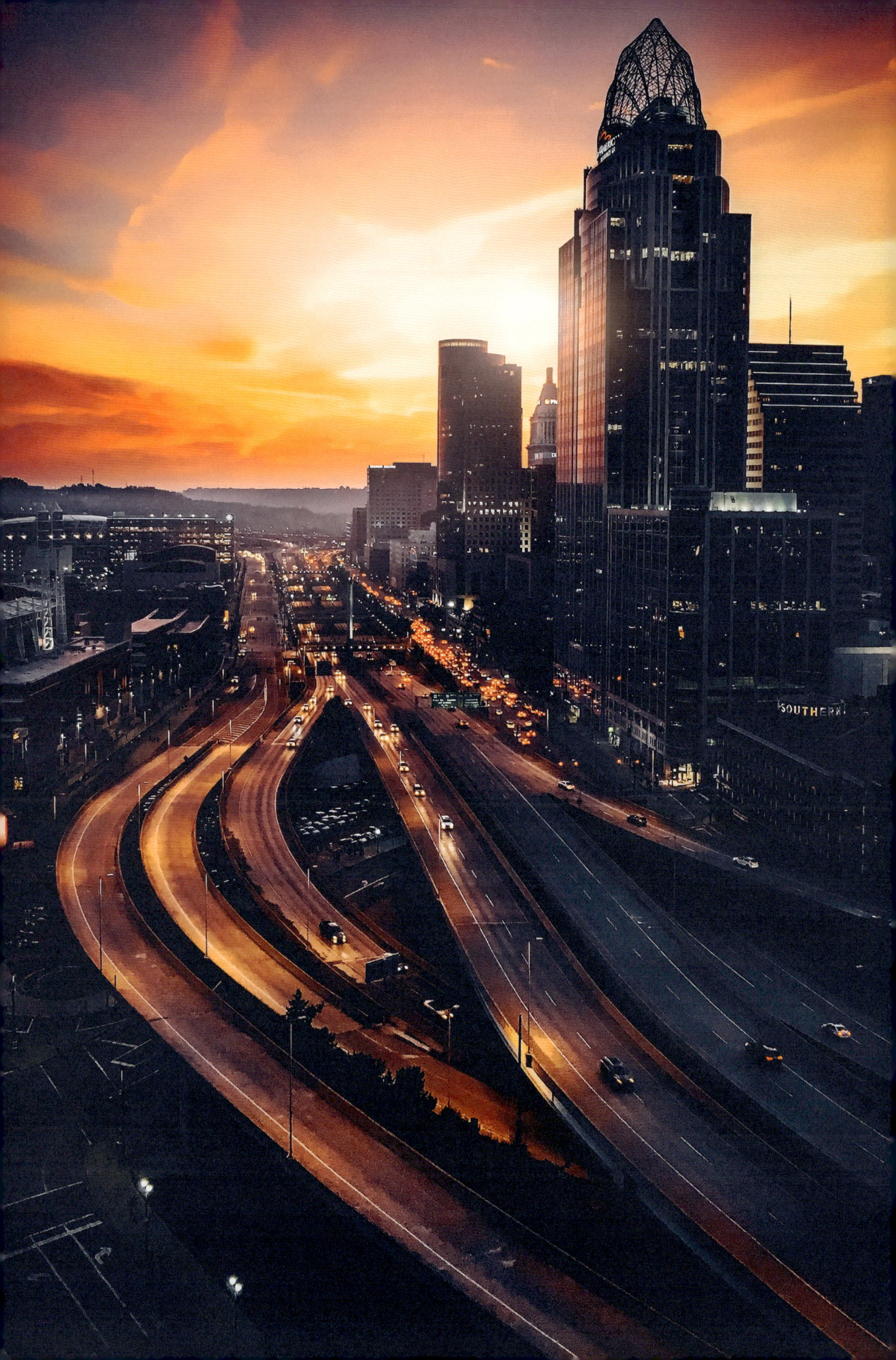
SOUTHERN

MIKE POGGIOLI

Originally from just outside New York City, Mike Poggioli came to see photography as a serious creative outlet when he moved to Chicago in 2012 and became enamored by the beauty of the city's architecture. He then brought his newfound love for cityscapes with him to Cincinnati, Ohio, in 2015, where he studied clinical psychology. Photography became an opportunity to cultivate mindfulness – a way to see the world with a beginner's mind – in both his personal life and professional practice. In 2021, he listened to the call of the mountains by deciding to settle in Asheville, North Carolina.

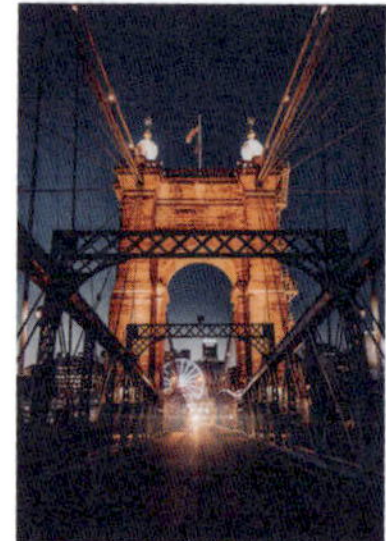

Cover John A. Roebling Suspension Bridge

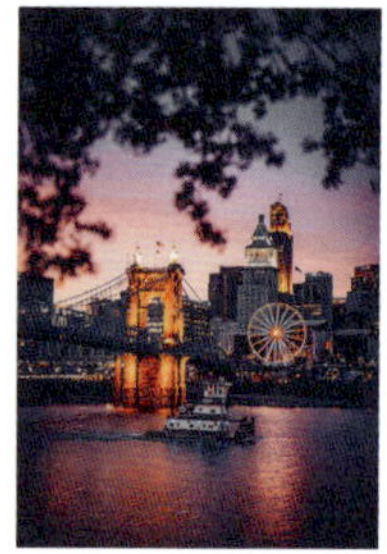

2 View of John A. Roebling Suspension Bridge and the Ohio River

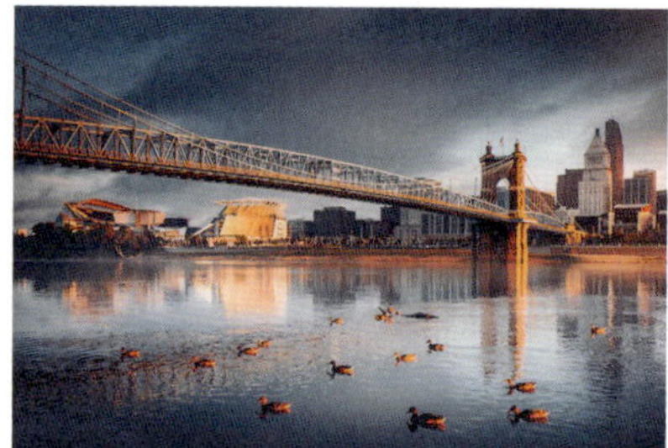

4-5 View of the Ohio River and John A. Roebling Suspension Bridge

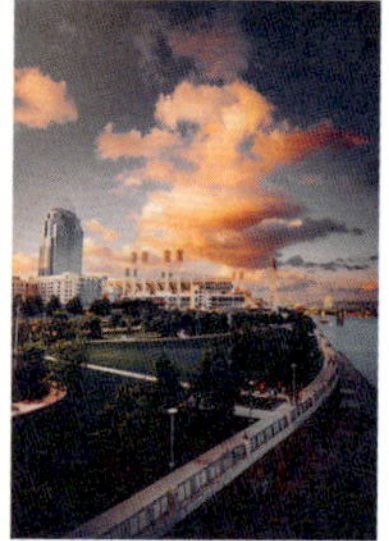

6 View of Smale Riverfront Park and Great American Ball Park

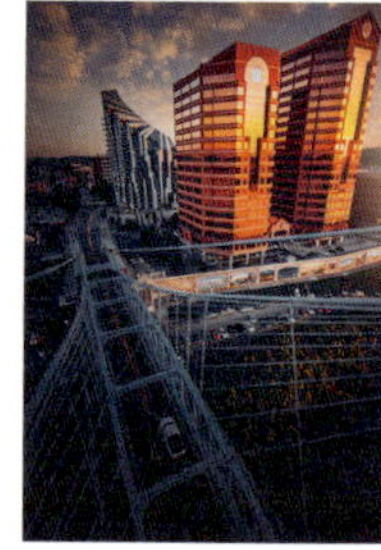

9 View of River Center Towers

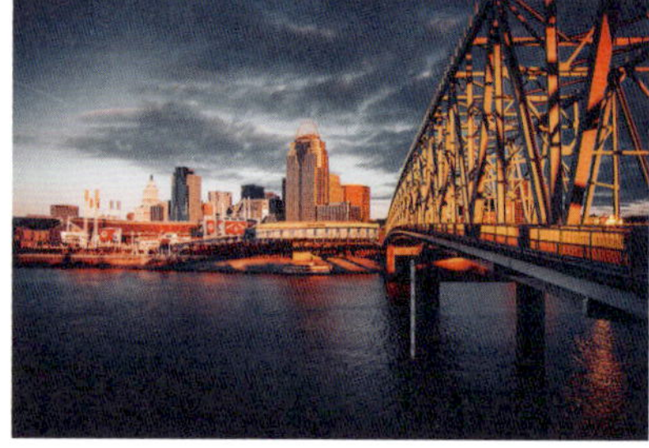

10-11 View of Cincinnati skyline alongside Taylor Southgate Bridge

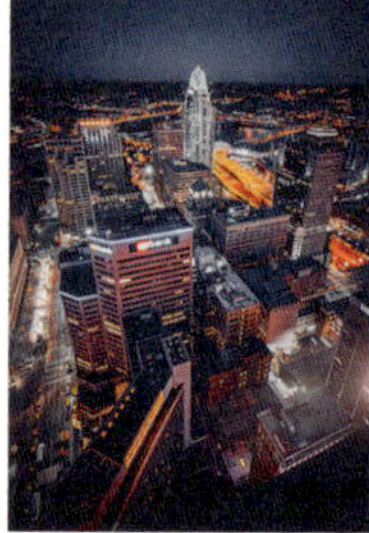

12 View of Downtown Cincinnati from the Carew Tower

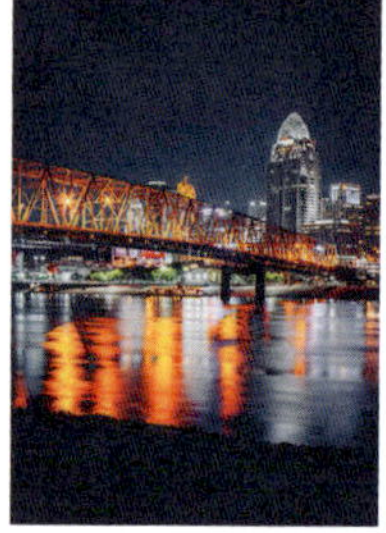

13 View of Taylor Southgate Bridge from Newport on the Levee

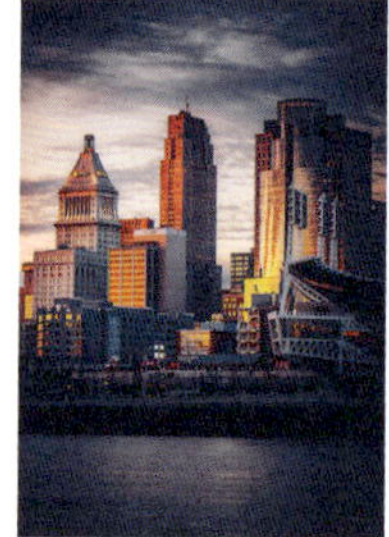

15 View of Downtown Cincinnati from General James Taylor Park

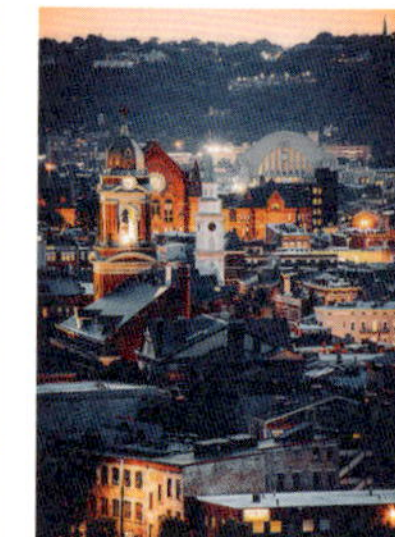

16 View of Over-the-Rhine from Mount Adams

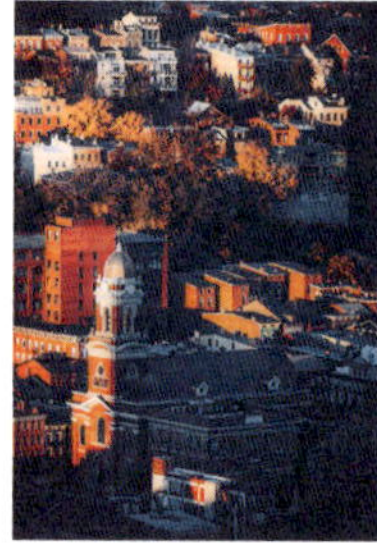

17 Above St. Paul Church and Pendleton

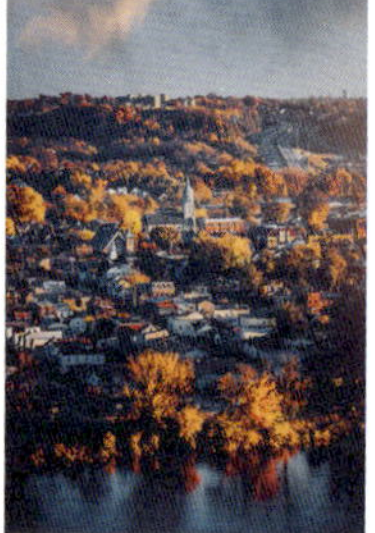

18 View of Kentucky from Eden Park

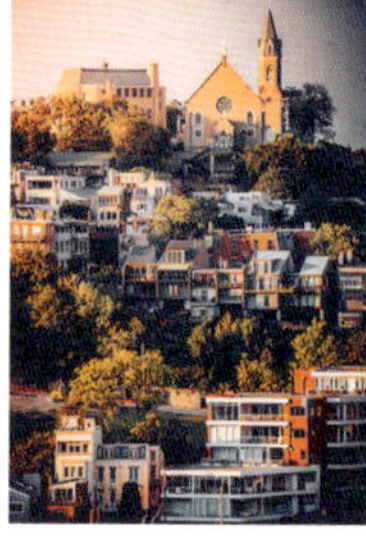

19 View of The Church of the Immaculata atop Mount Adams

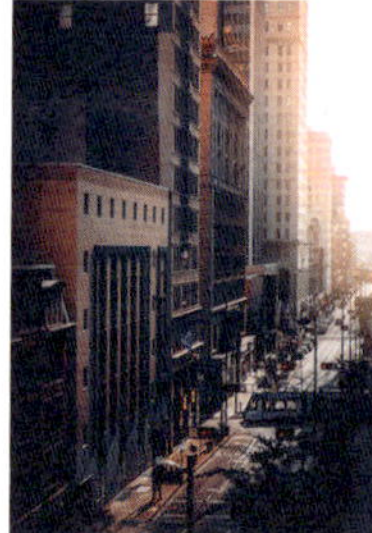

20 View of E. 4th Street

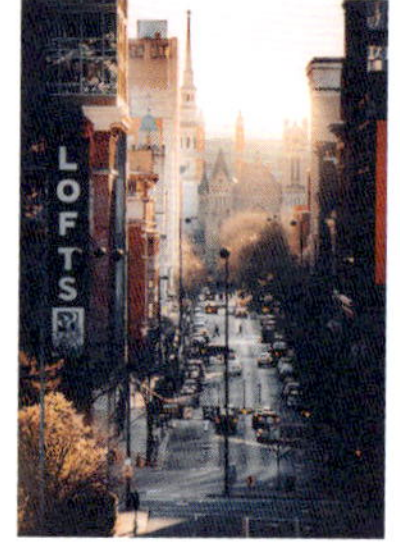

21 View of Covenant-First Presbyterian Church from Mount Adams

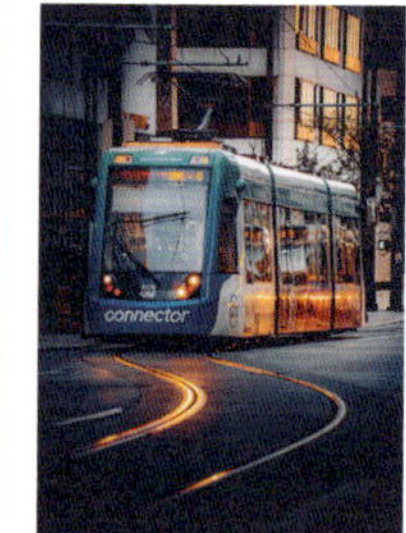

22 View of E. 6th Street and Main Street

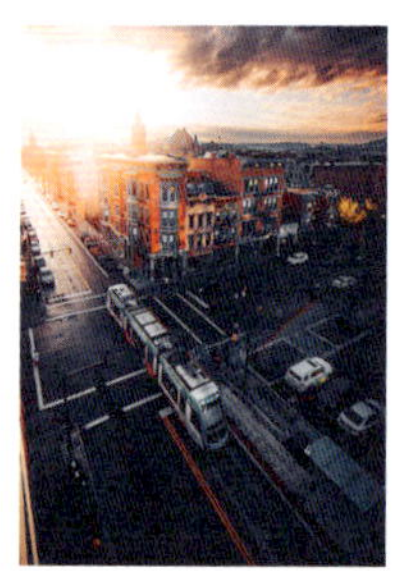

23 Intersection of Vine Street and W. 12th Street

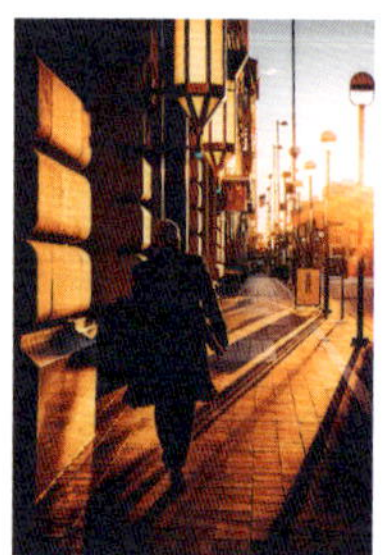

24 View of E. 4th Street and Vine Street

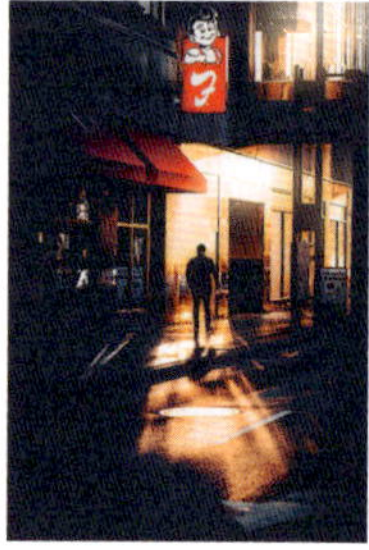

25 View of W. 5th Street

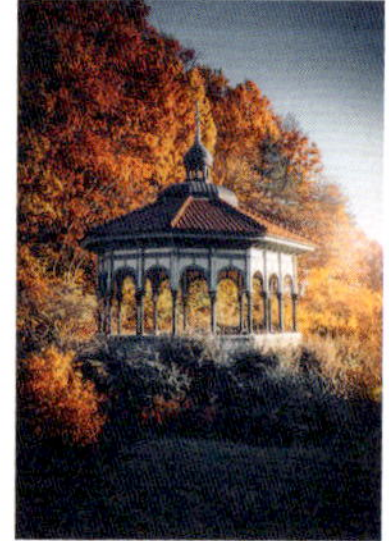

26 Eden Park Gazebo

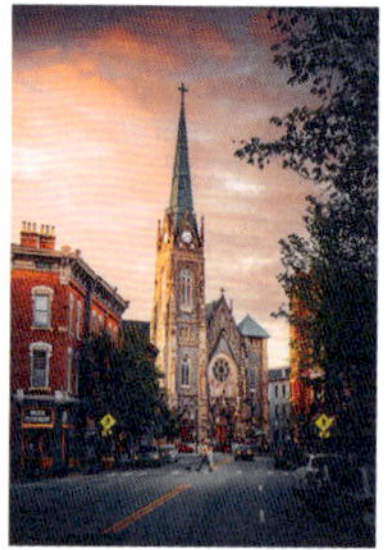

27 View of St. Francis de Sales Catholic Church

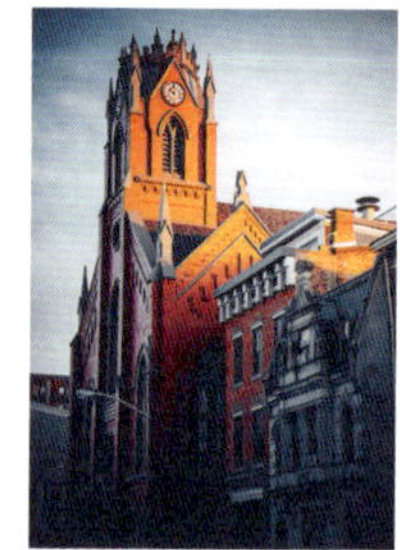

28 View of Apostolic Bethlehem Temple Church

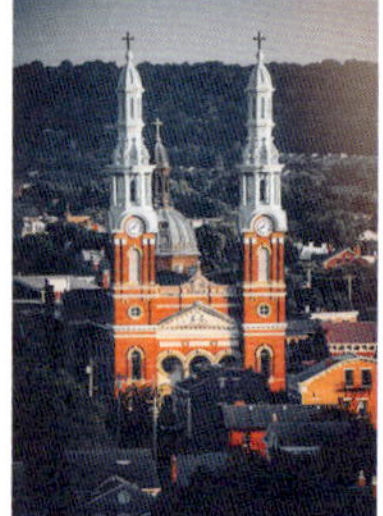

29 View of Mother of God Roman Catholic Church

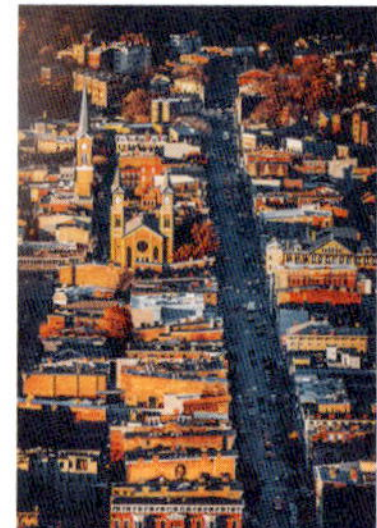

30 View of Vine Street

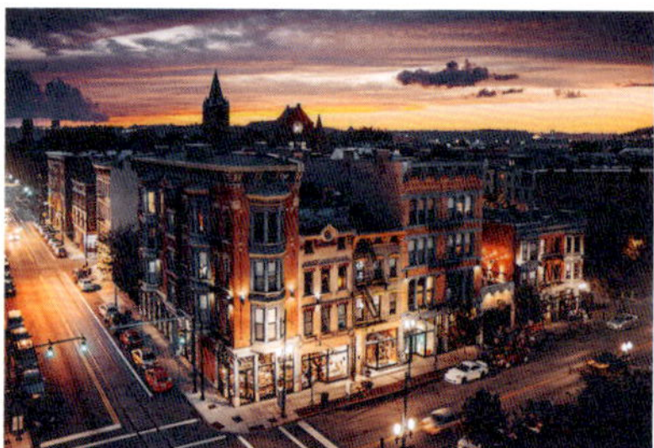

32-33 Intersection of Vine Street and W. 12th Street

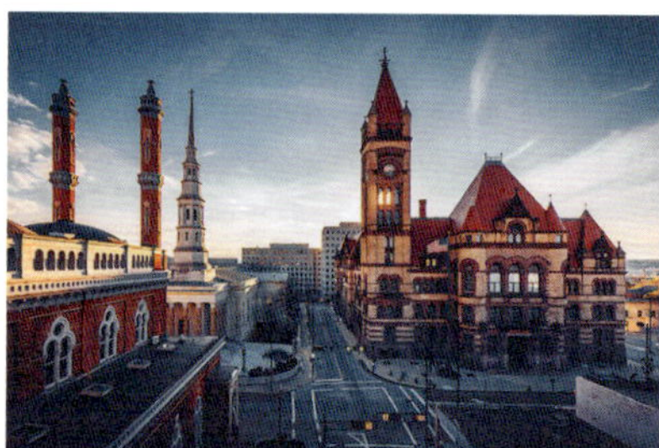

34-35 View of Cincinnati City Hall

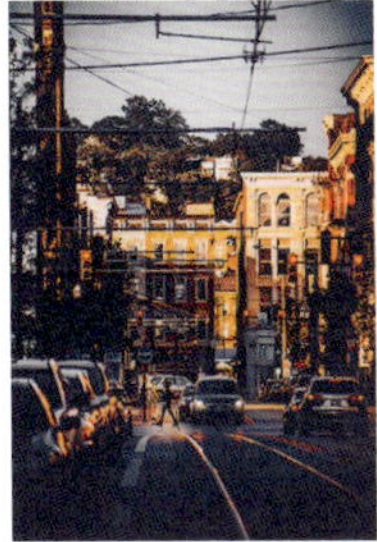

36 View of E. 12th Street

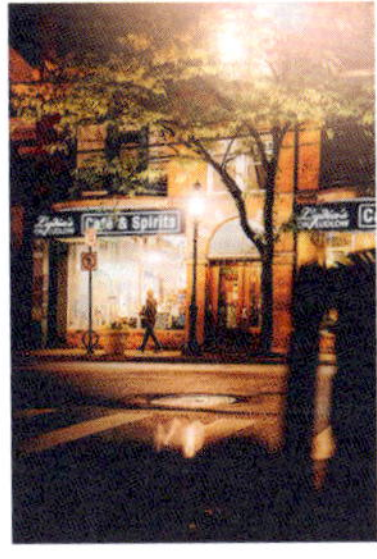

37 View of Ludlow Avenue

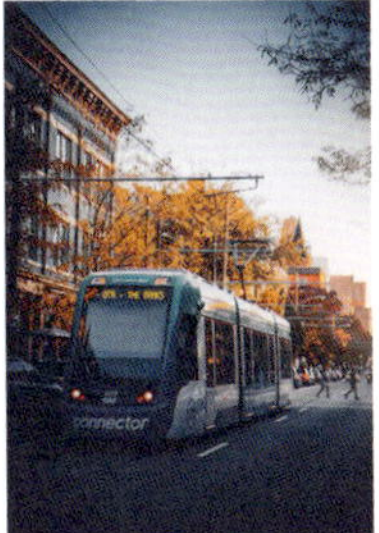

38 View of Race Street

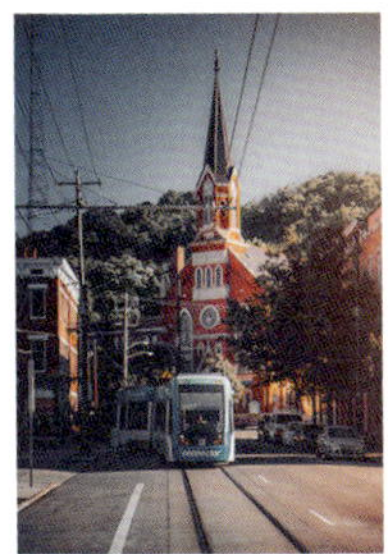

39 View of Philippus United Church of Christ

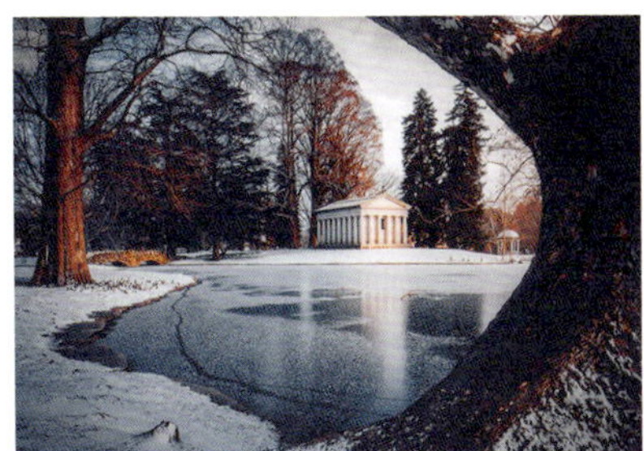

40-41 View of Fleischman Mausoleum, Spring Grove Cemetery

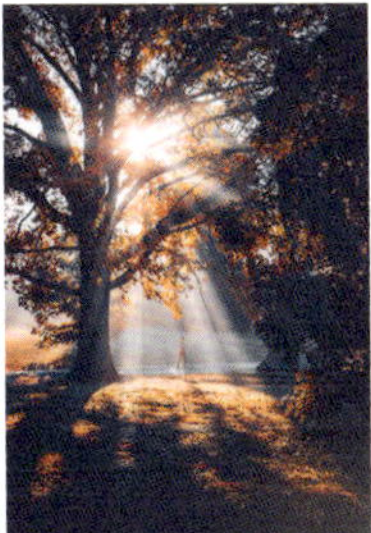

42 View of Spring Grove Cemetery

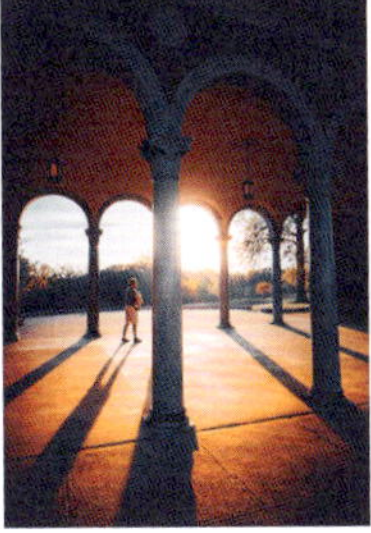

43 View of Mt. Echo Park Pavilion

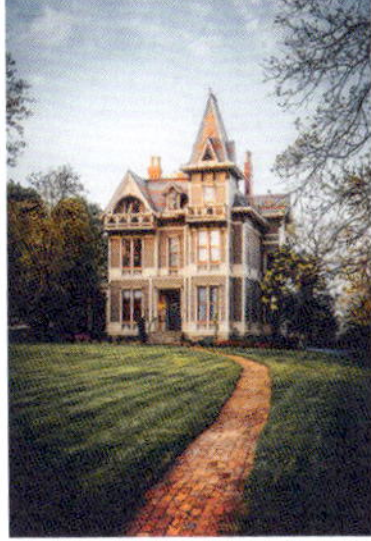

44 View of The George Stone House, Hyde Park

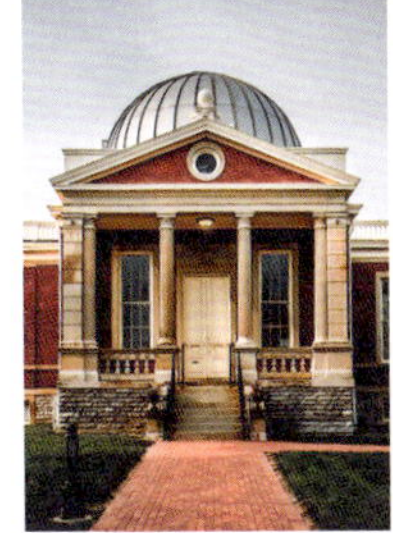

45 View of Mt. Lookout Observatory

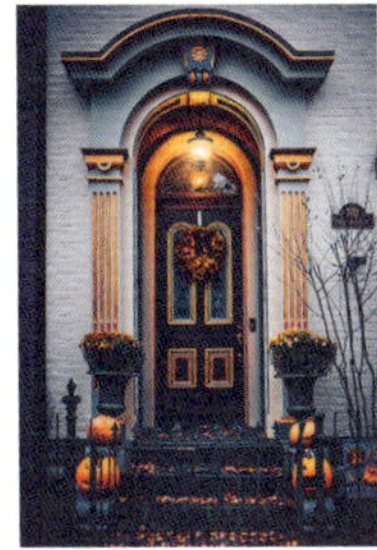

46 Historic Newport District, Kentucky

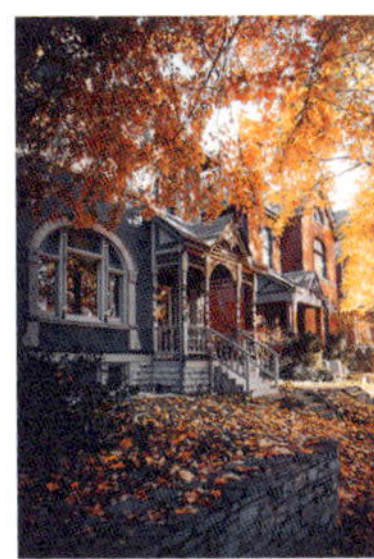

47 Historic Newport District, Kentucky

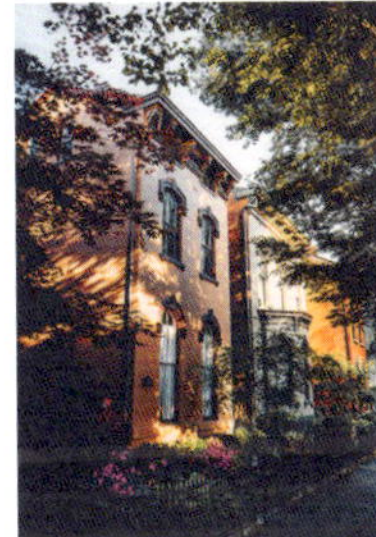

48 Historic Newport District, Kentucky

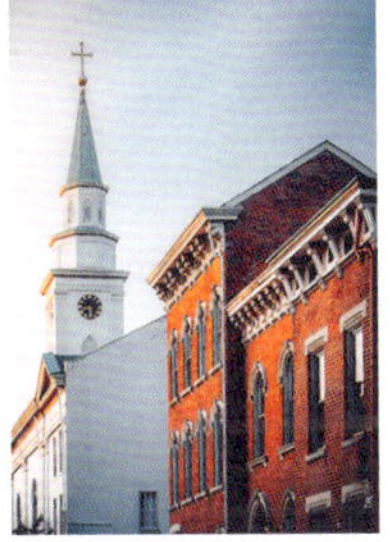

50 View of Old St. Mary's Catholic Church

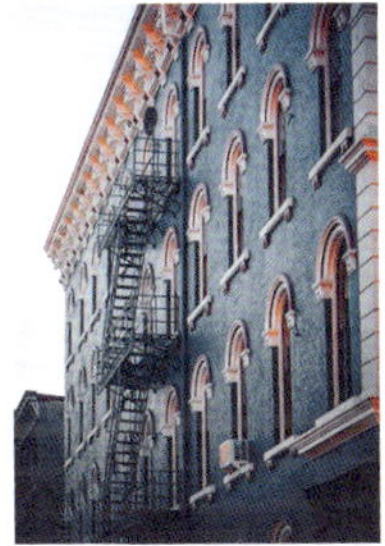

51 View of E. 12th Street and Main Street

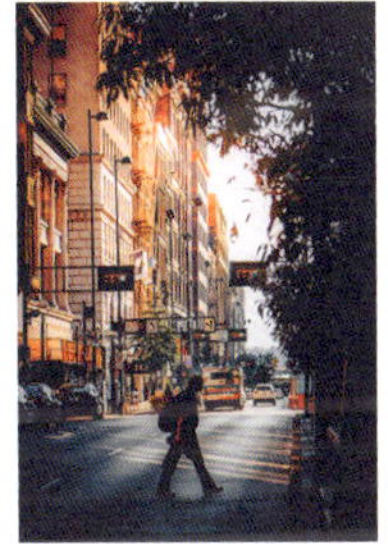

52 View of 4th Street and Vine Street

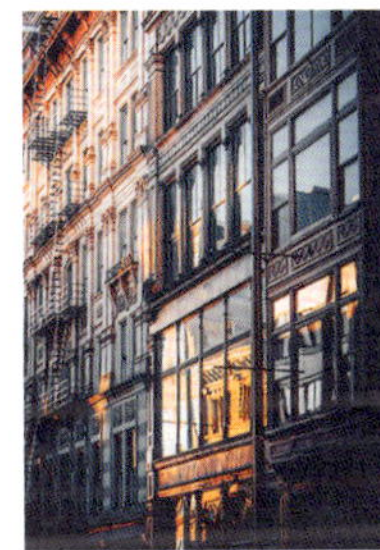

53 View of 4th Street

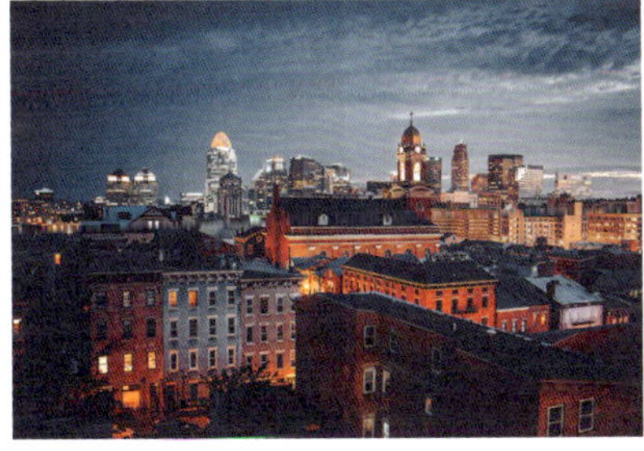

54-55 View of Cincinnati skyline from Pendleton Art Center

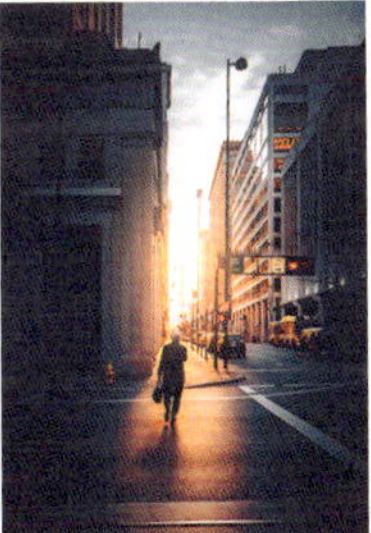

56 Intersection of Main Street and E. 4th Street

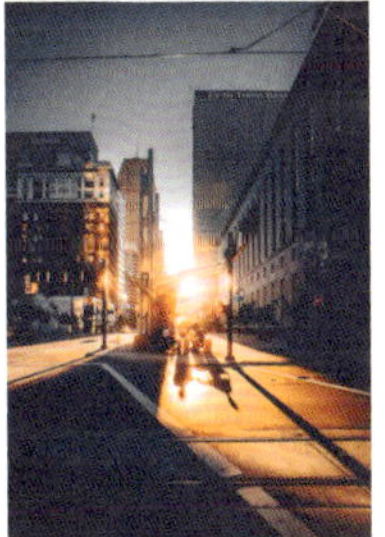

57 View of Fountain Square

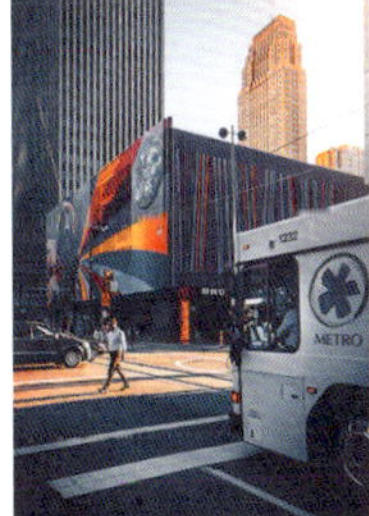

58 View of Armstrong Mural from E. 6th Street and Walnut Street

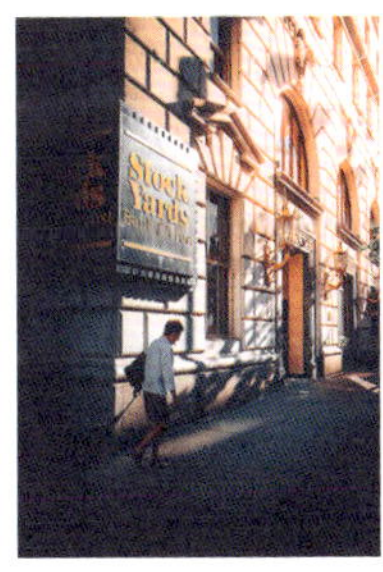

59 Corner of Race Street and W. 4th Street

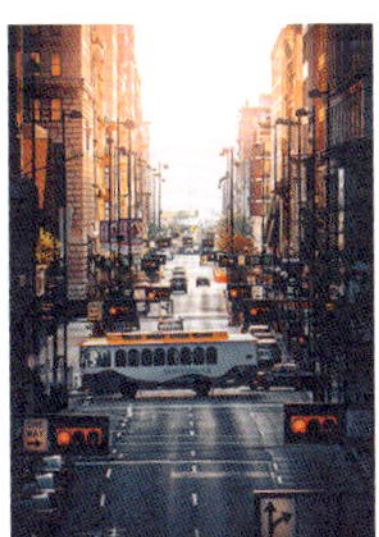

60 View of E. 4th Street

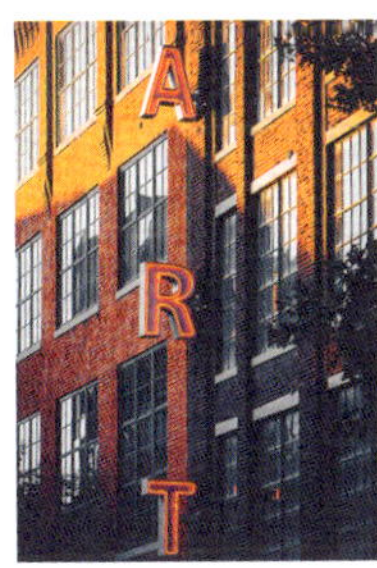

61 View of the Art Academy of Cincinnati

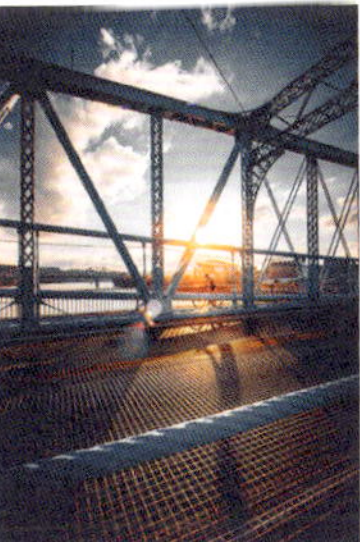

62 John A. Roebling Suspension Bridge

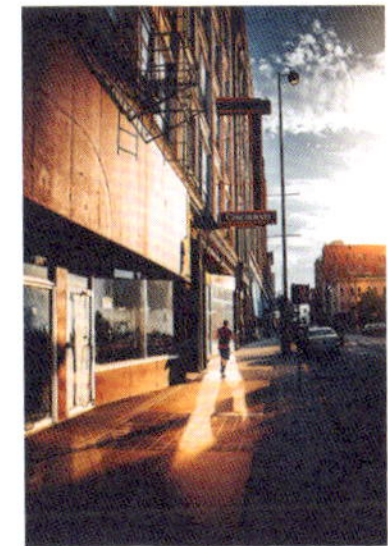

63 View of W. 4th Street

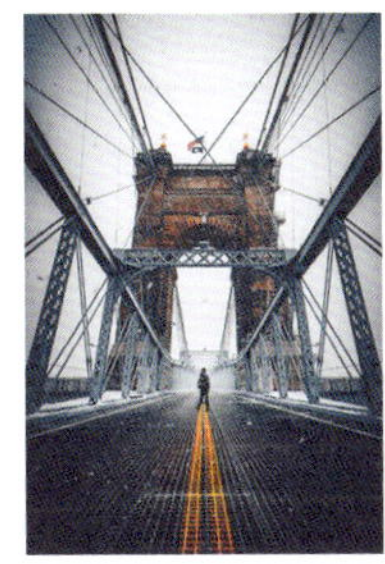

64 John A. Roebling Suspension Bridge

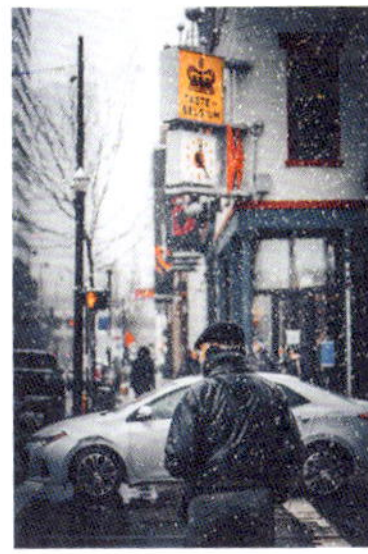

65 Intersection of Vine Street and W. 12th Street

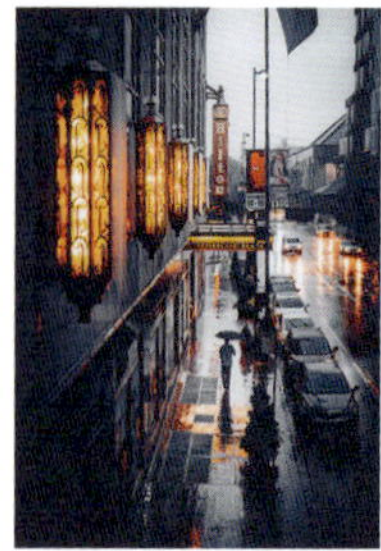

66 View of Hilton Cincinnati Netherland Plaza

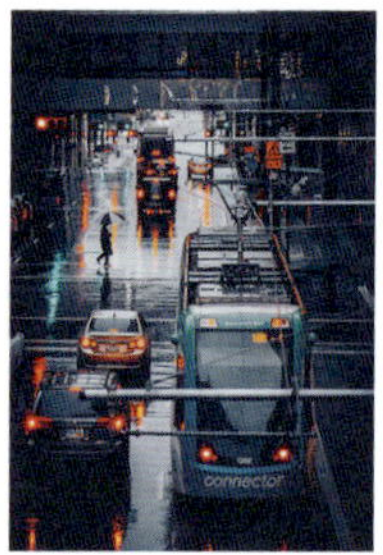

67 View of Fountain Square Connector Station

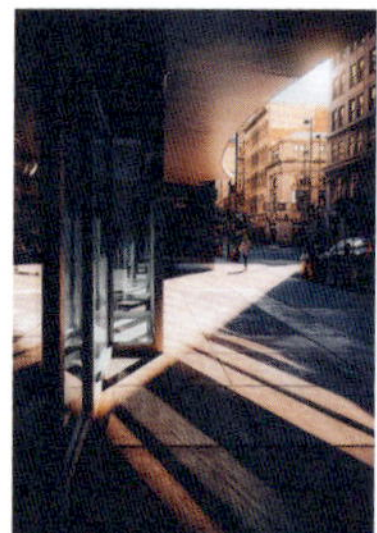

68 View of E. 4th Street

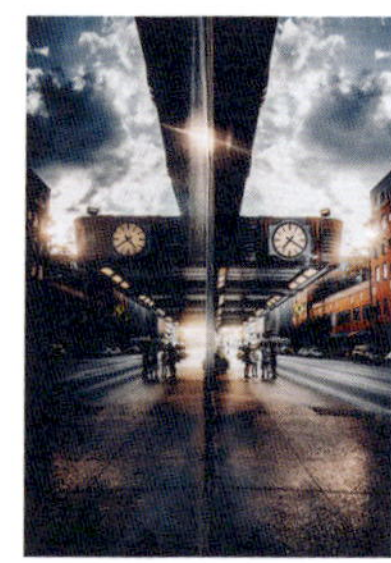

69 The Lofts at Shillito Place

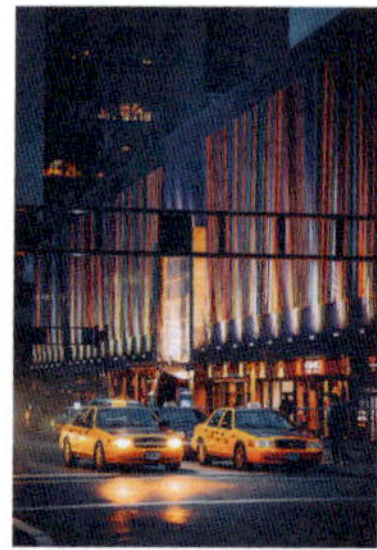

70 View of E. 6th Street

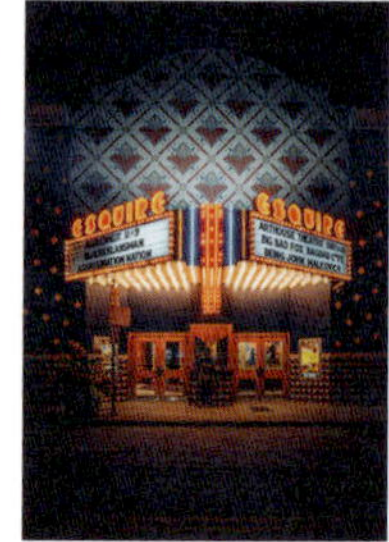

71 Esquire Theatre

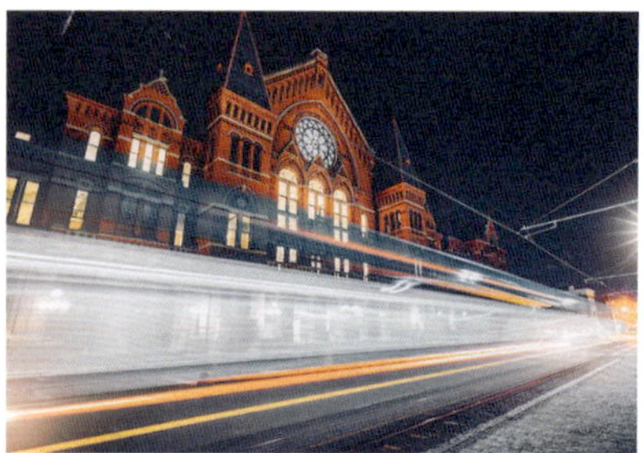

72-73 Cincinnati Music Hall

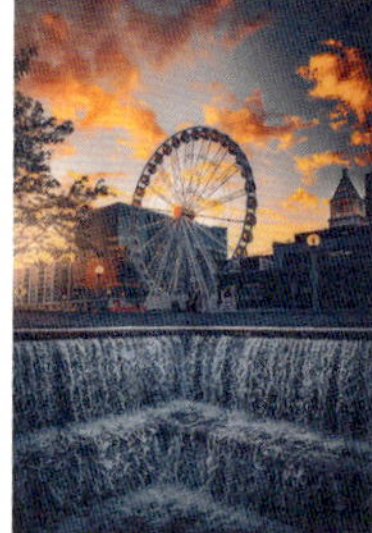

74 View of SkyStar Wheel from Berry Way Fountains

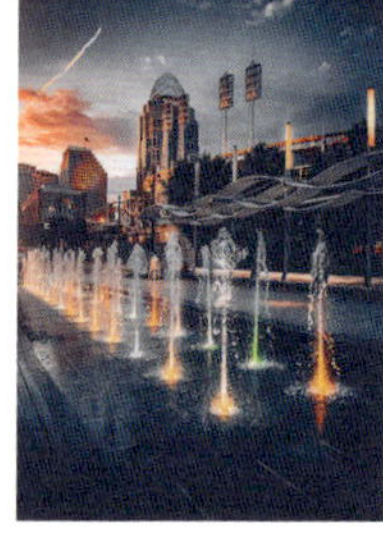

75 View of Great American Tower from Berry Way Fountains

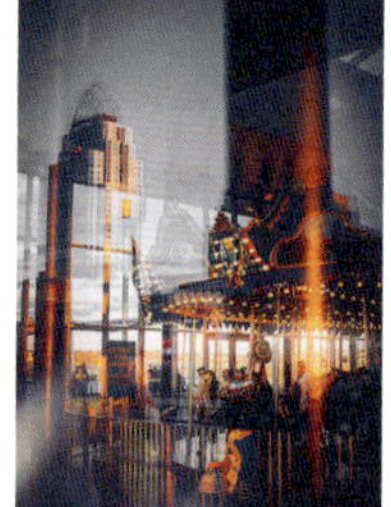

76 Carol Ann's Carousel

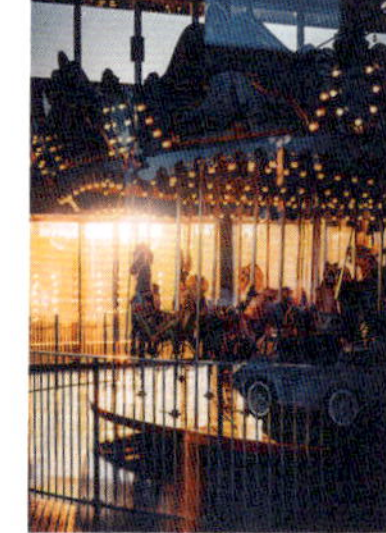

77 Carol Ann's Carousel

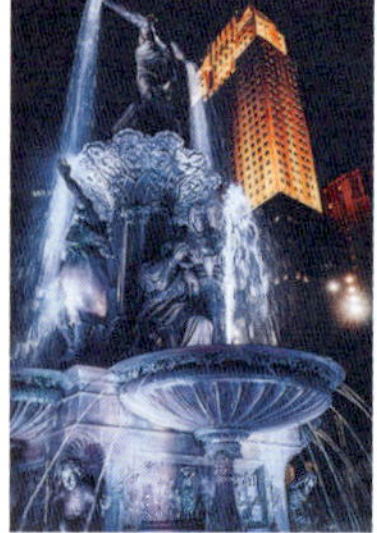

78 View of the Tyler Davidson Fountain

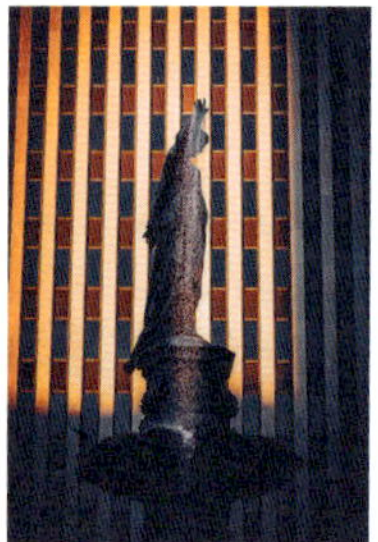

80 View of the Tyler Davidson Fountain

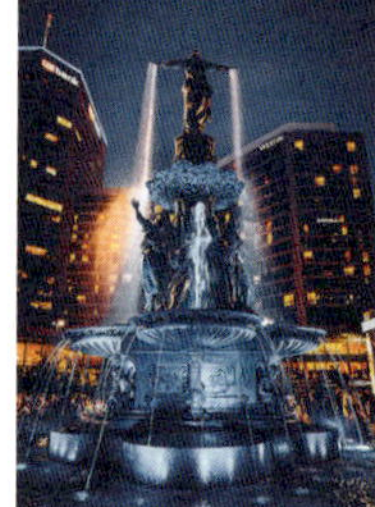

81 View of the Tyler Davidson Fountain

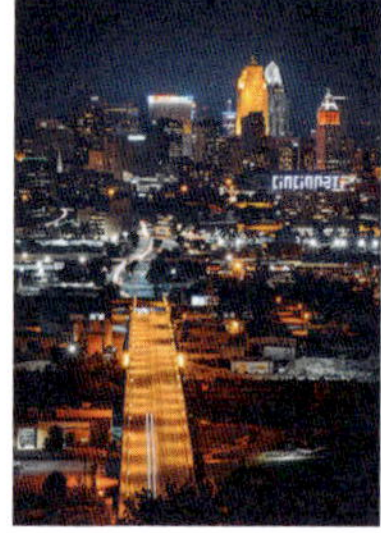

82 View of Cincinnati skyline from Olden View Park

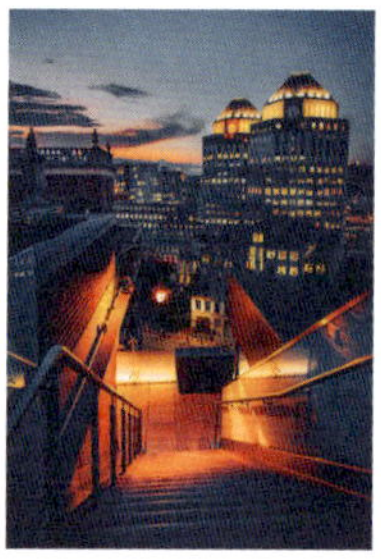

83 View from Top of the Park at Phelps Hotel

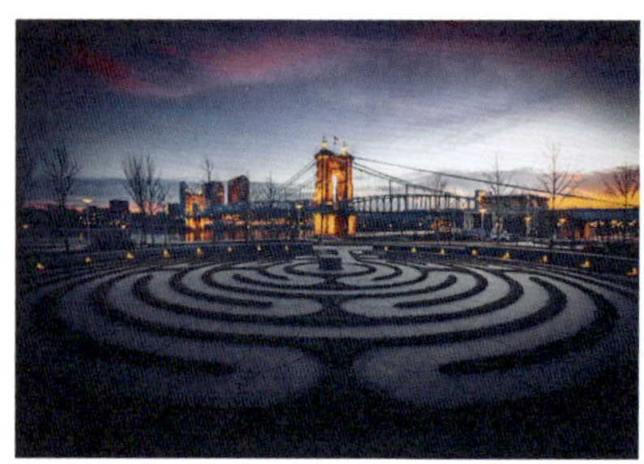

84-85 View of John A. Roebling Suspension Bridge from Smale Riverfront Park

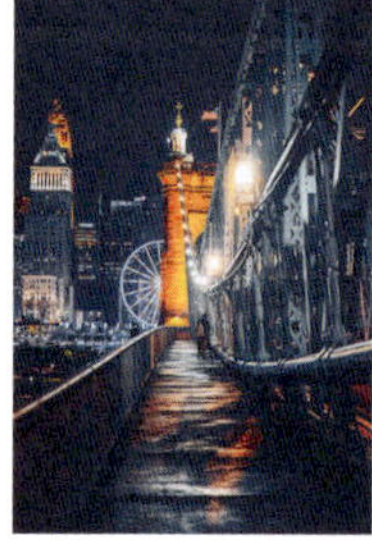

86 John A. Roebling Suspension Bridge

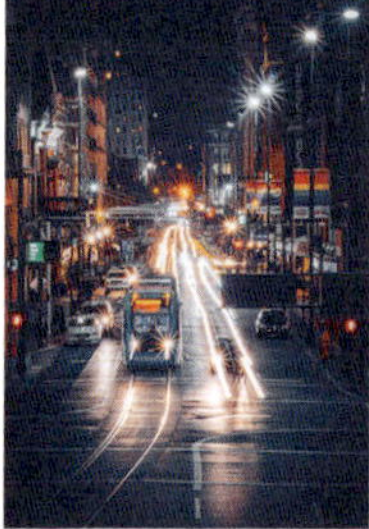

87 View of Walnut Street

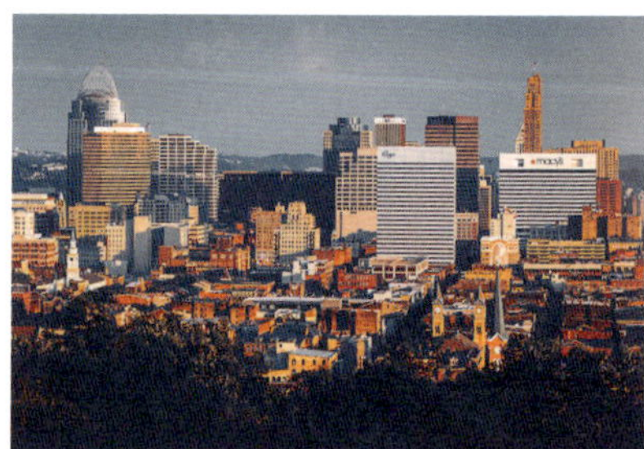

88-89 View of Downtown Cincinnati from Bellevue Hill Park

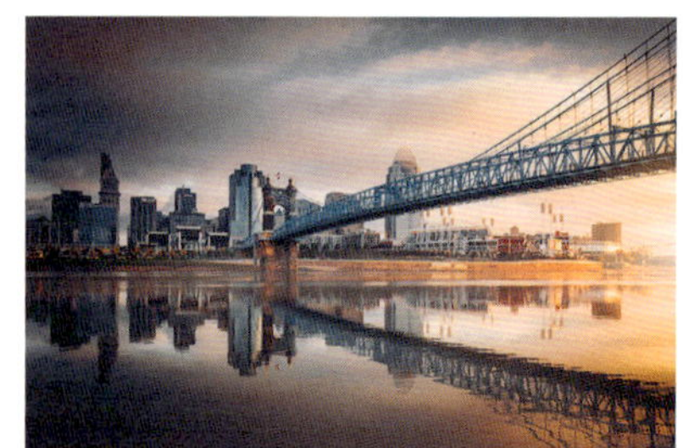

90-91 View of the Ohio River and John A. Roebling Suspension Bridge

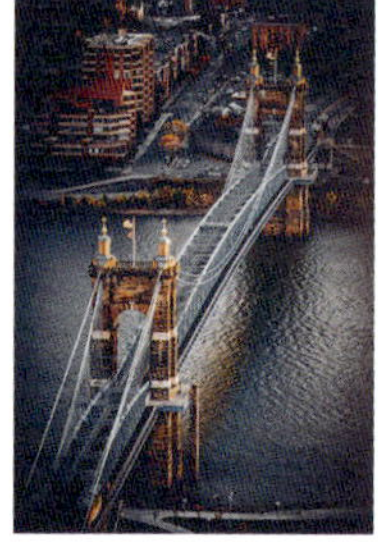

92 Above John A. Roebling Suspension Bridge

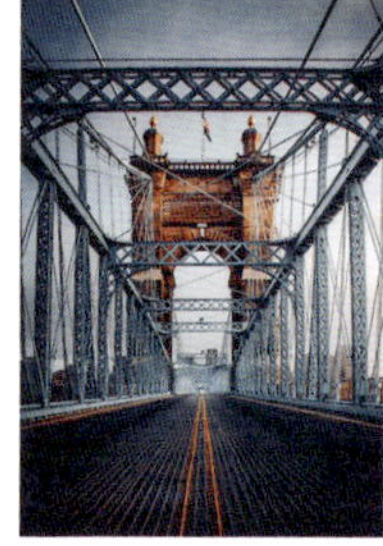

93 John A. Roebling Suspension Bridge

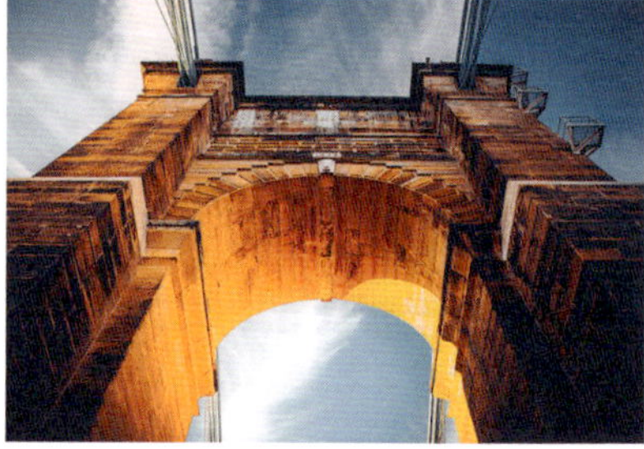

94-95 Looking up at John A. Roebling Suspension Bridge

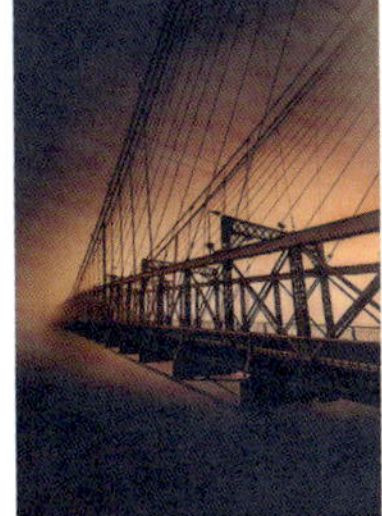
96 John A. Roebling Suspension Bridge

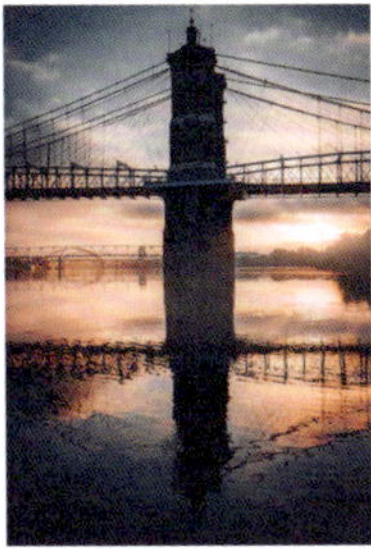
97 View of the Ohio River and John A. Roebling Suspension Bridge

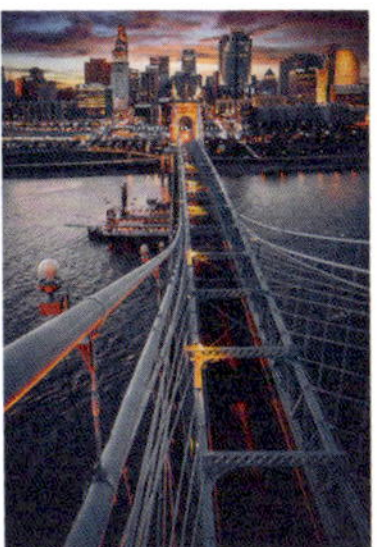
99 John A. Roebling Suspension Bridge

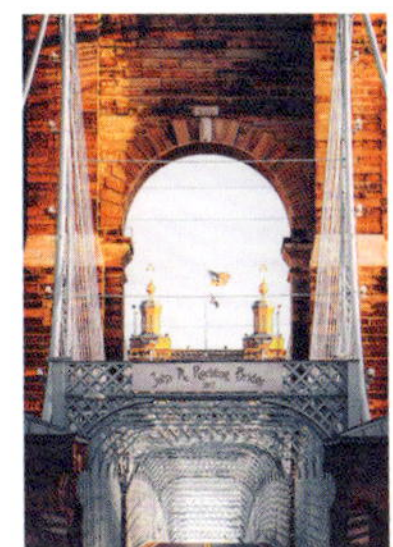
100 John A. Roebling Suspension Bridge

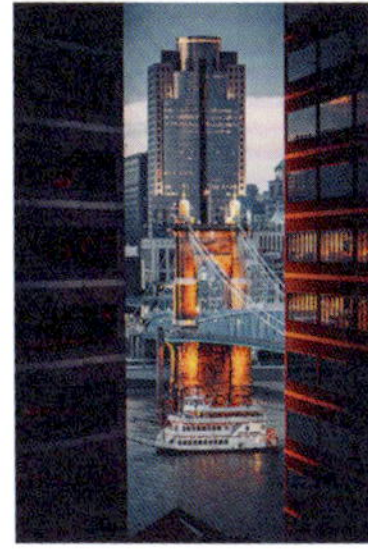
101 View of John A. Roebling Suspension Bridge and Downtown Cincinnati

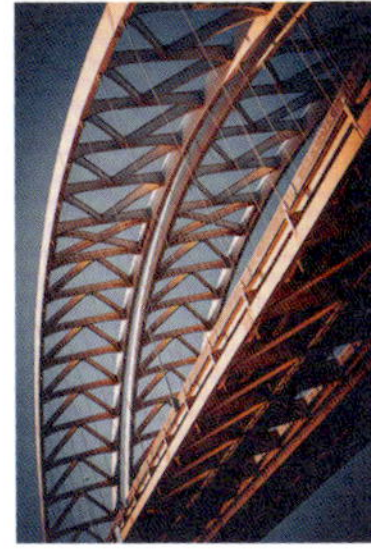
102 Looking up at Daniel Carter Beard Bridge

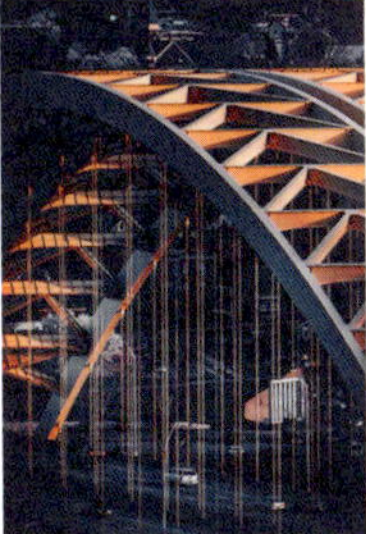
103 Daniel Carter Beard Bridge

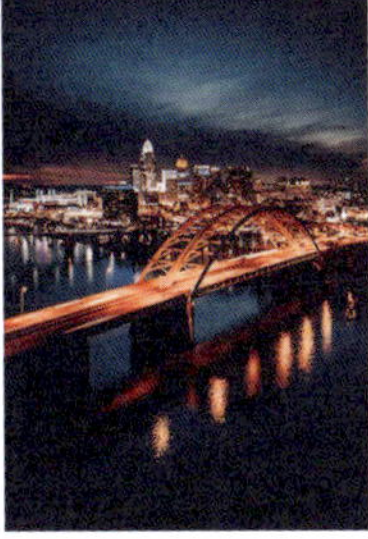
104 Daniel Carter Beard Bridge

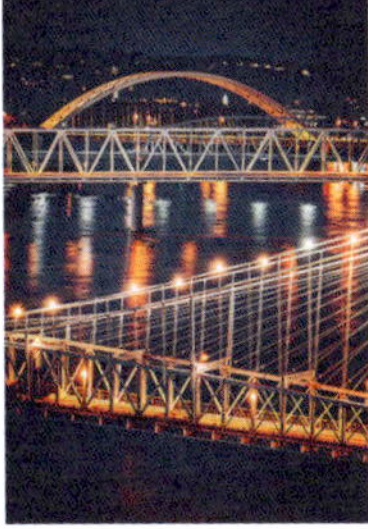
105 View of the Ohio River bridges

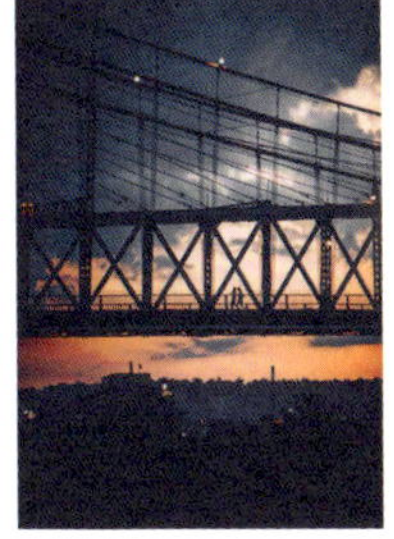
106 John A. Roebling Suspension Bridge

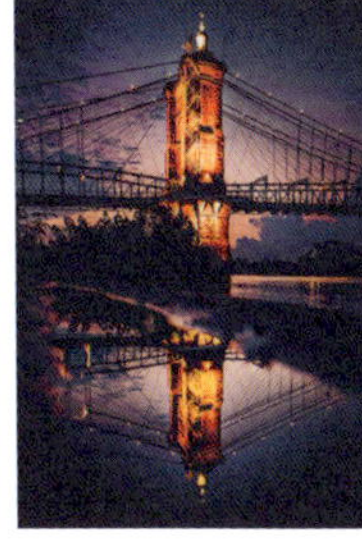
107 View of the Ohio River and John A. Roebling Suspension Bridge

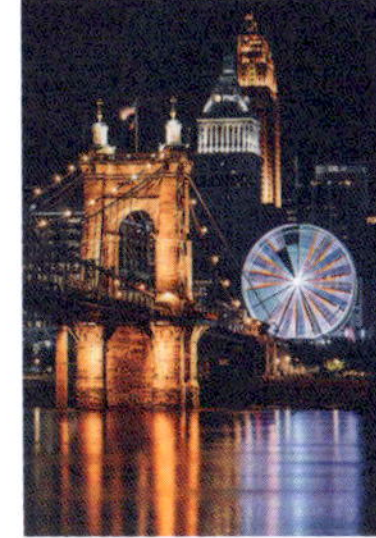
108 View of the Ohio River and Downtown Cincinnati

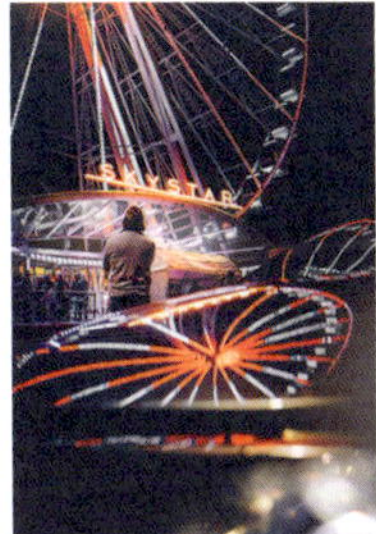
109 View of the SkyStar Wheel

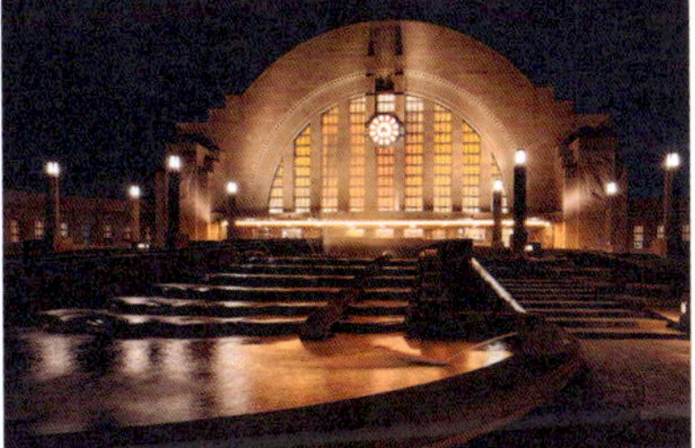
110-111 Cincinnati Union Terminal

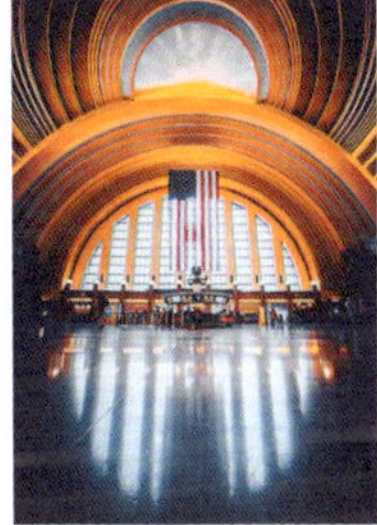
113 Inside Cincinnati Union Terminal

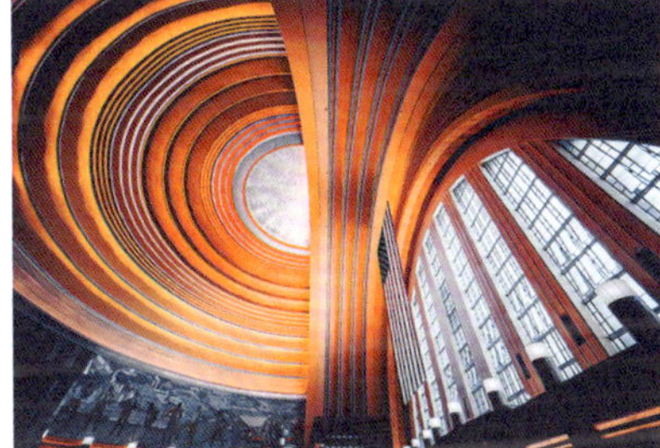
114-115 Inside Cincinnati Union Terminal

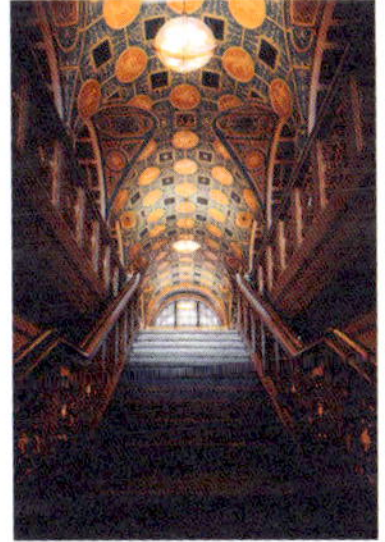
116 Inside the Dixie Terminal

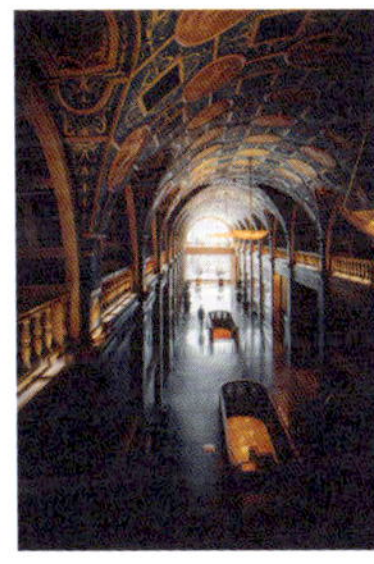
117 Inside the Dixie Terminal

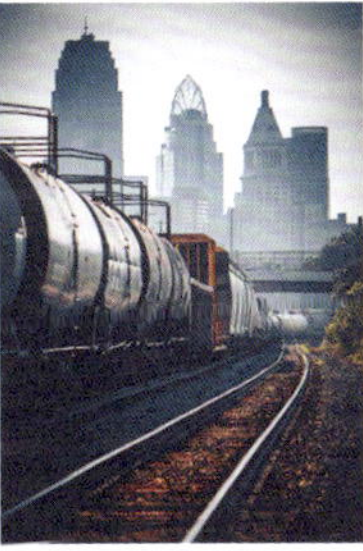
118 View of Downtown Cincinnati from train tracks near W. Mehring Way

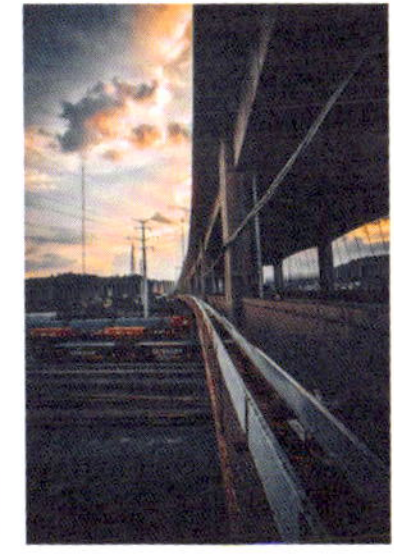
119 Train tracks under Western Hills Viaduct

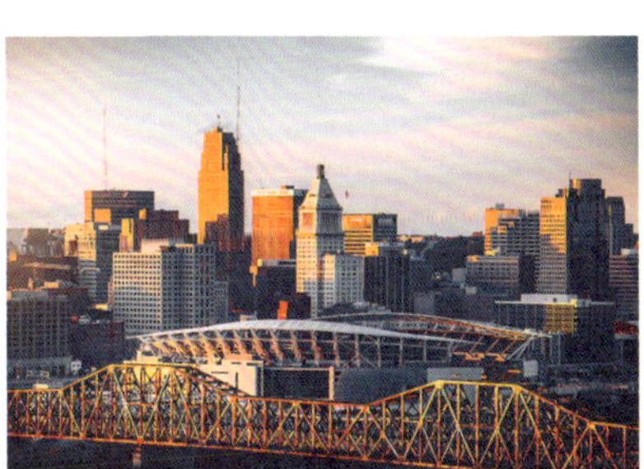
120-121 View of Cincinnati skyline from Devou Park

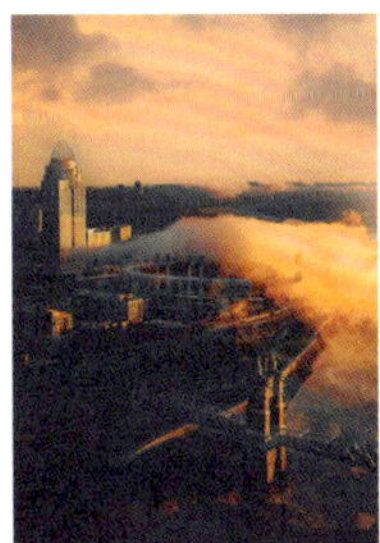
122 Above Great American Ball Park

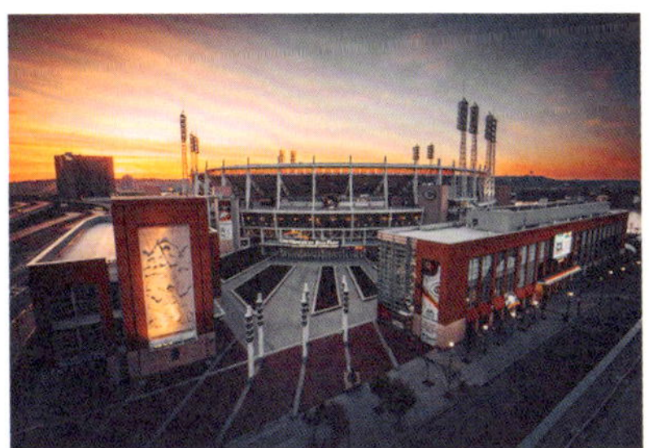
124-125 Great American Ball Park

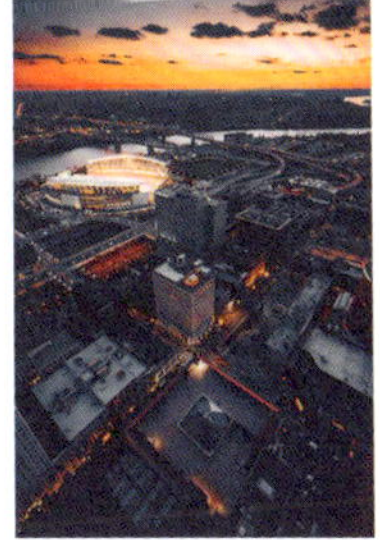
126 Above Downtown Cincinnati

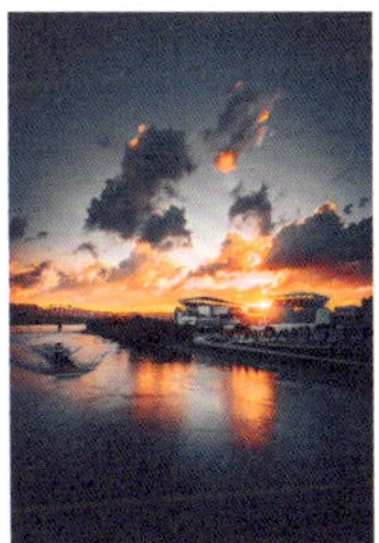
127 View of the Ohio River and Paycor Stadium

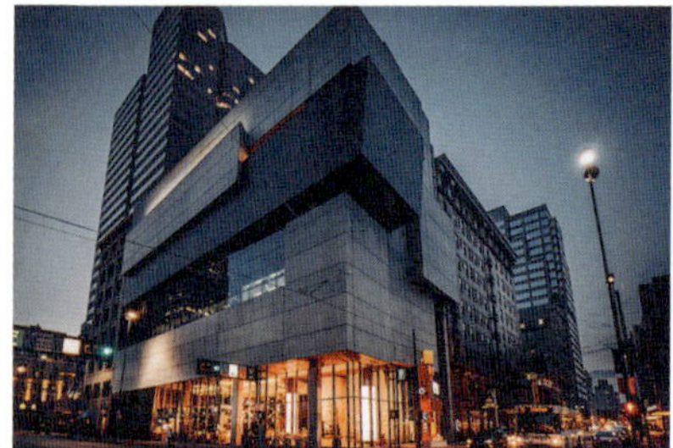

128-129 Contemporary Arts Center

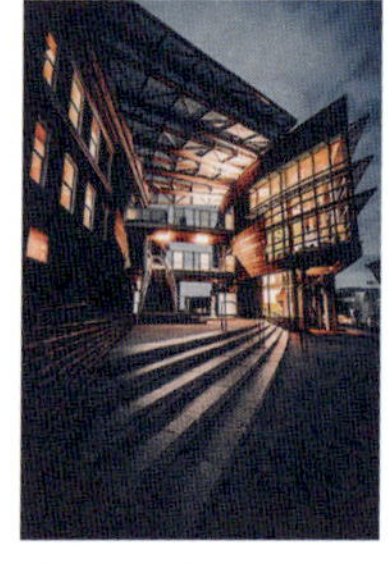

130 View of University of Cincinnati Steger Student Life Center

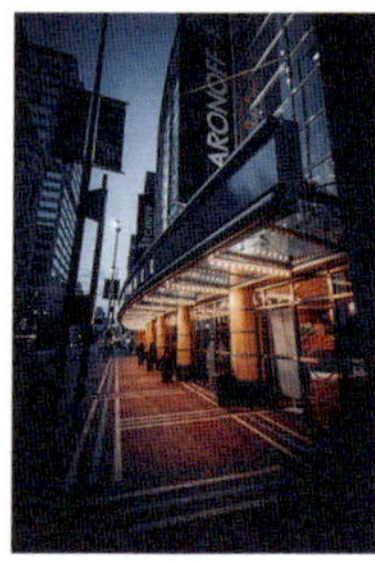

131 View of the Aronoff Center

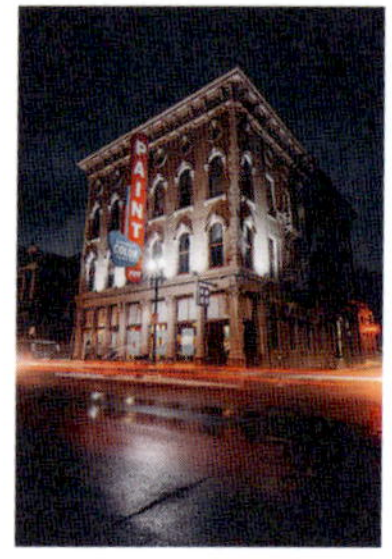

132 View of Cincinnati Color Company building

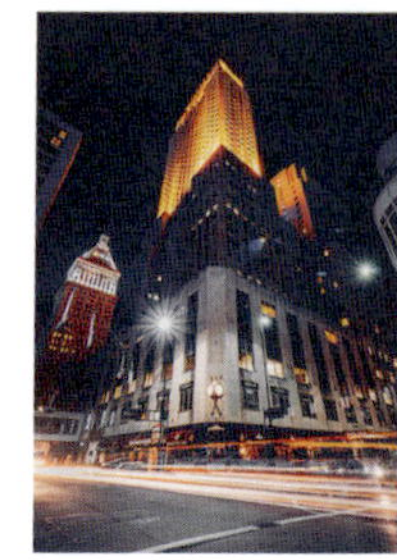

133 View of Carew Tower

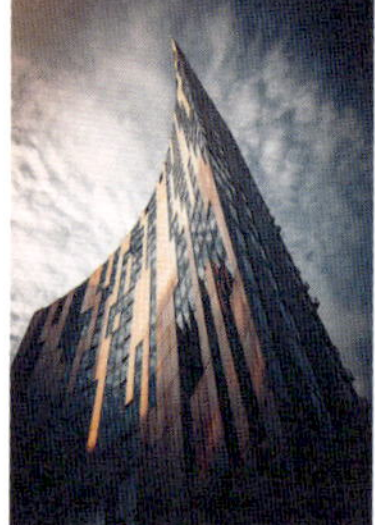

134 View of The Ascent at Roebling's Bridge

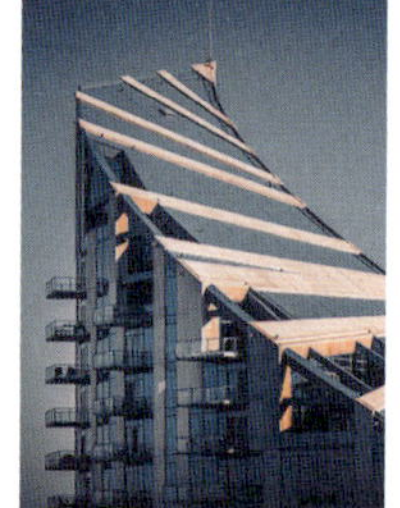

135 View of The Ascent at Roebling's Bridge

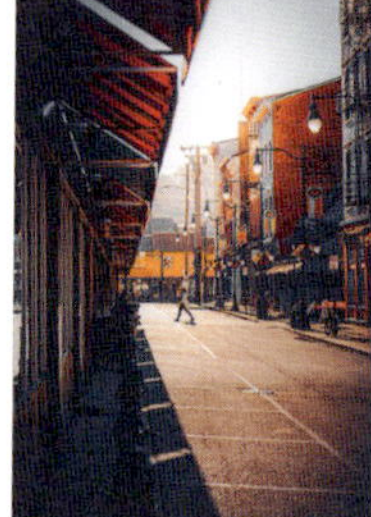

136 View of Findlay Market

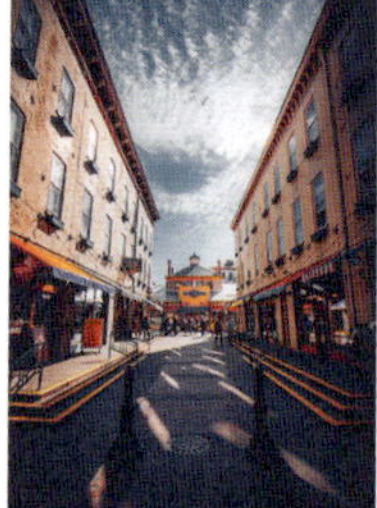

137 View of Findlay Market

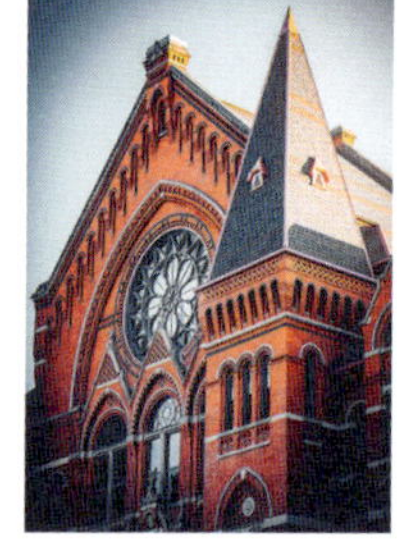

139 Cincinnati Music Hall

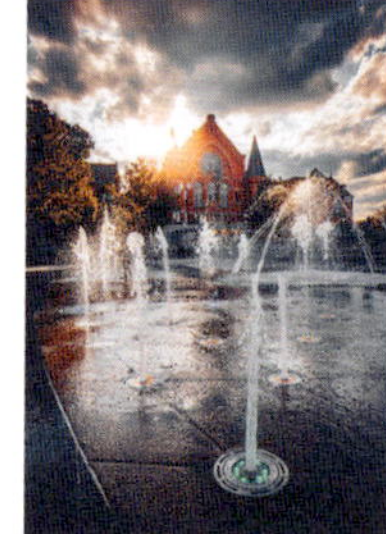

140 View of Cincinnati Music Hall and Washington Park

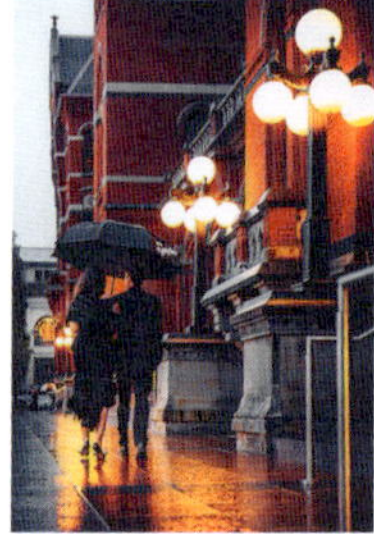

141 View of Cincinnati Music Hall

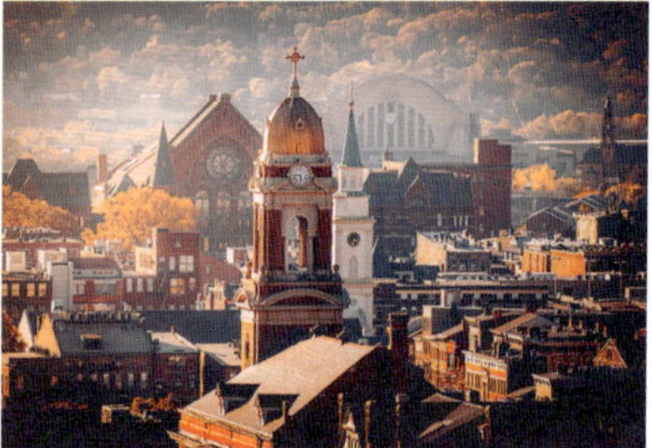

142-143 Above Over-the-Rhine

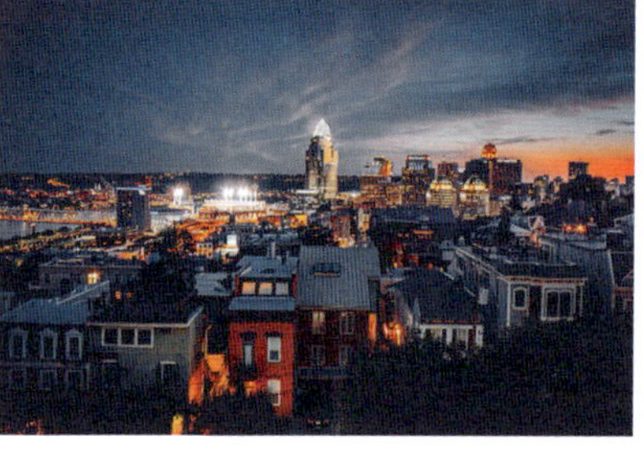

144-145 View of Downtown Cincinnati from Mount Adams

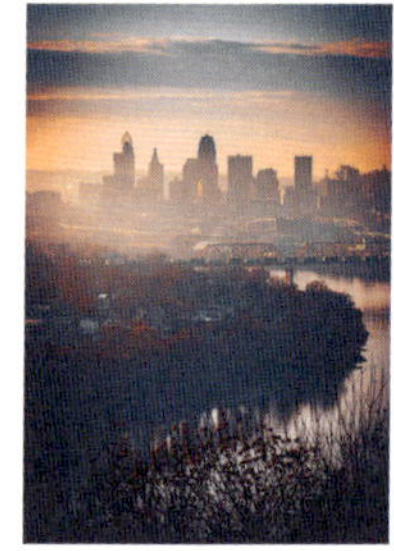

146 View of Cincinnati skyline from Mt. Echo Park

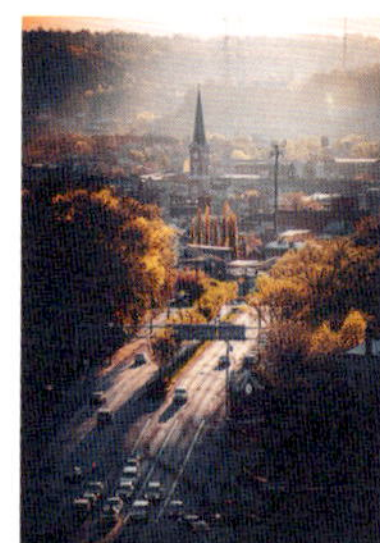

147 View of Liberty Street

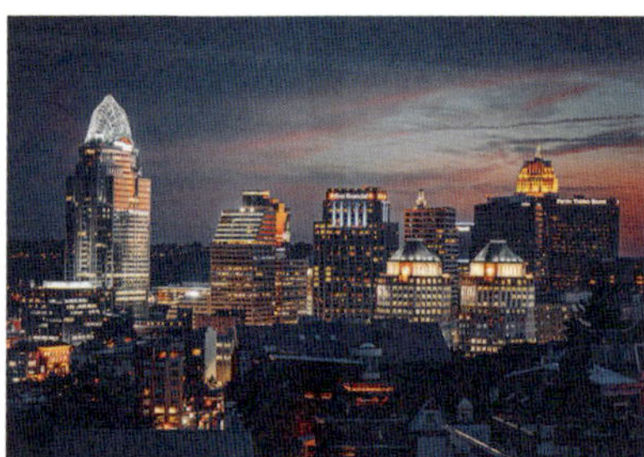

148-149 View of Downtown Cincinnati

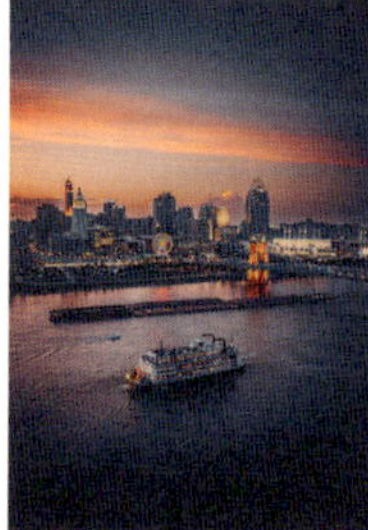

150 View of the Ohio River from Madison Place

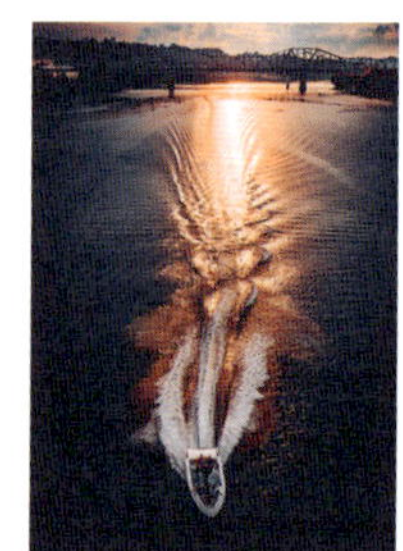

152 View of the Ohio River

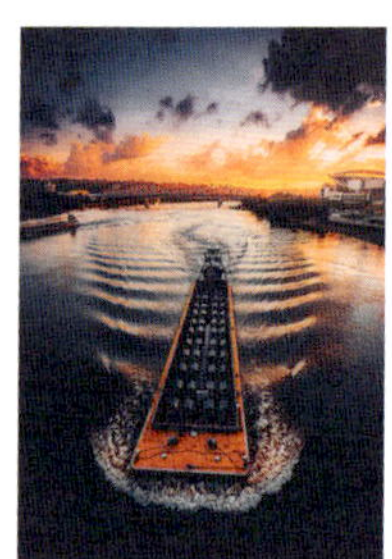

153 View of the Ohio River

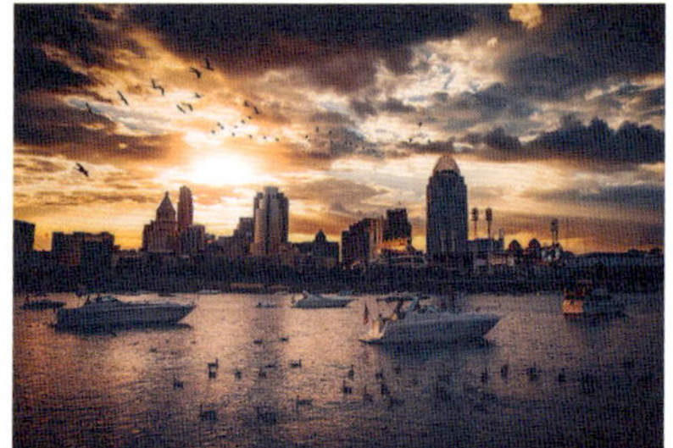

154-155 View of the Ohio River and Downtown Cincinnati

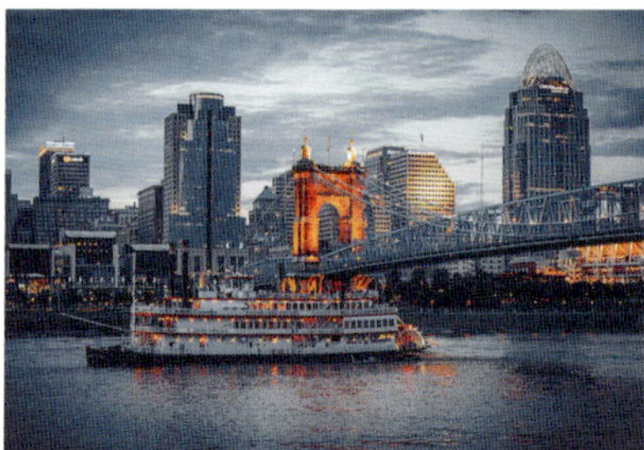

156-157 View of the Ohio River and Downtown Cincinnati

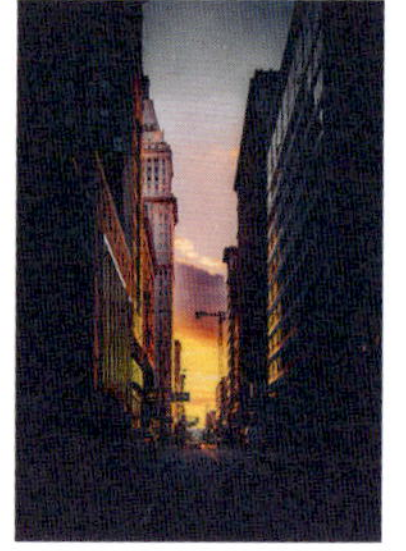

158 View of Vine Street

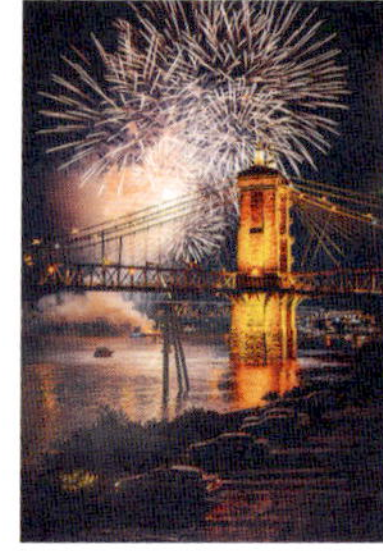

159 John A. Roebling Suspension Bridge

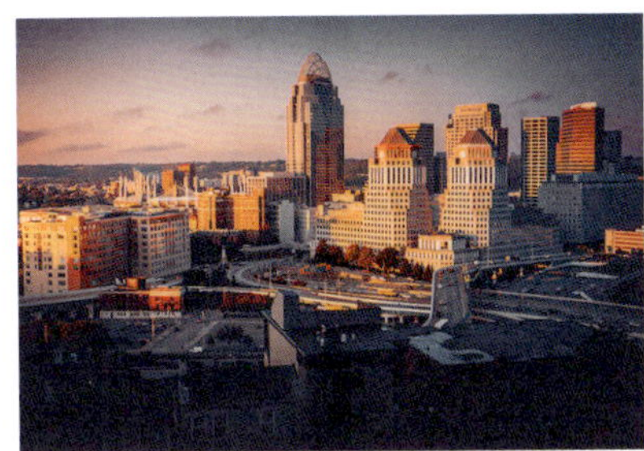

160-161 View of Downtown Cincinnati from the Rookwood Pottery Building

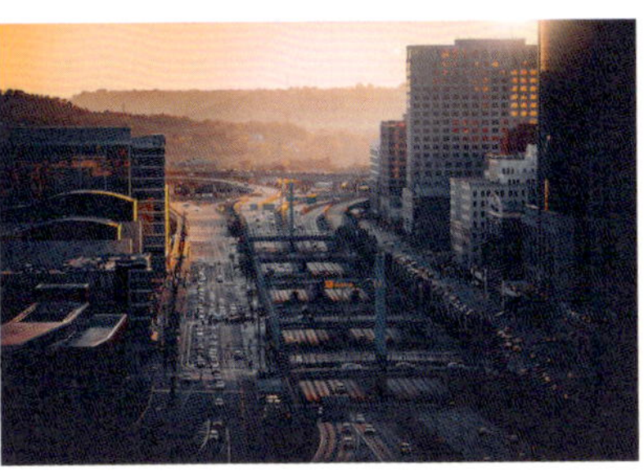

162-163 View of Interstate 71 from One Lytle Place

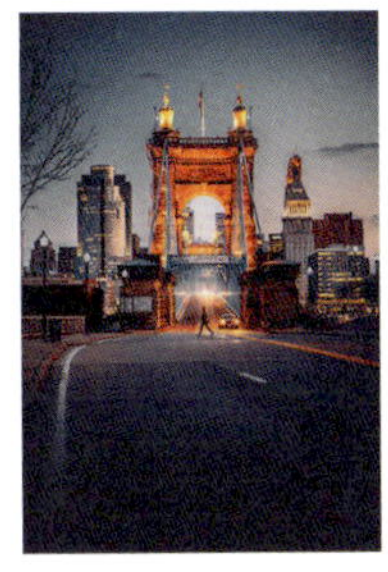

165 John A. Roebling Suspension Bridge

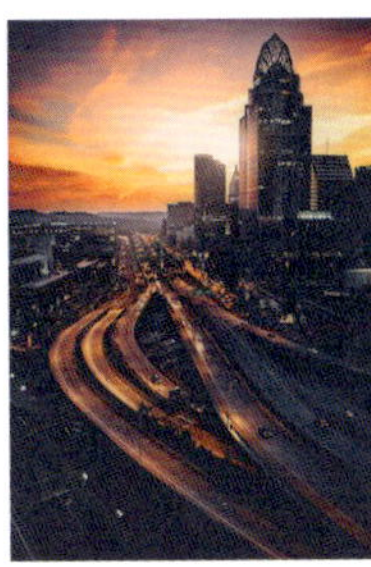

166 View of Interstate 71

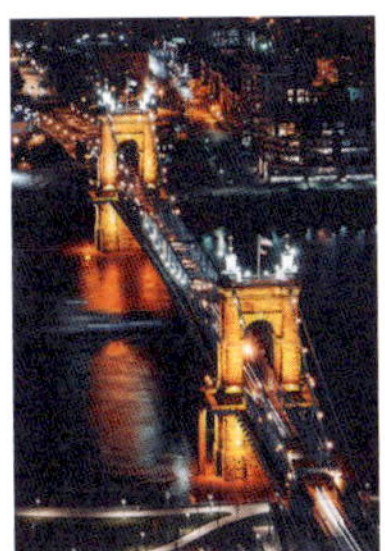

175 Above John A. Roebling Suspension Bridge

All photos by Mike Poggioli with exception of
page 122, photo courtesy of Patrick Donovan

Special thanks to Andy Keene
and Kristen Erwin Schlotman

LCCN: 2024947908
ISBN: 978-1-951963-31-6

Printed and bound in China
First printing, 2025

Trope Publishing Co.

Mike Poggioli's photographs are available
for purchase. For inquiries, email the
gallery at info@trope.com

+ INFORMATION:
**For additional information
on our books and prints,
visit trope.com**

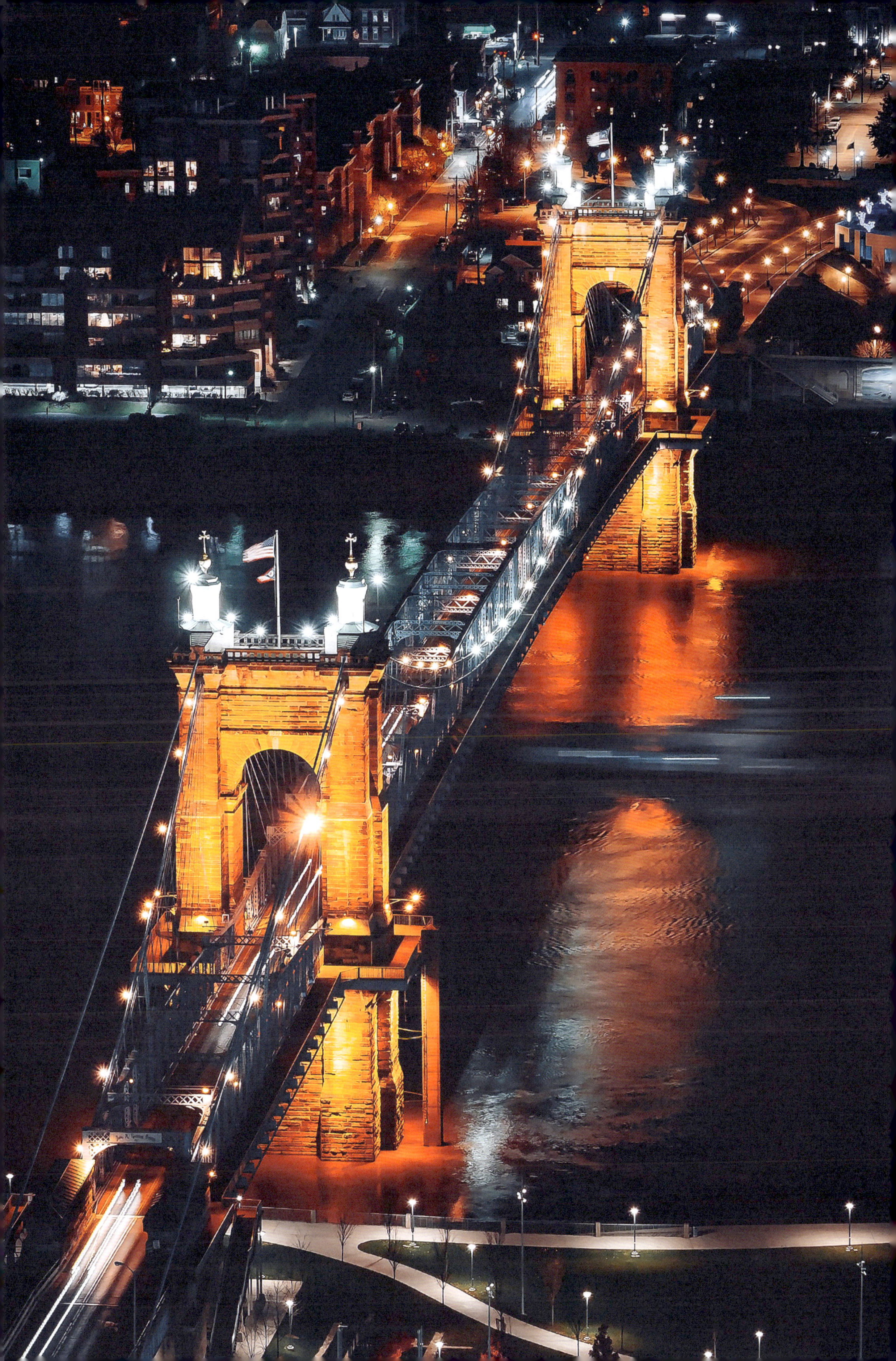

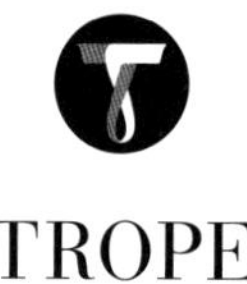

TROPE

TROPE PUBLISHING Co.